D1339623

Praise for *The Compassionate Mind*

'Anyone who struggles with their inner critic should make sure to read this book. Professor Gilbert writes in a masterly fashion about compassionate mind training – an innovative approach which is likely to grow in importance over the next decade as the evidence for its benefit continues to build.'

David Veale, Institute of Psychiatry, King's College London

'Like so frequently in the past, Paul Gilbert has come forth again with a book about the mind, its unused potential, and how to harness that potential to one's and others' benefit. *The Compassionate Mind* is a roadmap to compassion for the self and towards others. It is a book for those curious enough to explore their hidden potential to attain a special kind of humanness and happiness. A 10 on a scale of 1 to 10.'

Michael McGuire, author of *Darwinian Psychiatry*

'Internationally-renowned psychologist Paul Gilbert has provided all of us with a much-needed book. Written with wisdom and warmth, Gilbert takes us on a journey through the far reaches of evolution to the very depths of our own hearts. This helpful and thoughtful guide to living a compassionate life – for yourself and for others – will be a reminder for many of us that we are all human but that we need to be more humane toward our own troubled selves. Throughout this book the reader will feel like the author is speaking directly to him or her – and will recognize that you can use the tools of modern psychology to fix what feels broken inside of us. A timely book for a time when competitiveness, materialism and narcissism have failed us. This book provides timeless wisdom that you can use every day. It will make a wonderful gift for someone you care for – especially, if you give it to yourself.'

Robert L. Leahy, author of *The Worry Cure* and President of the International Association for Cognitive Psychotherapy

'Paul Gilbert is one of the most brilliant scientists studying compassion today. In this wonderful book, he makes his theories very accessible and down-to-earth. You feel like you're having a chat in his living-room with a warm cup of tea. I also love his easy-to-follow exercises, which offer concrete ways to help you develop greater compassion in daily life.'

Kristin Neff, Associate Professor of Human Development, University of Texas at Austin

'The increasing drive to find a competitive edge in all aspects of our lives may create efficiencies but they are cold, heartless and unpleasant to live with. Gilbert shows how and why this occurs, and explains why our capacity for compassion is the antidote.'

Oliver James, author of *Affluenza* and *The Selfish Capitalist*

THE COMPASSIONATE MIND

THE COMPASSIONATE MIND

A New Approach to Life's Challenges

PAUL GILBERT

Constable · London

Constable & Robinson Ltd
3 The Lanchesters
162 Fulham Palace Road
London W6 9ER
www.constablerobinson.com

First published in the UK by Constable,
an imprint of Constable & Robinson Ltd, 2009

A copy of the British Library Cataloguing in
Publication data is available from the British Library

Important Note
This back is not intended as a substitute for medical advice or treatment.
Any person with a condition requiring medical attention should consult
a qualified medical practitioner or suitable therapist.

ISBN: 978-1-84529-713-8

Printed and bound in the EU

Contents

Acknowledgements

I'm delighted to thank many people for all their contributions to this book. I must begin with the many patients whom I've seen in psychotherapy over the past 30 years – for their courage and insights into the difficulty they have in being compassionate to themselves and their efforts to become so. It was with them that the central idea – that a 'lack of self-kindness and warmth' is central to the many states of mental suffering – took root.

We have sought to research this in some detail – in particular, with regard to issues linked to shame and self-criticism. Here I would like to thank my research colleague Chris Irons who, over many years, worked on various models of compassion with me. I'm also delighted to thank enthusiastically my current, wonderful research team of research coordinator Corrine Gale and researcher and data analyser Kirsten McEwan. They work fantastically hard and with dedication. Special thanks, too, go to Helen Rockliffe for her enthusiasm and hard work while with us. My secretaries – Diane Woollands over many years (now retired – sorry if I wore you out) and recently Sue Branningan and Lesley Fulter – offered excellent support with proof-reading and reference checking. Special thanks also go to Keith Wilshere for his masterly management of our research unit, for keeping us all afloat and getting me back into guitar playing and recording with 'Still Minds'.

In 2007, I set up a charity to advance research and therapy work in compassion – the Compassionate Mind Foundation (www.compassionatemind.co.uk). It's a pleasure, therefore, to thank the current trustees: Jean Gilbert and Drs Chris Gillespie and Tom Schroder. Thanks also to our board members Diane Woollands (who is also the charity's coordinator) and Drs Ken Goss, Deborah Lee, Mary Welford, Ian Lowens and Chris Irons. All of them have worked on these ideas for a number of years and have developed compassion-focused therapy in their own domains, covering eating disorders, anxiety, trauma and psychosis. I'm also indebted to clinical colleagues Sue Procter and Drs Sophie Mayhew, Sharon Pallant and Andrew Rayner with whom

I've worked clinically and on developing outcome data for compassion-focused therapy. Thanks to the staff of the day centre at 63 Duffield Road for their continuing work with compassion-focused therapy and for making available facilities for our regular fortnightly supervision groups – a source of passion and a space in which to share ideas and research findings. Michael Townend and Louis Spry at the University of Derby have been highly supportive and helpful in moving training forward, and we hope to develop a structured training shortly.

I would also like to offer my thanks to my friend Professor Meinrad Perrez for offering me over many years the visiting professorship at Fribourg University in Switzerland, and for sharing his fascinating work on emotion regulation in families. Thanks also to my friend Professor Jose Gouveia of the University of Coimbra in Portugal, for again offering me a visiting professorship; and for stimulating important research in shame and compassion; thanks too to his students Paula Castilho, Marcella Matos and Alexandra Dinis. Special thanks also to Dr Giovanni Liotti for, over the years, his insights and work on attachment theory and therapy and guidance. I'm also indebted to various mentors at various times, including Dr John Price and Professor Leon Sloman who developed the social rank theory of mood disorder, Dr Anthony Stevens for his guidance on archetype theory, and Professors Michael McGuire and Dan Wilson for their considerable knowledge on evolutionary approaches to mental disorder.

The Mental Health Research Unit was established in 1996 as a joint venture between the University of Derby and the (now) Derbyshire Mental Health Trust. Without their support, our research and new approach would not be possible, so I'm extremely grateful for their vision and long-term encouragement. I would also like to thank the British Association of Behavioural and Cognitive Psychotherapies, which has always given me a sense of belonging and welcome, and asked me to be president in 2003. Here are folk dedicated to research on both process and outcome and who remain dissatisfied with all current psychotherapies and want to improve them. Although I'm rather more focused on biological and evolved processes, deeply flavoured with attachment theory, Jungian archetypes and non-conscious processes than some colleagues, they have always treated me kindly and given me many platforms from which to present my views. Without their support and openness, we wouldn't be where we are today. Whether any of our current psychotherapeutic schools and tribes can maintain themselves in the face of psychological research and not become simply 'evidence-based psychological therapies' is unclear. With things changing so fast now, who knows what will exist in the future? Special thanks go to Professor Bob Leahy, fellow cognitive behaviour therapist from New York, for his scholarship, friendship and passion for passion (emotions) in therapy – I said I wouldn't mention the pub singing.

Nick Robinson of Constable & Robinson has been a very enthusiastic supporter and publisher of this book. I could not wish for a more helpful publisher, friend and guide. Good on the red wines, too. Many thanks also to Fritha Saunders, the commissioning editor, who is enthusiastic, incredibly efficient and always helpful and very friendly. She was also extremely calming when I got into states of anxiety over deadlines. Nancy Duin, the freelance copy editor for this book, was wonderful in taking a difficult-to-understand text and turning it into something readable. There's hardly a sentence she didn't improve, and she then worked as hard on my corrections and additions. She also moved paragraphs around to make better sense of the text, and checked things I should have on the internet (she saved me from some embarrassing errors). If you understand what I've written, that is due in no small measure to Nancy's brilliance. To her, I owe my deep gratitude. Any remaining errors are, of course, purely my responsibility, but by the end of the book, you will be well into forgiveness.

And as always, love goes to my children Hannah and James, who have taught me so much about the power of love of kin. Love, too, to Jean – my wife, drinking partner, cricket sharer, collaborative researcher and love of my life for well over 30 years. God, are we that old? The NHS doesn't allow sabbaticals for book writing, so for the past years, it's been 5 a.m. starts trying not to wake my beloved.

In the months before this book was complete, Dr Simon Thomas, a long-term clinical psychology and therapy colleague and a truly lovely man of whom we were all deeply fond, died at the age of 48, after a long battle with cancer. And then my father developed a fast-growing cancer that changed him rapidly from being bright-eyed and active to confused and wanting to go. I was able to be with him in the last days. These events somehow harmonized for me what compassion is about – facing the realities and tragedies of life – and made me understand why I was writing in the early hours. So I dedicate this book to all of us who may take joy in life but suffer from being alive.

Introduction

Compassion can be defined in many ways, but its essence is a basic kindness, with a deep awareness of the suffering of oneself and of other living things, coupled with the wish and effort to relieve it. Although humans can engage in intensely cruel and callous behaviour (and, looking back at human history, they often have), for more than 3,000 years, compassion has been understood to be one of the most important and distinctive qualities of the human mind. Not only has it been encouraged as a spiritual and moral pursuit in many religions, but compassion has also been seen as a major healing process for our turbulent minds and relationships.

Although most religions recognize its power, it was within the Eastern traditions – and especially Mahayana Buddhism, the school of the Dalai Lama – that exercises and mental practices were developed to train the mind in compassion. In these traditions, developing compassion is like playing a musical instrument – it's a skill that can be enhanced with dedicated practice. These traditions also portray the development of compassion as having far-reaching consequences in terms of how the mind organizes itself, how we experience ourselves and the world, and even the ultimate reality of our sense of self.

Until relatively recently, the impetus for developing compassion and the way of doing it came primarily from spiritual and religious traditions. What is extremely exciting is that the last 30 years or so have seen the science of psychology and studies of the human brain begin to put compassion, caring, and pro-social behaviour centre stage in the development of well-being, mental health and our capacity to foster harmonious relationships with each other and the world we live in.

Shortly after the Second World War, researchers such as Harry Harlow (1905–81), who worked with monkeys, and the child psychiatrist John Bowlby (1907–90) began to study the impact of the caring relationship that infants had with their mothers. It was found that a mother's love and affection had a huge impact on the emotional development of the infant, child and subsequent adult. In the 1950s and 1960s, John Bowlby outlined the approach to human development that he called 'attachment theory'. This focused on the quality of the attachment relationship in terms of the accessibility and affection of the parent in soothing and regulating the infant's emotions. Indeed, we have probably all seen how young children become distressed if they lose contact with their mothers and how, in the normal course of events, the return of the mother calms the infant down. Bowlby helped us to recognize that, from the day we're born, our brains are *biologically designed* to respond to the care and kindness of others. Indeed, his work has stimulated a revolution in our understanding of the importance of affection at many stages of our lives. When we're distressed, kindness helps; if we're facing tragedies such as the loss of loved ones, the kindness of others helps; if we're having to face our own death, then feeling loved and wanted is important to our ability to face it. We now know that close friendships and affectionate relationships play a huge role in our mental health and well-being and influence how our bodies work. For example, people in affectionate relationships show lower levels of stress hormones and higher ones of 'happy' hormones than those in relationships characterized by conflict. Research has also shown that the way we relate to *ourselves* – whether we regard ourselves kindly or critically, in a friendly and affectionate way or hostilely – can have a major influence on our ability to get through life's difficulties and create within ourselves a sense of well-being. All over the world now, researchers in many different fields are beginning to explore the power of kindness and affection and the ways to harness it.

This is not a moment too soon, of course. We are confronted with considerable crises linked to a lack of compassion and of care for each other and our environment. We have become trapped by a competitive world that only seeks efficiency and profit maximization. Each of us has a brain that has evolved over millions of years and is very sensitive to the social context in which it lives. So while we can be compassionate, kind and selfless in some (cooperative and supportive) contexts, in others (competitive and threat-focused), we can be ruthless, cruel and very self-absorbed. So from understanding the importance of affection on how our brains and bodies work and how modern culture operates on our psychology and our brains, tuning compassion up or down, we're learning more and more about the importance of deliberately harnessing and focusing compassion.

A personal journey

My own interest in compassion and the eventual writing of this book grew out of lots of different strands in my life. So let me take you behind the scenes and consider some of them. We can go back 40 years to when I was introduced to Jungian concepts of archetypes while doing my A-levels in the 1960s. These were the days of 'liberal studies', and we had a fascinating young teacher who lectured from his just-finished PhD on something like 'A Jungian Analysis of the Novel'. We'd look at the plots and characters of various books in terms of underlying archetypes and the common themes in human history, such as the hero, the villain, the sacrifices of love and loyalty, vengeance from betrayal, the death of the hero and so on – great stuff. Archetypes, which George Lucas used to write his *Star Wars* movies, speak to the innate aspects of our minds, the source of the repeating desires and relationships that echo down through history – as we will see later in this book.

However, although even as a teenager the idea of becoming a psychologist was starting to shimmer in my mind (assuming I couldn't make it with my rock band), my main studies were in politics and economics and so I pursued those at university. I became very interested in how economic relationships impact on lifestyle and life quality, a theme that Karl Marx addressed. Marx was also a great fan of Darwin and Darwin was 'honoured' to received a copy of Marx's *Das Kapital* in 1873 and wrote to him that '. . . we both earnestly desire the extension of knowledge and that this is in the long run sure to add to the happiness of mankind'. According to Marx's biographer Francis Wheen, on 17 March 1883, 'As Marx's coffin was being lowered into the earth of Highgate cemetery, Engels declared: "Just as

Darwin discovered the law of evolution in human nature, so Marx discovered the law of evolution in human history."'[1]

The link between our evolved psychology and the economic systems in which we live, in the creation of misery or happiness, has never been well articulated. Unfortunately this evolutionary approach was to falter following the over-medicalizing and pathologizing of human misery – something that it has constantly tried to pull back from. As you will see, this link – between our evolved minds and our social conditions in the creation of compassion or cruelty, happiness or unhappiness – permeates this book.

Suffice it to say that, at this youthful time of my life, economic justice and equality were very much the concerns of myself and my friends. But my dream to become a psychologist had grown even stronger and so, lucky for me, I had the chance to retrain in psychology at Sussex University in 1973–75. Unfortunately I failed my neurophysiology paper and had to study for another year. This rather fitted with my style as a dyslexic, academic limbo dancer – just getting through. So I worked as a night psychiatric nurse, met my wife and got to play lots of cricket. Failures often have a bright side. I'm still happily married and play some cricket and my time on a psychiatric unit taught me a lot about the suffering of mental illness. My PhD studies at Edinburgh were on depression, and then, in 1980, I became clinically qualified and released on to an unsuspecting world.

My long fascination with Jung and archetypes led to what became known as evolutionary psychology and then, for me, studies of how our evolved minds set us up for all kinds of difficulties, including anxiety, depression, paranoia and the rest. I was fortunate enough to get to know and converse with Professor Aaron Beck, the pioneer of cognitive therapy, on a number of occasions. He, too, was interested in the deep evolutionary dynamics of our minds, but felt we should focus our therapy on people's conscious thoughts and teach them ways to help themselves. In his view, it's what goes through your mind today that affects your suffering rather than reflections on the past. This remains a controversial position, and while many psychologists still recognize the importance of and work with the past, the common-sense approach of cognitive therapy became very popular with a number of professionals – not only psychologists but also nurses, psychiatrists and social workers. The psychologists who adopted it then rushed off to develop its research base.

Still, although working with people's current thoughts, behaviours and feelings is immensely helpful, there's the little problem of the human brain and the fact that it's been designed to respond to kindness and affection. Now my own research focused a lot on issues of feeling inferior and defeated; indeed, I called my second book on depression *Depression: The evolution of powerlessness*. Some of my ideas were influenced by my economics degree, which had planted the idea that oppression is linked to mental illness. So I was interested in understanding the mechanisms by which our brain links to feelings of inferiority, defeat and oppression. This led me on to the study of shame and self-criticism – the way we can oppress and depress ourselves. However, the issue of *kindness*, which both attachment theory and my interest in Buddhism had alerted me to, haunted me in my therapeutic work and I knew it needed to be integrated into therapy and models of mental disorder. I was lucky in having as PhD students the talented Steve Allen and Chris Irons, who studied the interaction between attachment experiences and those of power and subordination. Their work and our many conversations helped to sharpen my thinking.

I was also fortunate that, during the 1980s, a group of us were able to meet every few months to share ideas about the interaction between the innate aspects of our minds and the way our early and social environments can bring out the best or worse in us. Those attending included: my wife Jean, who had studied social hierarchies in cockroaches and later undertook qualitative studies with depressed people and those suffering from schizophrenia; ethologist Michael Chance, who had explored different types of social rank hierarchies in monkeys; psychiatrists John Price, who was the first to link mood disorders to feelings of inferiority and defeat as evolved safety strategies, and Leon Sloman of the Clarke Institute, Toronto, who integrated John's ideas with attachment approaches; the Jungian analyst Anthony Stevens, who in the 1960s had studied attachment relationships in a Greek orphanage; and two other psychologists: Dave Stephens, strong in Buddhist interests and practice, and Dennis Trent, who had studied what are called 'pseudo attachments'. John and Anthony went on to write their book *Evolutionary Psychiatry*,[2] which suggests that the search for status and for connectedness/attachment figures are both powerful archetypal processes in each of us and that mental health problems can emerge from the thwarting or distortion of one or both of these. Those group discussions were exciting – the sharing of research papers mixed with the usual laments about the world . . . and too many chocolate biscuits.

In 1983, two Italian therapists, Victor Guidano and Giovanni Liotti, wrote a very influential book[3] that linked early attachment relationships to various processes that cognitive therapists had been looking at – our styles of thinking about ourselves and others. Some years later, I was lucky to become friends with Giovanni and learned much from his wisdom and insights into the role of early caring relationships on later difficulties.

I was interested in how I could bring these ideas to my more basic cognitive and behavioural work. I did some training in Kleinian psychoanalysis (not my cup of tea) and, in the 1990s, was able to spend four years working in a day hospital run along Jungian lines with Dr H. Ghadiali. I also liked the more open, sharing and collaborative aspects of cognitive behavioural therapy and had spent some happy years walking the streets with agoraphobic people and developing support groups. There's no doubt that gentle exposure to things feared and avoided and practising thinking differently, in an atmosphere of support, were both helpful. However, while some cognitive therapists were increasingly interested in techniques – teaching people logic and testing the evidence of their beliefs – I had become more convinced that that was only part of it. For me, it was how people could begin to 'feel' safe and soothe themselves that was key.

To tackle that, I had to work with how the brain is designed and that took me back to neurophysiology, attachment theory and my interest in Buddhist compassion, and I gradually introduced the idea of kindness into therapy. For example, I'd help people who had negative thoughts about themselves to explore the validity of such thoughts, to see what archetypal patterns they seemed linked to (e.g. fear of abandonment, the heroic need to succeed, the shamed self and its repair) or to discover if they were hiding other, more frightening ones. We'd then try to generate various alternatives and, with practice, bring them into real life. However, patients would sometimes say, 'I understand the logic and agree I'm not a failure, but I still *feel* like one.' So why was their obvious understanding of their problem not helping them feel better?

In my 1989 book *Human Nature and Suffering*,[4] I had explored research that suggested that we have special brain systems to enable us to feel a sense of safeness, reassurance and pleasurable, calming relief, and that this is linked to being cared for and receiving affection. Slowly the penny dropped: if the emotion system that enables us to feel reassurance, relief and safeness isn't working or accessible, people may indeed understand something but not feel any reassurance or relief from that knowledge. Just like you can have all the sexual imagery in your head that you like, but if your pituitary gland isn't responding to those images, nothing happens in your body. Other pennies began to drop. It became clear that we had to do much more about exposing people to *positive emotion* and helping them to develop and feel it. However, in a fascinating twist, research was starting to show clearly that there are different types of positive emotion. One is linked to drive and excitement and another is connected to feelings of reassurance, security, safeness and calm peacefulness (*see* pp. 21–5). I realized that, as therapists, we need to separate these two positive emotion systems very clearly in our minds because, although they're integrated, they also work in very different ways. Indeed, some people will try to create achievements and excitement in their lives precisely because, without that, life seems empty or they find it difficult to feel safe or content. Compassion is very much about stimulating the second type of emotion system. So for me, Buddhism, evolution, Bowlby's attachment theory and studies of the brain and positive emotion started to fall into place. I became convinced that, whatever intervention you used, you had to ensure that the patient experienced it with feelings of kindness and warmth.

However, it turned out that helping people develop compassion for others and, especially, themselves is not always easy. Indeed, some people are positively frightened of it and resistant to the idea. They see self-compassion and self-kindness as a weakness or an indulgence; to them, it means that you're going soft or letting your guard down. If they started to feel self-kindness or compassion, it could ignite feelings of grief because they would recognize how alone they'd been feeling for so long. John Bowlby suggested that, if you show kindness in therapy, you can activate your patient's attachment memories. If those memories are of neglect or unkindness, the feelings that result from neglect or unkindness can re-emerge. Far from experiencing the therapist or the procedure as kind, patients experience it through their emotional memories – they feel awkward, anxious and resistant to compassion.

This can be understood through what we call behaviour therapy, which goes back to the work of Ivan Pavlov (1849–1936) and his salivating dogs. Let me give you an example. Children have a natural desire to want to play. However, suppose that, every time children start to play, their parents punish them and withdraw affection. Over time, the children will learn that their own desires for play result in punishment, and so they'll inhibit these desires or become anxious if they feel such desires within themselves. We can learn to become anxious about our feelings because of how others have responded to them in the past. Let's look at the desire for care and affection. What happens if children's desire for care and affection results in neglect, rejection or even abuse? You can see the problem. So when the therapist behaves in a kind way, this can reactivate their patients' (innate) desire for care and affection, but of course, these feelings are associated with great fear, and that's what can flood through the patients – so they turn away from kindness. This realization led me and my team to our most recent research – looking at the fear of compassion. It turns out that, for all kinds of reasons, compassion can be tricky for people.

So that's the background to this book and to my thinking. I wanted to write a book to share with you the excitement and passion of modern psychological research as it explores in detail how we can develop more pro-social behaviour and create compassion and kindness in our world and ourselves. For many years, aggression, anxiety and depression have taken centre-stage in our research, but this is changing.

I also wanted to share with you the struggles we have in being compassionate to ourselves and others. You'll find many self-help books that talk to you about the importance of learning to accept and love yourself, but they don't explain to you why this can be important and why it can be so difficult. So this book is different in the sense that it tries to give you quite a lot of detail about how our minds work. It will explore with you the challenges in life that we all have to face because of the way we've evolved and the societies we've created. There's nothing easy in following a compassionate path, and at times it requires courage (not my strong point). But the evidence is now overwhelming: feeling love and compassion for ourselves and others is deeply healing and soothing, and helps us face the many challenges that will come our way.

Throughout the world now there is a gradual movement towards seeking a more compassionate way of living. Although we've learned that we can build efficient systems, cut our costs and do things increasingly cheaply, this is not a very pleasant way to live. We can end up in an efficient world that is uninhabitable – except for the relatively few wealthy. So developing compassion may not be the most efficient way to live but it will add to our well-being. Indeed, when we look around ourselves today, many of us will recognize that we're confronted with a world of gross injustice and suffering, and that we find it difficult to be compassionate because we live in deeply non-compassionate societies. We need to think about why this is and what we can all collectively do to change the way we live – but first we have to decide that building compassionate minds and societies *is* what we want to do.

This book

You will see there are two key sections to this book. Part I (Chapters 1–6) comprises my efforts to share with you the excitement of how science can illuminate the way our minds and brains work and why compassion can be a powerful healing process. To develop compassion, it helps to know the details of why this is important and how it works. Part II (Chapters 7–13) gives you a series of discussions and exercises that you can try out to develop your compassionate mind and see if they help.

Part I: The Science behind Compassion

Chapter 1 explores some of the common ways we experience our lives these days, especially being rushed in our hurry-hurry and 'competitive edge' society. Our emotions, desires and fears can run away with us and we may find it difficult to discover a meaning to our lives. It's also difficult to stand back from the hustle and bustle of everyday life and worries and see ourselves as emergent beings on this planet, in this universe. We can feel disconnected from the 'flow of life' of which we are a part. However, our desires and emotions were built in this flow and we share them with other beings. Understanding where our desires and feelings came from and how they work can be helpful as we embark on the road to compassion. We'll learn that much of what goes on in our minds is not our fault and certainly not our design.

Chapter 2 looks at the implications of our having evolved within the 'flow of life' and of our being part of it. It introduces ten of the challenges that face us. These relate to the fact that we've an evolved brain full of old-fashioned passions and lusts, and a 'new mind' that can activate, amplify and fantasize about these feelings, wants and lusts. Our ability to think and fantasize like this means that our fears and desires can be taken to extremes. As I mentioned above, we've evolved to require enormous amounts of love and affection, both of which influence our brain. We're a species that searches for individuality but also connectedness, conformity and belonging. We have a sense of *self-*awareness that can be a blessing and a curse. We may become aware that life can be full of suffering and tragedy in the form of illness, injury and death and various losses to ourselves and those we love. The final challenge focuses on our fear and anxiety about compassion and kindness. Compassion, fairness and justice are not cost-free. Learning to face up to the hardships of compassion is important to its development.

Chapter 3 explores the idea that all of us 'just find ourselves here' with a brain built by genes that have been evolving over millions of years to pursue desires, passions and ways of relating to each other, and into families and cultures that we never chose. We'll explore the evolved nature of our minds and how being tribal and cruel is as much a part of our innate potential as kindness. However, with the evolution of caring behaviour, especially between mothers and infants, there came into the world, for the first time, the capacity to protect, care and look after another living being. This was to bloom into various forms of compassion. The more we understand the way some of our lives are scripted by inner archetypes and mentalities, the more we can begin to stand back, take control of them and develop those we choose to develop.

Chapter 4 investigates one of the most important mechanisms in our minds – our ability to detect and respond to threats. All living things must be able to do this. However, this system, which harbours our emotions of anxiety, anger and disgust, can also cause major difficulties for us. We will see that our threat system, although designed for self-protection and the protection of those we care about, is quite complicated and can become a dominant process in our lives such that we are easily made anxious, irritable or depressed. We'll come to see that the more threat-absorbed we are, the more difficult compassion can be to achieve.

Chapter 5 will look at the fact that we have two very different positive emotion systems. One is related to drives and pleasures. Winning the lottery, going on holiday and falling in love can make us excited. Knowing that we're going to enjoy something or that it's going to enhance our lives is important because it makes us want to make the effort to do and achieve things. We'll also explore our contentment/ soothing system. The feelings that flow from this include peacefulness and a sense of inner calmness and well-being, which are often associated with connectedness – feeling socially safe in the world and valued by others. From the day we're born, kindness, love and affection soothe and calm us and help us to feel less threatened. So, we'll arrive at the fascinating discovery that our contentment system is also linked to affection and kindness. Learning how to harness the capacity for self-soothing through the development of self-kindness and self-compassion is a key part of this book.

Chapter 6 explores how our capacity for imagination and fantasy can be used to stimulate different brain systems. This is the principle on which training our minds in compassion is based, because we can learn to understand how compassionate imagery and thinking can stimulate the contentment/soothing system. We will, of course, need to be very clear about what we mean when we use the term 'compassion'. So we'll look at some Buddhist and other spiritual views of it before looking at compassion from a more Western, scientific point of view. We'll see that it's made up of various attributes such as being motivated to care, being sympathetic, being able to tolerate our emotions, being empathic and understanding of what we feel, and being non-judgemental. There are also related skills that we can learn: compassionate attention, thinking and behaviour, and how to generate compassionate feelings.

This chapter is the last in our section on the science behind compassion. Part I is not fully comprehensive, of course, and over the decades to come, we'll understand far more about how our brains work and how important compassion is. But these six chapters will give you a flavour of it, a springboard to think about yourself in new ways, and also prepare you for the exercises to come.

Part II: Building the Compassionate Self: Skills and exercises

Part II brings us to the exercises that will help you to develop your compassionate mind.

Chapter 7 begins the journey with understanding the importance of what is now called *mindfulness*. This means learning to pay attention in a particular kind of way and recognizing how your brain can go off on all kinds of tangents because of your thinking and fantasies. In mindfulness, we learn how to hold attention 'in the present moment' without judgement. So you'll recognize that your mind naturally tends to wander all over the place and it's very difficult to stay focused, but with training you can develop a 'calm mind'. All the exercises in the rest of the book will be engaged with 'mindfully' – that is, when the mind wanders, we will gently and kindly bring it back to its task without judgement or criticism. Without training, 'wandering' is the natural way of the mind, just as when we learn a musical instrument our fingers at first won't go where we want them to.

Chapter 8 will take us into a world of using imagery and creating certain kinds of fantasies to stimulate different emotion systems within ourselves. You'll learn that, just as you can create fantasies of a sexual type which will stimulate your body, so you can also use your fantasy mind to create images that will stimulate your contentment/soothing and affection systems. There are many ways of doing this, but the key is learning *how* to practise, paying attention and creating in your mind thoughts and images that are deliberately designed to stimulate your feelings of compassion and your contentment/soothing system.

Chapter 9 explores compassionate thinking. It's very easy for our emotions to have us reasoning in anxious, angry, fretful or lustful ways. Compassionate thinking is a way of directing your thoughts to be helpful to you. We'll be examining ideas from cognitive and other psychotherapies about how our thinking enables us to construct a world for ourselves in many ways. Learning to recognize the content of our thoughts and how to stand back from them and look at them in different ways can be very conducive to developing compassion and compassionate thinking.

Chapter 10 brings us to a very important theme: how we relate to and treat ourselves. Sadly, the Western world is riddled with people who don't feel happy with themselves, who are critical and self-blaming. Treating yourself unkindly and critically is not good for your brain; it stimulates all kinds of stress. So we'll be addressing this issue very directly, looking at why we become self-critical and what we can do to spot it and to change it. Developing self-compassion, guided by your knowledge of how your brain works (from Part I), can move you forward in important ways.

Chapter 11 focuses on the emotions that can cause a lot of trouble – the self-protective emotions of anxiety and anger. We'll look at these in turn and think of ways in which we can deal with them compassionately, once we've decided that we sometimes need to work in new ways to cope with these powerful emotions.

Chapter 12 takes us on a journey into more complex areas of compassionate behaviour. You'll come to understand why being compassionate is not a soft option or just 'being nice' but can be very difficult, because it means standing up to some of our own desires and refusing to act on some of our lusts or fears. It can also mean recognizing that our intense desire for belonging and connectedness, to be one of a tribe and defend our own interests, can be the source of intense cruelty and atrocity. The tough issue in compassionate behaviour is addressing our own inner tendency towards cruelty. Compassion for ourselves can be important when we see that our capacity for cruelty arises because our brains are designed for self-protection and genetic advancement. This isn't our fault, but feeling compassion for this very fact allows us to take control and to turn against this side of ourselves.

Chapter 13 reflects on how we can bring a compassionate orientation into our lives and eventually begin to build more compassionate societies. The challenges ahead are major and serious, but at the same time, we're gradually waking up to the fact that we're all here without having chosen to be, caught up in the flow of life, and that by learning to harness the power of kindness and compassion, we can begin to exert more control and create a world that's more fun and harmonious to live in. We're also gradually developing our sciences of the mind so that we'll be better placed to understand how to build lifestyles that are conducive to fostering physical and psychological well-being. This will mean finding new ways to organize and reward our labour because 'competitive edge' economics is driving us all slightly crazy.

It's a long and winding road but, I hope, one that you'll find fascinating and one that will inspire you to bring more compassion into your life. And remember that this is all about *training*. There will be many times when, like me, you'll falter, fall over, have a tantrum or panic attack, be self-focused, and eat all the wrong foods. But that's life and we can all learn to be compassionate about these, too.

Throughout the book, I've included various case examples to emphasize certain points. Now, for obvious reasons of preventing identification, the true names and facts have been significantly changed or a case study has been created by combining a number of cases.

Part I
The Science behind Compassion

1 Compassion: The start of our journey

Life can be tough and perplexing, can't it? Human history is full of stories and reflections on life's tragedies and suffering, as well of its joys and triumphs. Indeed, given the reality of the many challenges that life puts our way, it's hardly surprising that poets, playwrights, authors, artists, philosophers and spiritual seekers – well, just about most people, actually – have all pondered on how to understand life and make our relatively short ones here on Earth meaningful and happy. The challenges may come in the form of coping with our own emotions of fear, anxiety, anger or depression, or with the loss of loved ones, setbacks in our life plans, difficult relationships or painful memories. Then there's the issue of our own fragility in the face of viruses, bacteria, genetic error and injury, all of which can turn our lives or those of the people we love into painful tragedies and remind us of our own eventual decay and death. You can understand why humans were delighted when they discovered red wine!

Even if we are personally at peace with ourselves, we're increasingly aware of the immense suffering in the world and feel inner calls to create a more fair, just and nurturing environment for us all. Our pursuit of meaning, justice and happiness is as much a part of us today as it was centuries ago when humans could first give thought to these things. We can, of course, seek solace in all kinds of ways for the anxiety and anger we feel at 'finding life like this'. Although we in the West now live in a world with advancing medical science, material comforts and pleasures, we still yearn to find deeper meaning and sources of inner peace and joy.

This book will offer a guided tour of ways to approach this quest. First, we need to explore what kind of species we are and where we have come from – that is, what's the basis of our nature? Our search will help us recognize that ancient spiritual wisdoms and new studies in psychology and of the brain all point to the same source for meaning and happiness:

the cultivation of compassion for ourselves and for others. So in these pages we'll concentrate on the benefits of developing compassion, with a special focus on self-kindness and self-compassion.

The road to compassion

Although many spiritual traditions have long stressed the importance of compassion for our well-being and good relations with other people (see below), it's only recently that researchers have found out just *how* compassion exerts its beneficial effects. This is exciting. One way they've used to discover that compassion is good for us is by studying the brains of people who either are very well practised at compassion or engage in compassionate thoughts and fantasies. Now the thoughts, imaginings and fantasies that we choose to focus on can have very powerful effects on our brains, bodily states and behaviours – something you're probably already aware of. For example, you know that your own sexual thoughts, images and fantasies (even when at home alone) can do 'interesting things' to your brain and body. So it will come as no surprise to learn that, when we fantasize and think about compassion, this does 'interesting things' to our brains and bodies, too. In fact, focusing on kindness, both to ourselves and to other people, stimulates areas of the brain and body in ways that are very conducive to health and well-being. Researchers have also found that, from the day we are born to the day we die, the kindness, support, encouragement and compassion of others has a huge impact on how our brains, bodies and general sense of well-being develop. Love and kindness, especially in early life, even affect how some of our genes are expressed![1] So it turns out that kindness and compassion are indeed paths to happiness and well-being.

Old ideas on the nature of suffering

Over the centuries, many spiritual traditions have come to see this life as essentially one of suffering from which we are seeking to escape:

Muslims believe that we are separated from God and are seeking to return. Sufi music can touch the grief of disconnectedness and the yearning/searching for re-connectedness.

Christians believe that suffering in this world is intimately bound up with our relationship with God and that only through God can we end suffering by a return to heaven.

Gnostics think that the creation of the material universe and all life was a mistake, possibly made by an evil deity. Suffering comes from the 'flesh' and its desires, all of which we should renounce.

Hindus believe that we are caught up on a wheel of constant birth and death and we are unsure how to get off of it. They believe that, with the help of Shiva and good works, we can disembark from the wheel of life and its death-and-rebirth cycle.

Buddhists also believe in a cycle of reincarnation in which we are trapped. For them, suffering arises from our attachments and grasping after things and achievements, and we can free ourselves only by developing an enlightened mind. We do this by recognizing that the mind we're born with is chaotic and grasping, but through training it in mindfulness and compassion, we can experience a different reality.

Other spiritual traditions explain suffering as the result of being tested by God and, if found wanting, discarded. Others believe that the soul has to learn spiritual lessons through suffering, which is the point of reincarnation. The soul must take a developmental journey, like in the game Snakes and Ladders: in some lives, you go forward and in others you can go back. Many religions believe that bad lives are punished after death – some of them rather nastily.

All of these traditions have little to say about genetic variation, brain damage or how being born into loving or abusive families can affect the way our brains grow and our (bad) behaviour. Those who believe in reincarnation also don't explain why, just as you acquire some wisdom, you die, forget everything and have to start all over! Some scientists, once they'd discovered how genes and evolution are the basis for all life forms and that 'male' and 'female' were fairly recent genetic solutions to the survival of genes, argued strongly against belief in these traditions. However, these traditions were never intended to be seen as factual, but instead came into being to help us cope with a harsh life of suffering and to unite people in common purpose.

Compassion and kindness

However, in *all* these traditions, you'll also find a strong emphasis on the importance and power of compassion, both as a spiritual focus and as a way of enhancing our social relationships, our relationship with ourselves and happiness. Buddhism, in particular, has been very focused for thousands of years on deliberately developing compassion.[2]

Within Buddhism, 'compassion' and 'kindness' have different meanings:

- *Metta* is loving kindness or friendly care, which is an orientation to self and others.

- *Mudita* is appreciating and taking joy from being alive 'in this moment' (e.g. the colours of clouds, a rainbow or sunset, the taste of food). It also refers to 'sympathetic joy' – joy from the well-being of others. It is the wellspring of peaceful well-being.

- *Karuna* is compassion that involves ethical behaviour, patience and generosity with action.

- *Upekkha* is equanimity and a sense of connectedness/similarity to other humans and all living things – that all seek happiness and none seeks suffering, that we are all the same in our struggles in life.

Western psychology makes different distinctions between types of positive feelings, their evolved functions and their focus. Note, too, that 'feeling compassion' can involve sadness and grief for the tragedies in which living things are caught up.

Now compassion is not just about a moral position or anything as simple as 'if I'm nice to you, you'll be nice to me', but is actually a way of *training* our brains that affects connections in them in a very important way.[3] In the second half of this book, you'll find a number of exercises that will help you develop compassion for yourself and others and stimulate feelings of safeness, acceptance, peacefulness and contentment.

So that's the good news. However, it turns out that the road to compassion is not an easy one. Indeed, if it were, then given that we've known about the value of compassion for thousands of years, we would now be living in a rather nicer world than we are. So we need to arm ourselves with an understanding of the *challenges* that lie before us at the start of our journey into developing our compassionate minds – these we will explore in the next few chapters. We will also see that compassion can require courage, but courage is easier to summon up when we have compassion (*see* Chapter 11).

Life in a rush

Now, if you are anything like me, you probably find life a bit tricky – well, at least sometimes. On the one hand, there are many things in life we love and enjoy: the affection of those close to us; waking up on the first day of a holiday; walking in the hills where the air is fresh and the sky is a crisp blue and white; sex; food; and, of course, that glass of wine at the end of a hard day – quite a lot of things when we think about it. On the other hand, we can have days of feeling rushed and harassed, when we might feel a bit lost, stuck, tired, anxious, frustrated and in low spirits, when life seems somewhat pointless and meaningless. On top of that, there's constant news of all the wars, traumas, conflicts and problems in the world. Despite our desire to be happy, prosperous and good, many of us have feelings, emotions and moods that we don't particularly like or want but which just come and sweep over us. We might even feel them on that holiday. You know the kind of thing. Maybe we wake up feeling a bit irritable, on a short fuse, or anxious and tired, or down in the dumps. Our moods just seem to fluctuate sometimes, don't they, without us being able to pinpoint any particular reason – we simply have good days and less good days. Or we might start the day okay and then we get time pressured or something frustrating happens that puts us in a bad mood.

The problem is that, once we are in a bad mood, things can spiral. We can start to feel rushed and then forget things, and that annoys us even more. We get home and then, unintentionally, are irritable with our partner and they, not surprisingly, are irritable back. We might have been hoping for a romantic evening and now that has all gone pear-shaped. Or it might be that we are very tired and snap at the children, at their extra demands, bickering and fighting. We feel frustrated with them, frustrated with ourselves and frustrated with life – even with the family cat. We can find ourselves simply reacting to things with whatever emotions seem to be at hand. Even though, aware that this is not what we want to feel or do, and a voice in our head suggests a change to our behaviour, our emotions appear to pull us right on along, seeming to be so 'in the body' and at the root of us. So before we know it, we have rushed through the day leaving a swirl of half-done things, abandoned aspirations and personal disappointments in our wake. A friend of mine who read this chapter smiled and said, 'And that's just on the good days.' Well, it's not always so bad, but life *can* be tricky at times.

It's really quite strange because many of us live in a world of unprecedented wealth and comfort. Yet despite our apparently insatiable drive for efficiency, the competitive edge and the 'business model' influencing all aspects of our lives, there is no evidence that this is making us any happier than we were 50 years ago. Actually there is evidence that we are becoming more unhappy and irritable as levels of stress increase in our hurry-hurry society.

After the Second World War, the focus was on welfare and building better communities. So, in Britain, we built the National Health Service, new universities and a rail service that actually worked and didn't treat people like cattle. These were institutions that were, in many ways, the envy of the world. During the 1960s, we were led to believe that science and technology would gradually increase our leisure and family time, would enable us to retire earlier and earlier and generally would concentrate on increasing human well-being.

This philosophy of building societies for our 'welfare' is now all but gone, replaced by the need to maintain 'competitive edge' and make 'efficiencies', fear of unemployment, and the problems of running increasingly complex and expensive services such as health, education and transport. In fact, we're experiencing exactly the opposite of a release from the drudgery and time pressures of work. As Madeline Bunting[4] points out in her provocative book *Willing Slaves*, we are working longer hours, the retirement age has just been extended, the insecurity of a job market with short-term contracts is worse than ever and, in profession after profession, one hears stories about too rapid change, under-resourcing and not enough time to attend to quality. There is a depressing shift away from welfare-focused and 'quality of life' politics towards the business model, which is focused on shareholders' dividends and 'efficiencies', often at the expense of quality and a concern with human welfare.[5]

In fact, since the 1970s the profit-maximizing business model has infiltrated every aspect of our waking hours. In many facets of our lives, both personal and at work, we are consumed with meeting targets – the things that we feel or are told we must do. A businesswoman friend, lamenting the focus on individual targets and the demise of supportive working in her job, noted with a half smile, 'You know, the other today I found myself thinking about my sex life as a target – and whether I could keep up the 2.5 times a week average! At the moment, I think I can only manage the 0.5 – and, of course, I feel a bit of a failure and let down.' I never quite worked out what she did for the 0.5.

Despite our wealth and comforts, half of us will have some kind of mental health problem at some point, with depression, anxiety, alcoholism and eating disorders topping the list. The World Health Organization has worked out that depression will be the second-most burdensome disorder on Earth by 2020 and other mental health problems will be in the top ten. At the time of writing, this is only 12 years away, and by the time you read this book, it will be even less! For women between the ages of 15 and 45, depression is already by far the biggest burden and blight on their lives.

We are also becoming less trusting and feeling more threatened. My wife trained in radiography in the 1960s, when it was unheard of for staff to be threatened in hospital accident and emergency departments – even by the intoxicated. Now in some hospitals, security staff need to be on hand, especially at night, because threats are so regular. Closed-circuit cameras are perched everywhere; the days of leaving one's door unlocked are long gone.

So why aren't all of our advances in medicine and our ability to travel the world, nip down to the local supermarket for any number of things to eat, have the most fantastic flat-screen TVs with hundreds of channels – why aren't these things making us wonderfully happy as individuals and happy with each other? Well, many reasons have been given to explain this. According to Madeline Bunting, we've become 'willing slaves' to accountants and the need to compete. Oliver James suggests that we're suffering from 'affluenza'[6] – an addiction to affluence and a need 'for more and more'. John Naish[7] makes essentially the same point. He notes what evolutionary psychologists have been saying for a long time, that our brains evolved to cope with scarcity, not 'abundance and plenty', and we are born 'seekers' and 'wanters' because, for millions of years, that was often the state we were in. So while we have an evolved mind that seeks out more and more, we are also struggling to say 'no' to our wants and that 'enough is enough'. Add to this little evolutionary glitch the fact that we have a marketing industry that spends billions every year ensuring that we are not content and that we do want more and more . . . and you can see the problem.

All these views have much to recommend them. However, there are two other aspects that need to be added. First, we haven't learned how to train our minds for happiness and contentment. Moreover, every message within our families, in school and at work teaches us not to be content because this is 'resting on our laurels', which somehow smacks of laziness or lack of ambition or 'backbone' and dooms us to the backwaters of life. Consider the commercial world: who would regard as a good business any firm that was content with itself, had 0 per cent growth or might even be prepared to shrink?

Second, we have forgotten a key point that Karl Marx made a century and a half ago: the means of production shapes our very consciousness. But of course you don't have to be a Marxist to understand that our working lives are becoming so devouring of time and stressful that we think that only by having more and more can we compensate for that time and offset that stress; each of us is a dog chasing its tail. How often have you heard other people say, 'I worked so hard I deserve this pay increase/a new car/a better holiday/a night out.' It's odd – we feel we have to reward ourselves because we've treated ourselves so badly and are knackered. And we're locked into this because there are mortgages to pay and lifestyles to maintain and no other way of sustaining them without selling our souls to the business model. So it is not (just) our pursuit of affluence that is driving us all slightly crazy, irritable, aggressive, exhausted and self-focused, but the fact that our competitive lives are *incredibly stressful*. In our exhaustion, we are losing contact with each other; watching television has become easier than socializing; drinking a bottle of wine has become easier than practising relaxation, meditation and 'mind replenishment'. Mine is the Merlot. The most common complaint that GPs hear day in and day out is, 'Doctor, I'm so tired,' and one of the reasons why television is so popular is because, although it's rather brain numbing, the very passivity of it is just what appeals when you feel so tired. Our lifestyles are physically, mentally and spiritually exhausting us – and we know it!

Karen's story

Karen's situation is rather typical. She worked in a university department, and when a colleague left, budget cuts meant that that person was not replaced, so other people just had to absorb the work. A year later, the same thing happened. Slowly the department was afflicted by the 'creeping hours' effect and a mixture of worry and anger permeated it. Within a few years, a department that had been a pleasure to work in, where people had had time for each other and had helped each other in their tasks, had become a non-stop 'Sorry, I really haven't got time for you today' and 'How come you haven't finished that report yet?' sort of place. People were cynical about their work and had lost pride in it, with an attitude of 'Don't worry too much about that report – anything will do – anyway, it will all be changed tomorrow in some new reorganization.' (The NHS is riddled with this type of thinking.)

In my work as a clinical psychologist, time and time again I meet people who tell me that quality is constantly being sacrificed in the pursuit of profit and competitive edge. Yet humans derive a sense of satisfaction from being *able to spend time* creating quality. We get pleasure from our creations, and need to see appreciation in the eyes of others. The business model is more interested in growing larger and satisfying stakeholders, not in the job satisfaction or the well-being of its workers.

In Karen's department, new tough managers were brought in to make tough decisions, with their behaviour sailing close to bullying. Karen felt that the aim of providing quality education was being replaced with the 'need to compete in the marketplace'. Everybody increasingly felt that the reason for their existence was to put 'bums on seats', cheaper and more quickly.

Now this is not an uncommon story, from the top to the bottom of society. In our hearts, we know there is a problem with all this. Economic systems are falling more and more out of tune with what our minds and social relationships actually require: to have a sense of connectedness, safeness and well-being. What is the point of creating a world of more luxurious cars and homes, more TV channels, more brightly lit supermarkets and their ready meals, if most of us are so tired, work-focused, stressed out and miserable that we hardly notice them anyway – or just see them as expected rewards for our hard work. Even more problematically, as we struggle with the stress and to keep up, we could actually become more vulnerable to mental health problems and, if we can't keep up, *self-critical.*

Karen noticed that, as the months passed, it was becoming much easier for her to become frustrated and her anxiety was also increasing. She often had a worry in the back of her mind about whether she had done all she was supposed to – had she forgotten anything? Previously she had been happy and relaxed on Sundays, but now she was often anxious and unsettled, thinking about work on Monday and what she had to do. She started to feel rather trapped in her job and wondered how she might change. She also noticed that, at times, her anxiety would just kick in from nowhere: when waiting for a train that she knew was likely to be crowded, she would start to worry frantically that she would not get a seat or that it might break down. In addition, she was feeling increasingly claustrophobic. Going into a meeting, she started to panic that she might have to fight her corner all over again because budgets were increasingly tight and the finance people had long lost any concern for quality – it was just about surviving now.

A few years earlier, Karen had enjoyed her 'intimate moments' with her husband and reading a book before sleep. Now she often felt too tired for intimacy, and she'd be able to read only a page of her book before falling asleep. 'It's taken me nearly a year to read one novel,' she reflected sadly. 'Trouble is, by the time I get to the end I can't remember what happened at the beginning!' And at the back of her mind was the constant worry that her relationship with her children was suffering, again because of a lack of time and her own fatigue, but the family desperately needed her salary to pay the mortgage. She said tearfully, 'You know, the years are going by so fast. I'm going to turn around to find that my children have left home and I hardly know them.'

Karen was experiencing the effects of the increasingly common problem: living in a society that is continually demanding more and more of her, with no concern whatsoever for her welfare, that is overstimulating her threat and stress systems. Her mild depression was a *natural*, *normal* consequence of that; her loss of confidence was actually her brain saying, 'Give up, get out of this fight' – but, of course, how would she then pay the mortgage?

Like Karen, many of us are now caught up in a culture driven by the 'business model' and the need for profit, not by a human 'psychology model' or a human welfare or a well-being model. We are so caught up in the drive for profits and efficiency that we are losing contact with each other and the things that nourish, support and nurture us through life. In fact, I was thinking of writing a book called *Why Efficiency is Bad for You*! Think of all the things in life that, if we focus only on efficiency, wouldn't be much fun. The drive for efficiency is actually making our lives uninhabitable. So the business model of life will create haves and have-nots and have-lots and will keep anxiety high as we try to maintain a 'competitive edge'.

Of course, modern life beats that of our ancestors, living in damp caves, often near starvation, fighting off wild animals and being subject to a range of diseases that are easily curable today. And of course, most other socio-political systems that have operated in human civilization have been ruled by despots. Competition between tyrants of one kind or another kept people poor, feudal and focused on fighting and defence. So freedom, invention, innovation and enterprise have helped us in various ways. Unfortunately the drive for profit and competitive edge (which was the motivation of the tyrants, after all) is now being played out between firms and corporations who have hijacked these qualities, and they are seriously failing to provide for our human needs. We are increasingly creating divided, grasping and exhausting environments that are not conducive to happiness or well-being. In the decades to come, we must, as a society, think what all this work is for. Given all the billions and billions of hours of labour and effort by all the humans in the world every day – what are we doing? Our human effort, the sweat of our brows, is being frittered away in the manufacture of trinkets.

A compassionate approach to life asks us to face these issues head on, and on our road to compassion, we will encounter a number of challenges. Each one will require careful thought, with solutions emerging as people work together pooling their ideas, knowledge and talents. But ultimately the solutions to all the challenges we will now explore point in the same direction, to the importance and urgency of developing compassion for ourselves and for others. Each of the challenges I will discuss in the next few chapters have important implications for our own personal lives, our sense of contentment and our well-being, and also how we might start to think about how to organize ourselves as collections of individuals and societies living on this resource-limited planet. Compassion is not just about being reactive to things that have happened but also about 'trying to create' for the future.

The flow of life

Many currently available books on compassion are written from a Buddhist perspective or spiritual tradition. This book is rather different because it will integrate these insights with our modern understanding of the origins and functions of the brain. It is, in fact, a recognition of our evolutionary history – what evolution has set us up with – which opens new insights into our desperate need to develop compassion for ourselves and others. Indeed, many of the challenges that we will meet shortly have become challenges in part because of how our minds have evolved and what they have evolved for. Understanding how our minds got to be what they are and why we have the range of emotions, desires and passions that we have can be extremely valuable in helping us to stand back from those emotions, desires and passions and recognize that we didn't design or create them – we simply have to understand how they live and flow through us. By understanding how our minds work, we can see what we're up against.

So, the major context for a lot of the challenges we face is to come to terms with the fact that we are *evolved beings*.[8] This means that we have emerged from the *flow of life* on this planet; we are the result of the struggles of millions of other life forms, 99 per cent of which are now extinct.

A key message that modern science provides us with is that evolved design is not necessarily good design. For any strategy or trait to evolve, it simply has to out-compete other designs. There is an old joke which goes: 'You don't have to run faster than the wolf. You just have to run faster than your friend.' Okay – so it does nothing for friendship, but it does demonstrate that some of the things that evolution has bestowed on animals to give them an advantage in one area can compromise their abilities in another. This trade-off can be seen in the peacock's tail, which is great for attracting mates but a handicap when trying to escape from predators. Also consider how giraffes have to struggle to get their necks down to drink water. Sex is none too easy for them either. Any alien visiting this planet would regard them as rather bizarre animals – how could such an animal have evolved? Then we discover that the long neck is actually an adaptation that allows giraffes to eat leaves from the higher branches of trees. So an advantage in one area can actually produce serious disadvantages in others.

There are many examples of this in our own human genetic profiles and our human psychology. A gene that confers protection against malaria is the same gene that gives rise to sickle cell anaemia – a dreadful disease that affects some individuals from a number of different ethnic backgrounds.[9] If we look into psychology, we also see trade-offs. For example, our stress systems were designed to cope with relatively short-lived stressors such as predators or short fights and interchanges, but not chronic stress. There is now good evidence that the stress hormone cortisol is useful for short-term defensive behaviour, because it mobilizes fats, energizes the body and focuses attention, but it can actually damage the immune system and the brain if it remains elevated for too long.[10] Our big brains give us our intelligence. However, having a big brain means having a big head, which can make birth difficult and very painful for the mother and increases the risk of death in childbirth. Billions of women have died as a result of these adaptations. Still, we are born small and completely helpless and require a long period of attachment and being cared for. Our dependency and interactions with our parents as we grow up stimulate our brain to grow in various ways. However, our dependency also opens us up to harm from our carers if they are abusive or neglectful. The kind of care we receive affects how our brain matures.[11]

Another reason why evolution does not always come up with good designs is because it proceeds by adapting pre-existing designs. It cannot go back to the drawing board and start again. It can't press the 'delete' button on previous designs. Thus, our brains did not appear *de novo*, but are the result of millions of years of evolution. This means that new adaptations can run up against old ones and cause problems. We will look at this in more detail in our next chapter when we discuss the difference between 'old brains', which reflect the range of emotions and social behaviours that we share with many other animals, and 'new minds' that enable us to think in complex ways. Our human imaginations can give rise to wonderful art but also the most hideous of tortures. Our high-level thoughts and fantasies can be directed by much older, primitive desires and emotions that evolved long before the capacities for imagination and complex thinking.

We should also be aware that many of our human adaptations evolved to fit social and ecological contexts that existed many thousands of years ago when there was a high infant mortality rate, when people lived in small, close-knit, isolated groups that may have been hostile to each other, when a person would interact with the same few people (maybe only 100–150) throughout life, and when the style of life was primarily hunter-gatherer. Hence quite a few of the typical ways we now think about relationships (e.g. as kin, friend, enemy) tend to reflect ways for organizing social information that fitted this ancient lifestyle.[12]

Modern life may serve us well in many respects, but it can also produce *contextual overload*. For example, modern lifestyles can overload physiological systems – e.g. the cardiovascular system was not designed to cope with high-fat foods, low exercise and smoking. Obesity is a problem for us because we evolved in a world of scarcity, having to be on the move to find food. We did not evolve inner mechanisms for restraint. We now live in a world of plenty, of supermarkets and cars, with food manufacturers spending billions creating tasty 'addictions'. We've also created environments in which we marinate ourselves in artificial chemicals from various industrial processes and food production, and we've very little idea of how they impact on us. Research is gradually indicating that some of these chemicals in our environment and our food are having negative effects on our mood states and on children's behaviour.

Of our basic behaviours, it is likely that competitive behaviour, social comparison, social anxiety and fear of exclusion might each function quite differently in small, close-knit, familiar and stable groups than they do today in our large and constantly changing groups and mega-societies.[13] Modern environments can also produce *contextual constraints*, where new environments hinder the development of adaptive behaviours. For example, most primates are free roaming, living in groups in the outdoors where females and their offspring can, on the whole, avoid aggressive individuals. Humans, however, have created marriage, houses and households, all of which enforce proximity and can make escape from aggressive individuals extremely difficult, if not impossible. Domestic violence is, to some extent, created through entrapment. Another example of a constraint on natural escape and avoidance behaviour is needing to keep up the payments on an expensive house, which may stop you leaving a well-paid but highly stressful job. Indeed such 'entrapments' are very common in depression.[14]

Our modern environments can also frustrate evolved needs because they provide insufficient or the wrong kinds of signals/inputs. Children need love, affection, care and protection, and many studies, particularly those that have involved children neglected in orphanages, have shown that severe neglect can have a detrimental effect on brain maturation.[15] Although the need for affection and love is at its height in childhood, as we will see humans have evolved to need love, affection and compassion to varying degrees throughout life. These 'inputs' actually nourish our brains in part because affection, support, kindness and compassion cause the release of endorphins, opiates and hormones such as oxytocin that are good for our well-being and health. Modern environments may be limiting these inputs in all kinds of ways as well as providing brain stimulation that is not entirely helpful. In fact, some authors go so far as to say that the modern stressors of 'competing', the level of exhaustion due to our styles of working, and the forms of television that we watch and the computer games that we and our kids are playing all contribute to stress that can actually damage the brain.[16] Critics may say, 'Sure, but wasn't life tougher a hundred years ago?', and the answer is: 'Of course, it was.' But that was also a time when one in seven children died and the average life expectancy of people in London's East End was between 45 and 50 years. Of course, there are many lifestyles that are much harsher than ours and some that are better. The focus here is on how the business model is driving a wedge between what we materially want, can buy and sell, and what we actually need as sources of well-being.

The interaction between our evolved dispositions and our culture is powerful and transcends the personal.[17] What this means is that the very sense of ourselves, the kind of person one feels one is or wants to be is created within our societies and cultures. For example, in ecologies where men hunt in dangerous terrains – e.g. where there are many predators – or where there are other hostile groups or great inter-male competitiveness, masculine identity tends to focus on issues of bravery, traditional macho values and clear gender differences.[18] These social ecologies also impact on child-rearing practices, which can be harsh and punitive.[19] So the way you come to think of yourself as a person, the values that you believe are important to you are actually created for you in your social contexts. If you grow up in a safe, loving environment, your values will be different than if you grow up in the back streets, where violence and the threat of violence are never far away. If you grow up in a Buddhist monastery, your values regarding a whole range of things will be different than if you grow up in a fundamentalist Christian or Muslim family. We like to focus on individuals and target them if they do right or wrong, but the challenge is to recognize that we are far more *created* than we are the *creators* of our own identities and senses of self.

As I will discuss in the next chapter, this brings us to some personal implications. Basically neither you nor I *chose* to be here. We did not choose to be born, nor the kinds of brains that we have; we did not choose the kinds of emotions that we have to deal with (that is, our capacity for fear, rage, sexual desire); we did not choose how our brains and bodies would be educated and the values we would end up adopting; we didn't choose to be born into this century rather than another, or into a Christian, Muslim, Hindu or atheist social group. So when we emerge into consciousness at around the age of two, we *just find ourselves here*, trying to make sense of it all as best we can. We grow up automatically under the age-old instructions of our genes and the influences of our social relationships.

Conclusion

Science is now helping us make sense of 'being here' because it is reconnecting us to the *flow of life*, which takes us to our first challenge. Our lives can be compared to road maps, with places of origin, terrains that have been easy or hard, routes taken and those avoided, blocked roads, cul de sacs and intended and unintended designations – and, of course we can also think about which roads to take to desired destinations. In the next chapter, we're going to explore in detail some of the challenges that face us on our road to developing compassion, and how compassion will help us to face up to and deal with these challenges.

Developing compassion is seen as a key process for helping us develop happiness and meaning.[20] Recently, however, some researchers have pointed out that there are many aspects to well-being that focus on 'living one's life to the full'.[21] While happiness is primarily a feeling and an emotional approach, both compassion and 'living life to the full' shine a spotlight on our feelings of control, self-identity, personal meaningfulness and motivation. Compassion-focused approaches stretch across both.

We'll see that sometimes compassion requires us to act with courage and override anxieties. Developing compassion for self and others can help us with the many challenges of life, with learning how to cope with strong emotions that emerge within us and with conflicts with other people, and even how to think about world problems. Focusing on the inner development of self-kindness, social connectedness and contentment can help us on our way.

2 The Challenges of Life

Our road to compassion begins by trying to understand in detail the consequences that arise because we are emergent beings *in the flow of life*, part of evolution. By appreciating the way in which our minds and bodies have been created and have evolved, we can begin to understand the challenges in our own personal lives and those we face in building more compassionate societies. Some of these challenges will be very familiar because you meet them every day. You may well think of various other challenges in your daily life, so don't take this as an exhaustive list.

Challenge 1: Old brains and bodies

The first challenge is to (re)connect ourselves to the *flow and variety of life* on our planet, in this solar system and in this universe, and recognize that our minds are the product of that flow. It is called evolution. Our brains contain within them a range of potential feelings, fantasies and desires, the origins of which stretch back into the far distance of time, and which were designed in the flow of life. Many animals appear to have the basic emotions of anger, anxiety and pleasure to guide them through their lives, although how they experience them is, of course, probably quite different to the way we do. Many studies have shown that the brain areas that regulate these emotions in animals are similar to those in our own brains.

What science has also revealed is that our brains contain at least three types of major emotion regulation systems. Each one is designed to do different things, but also to work together as a system and to be in balance with and counterbalance each other.[1] Our *experiences* of emotions and desires emerge from the *patterns* they create in our brains and bodies. So if you're having one type of thought or feeling, one pattern – an array of many millions of brain cells – will light up in your brain, but when you feel differently, a different pattern/array will be activated. As we'll see when we work on the exercises in Part II, we may be able to take more control over the 'brain patterns' that emerge in us.

The three interacting emotion regulation systems are shown in Diagram 1. We'll be exploring them in more detail in Chapters 4 and 5, as they play a major role in how we'll think about compassion and compassion training.

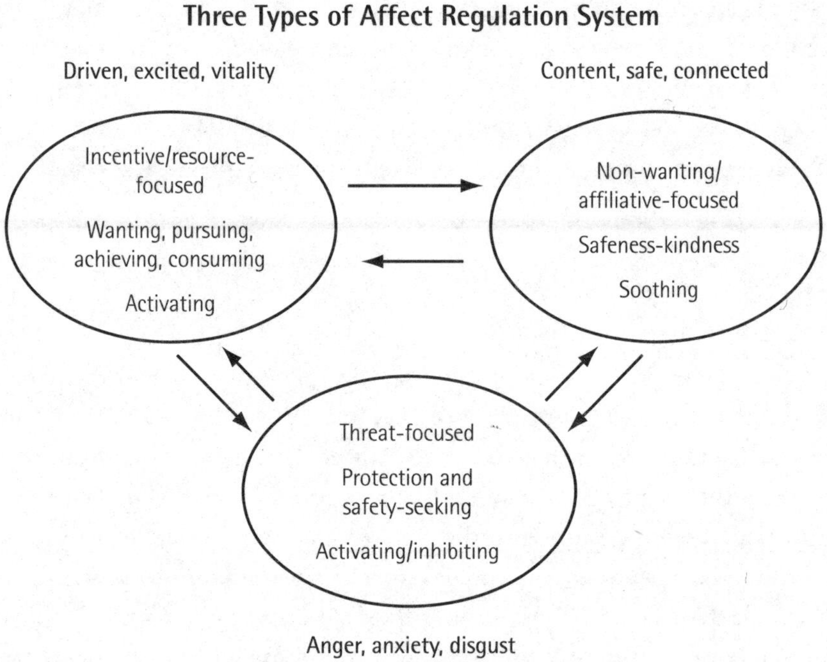

Three Types of Affect Regulation System

Driven, excited, vitality   Content, safe, connected

Incentive/resource-focused

Wanting, pursuing, achieving, consuming

Activating

Non-wanting/affiliative-focused

Safeness-kindness

Soothing

Threat-focused

Protection and safety-seeking

Activating/inhibiting

Anger, anxiety, disgust

Diagram 1: The interaction between three major emotion regulation systems

This is a simplified view of what are, of course, multi-component and complex systems. However, thinking in terms of these three can provide a helpful framework for exploring how our brain gives rise to different feelings, desires and urges such as anger, fear, excitement and various desires and lusts, as well as compassion. So let's look briefly at each in turn.

1 *Threat and self-protection system* The function of this system is to pick up on threats quickly and then give us bursts of feelings such as anxiety, anger or disgust. These feelings will ripple through our bodies, alerting us and urging us to take action against the threat – to self-protect.

The effect of this system is to activate us to run or fight, or inhibit us so that we freeze, submit or simply stop doing things. It also comes into play if there are threats to the people we love, to our friends or to our group. Although it's a source of painful and difficult feelings (e.g. anxiety, anger, disgust), remember that it evolved as a protection system. In fact, you might be surprised to learn that the brain gives more priority to dealing with threats than to pleasurable things. The threat system operates with particular brain networks, one of which is the *amygdala* (from the Latin for 'almond'). You have one of these groups of neurons on each side of your brain behind each ear. The amygdala is a fast-acting processor that picks up on things of importance to us, especially threatening things. The stress hormone *cortisol* also plays a major role in our sensitivity to threats and how we experience them, as well as to our general sense of anxiety.

2 *Incentive and resource-seeking system* The function of this system is to give us positive feelings that guide, motivate and encourage us to seek out resources that we (and those we love and care about) will need to survive and prosper. We're motivated by and find pleasure in seeking out, consuming and achieving nice things (e.g. food, sex, comforts, friendships, status, recognition). If we win a competition, pass an exam or get to go out with a desired person, we will probably experience feelings of excitement and pleasure. If you win the lottery and become a millionaire, you may feel so energized that it is difficult to sleep, your mind may be racing and you may want to party all the time. The reason for this is that your incentive/resource-seeking system has got out of balance and, in a way, over-excited. People with manic depression can have problems with this system because its activation point can shift from too high to too low. When balanced with the other two systems, however, this one guides us towards important life goals. Imagine what life would be like without it: you'd have no motivation, energy or desires – and, indeed, in depression people can lose the feelings that this system provides. Over-stimulated, though, it can drive us to wanting 'more and more' and to frustration and disappointment. When blocks to our wants and goals become a 'threat', the threat/self-protection system kicks in with anxiety or frustration/anger.

The incentive/resource-seeking system is primarily activating and 'go get'. A substance in the brain called *dopamine* is important for our drives. Lots of things can produce a flush of dopamine – falling in love, passing an exam, winning something you want. Because they're pleasurable, we'll seek out these things. People who take amphetamines or cocaine try to get the energized and hyped-up good feeling that dopamine produces naturally. The come-down is, of course, the opposite.

3 *Soothing and contentment system* This is the most tricky system to describe. It enables us to bring a certain soothing, quiescence and peacefulness to ourselves, which helps to restore our balance. When animals aren't defending themselves against threats and problems and don't need to achieve or do anything because they have enough of everything, they can be content. 'Contentment' means being happy with the way things are and feeling safe, not striving or wanting. It is an inner peacefulness that's quite a different positive feeling from the hyped-up excitement of 'striving and succeeding' feeling of the incentive/resource-seeking system. It is also different from feelings that are often associated with boredom or a kind of emptiness. When people practise meditation and 'slowing down', these are the feelings they report: 'not-wanting', an inner calm and a connectedness to others.

What complicates this system, but is of great importance for our exploration in compassion, is that it is also linked to affection and kindness. For example, when a baby or child is distressed, the love of the parent soothes and calms the infant. Affection and kindness from others helps soothe us adults, too, when we're distressed, and gives us feelings of safeness in our everyday lives. These feelings of soothing and safeness seem to work through brain networks similar to those that produce peaceful feelings associated with fulfilment and contentment.[2] Substances in our brain called *endorphins* appear to be important for this peaceful, calm sense of well-being. The hormone *oxytocin* is linked to our feelings of social safeness and, along with the endorphins, give us the feelings of well-being that flow from feeling loved, wanted and safe with others. This soothing system is going to be a central focus in our compassion training because it is vital to our sense of well-being. (Incidentally, I use the term 'safeness' to describe the experience of being safe. 'Safety' and 'safety-seeking' are aspects of the threat/self-protection system.)

A number of key points arise from understanding the nature and origins of our emotions – what they were designed for and what their functions are.

The first is that many negative emotions such as anxiety, anger, disgust and sadness are a normal part of our emotional repertoire. These protection emotions are the big players in our brains and can easily override positive emotions: if you're enjoying lunch in the park and a lion appears, you'd better lose interest in the pleasures of lunch and run! These emotions evolved to help us detect and cope with threats, but in our society, obsessed as it is with happiness, we sometimes feel that, if we experience them to any degree, there's something wrong with us. Importantly, we should note that our brains did not evolve for happiness but for survival and reproduction, so we need to learn how to accept, tolerate and work with difficult emotions or low moods. These aren't evidence of 'something wrong' with us but can be quite normal responses to things in our life.

Second, it naturally follows that our emotion systems may be working perfectly normally but the inputs are problematic. Someone who feels trapped in, say, a loveless relationship may become depressed. The depression can be a *normal* consequence of this situation in which they find themselves. As we will see in Chapters 10, 11 and 12, compassionate behaviour sometimes requires courage, to make changes in our lives. Some people's lives *are* stressful – that's why they feel stress – or they may have experienced tragedies and losses and that's why they feel sad or are grieving. Of course, there are things we can do to improve the quality of our lives and feelings and we will be exploring how compassionate thinking and behaving and compassionate feelings can help us, but it is also important to recognize that some of our unpleasant feelings and reactions are usually not abnormal and we should not feel ashamed of them.

The third issue is to recognize that we become stressed and distressed when our incentive/resource-seeking and threat/self-protection systems get out of balance with the soothing/contentment one. Modern societies are, in a whole variety of ways, over-stimulating both our threat system and our incentive ('want more' and 'need to do more') system.[3] However, happiness does not lie in over-stimulating these brain patterns, but in balancing our emotions and desires, recognizing the ups and downs of life and learning how to stimulate and develop the soothing system. The latter gives rise to feelings of peacefulness and helps to regulate the threat-based emotions of anxiety, anger, disgust and depression and the excessive 'need and want' feelings of the incentive system. This soothing system responds to kindness, as we will see in Chapters 4, 5 and 6, and learning to focus on kindness to self and others can help stimulate it. Much of the second half of this book is devoted to exercises to do precisely that and to bring your systems into balance – because as in most things in life, it's all about balance.

So the early roots of our emotions are buried deep in the evolutionary past, stretching back to the reptiles and early mammals, in fact. Of course, we know that our emotions can be wonderful because they give colour and texture to our lives: they give the pleasures of love, are moved by music and sunsets and create the fun when your friend tells you a new joke or the excitement of going on a date with someone new, as well as anxieties and angers. Some theorists believe that emotions are actually key to understanding the whole nature of consciousness; to them, consciousness is actually based on emotions. In fact, so important are emotions that they play a very fundamental role in our ability to function at all. Indeed, research on people who have damaged the parts of their brain that register emotions has shown that they are at a severe disadvantage.[4] You might think that without emotion to worry about they would be like Mr Spock in *Star Trek*, clear, logical and precise, but far from it. Without emotions, we can become easily confused, can find it hard to make decisions or weigh up the importance of things, can lose motivation, become disconnected from others and generally find life aimless, grey and drab and so lose the ability to function. Well, Mr Spock was actually always quite an 'illogical' construction!

However, as with all things that have developed through evolution, our emotions come with challenges as well. As wonderful and important to our functioning as they are, our emotions can also get us into serious trouble – especially when we are taken over by them. Remember that bad day we were having in Chapter 1, getting frustrated, irritable and so on? That's 'old brain' emotion running things for you. People come into psychotherapy in their droves because of problems with their emotions and feelings. Some behave immorally against others, acting cruelly because of their emotions and feelings or, at times, their *lack* of feelings. Indeed, for thousands of years philosophers and religious people have pondered the problems that come from human behaviour being guided by rather primitive emotions and what we can do about them.

Evolved social lives

So some of our basic emotion potentials have their roots in 'old brain/ mind' systems that have been knocking about on this planet, doing their thing, for many millions of years – indeed, long before us. But if you look closely, you'll see that it's not just emotions that have been doing the rounds for eons – this is also true for a whole variety of social-relating styles and patterns. For example, if you look at a species that is somewhat like us, such as chimpanzees, you will see them engaging in lots of social activities that we engage in, too, and forming types of relationships that we also form. So you will observe them pursuing sexual opportunities; fighting and challenging each other for status and social position; forming close friendships and bonds; caring for their children; answering distress calls and clinging to each other when frightened; reconciling their conflicts and working together in groups, as in hunting. Sadly they've even been seen to engage in warlike behaviour, when a large group split into two smaller groups and then one group exterminated the other.[5] Taken all together, these are what we call *archetypal life patterns* (or 'strategies', as evolutionists describe them) and they work in us too – as we will explore in more detail in the next chapter.

Now for the moment and for convenience and ease of discussion I am going to refer to these basic emotions and relating styles as *'old brain/mind'* abilities or attributes. They are the age-old motives that guide us (as they do other animals) to seek out sexual relations, status, friendships, family connectedness and having our own children, and our emotions help keep us on track to secure them. So we have positive feelings when we are succeeding at these things, such as gaining status and friendships, having a sense of connectedness to friends and family, having our own families. But we can experience very negative emotions when these important aspects of our lives are blocked and we feel like outsiders, disconnected from family or friends, and / or feel as if we have been reduced to a lowly status and are inferior.

So our first challenge is to recognize and cope with desires, motives and dispositions that have been written *for* us, rather than *by* us long ago, and which operate within many of our animal cousins too. When we put ourselves in the *flow of life*, we become aware that we're actors on this planet, playing very similar parts to other life forms in our struggle for survival and reproduction. We have kinship with other life forms; we reconnect with the flow of life. However, as we will also see, new thinking and our self-aware brains greatly influence our basic feelings and the importance of our social relationships.

Challenge 2: New brains and new minds

The second challenge is, in a way, the opposite of the first. It is about coming to terms with the fact that we are also *very different* to all other life forms on this planet. This is because we have what we can call *'new brain/ mind'* attributes and competencies.

So let's consider exactly how we are different from every other species, including chimpanzees, with whom we share more than 98 per cent of our genes. Something happened in the evolution of the human mind a few million years ago that made our minds radically different to those of other species. Actually scientists don't think it was one thing that happened but a series of interconnected adaptations.[6] Humans eventually evolved into the primate who remains dependent the longest with a brain maturation process that far exceeds that of all other species.

To appreciate just how far humans have evolved in this direction, consider that, at the time of birth, the brain of our nearest living relative, the chimpanzee, has a volume of about 350 cubic centimetres. During maturity it will grow to around 450cc – the shape of the skull does not allow for more. Around two million years ago, early humanoids known as *Homo habilis* first appeared on Earth with a brain capacity of 650–700cc. They walked upright, lived in family groups, developed simple tool use, followed a hunter-gatherer way of life and may have built shelters. After *Homo habilis*, evolution came up with *Homo erectus*, Neanderthals and *Homo sapiens* (us), and today our brain capacity is around 1,500cc. So in just two million years the expansion of the brain, and especially the *cortex*, the outer, convoluted layer, has been rapid and dramatic. The ratio of cortex to total brain size is estimated to be 67 per cent in monkeys, 75 per cent in apes and 80 per cent in humans. Much of this extra cortical mass is present in the motor areas, which are responsible for movement and the skills of fine coordination, and in the frontal cortex, where our ability to empathize and imagine sits and where the internalization of social regulators (values and social rules) occurs. Big brains and the competencies they support need energy and are costly to run, so there must have been some important pay-offs to evolving them. There are: they are what make us intelligent.

The human brain starts out about the same size as a chimpanzee's, 350cc, but during its first four years of development, it will triple in size, then grow more slowly until it reaches around 1,500cc. Not only is there a rapid increase in size post-birth, but there is also considerable development in the branching and connecting-up of neurons (nerve cells). In the first years of life, the human brain undergoes a radical transformation as millions upon millions of new connections are formed and laid down in increasingly complex networks day by day. The maturing, branching, networking and organizing trajectories of the brain give rise to increasingly complex potentials for thinking, feeling and behaving in a multiplicity of social ways. Two key processes direct these abilities: the genes we are born with and our experiences in life. When some event occurs, the brain responds and neurons fire in complex patterns like fireworks. When they do, they start connecting to each other. A well-known finding suggests that 'neurons that fire together wire together'. So you can imagine how extensively the brain of an infant receiving soothing and affection will be getting wired up compared to one of an infant receiving little soothing, who is also neglected or often being stressed.

Genes give us our basic abilities – e.g. to learn a language, form attachments to our parents – and influence our personalities, but the types of language we learn and how we use that language in our thinking are dependent on our experiences and where we grow up. We also know that experiences that are stressful affect our brain in various ways. Powerful early experiences of feeling loved or stressed – and even the environment of the womb – can actually turn genes on and off. So our experiences can have powerful effects in shaping us, the kind of people we'll become, right down to our genetic expressions. Our genetic potential is called the *genotype*; the actual way our experience shapes us, and affects what we actually feel and do, is called the *phenotype*. People can have very similar genotypes but very different phenotypes. You might have the genotype to be a world-class athlete but grow up in poverty, take to smoking and drinking and never make your phenotypic possibility of winning gold medals a reality. In addition, our thoughts, values and social engagements can play a huge role in our behaviours and phenotypic expression. As a result, because of our new brains and cultures, we have a far greater range of phenotypic possibilities than any other animal.

These controlling processes – our genes and experiences – are inter-dependent; it's not a case of genes on the one hand and life experiences on the other. Researchers have recently discovered that the brain changes throughout life as we learn. This is called *neuroplasticity* – cells that are stimulated together and fire together wire up to each other *throughout life*. So what you focus on, aspire to and *practise* will make a difference to your brain and that is true for compassion training, too. We also know that we are producing new brain cells every day (maybe 5,000) – a process called *neurogenesis*. So our phenotypes are always changing to some degree.

So we can see that experience and learning are vital to shaping the brain. And evolution gave us our 'new brain/mind', with huge advantages for us in our ability to think, imagine, learn and use symbols and language. You can see how radical these new qualities are when you think about how difficult it would be to train chimpanzees to do something that many humans learn fairly easily, such as driving a car. This requires an extraordinary capacity to *integrate* competencies such as memory, conceptual understanding, attentional control and motor coordination, and yet we can sustain that level of coordinated activity for hours on end! We might even talk on our mobiles while we do it (although the police will be after you if you do, of course, because that is actually one task/step too far). Think about what goes into learning how to play a Rachmaninov piano concerto, which again requires an extraordinary capacity for dedicated training, memory and fine motor coordination. Or imagine something a bit more mundane – how we learn the rules of a game such as football and can sustain the play over 90 minutes, then talk about it for the next week, reflecting on 'If only Sam had done X and Joe had done Y' and 'Isn't it time to sack the manager?' My favourite game is cricket and we can sustain that over five days, although I am not sure if that is a measure of intelligence or endurance. The point is that we are able to coordinate different elements of our minds and their competencies in extraordinary ways. It seems that our brains work as a *system* in a slightly different way to those of other life forms, and because of this integrated type of functioning, many other competencies arise.[7]

But that's far from all. Our use of *language* and *symbols*, our ability to *conceptualize*, to think in terms of systems – to think about how things work, to understand the rules, which is the fundamental skill required for science and progress – have opened up a whole new domain of 'mind' in the universe. We have a brain that can reflect, ponder and conceptualize the world; we can be observers and experimenters, making purposeful interventions to see what happens and discover how things work; we can peer below the surface of things, have theories and test them out. Because we have such a complex, meaning-conveying language, we can pass on our learning so that we now increasingly live in a world built by human knowledge and creativity accumulated over thousands of years.

The human brain is also highly creative and we are always trying to share our creations. These may be music, songs, stories, poetry, paintings and sculpture, or scientific discoveries. How often do we find ourselves wondering what other people think about what we've done or even what their opinion is of the ideas we are expressing. If you're a cook (sorry, chef), you'll be trying to work out how to bring ingredients together to create new tastes and textures and dishes with an aesthetic appearance. Sports people make rapid decisions and try to be innovative in their play. We have strong desires to seek innovation, to be creative, to improve things, to have some element of originality and to be appreciated or praised for that.

'Fantastic!' you may say, and indeed that's true. Our 'new brains/minds' have given rise to agriculture and complex food production, science, TVs and mobile phones, medicine, culture, story-telling, history recording, the arts and an increasing deep understanding of our own minds (and, yes, cricket, too) and, one day perhaps, the ability to live on other planets. But what about the downside? What price have we paid for these abilities? Or if you want a more spiritual question: what responsibilities come with these 'new brain/mind' abilities? You see, this is something we will note time and time again in the evolutionary story – that benefits often come with potential disadvantages, or 'trade-offs'. The downside in this case is not hard to find. *The problem comes when you put 'old brain/mind' dispositions, emotions, wants and desires together with 'new brain/mind' talents.*

I suspect that our ability to imagine and fantasize came before our ability to integrate our attention, thoughts and feelings in the ways described above. But, however they evolved, our ability to fantasize and imagine gives us major advantages. Coming up with an innovation can occur by accident, but more commonly it results from our inner effortful creation and fantasies. The prehistoric makers of early flint spearheads had an image or notion in their minds of what they were trying to make and achieve. We humans don't just respond to external cues – we try to bring our inner fantasies and imaginings into existence. For example, I pick up my guitar with a rough idea for a song in my head and then try to work it out.

Unfortunately, our fantasies and imaginings can also be a source of great disappointment and conflict. We can fantasize about the lives we'd like, the careers, the money and the houses, the friends and lovers we'd like, the children we'd want to have. In our minds, our lovers are always admiring, ever ready for physical pleasure and never tired, grumpy, headachy or farty; and our children are always well behaved and respectful and study hard, are never rebellious or come home drunk and vomit on the kitchen floor. We fantasize the best for ourselves to want more and more – never satisfied because we can always imagine having more or better. Fantasies can fuel our greed. We can be constantly disappointed because reality is never as we'd like it to be – my songs are never as good as I'd imagined they would be.

Fantasies can also be a source of fear and anger. Thirty years ago, my wife Jean and I lived in a lodge cottage in Scotland. There were no other houses around us. When she did night duty in the hospital, I was left in the house on my own. At times in the dark night I would hear sounds in the attic or outside and my heart rate would increase as my fantasies of what could be there ran riot. I told myself that I was a psychologist and a man, to be sensible, but sadly that didn't really help me. I was easily spooked! People can develop all kinds of anxiety conditions because of their fantasies about what's going to happen to them, or what might happen if they do certain things. Some people believe that the way we relate to God is through our fantasy world. So all kinds of difficulties are associated with fantasies and our capacity to fantasize and imagine. And, of course, we can have fantasies and thoughts about what others are thinking and feeling about us, without much idea if they are true or not.

While our 'new brain/mind' may yet save us from environmental disaster and help us see the value of compassion training, it might also finish us off. Consider what happens when our 'new brain/mind' talents are recruited into the service of 'old brain/mind' motivations such as tribalism. Many animals operate within groups and defend the boundaries of those groups;

they are tribal and can be very aggressive to outsiders. We don't need to go into genetic explanations of why that is; we simply know that is the case. That same motivation for defending, retaliating, punishing, attacking or destroying others, when harnessed to 'new brain/mind' competencies, becomes deeply problematic – indeed terrifying and tragic. Many of the atrocities that have taken place over the last few thousand years have been the result of 'new brain/mind' competencies linking up with 'old brain/mind' motives and defences. We can even use our 'new brain/mind' competencies to justify our actions and give us very sophisticated ways of acting them out. Animals will defend their groups and territories at all times, but only humans can think about how to do it more effectively with guns, or sadistically by torturing those who are either not in the group or who have betrayed it. At least a third of all the world's research money is spent on weaponry. Rich nations sell poor nations armaments, crippling their economies, maintaining tyrants and causing untold harm, with the profits from the arms sales flowing back to the rich nations. It is, of course, disastrous, but is the consequence of a fantastic 'new brain/mind' not being able to sort out the tribal motives of the 'old brain/mind' – greed and a belief in the importance of aggressive power. Even religions can feed into this tragedy.

These are just a few examples of our problems between 'old brain/mind' and 'new brain/mind' interactions – we see these tragedies enacted every day. On a personal level, the way we use our 'new brains' to think and ruminate about ourselves can be a source of stimulating, powerful, primitive emotions and feelings, which we can become locked into and, in that way, drive ourselves deep into anxiety and depression.[8] The moral is, of course, that we require both a sophisticated and an agreed form of welfare-focused social organization to contain our potential tribalism and abusive power hierarchies, and we must also recognize that, if we don't understand and train our minds very carefully and learn to be wary of the dangers of allowing 'new brain/mind' competencies to be directed by 'old brain/mind' passions, we're going to be in trouble.

Compassion invites us to use our 'new brains/minds' in new ways – to stand back from some of our primitive passions and desires, such as tribalism, and remember that we're all human beings, in the flow of life, who feel pain and suffer the same way; we've all just somehow 'arrived here' and are actors of the narratives of life. As the Dalai Lama is fond of saying: 'We all want happiness and we don't want suffering.' It is a meditation that we will visit later in this book. Our 'new brain/mind' gives us choices – it's the bite from Adam's apple – but we've yet to really understand how to train and use it.

To summarize, you can see that we have two types of brain and two types of mind. This makes life very tricky for us because they don't always work well together. The 'old brain/mind' that reaches back over many tens of millions of years operates through fast-acting brain networks linked to our emotions and desires. Our feelings are automatic and effortless, flushing through us with little reflective or conscious thought, and, as they do for many other species, they alert us to threats, activate emotions and guide us to important life goals (food, sex, alliances and status). By contrast, our two-million-year-old (or less) 'new brain/mind' is slow and reflective, can use symbols, can conceptualize and understand how things work, is creative and ever improving. It fantasizes and creates images of 'wants' and desires or things to fear. Our 'new brain/mind', especially the frontal cortex, also provides much of our ability to empathize and understand other people's thoughts and feelings and makes us an especially social and mutually influencing species.

The relationship between these two types of brain/mind is complex. Our insightful ability to empathize and understand others can be used to help them or find out how to frighten and threaten them, to 'hit them where it hurts'. The passions, motives, wants, lusts, fears and vengeances of our 'old brain/mind' can hijack the capabilities of our 'new brain/mind'. When it does that, we simply find ways to satisfy those desires or find reasons for feeling what we feel, supporting our prejudices. Emotions can suggest their own self-justifying reasons. 'I *feel* it, so it must be true,' we say. 'I *feel* anxious, so this must be dangerous and I should avoid it.' 'I *feel* disgusted, so this means it's bad.' 'I *feel* that this is wrong; therefore it is.' 'I *feel* that I can't trust you; therefore you are dangerous to me.' We don't question what we feel or do because we have 'gut feelings' and urges that we're right.

In fact, we can actively look for reasons to support our feelings, even ignoring or dismissing alternative, more reasonable views. Many psychotherapies these days try to help people pay more attention to their reflective thinking and to stand back from their feelings and use their 'new brain/mind' abilities to regulate and change emotions (*see* Chapter 9). However, it's also important to work with the motives and emotions of our 'old brain/mind', learn to understand them better, to tolerate and not act them out. We can learn to act against them, and replace them with new motives and emotions that are orientated towards compassionate ways of living and being. Note, though, that the many human tragedies that have arisen from us humans having these different brains *are not our fault* because, until now, we've had so little insight or understanding of how our brains evolved and work. Moreover, the passions and fears of the 'old brain/mind' were *designed* to be very powerful and not easily overruled.

Challenge 3: The curse of the self

The Curse of the Self is actually the title of a fascinating book by one of the United States' leading social psychologists, Mark Leary.[9] It illuminates our third challenge, which is related to the second. Along with the amazing talents of our brain to coordinate and organize its interconnections in numerous ways for, amongst other crucial tasks, driving, playing the piano and making pizzas, we have evolved abilities to be more *self-aware*. 'New brain/mind' abilities can now be used to give us a *sense of ourselves*. So we can develop a self-identity, a sense of 'me-ness' and 'I-ness' with feelings about who we are, who we want to be and how we want other people to see and relate to us. Self-awareness allows us to appreciate 'being alive'. We can stand and look at the stars in the inky night sky, feel in awe of the universe and know that we exist 'here'. Cool stuff. It also means we can exert some control over our feelings. For example, I can decide to reduce my eating because I want to be slim, healthy or even more handsome (okay, don't laugh – not much chance of that, but there's always hope). So having self-awareness has lots of benefits for us, but like so many things, it comes with a challenge and a 'handle with care' sticker.

It turns out that, because our brains are complex and can integrate systems and abilities in many different ways, we need some kind of organizing process; otherwise we'll be presented with too many possibilities, values and conflicts in what we do or think. We have to have some way of giving priority to different potentials within us. This is where a sense of self and self-identity come in. Our sense of self is linked to memory and to a feeling of consistency in our values, behaviours and emotions. So my sense of myself is linked to the person I would like to be, the person I don't want to be, the person I am capable of being, and of course, my memory of 'being me' yesterday, the day before and so on.[10] Within the sense of self are a number of abilities – introspection, an awareness of what one feels, and the capacity to contemplate the self as feeling and existing (or not existing) in the future. Now these self-aware and self-reflective abilities can have a very powerful impact on 'old brain/mind' emotions. I mean, I just get used to being here, in this life that I never chose, with feelings and desires I never asked for, and then I discover that my body is decaying around me and I'm soon not going to be here at all. I've got 25–30,000 days of life – if I'm lucky, that is. I've fallen deeply in love with my wife and my children, and then I find out that they aren't going to be here long either; we'll all just fade away. It seems a bit of a rotten deal, really.

But there are other problems with waking up to a sense of self. This is because our 'old brain/mind' makes us very *socially* aware and recruits 'new brain/mind' abilities to think about the self in relation to others. So it's quite possible for me to think about myself as inferior and a failure *compared* to others and, in that way, activate feelings of depression. I can worry that I don't fit in, or that people don't like me or see me as weak. My self-aware mind can also worry about my efforts to control *future problems* and *future me's*. I can worry about paying the mortgage, whether I'm keeping up at work, about my weight, my appearance – even my guitar playing! (Yes, I wanted to be a rock guitar player in the 1960s, and only went to university because I wasn't actually very good at it.) Animals don't usually get depressed about such things. Like us, they can get depressed if they are beaten down by others or if they suffer major losses in their relationships – they respond to the world as they experience it.

But as we have noted above and will revisit in later chapters, we humans can respond to the world that we have *created in our heads*, the one that we have imagined, the one that we think about, and can experience *ourselves* within that world within our heads. Our self-awareness and our capacity 'to think about our self', to recognize we are, for instance, a self that we may not want to be, an ashamed self, a 'less than self', an 'out-of-control self' – all those reflections seriously add to our miseries.

So although self-awareness is a fantastic feat of evolution and brain complexity, this very sense of 'me-ness' and 'I-ness', which Buddhists call the 'ego self', will want to defend itself, protect itself, promote and give itself pleasures, and it can judge itself, criticize and even attack itself. Okay, let's be honest: we actually become quite egocentric and narcissistic! Of course, all animals are egocentric, because they are focused on their own needs and wants, defending their territory or social position, protecting their own offspring and so on. So the desires and wishes of the ego self are rooted in the basic survival and reproduction mechanisms that exist in *all living things*. However, having this ego self makes our struggles in life all very personal, and we now seek to defend and enhance the ego self *itself* when, in fact, it emerges from patterns of chemical transmissions in our brains. You can look all you like into my brain (well, not literally, of course, because I'm rather attached to it) and all you'll find are brain cells signalling to each other, extraordinary patterns of millions of cells firing in a mosaic. However, there's no 'me' lurking about somewhere in that maze. My experience of 'me' *is* the pattern and is nowhere else. If the patterns change – for example, because of brain damage – then the essence of 'me' changes and I might become a very different person to how I am now. Consider also that there's not a single atom left in my body that I was born with; 'me-ness' is not an entity, it's a vast number of complex patterns of neuronal connections, the firing of brain cells in their millions, and countless relationships. The sense of 'me-ness' is an emergent experience within consciousness.

Now some scientists suggest that consciousness is actually created by the brain in its complex net of connections. Others say that the brain creates patterns *within* consciousness – consciousness is in some way a property of the universe. Thus my pattern can be created through my physical form and can then exist somehow as a pattern in consciousness. Who's right – or are they both wrong? Well, you'll have to wait on this one; they're likely to be debating this thesis long after you and I are gone. If you type 'studies in consciousness' into any search engine, you will be taken on a fascinating journey. I just mention it here to show how our sense of self-awareness butts up against these issues.

A key problem with a sense of self and self-awareness is that just about any problem can become linked to it. If I put on too much weight because I don't control my eating, if I make mistakes, if others reject me, if others criticize me, if I struggle to understand how my computer works when others seem to do this easily – just about anything can become a way of judging and experiencing myself negatively. I then have two problems: the annoyance or disappointment about *the thing itself*, and the experience of *me* as inferior, bad, defeated, unloved or inadequate in some way. The annoyance or disappointment over the thing itself may dissipate quickly, but my ruminations about myself as inferior, incompetent, lacking will-power or whatever can stay with me for hours, days, weeks or even years, constantly undermining my happiness.

In addition, feelings about oneself, according to whether we are doing well or badly, can be linked to how we think others perceive us. Being overly worried about this and then judging ourselves as a result can rob us of many things in life. For example, one person may go to the park and paint, enjoying the activity, the landscape, the colours, the way the light dances in the trees, the smell of the air, the application of paint on canvas or paper. However, another person starts painting and then begins to think, 'It's not very good – other people walking by will be critical,' and they become self-conscious and don't want others to see their efforts, so they pack up, disappointed, and go home feeling miserable. These self-judgements have robbed the second person of the ability to simply engage in the pleasure of an activity. As we will see in Part II, developing self-compassion can help us get back into the pleasure of 'the activity' and to suspend a sense of self – to get back into experiencing rather than judging.

Awareness of pain

Both our new type of awareness and our self-awareness are coloured and textured by 'old brain/mind' moods and feelings. As far as we know, animals can feel anxious and angry and depressed, but they don't really know that they do, they don't have a sense of self as living in these mood states. If we are in physical pain, we have an acute self-awareness of that pain, which can create fear and depression. One of the things that makes morphine so effective is the way it changes the experience of pain and our feelings about it.

Think about depression. Depression is a state of mind where the systems in our brain that regulate positive emotions are toned down, and the systems that regulate negative emotions are toned up. This brain pattern may have evolved because it helps animals cope with threatening environments: it's a 'go to the back of the cave and stay there until it's safe' response. But to give self-awareness to a brain that can go into that state or pattern is to add another level of suffering altogether.

Now evolution didn't do this on purpose just to give us a hard time. 'New brain/mind' abilities evolved because they gave us many advantages in dealing with threats and relating to other people, but evolution can't control how these new abilities are used or the downsides they have. It is, if you like, a glitch and quite a serious one, because self-awareness and emotion awareness can be captured and textured by 'old brain/mind' patterns such as depression. And when they are, we experience the world with the light of positive feelings extinguished and feelings of fear and dread heightened – a nightmare world. Not realizing that our conscious self-aware minds have been captured by an old defensive program, we start to dwell on how terrible we feel, our fatigue and what we see as a grim future and create horrible thoughts and fantasies about ourselves. In this way, we start driving the positive emotions even further out of bounds.

Sometimes it helps to realize that, perhaps due to stress or a lack of social support or for some other reason, our 'old brains/minds' revert to what is to them a perfectly sensible defensive pattern. They have no knowledge of our new self-aware brain and just run their programs, turning off positive emotion systems and turning up threat-based ones. As we will see in later chapters, to be compassionate is to stand back from these emotion and mood states of, say, depression, anxiety or the urge for vengeance and neither pathologize nor indulge them. Rather our thoughts can be directed towards what we need to do to see these as often 'normal though undesirable' aspects of our minds while at the same time making an effort to change our brain-state patterns to ones more conducive to acceptance, contentment and well-being. For some, this might involve medication that changes brain chemicals and creates new 'states of mind'; for others, psychological therapy and a change of thinking style; and for still others, changing their lifestyle (e.g. downsizing from a stressful job) or social-relating style (e.g. becoming more or less assertive or more forgiving or tolerant). The point here is that, while our self-awareness flows in and through our brain states, it is also different from them.

Aloneness

Evolutionary psychologists have also pointed to another sad downside of self-awareness. Ultimately, we all live inside our own individual, separate heads. We are self-aware, but we are also aware that we are alone. We can reach out to others, we can touch them, we can talk to them, we can get a sense of what they're thinking about the world and about us. But in another sense, we are alone inside our skulls – we are born and die individually. Yet we crave connection. We like to do things in teams – to play in an orchestra, to work on projects – to have a sense of 'we-ness', not just 'me-ness'.

Many spiritual traditions speak to this sense of disconnection and aloneness and, except for those personalities with extreme introvert traits, our yearning for connectedness. In some traditions, it is about a wish to return to a relationship with God; in others, it is a wish to transcend the self, to lose ego boundaries, to have oceanic feelings of linkage. Our sense of disconnectedness is the price we pay for having a brain that gives rise to a sense of our being an individual self.

Some believe that, by training our minds in certain ways (which will include meditation), we can have insights about this whole 'nature of self' business. We may come to see it more as an illusion, that the sense of a separate self evolved partly to help direct and regulate those 'old brain/mind' systems in their pursuit of survival and the reproduction of genes.[11] Tricky that one, isn't it? When you stand back from the sense of 'being an individual self' and recognize that you are the repository of passions and feelings that have been knocking about for millions of years, that in a way they live *through you* but they're *not you*, you can develop new insights into the very nature of your mind. Consider, too, that if the 'me-ness of me' is a pattern of firings in my brain, I might be able to train it to adopt certain patterns that will give me experiences of well-being and very different experiences of 'me-ness'. I might be able to exert some control over the patterns that get etched on to my 'field of consciousness'. Now we are going to be touching on some of this, but if you want to pursue these ideas further, you might wish to seek out people who are practised in the ways of meditation.

So let's get back to our main point – the curse of the self. We humans can shape, construct, blend, amplify, suppress and make more complex our feelings of happiness, anxiety, anger, jealousy, depression and so forth in ways that animals never can – thanks to our 'new brain/mind' abilities. Our self-aware field of consciousness can be coloured by emotions and moods resulting from patterns generated by our 'old brains/minds'. We can think ahead, ruminate on regrets, feel ashamed or guilty, and generally focus on negative things about ourselves. We can 'hold' them in our minds and, in doing so, constantly stimulate negative emotions. None of that is very compassionate or nourishing, is it? The challenge here then is to understand our minds and recognize that the way we think about ourselves – whether we are harsh or kind to ourselves – is going to play a very major role in the way some of our 'old brain/mind' emotions and feelings get acted out within us; it's going to affect how our bodies and emotions work. We can also recognize that somewhere inside each of us is a sense of aloneness. At times, we crave solitude and grow with it, but this is when we choose it. The yearning for connectedness is one of the motives of people looking for spiritual meaning – to connect with something greater than themselves.

When we set out to develop compassion, we adopt the basic idea that, if we learn to concentrate our attention, thoughts and behaviours on compassion, imagine ourselves as compassionate and think about how to be compassionate for others, we'll be stimulating particular systems in our brain. Indeed, there's now a lot of evidence that this is so (*see* Chapter 8). It turns out that, if you get those compassion systems in your brain working, they will create feelings of peacefulness, calmness and connectedness, not to mention insight into the nature of the self and one's role in the flow of life. Furthermore, the physiological changes you create in your body as you become compassion-focused will affect your immune system and other systems relating to health.[12] This, of course, is not so easy, so here's the real challenge: to develop within yourself a compassionate self-nourishing orientation that will stimulate your mind and body in certain ways – in contrast to the angry, frustrated, disappointed, self-critical style that so many of us adopt in our hurry-hurry, 'no time for me or you', competitive societies that force us to focus on targets. Yep, the more you think about it, there's no doubt about it – efficiency is bad for us.

Challenge 4: The importance of love and caring

The fourth challenge relates to a key aspect of our humanity, which is our interdependence with each other. It is very easy to think of our 'old brain/ mind' as containing only the difficult emotions of anger, anxiety, tribalism and so forth. However, the evolution of mammals brought new emotions and motives into the world – this was a brain that could care about others. Now, of course, the way early mammals cared for their offspring was automatic, their brains responding to specific cues or stimuli such as the cries of the chick in the nest – not much thought there. But it was the first glimmer of a brain that would build a nest to protect an infant, that would detect, recognize and respond to distress calls (e.g. from an infant) and behave in ways that would benefit an infant. In other words, its behaviour was aimed at supporting, protecting and helping another living being (its infant), not just itself. Okay, some would say that this behaviour was aimed at supporting, protecting and helping its own genes. However, over millions of years, such caring was so successful as an evolved strategy to maintain genetic lineages that, in the flow of life, it has flourished into complex potentials within the human brain, including building the competencies that gave rise to our abilities for compassion.

By the time of humans, our brains have evolved *to be caring* and *to need caring* to such an extent that the way they shape and wire themselves throughout life, the pattern of their interconnections, is significantly influenced by the affection, love and caring they receive.[13] Parental caring not only soothes children when they're distressed, but it helps them to understand and come to terms with how their minds work; they can talk about their feelings and things that have happened to them. Knowing that they exist in the mind of another as a loved person stimulates their soothing/contentment system and makes their world feel secure. This is the way our brains are built. We depend on care and love.

Children (and adults) who receive kindness, gentleness, warmth and compassion are, compared with those who don't, more confident and secure, happier and less vulnerable to mental and physical health problems; they are also more caring and respectful of others.[14] Receiving kindness, gentleness, warmth and compassion tells the brain that the world is safe and other people are helpful rather than harmful. Receiving kindness, gentleness, warmth and compassion improves our immune system and reduces the levels of stress hormones. Receiving kindness, gentleness, warmth and compassion helps us to feel soothed and settled and is conducive to good sleep. Kindness, gentleness, warmth and compassion are like basic vitamins for our minds.

So from the very first hours of our lives right through to our last moments, kindness, gentleness, warmth and compassion are the things that can sustain us and help us bear the setbacks, tragedies and suffering that life will rain on us. What I have described above is now standard psychological knowledge.[15]

Love and affection stimulate the soothing/contentment system, and the sense of security that results helps to tone down negative emotions. One of the major difficulties for children who come from disadvantaged backgrounds is their inability to feel safe. Studies have shown that their levels of stress hormones (e.g. cortisol) can be quite high and that parts of the brain that are involved with kindness and empathy for others may not be as well developed as in those children who come from loving homes.[16] This occurs because growing up in a threatening environment means that you need a brain that is going to be able to deal with threat. So the brains of these deprived children are organized for threat and defence, which means that they will also be organized for aggression or anxiety, the brain's two protection emotions. If we are to help these children develop their brains to be more orientated towards kindness to others and their own well-being, we need to help them feel safe, loved and wanted. We need to develop the science of brain maturation to such a point that we can ensure these children's brains are getting what they need to nourish and nurture them. The priority should be to ensure that these children experience safeness and receive kindness, gentleness, warmth and compassion (and compassion can mean firm boundaries, too). Indeed, we can now monitor many aspects of children's bodies and brains to make sure that their stress levels are dropping and that their frontal cortexes (important areas for emotional development) are maturing in a way that is conducive to their well-being and the development of abilities to be empathic and kind to others. We are, however, a long way from caring for our children's emotional health like this, compared with how we look after their physical health.

If we think about the other end of life, the way in which we age and come to terms with limitation – indeed, even the process of our own death – this, too, is greatly influenced by the degree to which we experience love, kindness and affection around us. Facing the great unknown can be even more terrifying when we feel unloved and disconnected from those around us and cannot rely on the kindness and support of others. We all know this in our hearts, it will hardly be news to you, and yet we have to struggle to build societies that put these qualities at the forefront of our endeavours. Instead, we are more concerned with the business model and the 'costs of care'. We have yet to confront the issues of living wills and having more choice over the process of death. Although we find it difficult, we all know in our hearts – and anyone who has seen their parents die slowly and painfully will certainly know – that the way we deal with death in our society is far from compassionate. Medicine can prolong dying, which is not the same as prolonging life.

So we have to recognize something very fundamental about ourselves – *we are a species that has evolved to thrive on kindness and compassion*. The challenge here is to recognize the importance of kindness and affection and place them at the *centre* of our relationship with ourselves, with others and with the world. So ask yourself: Have you really put warmth, gentleness, kindness, support and compassion at the centre of how you relate to yourself and the way in which you try to help yourself through life's tragedies? Have you put those qualities at the centre of your relationships with others, even people you don't like very much? If you think you have, that's fantastic, but I suspect that many of you know that you haven't, that you are much more self-critical than that – and we aren't always as loving and as kind as we could be to others, are we? And yes, of course, I've lost my temper with members of my family, too. In fact, my wife thinks I'm becoming a bit of a grumpy old man despite my best efforts. Compassion can be quite hard work.

Challenge 5: Interconnectedness and interdependency

Humans evolved many of their 'new brain/mind' abilities over the last few million years. During this time, they lived in relatively small isolated groups of between 100 and 200 individuals. There would have been some genetic links between most people, and of course, all members of your own group would be familiar to you and you'd have some kind of relationship with them. Many researchers believe that, at a time when survival depended on sharing and mutual support, these groups would have been relatively egalitarian. Indeed, one's status within a group might have depended on one's altruism – having a reputation for caring, sharing, honesty and reliability – along with other talents such as being good at hunting or being wise. Moreover, many of our 'new brains/minds' developed the ability to think about, and work with, other brains/minds in complex cooperative ways. Hence another aspect of compassion relates to the recognition of our interdependency with each other.

The importance of feeling that others care about us (at least to some degree) textures many of our relationships and feelings throughout life. Some years ago, social psychologists Roy Baumeister and Mark Leary[17] wrote a famous paper on our need to feel that we 'belong'. They brought together a lot of evidence to support the view that we humans have a very deep need for a sense of belonging and a group identity. Such feelings also accompany certain assumptions about how others will support you. Imagine that you are living 10,000 years ago in a small group and you go out hunting. You know that, if you don't come back on time, members of the group will worry about you and maybe even come to look for you. You are likely to feel far more secure than if you think nobody cares much whether you return or not – that is, the people in your group are not being unkind or critical, but they are fairly indifferent to your well-being and fate. Humans want to be thought about when 'out of sight', and not be forgotten. We have evolved to have a need to *live positively in the minds of others* – another form of interconnectedness, thinking about how we exist for other people. Consider how many stories and movie scripts make it a virtue for a team to go back and find the member who has been lost or left behind. Indeed, humans are renowned for extraordinary acts of heroism and rescue. It is almost certainly our interdependence and mutual support that have got us through the last few million years, including the Ice Age.

Interconnectedness gives us the basis for positive relating, a sense of togetherness and friendship. It is our ability to cooperate and work together, to learn from each other and to support each other that makes us capable of science, technology and landing people on the moon. We gain enormous joy from doing things together – be this playing in a football team or in an orchestra, or simply watching a film with friends or family. It gives us a sense of 'we-ness', not just 'me-ness'. Humans like and will seek out friendly togetherness (although, of course, we also like solitude and our own space from time to time). As we have already noted, the way we depend on each other and the importance of affection from others can be crucial for our brain development, sense of security and well-being.

There is now a lot of evidence that having friendships and feeling supported and valued within a network of individuals are important for mental and physical health. We know that feeling valued and supported in a network also lowers stress and is good for our immune systems. Think of viruses: they played a huge role in evolution – they have actually affected our DNA – and have been responsible for some species disappearing altogether. The flu pandemic of 1918/19 killed more people than died in the First World War. So anything that gives us an advantage in our ability to fight viruses and have a robust immune system is beneficial. Positive social relationships not only provide individuals who will look after you if you're sick, but they can have an impact on your immune system, too. Today some economists use the term 'social capital' to describe the benefits we gain from our mutual supportiveness and connectedness, but it is useful to keep in mind the physiological benefits of supportive, interconnected relationships, too. Such relationships also have a major impact on the soothing/contentment system.

The shift from the Stone Age to the age of the iPod has been rapid indeed – just 10,000 years. From small isolated groups, we have become a global community. However, while among ourselves we are constantly trying to re-create networks, we are often unable to do it. Increasingly we live in segregated communities. The idea of young mothers looking after children at home alone would have been an abomination to the Stone Age brain. The way many of the elderly are segregated and live alone, often distant from family, would also be considered an abnormality. The way we segregate our children and adolescents in schools, educating them outside the adult community, and fail to offer them any sense of belonging is another abnormality. And the huge differentials in resources that can be obtained through individual competitiveness that positively discourages sharing is another aberration. There are clear benefits to living in a modern society, of course, but any review of history tells us how miserable the lives of the poor have been in most societies in the last 10,000 years: too many people living lives that are disconnected and resource starved, trapped in unpleasant environments.

From time to time, there are moves within human thinking and politics to try to shift us into more egalitarian societies, but time and time again, these efforts are undone by group conflicts, protective elites, competition and the attractions of controlling resources for ourselves and constructing our own little 'others-like-me' networks. The shift in Britain from the welfare-orientated politics of the 1950s and 1960s to the 'need to maintain competitive edge' politics of the last 25 years is as tragic as it is typical. Unfortunately, in nearly every aspect of our lives, the 'competitive edge' approach may be slowly dissolving interconnectedness. Part of the reason is that people have far less time to spend on nurturing and nourishing their supportive networks.[18] It is more common to come home, open some wine and flop goggle-eyed in front of the TV. For exactly this reason, alcohol has become a major and increasing problem.

It is also worrying how many older people have noticed major changes in the sense of connectedness within their places of work. This is the result of the erosion of the things that once supported 'group mentality' working, to be replaced by a more competitive, 'me first' business model that is constantly time-pressured. One of the first casualties is often the time to think through issues with colleagues. Emails are fired off without much thought, responding to one emergency after another. Electronic communication means the loss of voice tones and facial signals, all of which normally stimulate the amygdala in the brain that is integral to how we interpret and 'feel' about communications. We can't tell if the person sending the message is being humorous, critical or just stressed. There is also constant reorganization, which changes whom one works with and relates to, undermining stability – all to try to find that competitive edge and increase efficiency.

The NHS used to work as a complex, interconnected set of people trying to cooperate together; now it's been split into competing business units/groups. The concept of clinicians and patients, primary-care and secondary-care providers, voluntary and statutory sectors all cooperating has been seen by successive governments as a *bad thing*; instead they must compete and seek to outbid each other. Stories of cheating – for instance, by recoding trolleys as beds – are, of course, legion, but it is the competitive, target-driven system that entices people to behave in these immoral ways, not the individuals themselves. General practitioners express sadness at the erosion of 'family [i.e. relationship] medicine' in favour of rapid body mechanic medicine where any doctor will do. The time to really listen and develop relationships with their patients is being pared away. Governments hope that cherry-picking private enterprise will be more efficient (and, of course, they define the parameters of efficiency, which rarely look at long-term effects). Unfortunately, whether we look at the railways, water companies or other national services, we see that competition and private enterprise actually produce *poor*-quality work. In reality, to provide national services we require individuals to cooperate and not be fragmented into small competing groups. The feelings we get from living in either a cooperative or a competitive group will have very different impacts on our minds, our values and how our brains and bodies work. As John Seddon points out brilliantly in his new book *Systems Thinking in the Public Sector*,[19] the whole focus on target setting is wrong; it sets people against each other and their customers. Is this soulless efficiency really what we want? It's a challenge because, in its place, we clearly don't want inefficient and poor-quality systems; but as Seddon says, we need to radically rethink how we organize ourselves into far more cooperative, interdependent networks.

The crisis gets deeper, though. A few months ago, I boarded an overcrowded train on my way to the airport and couldn't get a seat. Then I ran into large queues waiting to check in, which were poorly organized and within which other people were becoming increasingly angry. The lady behind me said, 'Because we pay little, they treat us like cattle.' It struck me that this is a common experience. Whether it's trying to get through to somebody on a helpline, get an appointment within the NHS or even take a train or plane – because services are so under-funded, we are all having the experience of being under-valued and treated like cattle. We are commodities on a conveyor belt, about to be processed. We experience our world as deeply uncaring and indifferent. In every aspect of our lives, we feel 'they just don't care' even if we are not quite sure who 'they' are. Business efficiency is crippling our hearts. We can do things on the cheap but we will then be treated as such. Feeling valued in our group is waning fast, adding to the failure to create a world conducive to happiness.

Another reason why interconnectedness is being fragmented around us is because we now have to work with so many different audiences. Ten thousand years ago, you grew up in your group, knowing everybody more or less from the day you were born to the day you died. Relationships were based on people's reputations for honesty, their contributions to the group and their consistency. Today relationships are more about impressing. People often feel like actors on a stage with their lives increasingly like a performance, up for judgement, and judges – overt and covert – are everywhere.

How can you impress other people with your talents and usefulness? Social comparison creeps in here. Jane was often bothered by questions like 'Do my friends think I'm a good mother?' and 'Shouldn't I be doing more with my children?' Our brains have been designed by evolution to be very sensitive to what we believe others think and feel about ourselves because fostering good relationships with others is good for our mental and physical health. But if we are overly sensitive in a field of comparative strangers, we risk becoming lost to our own theatricals and performance judgements.

Fostering good relationships

Now, rather than trying to impress people with how talented, competent and in control we are, there is actually another way to go about fostering good relationships, one that can make us all happier. In 1939, the businessman and educator Dale Carnegie wrote *How to Win Friends and Influence People*,[20] which was to become a multi-million seller. It is an extraordinary book – simple, direct and clear. Its message was: 'Learn how to listen, and take a genuine and sincere interest in other people and focus *on them*.' In some ways, Carnegie tapped into the very old spiritual tradition of the value of developing a compassionate orientation to others. For Carnegie, we should foster these ways of being with others, not because they are required by some deity, but because they work and are conducive to our well-being. In fact, we now know that Carnegie was absolutely right: cultivating caring relationships with others is a key element of feeling happy and is beneficial for our well-being. However, we have built societies that neither teach nor inspire this. Even our entertainments are recognized as being increasingly designed to thrill and grab our attention with violence and simplistic views of good versus evil.[21]

A downside

However – and you're probably getting the hang of this now – many of the things that evolution has given us can be both a benefit and curse, and so it is with interconnectedness. The downside, of course, is that, if we feel disconnected, isolated, alone, unwanted and unloved, we can suffer terribly. Moreover, our need for interconnectedness is what also leads us to compare ourselves with others and wonder if we are 'like' them and up to their standards, whether we are accepted by them, whether we fit in, are part of the team. Or are we marginal outsiders who must always struggle to prove ourselves 'worthy'? As our moods go up and down, we can have a sense of being part of, or not being part of, the social world in which we live. When we become depressed, we can have a very acute sense of not belonging and not feeling part of our world, feeling separate and cut off from others, and those feelings can be extremely painful.[22] So the challenge is to learn how to understand these aspects of ourselves, develop the skills to create feelings and behaviours that facilitate inter-relatedness and connectedness and then practise them.

In later chapters, you'll find a number of exercises through which you can practise imagining feelings of connectedness and reaching out to others. In many spiritual traditions, people focus on connectedness to spiritual beings. In Buddhism, for instance, one can focus on a sense of connectedness to the Buddha, to the community and to the teachings, which together are known as the 'three jewels'. At the same time, one shouldn't turn connectedness into a drug-like attachment or 'must have'. So we can learn how to accept the experience of separateness, too. We will find this a lot easier if we have within our own heads kindness and warmth towards ourselves.

Another downside of our need to belong to small groups is the fact that, to feel connected, we sometimes believe that we have to give up our individuality and merge ourselves with the group, clothing ourselves in their values, attitudes, and behaviours in order to be like them. We dress like those around us, eat the same food, listen to the same types of music, adopt the same religious values. It is easy for us to look at other cultures – at, say, children on parade, all dressed the same, waving flags, chanting slogans in praise of their president or chairman – and conclude that they have been 'brainwashed'. We can observe other people being led like sheep and see them as a submissive lot in many ways. Yet we don't turn around and realize that we have fallen victim to exactly the same pressures, that our values are very much created for us, that if we lived in those cultures we would behave and think as they do, we'd be the flag wavers, and we'd be looking at us through their eyes. Why do you think the fashion industry is worth billions? Why are people so busy comparing themselves with each other and wanting the same things? Where does the desire to be a certain body shape come from? We all submit to group norms because of our need for interconnectedness – but it carries risks. The obvious one is to our sense of self, but such a need for conformity can, as I have discussed earlier, also result in tribalism, which can be (and has been) the source of our greatest terrors. It is estimated that, in the last century alone, humans have killed over 200 million of their own kind in various wars and conflicts, not to mention those they have tortured and maimed, locked up and beaten.

So you can see that the need for interconnectedness is at the root of some of the most wonderful feelings we can experience, and by working together and supporting each other, we can achieve so much. But, without care, it can also be the stuff of nightmares: alienation, deep loneliness, despair, destructiveness, tribalism and hatred. So our fifth challenge then is to recognize the enormous importance of our need of and desire for interconnectedness and also its dangers.

Challenge 6: Not the same – the importance of the individual differences between us

Humans clearly belong to one species, and in many ways, we are identical to each other and quite different from other animals. We make assumptions about this similarity all the time, and indeed we need to. If we couldn't imagine that other people see things or understand things as we do, we would be aliens to each other, but we are not. In fact, one of the reasons we are able to communicate and cooperate in the ways that we do is because we use our own minds to make judgements about what is going on in those of other people. However, here's the catch – this assumption of similarity can cause confusion. How often have we found ourselves thinking: 'If I was in that person's shoes, I wouldn't have done/said/felt that. How can he/she do/feel that? I would never have done that'? We use our own inner experience of feelings and our sense of self-identity to judge the other person – when their values and ways of thinking and feeling may be quite different to ours. Research has shown that cyclists and pedestrians get annoyed with motorists for hogging the road partly because the cyclists and pedestrians think that they are quite visible but, from the motorists' point of view, they are not. Research also suggests that, when we are young, we assume that people see the world in the same way that we do. Then, as we mature, we gradually realize that this is not quite the case, and so we have to alter our perceptions and start to think about all the ways in which other people can be rather different to the way we are, from their tastes, personalities, values and judgements through to their vulnerability to disease. This ability to have *empathy for difference*, to be open to diversity, to work hard at thinking about how other people may differ from you is a key step on the road to compassion – and it's not always easy.

When you train as a psychotherapist, you're taught to imagine what it might be like to be the other person, to see the world through their eyes. This can take some effort and isn't automatic – but it is possible. If you really had no idea at all, you would be struggling. Another important issue in learning to be a therapist is being able to visit the darker areas of your own mind. Therapists who are frightened of their own problematic desires and fantasies and only see them in the minds of others and never as part of the evolved minds of us all will struggle with some patients. Indeed, it is important for all of us to recognize that our minds have a 'shadow side', as the Swiss psychotherapist Carl Jung called it. Incidentally, this is why we are attracted to such things as horror movies – we want to see them scripted and acted out by others so that we can become voyeurs and not feel responsible for those kinds of fantasies or passions.

Shadows are partly created by the way our self-identity is shaped within social communities. The Spartans who lived in Greece more than 2,000 years ago and were noted for their fighting ability would have had no trouble with homosexual feelings and actually promoted them, whereas some Christians would find any such desires in themselves deeply troubling and would want to get rid of or repress them. Jung thought that some people who were vehemently against certain things could be 'projecting their shadows' – seeing and attacking in others things they couldn't face in themselves. This would include, for example, the man who is critical of or avoids his wife when she cries because it resonates with some deep sadness in himself; he's fearful of his own vulnerability and that he might collapse into tears, so he doesn't want to acknowledge such feelings or want anyone reminding him of them. So people differ in what they can face up to in themselves and what they might project.

We also make assumptions of similarity when it comes to issues of freedom and rights. Historically, of course, humans have tried to dominate other humans and have seen some groups as inferior and less worthy than others. In fact, history is full of cultures and societies literally cultivating contempt and even hatred for others to justify conquering, exploiting, enslaving and destroying them.[23] Societies have long blamed poor old God. At one point, it was believed that God decided and ordained people's lives – for the king to be the king and the peasant to be the peasant, for men to dominate women, and white people to dominate black people. And of course, God would want one tribe to enslave and persecute another tribe that He didn't happen to be favouring at the moment. Things have gradually changed, and some groups have now decided that God actually has another set of ideas: 'In the eyes of God, all are created equal.'

Now it is important to see this as a moral statement about how we treat, value and respect each other. Also important is the Buddhist principle that we all seek happiness and none seeks suffering. These moral perspectives matter because it is also clear that we are *not* all created equal. Our genes comprise one major area of inequality and difference because they are going play a big role in the sorts of talents we are going to have and also in our vulnerability to a variety of life difficulties including, of course, disease.

By studying identical (monozygotic) and non-identical (dizygotic) twins, we are now beginning to understand just how important our genes are. Identical twins come from the same egg and share 100 per cent of the same genes. Non-identical twins derive from two different eggs and have only 50 per cent of their genes in common. This allows researchers to do comparisons of various traits, and to explore differences in identical twins who were separated at birth and then met up again later in life. These first meetings have produced some extraordinary stories, such as brothers discovering that their wives have the same names and occupations, or turning up in very similar clothes bought from the same shopping outlet – some really quite specific things. So you may think that it's 'you' who likes the blue shirt or pink blouse with the dark jacket – but if our genes are playing a major role here, what do we mean by 'you' or 'me'? Maybe it's truer to say that we are experiencing the choice of our brain. Strange, isn't it?

These twin studies have also allowed us to look at vulnerabilities to diseases such as cancer, and also at important differences in our personalities. Researchers have distinguished five key personality dimensions: neuroticism, conscientiousness, openness to experience, extroversion and agreeableness. People vary in how much they experience and express these traits and also how they are combined in patterns. Agreeableness seems to be associated with a tendency to be compassionate, while neuroticism is associated with a tendency towards experiencing the world in rather threatening ways and a vulnerability to anxiety and depression. There is increasing evidence that some of the extremes of destructive behaviour, such as those seen in psychopathic and paranoid personalities, have a genetic element. All of that, of course, makes for some complex thinking around issues of responsibility for crime and punishment.

Another dimension of personality studied by Simon Baron-Cohen and his colleagues[24] in research on autism distinguishes between what he calls 'empathizers' and 'systematizers', which may also have a bearing on the ease of developing compassion. Empathizers' brains are oriented towards understanding the minds of others and being able to intuit and relate to other people's feelings. Systematizers, on the other hand, are good at understanding systems and mechanical things. They can see patterns in and rules behind systems very quickly; they like computers and can fix your car but may be less good at dealing with complex emotions and social relationships. So systematizers and empathizers experience the world and their relationships in slightly different ways. There is not, however, much research on the ease with which empathizers and systematizers take to compassion-focus development or on the possibility that they may feel and express compassion in different ways.

Businesses also have various ways in which they understand individual differences. They are aware that some people are good leaders and inspire us; others make good lieutenants and are conscientious, attend to detail and ensure that things get done; and still others are creative and ideas people. Good businesses work with the qualities that people have rather than trying to turn them into something they're not. Problems arise, of course, if you want to do things to which you're not really suited. For example, some individuals may want to be leaders because they like to be in charge and earn a lot of money, despite the fact that their leadership qualities are extremely poor and they are less inspiring than a blancmange. You can see that we should recognize and respect each other's individual differences. If we just assume that we see the world in the same way, we're going to run into problems. If, however, we can learn to appreciate differences, we can build on them.

Individual differences affect relationships between young and old and, of course, between men and women, who, through evolution, have actually developed different sexual strategies.[25] A woman will choose genes for her relatively few offspring very carefully. A man, on the other hand, can sire thousands of children and so it's in his genetic interests to be far less discerning and more opportunistic. Many self-help books on relationships have addressed this difference and the fact that men and women think about sex and, indeed, relationships in a variety of ways. Provided couples recognize this and work to explore it and are prepared to compromise, all may be well. However, each partner will want the other to be kind rather than unkind, compassionate rather than cold and heartless, to be interested in them rather than not – qualities that will sustain the relationship, rather than just pure sexual attraction.

Individual differences are very important when it comes to medical treatment, especially medications. For instance, think about how different people react to alcohol. Some, particularly those from certain Asian countries, have a gene that makes them very sick when ingesting even small amounts. Some drink and then gradually go to sleep (I'm one of those, waking up a few hours later with a hangover). Some become more and more uninhibited – and amusing or embarrassing, depending on your point of view – but others don't need very much alcohol before becoming aggressive. Sadly the prisons are full of individuals who are reasonably pleasant when they don't drink but, if they do, have a reaction that turns them combative and dangerous. Much domestic violence is linked to drinking. If alcohol has these variations in impact, think about drugs such as antidepressants: some people may benefit from them, whereas others have awful side-effects and do far less well. Recent studies have looked at possible genetic differences between responders and non-responders to one particular antidepressant.

We also know that people vary greatly in their talents and abilities. I would love to have been a rock guitarist. There is another Paul Gilbert who actually is a rather brilliant one, but sadly that's not me because I'm tone deaf, struggle with timing and don't have much musical talent. I still enjoy myself though, just plonking away. I would also like to have been a cricketer but was pretty poor at that, too, despite my best efforts and lots of practice. It can be a slow and rather sad realization that we are perhaps not suited for the things that we would deeply love to do or be. Of course, this flies in the face of all those rather daft ideas that say that you can do or be anything you want if you just want it enough. How often have teachers and parents told kids this, leaving them feeling that there must be something wrong with them if they can't make it? It didn't matter how much I practised in the cricket nets or how many hours I spent with my guitar turned up loud, annoying the neighbours – it just wasn't going to happen for me. We can take the same view towards our physical appearance, technical abilities and so forth. In fact, it is the recognition of these variations between us that is a key step towards compassion, both for ourselves and for others. We do not live in a world of equality; our genes and our life experiences will treat us unequally.

Now understanding that we are individually different in so many ways creates a number of challenges on our road to compassion. We have to learn how to be empathic and curious about the minds of others. We need to recognize that values, perceptions and ways of thinking vary between us. For example, there is some evidence that there may be a genetic component to why some people are attracted to right-wing politics and authoritarian ways of organizing society while others are oriented towards egalitarian principles and liberal values. Some people may be very sensitive to the feelings of others, whereas others may lack that sensitivity. Some seem to be able to ride the ups and downs of life like corks on the sea, whereas others sink quite easily. Because of their personalities, some individuals may find developing compassion much easier than others. That does not, however, mean that the latter cannot develop these qualities at all. I may not be a great guitar player, but I can play a bit and I enjoy my own level of competence now.

Recognizing that we are all individually different also means that we have to come to terms with envy and *accept our limitations*. Envy is linked to our tendency to compare ourselves with others and wish we were more like them. Sometimes we try to model ourselves on people we admire or on those we think are getting more of the action than we are. This is understandable, but it can easily turn to self-criticism when we're not able to accept our limitations, accept ourselves as we are *in this moment – right now*. Sometimes when we see the higher material quality of life that others have, compared to our own, it can make us angry. So it can be very hard indeed to come to terms with 'this is how *I* am' and 'this is the life *I* am in'. We need to recognize, however, that when we accept ourselves as we are, and life as it is, we may find it easier to find peace and contentment within ourselves. This is absolutely not a position of passive, defeated resignation but rather it is about looking around to see what we can do now with what we've got. It's about 'being in the moment' as opposed to living in regret and with 'if onlys' or 'isn't it unfair' or 'I could have been . . .' or 'I should be better, more able or competent . . . Why am I not good enough?' and so on. But as I said at the beginning, this is a challenge: it's not easy.

When I was younger and training to become a therapist, trying to help people who were very distressed, I used to say to my supervisor that my patients would be so much better off having somebody with far more experience than I had. To some extent, that was clearly true. However, my supervisor, who was a wise and gentle older lady, pointed out that this was the essence of life. We can live life in the 'if only' lane or make the best of it and appreciate where we are right now. So the question for me was not 'How can I have 20 years' experience on Day 1?' because that wasn't possible. Everyone has to walk exactly the same road as I was walking, from being inexperienced to experienced. There is no other way. Rather the question she wanted me to ask myself was 'How can I be the best young, inexperienced therapist I can be, given my limitations?' Because that was all there was for these individuals – there was no one else. It was a harsh lesson in some ways but it helped me confront the reality of my limitations: I could only be what I could be.

Not only do we have to come to terms with our different limitations but we also have to learn to recognize that, in some areas, others really *are* better than us. Indeed, this is why we enjoy going to the theatre, listening to music or watching sport. We are listening to or watching people creating and doing things that we can't possibly do ourselves and appreciating them for it – although, of course, in the case of sport if they don't win we can feel far from appreciative. But the ability to value the talents and attributes of others is a vital element of compassion but can be undermined by envy or self-insecurity. Compassion can, therefore, actually involve learning how to appreciate and take pleasure from the talents of others, *to be pleased for them.*

So individual differences between us are extremely important in many aspects of our lives. The source of such differences lies in our genes, the way they combine and interact, the way our life histories interact with our genes to shape our brains and bodies, the kind of social arenas in which we have grown up and the values we have adopted, the things that we have learned – and more besides. But as the Dalai Lama says, 'All seek happiness. None seeks suffering.'

Challenge 7: Our internal relationship and self-interconnectedness

Our seventh challenge brings us to how we think and relate to our own inner potentials, emotions, motivations and so forth. Many self-help books will focus on helping you to look at the way you think or interpret things, how your feelings work and how you plan and engage in behaviour that is likely to be useful to you, and on helping you to develop your skills and abilities. These are fine as far as they go. However, given that our brains evolved for social relating, it is useful to think about our internal world as being full of 'social-like' relationships. In other words, it's about how parts of ourselves or different systems in our brains relate to each other.

It's like having a number of different potential actors within our heads who all have to learn how to interact with each other. In this way, my angry thoughts can be seen as part of my angry self (linked to a particular pattern of activation in my brain), whereas my compassion thoughts can be seen as part of my compassion self (linked to a particular pattern of activation in my brain). So, for example, when we are self-critical and self-condemning we are relating to ourselves through the competitive, contemptuous part of the self and stimulating a particular pattern of firing of our brain cells. However, when we turn on, tune into, train up and listen to the words, motives and desires of the compassion self, we can create in our brains quite different patterns of activity that affect our feelings, behaviour and thoughts.

For some people, their emotions and memories can be overwhelming and frightening. They may believe that their feelings are abnormal and that others would make them feel ashamed if they found out what they were feeling. Others may believe that their feelings will drive them crazy or that they'll lose control of them. To cope with the power of such 'old brain/mind' feelings, they may try to avoid them or cope with them in various unhelpful ways such as by drinking or taking drugs or even by self-harming. As far as we know, only humans can choose to avoid internal feelings or try to control them in these ways. Research shows, however, that avoidance commonly leads to more trouble. Learning to develop compassion for our feelings can be an important step towards working with them. So it can be a challenge to acknowledge and face the power of feelings in our 'old brain/mind' systems.

Another important reason to really focus on self-compassion is because self-criticism and self-dislike seem to be growing at an alarming rate. I say 'seem to be' because obtaining accurate data on these sorts of things is difficult. Recently a colleague was looking for medical students to take part in one of our studies on 'self-compassion as an antidote to self-criticism'. There were many takers. He was surprised at how many admitted to having problems with self-criticism, saw themselves as a self-critic – to the point of making them anxious and undermining their confidence. When the Dalai Lama first came to the West, he was stunned by the levels of self-dissatisfaction, self-disappointment, self-criticism and self-dislike he encountered. For all our technology and comforts, he found us a people in conflict with ourselves.

Very few people who enter psychological therapies feel good, accepting, confident and at peace with themselves; there is usually some sense of dissatisfaction, a feeling of being flawed or inadequate in some way. If you want one recipe to make you unhappy, it would be to focus on the things you criticize or don't like about yourself. Given the way our thoughts, imaginations and fantasies affect our brains, you can imagine what it does to our heads to concentrate on the things we don't like about ourselves. But people do – day in and day out. Indeed, recent research has shown that, for many people who have mental health problems, a typical thing they have in common is self-criticism. This can vary from mild disappointment with the self through to outright self-hatred.[26]

In fact, it was the many conversations I've had over the past 30 years with depressed, anxious, lost and lonely people that convinced me that the one core element they seemed to lack was the ability to be kind, gentle, warm and compassionate with themselves. So I decided to teach them these skills and see whether they helped them. This was not re-inventing Buddhism exactly, which of course is centrally focused on compassion, because the approach I work with, and which we will explore in this book, is based on how our brains work. It was developed in collaboration with my patients, who taught me an awful lot about the road to compassion when one is feeling depressed, terrified or paranoid. On the other hand, there are very few aspects of the compassion approach outlined here that have not been heavily influence by the wisdom of Buddhist-informed psychology.[27]

The take-home message really is: We can stimulate patterns in our brains that are self-nourishing, supportive, encouraging and soothing, so that in whatever we do to help ourselves (say, change the way we think about ourselves or face up to and cope with things we struggle with), we practise creating in our heads an experience (brain pattern) of warmth, kindness and support as our *primary starting position*. If we do this, we may find that things will be slightly better for us.

So the seventh challenge is really about learning how to understand our (at times powerful) feelings and urges and our internal relationships with the different parts of ourselves. We can learn that, when we're critical of ourselves, it's often out of disappointment or fear. However, when we are kind to ourselves it is not just our thoughts but also our *feelings* of kindness that are key. The challenge is to create nurturing and nourishing relationships with the many parts of our selves, so that no part is split off, forgotten, ignored, hated or avoided. We will be looking at this challenge quite a lot in the second part of this book.

Challenge 8: The tragedies of life

In some ways, our eighth challenge lies at the heart of our distress. We know that life is basically tragic. From the great writers of the Greek tragedies and the ancient spiritual thinkers, to modern-day writers and philosophers, the big question was and is: 'Why is life so full of suffering?' We just get the hang of 'being here' and think we've learned a thing or two about life and then we have to get used to the idea of decay, death and not being here any longer. A doctor friend of mine pointed out the other day that, although we're giving people medications to prevent heart attacks, they'll die later of dementia or cancer. For many of us, it's not so much the fear of death but the way of death that haunts us. As Woody Allen is reported to have quipped, 'I don't mind dying. I just don't want to be there at the time.' But as I noted above, facing death can be easier if we have a sense of being cared for and of being connected to the flow of life as opposed to being alone and alienated within it; it is also easier if we are gentle and kind with ourselves as we look back on our lives, in contrast to being harshly self-critical and disappointed.

Thinking about the pervasiveness of the human tragedy is one of the first steps on our journey into compassion; indeed it is one of the inspirations of compassion. It may seem strange that some people's first move into compassion is through their rage at and sense of injustice about the suffering of life. Sadly some people get stuck there, going round and round in angry circles, rather than seeing their feelings as a *call to compassion*. One person I worked with some time ago reflected at the end of his therapy that he had seen life as rather unpleasant and had been quite angry at his own and other people's suffering. But then he realized that: 'If one finds oneself in hell, one can keep on having a tantrum about it, which makes hell even more hellish, or one can start looking for a bucket of water. If each of us finds a bucket of water, maybe we can put out some of the fire.' For him, developing compassion was a bucket of water.

Some suffering arises simply from the compromises that occur as a result of evolved design. The shape of the skeleton evolved originally in the sea and is not that well adapted to upright walking. This is why we can have problems with our knees, hips and backs, because of the weight they have to carry. Countless women have died in childbirth because the physical requirements of upright walking can complicate the shape of the birth canal – human babies can get stuck because the design is not that good. Disease-causing viruses, parasites and bacteria are also evolving life forms that interact with ours. They can be responsible for both mild inconvenience (say, the flu one gets on the first day of a longed-for holiday) and tragic disability and loss of life – the flu virus of 1918/19 killed more people than died in the First World War. Individual viruses that make their hosts blind or crippled, or actually kill them, stalk the earth in their billions in *their* effort to survive and reproduce. Most experts talk about 'when' the next killer virus will strike, not 'if', with all the suffering and grief that will follow in its wake.

Our bodies are based on the building blocks created by genes, but errors occur and genes, too, can cause serious suffering. There are many genetic diseases that will terminate life early or will create an existence of pain and suffering. It was probably genes that claimed the life of a colleague's beloved 48-year-old wife from breast cancer *and* that of their equally beloved 26-year-old daughter, just after completing her PhD. Such tragic stories are not so rare – they touch all of us in one way or another. And just a few hundred years ago, it would have been surprising if you did *not* lose some of your children before they reached adulthood. In some parts of the world, this is still the case.

We're a tragic species, too, precisely because we have these amazing 'new brains/minds', but they sit on top of old passions. We don't always appreciate how humans' disposition for cruelty, war and violence (seen as solutions to complex problems), which greatly contribute to human suffering, is linked to how our brains have evolved and been socially nurtured. Human history is riddled with leaders who have inspired their followers to carry out terrible acts; they have obeyed because, for them, as for us, tribalism and submissive following are powerful pulls. Such observations are far from new, and over the centuries, we've struggled to find meaning and make sense of them (*see* Chapter 12). Some people believe that the world was made by a benevolent God and that one day our suffering will end. They assume that God has His/Her own motives that are beyond human reason and so there is no point trying to work them out – we just have to bear the suffering until all becomes clear. For some, this type of faith disappeared in the Nazi concentration camps. Worse is the belief of others who think that suffering is God's punishment. When the tsunami hit the Indian Ocean on Boxing Day 2005, causing more than 250,000 deaths and dreadful grief and suffering to countless more, some religious leaders claimed that this was God's punishment for the world's decadence. Not much compassion there then. The Gnostics, an early Christian sect, thought the Earth and the material universe had been made by mistake or by a malevolent deity; passions of the flesh and possessiveness were parts of his game plan and so should be avoided. They became known as the Cathars and were wiped out as heretics by the Roman Catholic Church in the thirteenth century in what is now regarded as a campaign of genocide.

Today, there are increasing moves to rescue the concept of 'intelligent design', a form of creationism. As evolved beings in the flow of life, our bodies and minds are amazing, extraordinary and fantastic. But if they were actually designed by God or some other entity, one would have to say that the design is positively dreadful! Not only is the body poorly constructed in many ways (don't forget the high death rates following childbirth because of the way our upright walking has compromised the birth canal), but so is the brain. If there is a Designer, why would He/She create a system in which 'new brain/mind' competencies fuel 'old brain/ mind' motives, emotions, tribalism and goodness knows what else? Why design a body that is so easily vulnerable to viruses, parasites and genetic error? It doesn't make any sense to me. So I prefer to think of humans as part of a process, such as the flow of life, and spiritual questions arise within that. That for me is a key to compassion – recognizing that *we have not been designed*, that we all just find ourselves here, not because we (or some other power) chose for us to be here. So we need to use our 'new brains/minds' to support and help each other through the tragedies of life. The struggle of good and evil, beloved by the religious, actually turns out to be the struggle that occurs partly from the interaction of our 'old' and 'new' brains/minds, and partly from different innate strategies within us.

Some psychologists believe that our extraordinary and impassioned pursuit of pleasure, comfort, fast cars and nice houses is partly due to the fact that we really haven't got our minds around the reality of life as tragedy. At the heart of Buddhism is the recognition that all things are impermanent – including, of course, life itself – and pain and tragedy are inevitable. The flow of life in the universe is painful. Indeed 99 per cent of the life forms that have ever existed on this planet have become extinct; everything passes, everything changes. The point in Buddhism, however, is not just to casually observe this tragedy, to have a detached, 'well, you just have to come to terms with it and get on with it' approach, but to have a deeply heartfelt recognition of the suffering that we experience as a result of 'being here', of waking up in the flow of life for just a short while. Compassion comes from the recognition that life is tragedy, a recognition that forms the basis of a lot of compassionate mind training.

The Buddha also suggested that the ways in which we try and cope with the pain and tragedies of life can unintentionally cause even more difficulties for ourselves and for others. For example, by pursuing material possessions and enjoying our comforts, we don't have to think about the realities of life nor the tragedies and the suffering of the vast majority of people on this planet. There is, for instance, unseen suffering behind the production of cheap clothes and factory farming, and the Earth is being destroyed by our industrial processes, which will cause generations to come to suffer. There is the often unrecognized suffering that results from our social comparisons, self-criticisms and general inability to treat ourselves with kindness. Sometimes suffering can just seem so overwhelming, and we feel so unable to do anything about it, that it is easier not to think about it at all. Yet we know we live in a suffering world, and these thoughts, feelings and fears tick away in the backs of our minds.

So we're a tragic species because we're dying from the day we're born, because we're susceptible to so many genetic and infectious diseases, because we have two types of brain that together can drive us crazy and to commit great cruelties and allow terrible injustices, because we want, yearn and grieve to connect. But the open acknowledgement of this is not the road to despair but the call to compassion. If life is like this, how can we train our brains to bring some meaning and genuine joy into our lives?

Challenge 9: Morality and societies

There is one obvious aspect of life that compassion dovetails tightly into and this is morality and moral thinking. Not all moral concerns are related to compassion, nor is compassion related to all things moral. Concerns and questions about what morality actually is and how we arrive at it and enact it have been part of moral philosophy for many hundreds of years.[28] The general consensus is that our sense of what is right and wrong is related to complex interactions between genetic disposition, learning, conformity, learned social values, the 'feeling of things' and reasoning. Of course, people can also take moral stands because they are frightened to disobey dominant members of their group and simply adopt their values.

Moral feeling and thinking are not static but unfold as we develop, often in stages. As children, we have a basic empathy for others and a sense of justice that comes to be guided by parental punishment and praise. Later we become aware of our group's values, rules and expectations of good conduct. Our moral sentiments are linked to the morality of these group values. Early Roman morals and acceptable behaviour were rather different to ours, for example. A further development moves us to take a more detached, non-partisan 'view from the balcony', through which we become aware of humanity at large and the fact that our tribe or group has created artificial boundaries around parts of humanity. This leads to the thought that freedom, liberty, respect and compassion should be given to all humanity and, indeed, in some traditions, to all living things. These stages each become part of a self-identity.[29]

While we're growing up, it is not long before we recognize that moral thinking often involves conflict. For example, suppose two people are seeking medical care: one has only a mild health problem but has paid money to the health system for his/her care; the other has a major health problem but has not paid into the system. You can only treat one. A principle based on justice would be to provide medical care to the one who had paid for it; not to uphold this principle could result in people refusing to pay and the collapse of the system as a whole. A compassionate, care-based principle would see us giving help to the one more in need. If a poor person needs powerful drugs to treat his child, how should we treat him if he steals them?

Incorporated within this style of reasoning are the concepts of 'rules', 'deserve' and 'need'.[30] Carol Gilligan[31] also drew attention to two types of moral thinking: one based on concepts of rules, fairness and justice and one based on feelings of concern/care for others. Women may be more focused on nurturance because they invest more in their young and can depend on supportive, kin-based alliances.[32] Men may be more focused on problems of competition and the need for its regulation through systems of fairness and rights. Issues linked to rights (taken and bestowed) and systems of justice have concentrated on the recognition of people's autonomy to pursue goals and remain free from exploitation. Rights are important for cooperation and for the prevention of exploitation of the weak by the powerful, and they have often been hard won. However, recent data have questioned these gender differences and directed attention to situational factors that require different types of moral thinking.[33]

One interesting aspect of this is the way in which compassion actually incorporates both a justice and a caring orientation, although, as noted, while we would certainly not believe compassion to be unjust, caring and justice *can* conflict. A social or traditionally agreed form of justice for a victim may be a very non-compassionate response to the perpetrator. Justice does not necessarily require forgiveness, whereas compassion probably does. Justice, as a result, may be more socially and culturally constructed than compassion.

We know that different people, on different issues, apply different processes to judge different moral questions. Some have arrived at morality through increasing awareness of suffering or unfairness. For instance, awareness of the suffering endemic in animal farming generates an emotional concern to change one's behaviour; others are vegetarians simply because this is how they've been brought up. In the first example, morality is developed through an emotional reaction to the pain and suffering of other living things and, in that emotional sense, is linked to compassion. It is not a morality that is arrived at through reason, but neither is it a morality that is without reasoning. Thus developing morality can involve a complex interaction between feeling and reasoning. And indeed that's the problem, because *different types of emotion* are linked to morality. Feelings of sympathy and sadness and being upset by suffering comprise one sort, but feelings of disgust, indignation and/or fear are others. For example, it is all right to factory farm and kill animals for food but immoral (i.e. felt to be disgusting) to have sex with them.

So people argue for a *moral* position in a great number of domains in a whole range of ways. Some celebrate homosexuality, while others are disgusted by it and see it as sin. Some are appalled by abortion, while others fight for a woman's right to choose. Some see the arms trade as legitimate to one's national economy and right of self-defence, whereas others see it as corrupt and a stain on humanity. Some believe that criminals should be electrocuted, stoned or hanged, while others believe these are deeply immoral acts. Some believe that torture is a legitimate way to treat one's enemies, whereas others see it as a major moral test of a culture. Some believe that all cultures and religions should be free to follow their own beliefs and practices, while others believe that certain humanitarian rights – such as freedom from subjugation and from female circumcision – override individual creeds. Some hold that religious beliefs that originated in the eastern Mediterranean more than 2,000 years ago are a source of tribalism and aggression, whereas others believe that they are fundamental to morality. Some believe that human/animal stem-cell hybrids involving only a few hundred cells will open the door to cures for many horrible diseases, whereas others believe that this is the beginning of a Frankenstein world. And so we could go on and on. No wonder moral philosophers have their work cut out for them. They recognize that this combination of genetic disposition, learning, conformity, learned social values, the 'feeling of things' and reasoning raises complex questions about how we think about moral issues.

So it's not surprising that people can be confused about moral sentiments and will often rely on their emotions and social comparisons to make judgements, with their capacity for thinking obligingly coming up with justifications for whatever moral principle they have latched on to or indignation they have felt.[34] Some go to religious texts such as the Bible for guidance and in this way come to decisions about what God thinks of, say, homosexuality or some other issue. Since you can find in these texts arguments to support or object to just about any behaviour, because they were written for societies and cultures long ago and addressed very different social problems to the ones we have today, you're on to a winner. You can pick and choose. If you don't like what you find in the New

Testament, no problem – go to the Old, and vice versa. For some, the very issue of why one would want to appeal to a higher authority that one cannot discuss or debate with or question is itself a moral question. And it's a moral question because, if you appeal to a higher authority, you will be using that authority to threaten, cajole, reward, control or punish someone else because you know that your own authority and ability to persuade is not enough. Hence the very act of using ancient religious texts supposedly containing the words of God is a moral issue that we could take very opposing views on.[35]

So maybe we can approach the problem in another way and focus instead on *pro-social behaviour* and how we help people to become compassionate, kinder and more empathic.[36] If we do that, it may be a way by which we can approach moral questions and arrive at our own decisions. It does seem that people who come from loving and caring backgrounds, where compassion has been part of their lives, think about moral questions in a different way to those who have had a neglectful or abusive home life.[37] However, the ways in which compassion and compassion training may help us with our moral thinking and decision-making are unclear and in great need of research. For example, it has been frequently pointed out that, although Tibet had one of the most developed Buddhist compassion systems in the world, it also had one of the poorest and most feudal societies, which operated a complex caste system. The Tibetans also held many beliefs on the importance of subjugation and deference, particularly by the lower classes, as ways of earning merit. To some observers, this was a (perhaps unconscious) way of maintaining deference to the higher levels of the hierarchy.

Challenge 10: Resisting compassion and self-compassion

Much research has shown that focusing on compassion for others and on self-compassion has a range of health-promoting and relationship-enhancing benefits.[38] However, our final challenge relates to the fact that, although we can understand all that I have written so far and may agree with various points, we can still be quite resistant to pursuing the compassionate path.

According to Aristotle and ancient Greek tradition, the only people deserving of compassion are those who do not deserve their suffering, and that sentiment, which is alien to Buddhist compassion, has continued to ripple through Western thought.[39] The Romans thought compassion was a weakness in a society that needed to constantly demonstrate its power. Mercy was okay, however, because it was given by the victor to the vanquished. When David Cameron, the leader of the Conservative Party in Britain, recently suggested that some wayward youth probably require more love and support, he was ridiculed in the press as a 'hug a hoodie' politician. He was, of course, right, and we all know this but won't address it.

As for self-compassion, which we will focus on with some exercises in the second half of this book, we need to examine an aspect that is not well covered in Buddhism or other spiritual traditions that involve compassion: some of us have a great resistance to becoming self-compassionate and to training our minds in self-compassion (and, of course, to expressing compassion for others). This relates to what we discussed above in terms of individual differences: people differ in the ease by which they understand the value of compassion, and the ease by which they develop it. Our reasons for pursuing compassion or resisting it vary. Some of us might have been taught that we should always put others before ourselves. Self-compassion smacks of self-indulgence and even selfishness. I mentioned how Dale Carnegie's *How to Win Friends and Influence People* focuses on the needs and interests of others (*see* p. 51) – but this doesn't mean to the neglect of oneself or failing to be self-nurturing. In fact, truly caring about oneself and about others go hand in hand. We will see, though, that self-compassion is quite different from self-promotion, struggling to do better than others, fostering a sense of entitlement or just doing 'nice things' for oneself or giving oneself treats.

Some people feel that they are already pretty self-compassionate. I have met some patients like this, and it is only as you get to know them in depth that you find out that their self-compassion is rather superficial and a bit of a fair-weather friend. They are indeed kind to themselves when things are going well, but as soon as they make mistakes, fail at something or enter into a conflict, they are rather less than kind, understanding or forgiving.

For others, self-compassion smacks of weakness, softness and namby-pamby-ism! Having fallen on hard times, Jack, previously a successful businessman, had become depressed and unable to work due to anxiety, fatigue and concentration problems. He was 'very disappointed' in himself for getting depressed, seeing it as a basic character weakness – he should be at work. The idea that he could be kind to himself and compassionate to his depression made him uncomfortable; it even seemed 'a bit daft'. Having heard something about cognitive behaviour therapy (which I use a lot but with an evolution and compassion focus), he thought that I was going to teach him how to change his faulty thinking so that he could think *correctly* and get back to work. It was all very much of the 'pull yourself together' school of doing things. Jack thought self-compassion would make him weak and spineless: 'Well, you see, I didn't get where I am today by being gentle and compassionate with myself but by driving myself on. The harder things get, the harder I push myself – that's the way to succeed.' He felt that to become kind and gentle with himself would lower his drive and make him lazy, and then he would fail to achieve – one of his biggest fears.

Jack demonstrated a problem that afflicts many people. They are so concerned with achieving things, proving their worth and impressing others that, when they don't do so well, they get angry, frustrated or depressed. In therapy they may quickly discover that they're not quite sure why they want to achieve all these things and feel so threatened if they can't. Not uncommonly, it starts with trying to win parental approval or do better than a sibling. They've got rather stuck trying to sort out childhood problems using an adult solution. It doesn't work, of course, because achievement doesn't fulfil our inner yearning for a certain type of recognition and affection; only by facing up to those feelings directly can we heal them.

Forty-year-old mother and nurse Jane felt that to be kind, gentle and compassionate to herself would be 'letting herself off the hook'. Like

Aristotle, she believed that we should only feel compassion for somebody's distress and suffering if we feel that person does *not* deserve their suffering (*see* Chapter 12). Jane felt that she *did* deserve her suffering. In medieval England, one did not feel compassion for those suffering the torments of hell because it was believed that they deserved them. So there is a long tradition of thinking in the West that kindness and compassion should be for those who are not responsible for their suffering – their suffering is not their fault and they have not brought it on themselves or done something to deserve punishment.

Jane had another issue with developing self-compassion, which was linked to her belief that she did not deserve compassion. This was related to fear. In her opinion, you should never take things or aspire to positions that you don't deserve because they can be taken away from you and you will be humiliated for even thinking that you had deserved them. Carol had a similar problem. She was also frightened of and resistant to becoming compassionate and kind to herself, saying that it was the last thing she wanted to become. 'Look,' she said, 'I try to be nice and all that, but if you really knew me – if you *really* knew what goes on in my mind – you would know why I can't be compassionate with myself. I know I'm not that nice – not at all as I pretend to be. Not until you take these horrible things away from my mind and make me a better person could I even think about liking myself or being self-compassionate.' It was difficult for her to think about coming to terms with rather than ridding herself of her inner feelings and fantasies, by accepting that they are part of the human mind, as writers of horror stories easily show.

Another form of resistance to developing self-compassion can be produced when people begin to develop it, especially by doing the same sort of exercises as in this book, and this exposes a yearning in them that may have been buried for a long time. This yearning may be for a sense of closeness or for a feeling of being connected to others – not alone – or a desire to feel loved or wanted. As the candle of self-compassion starts to flicker, it can illuminate great sadness and yearning within us. For some people, that can be overwhelming at first, and so we must go a step at a time – compassionately.

And for others, the beginnings of self-compassion can trigger memories of times when people who had been initially kind to them later abused them. This can create real confusion in their minds about trusting compassionate feelings, and for these individuals, the beginnings of self-compassion can reactivate rather fearful or strange emotions. We can make sense of this in the following way. Each of us has a system in our brains that codes for experiences of close relationships: the *attachment system*, which links to our soothing and contentment system and lays down memories of being loved and soothed. However, if we have memories of others harming us and/or of ourselves feeling anxious and angry towards them, those memories are going to reactivated if a therapist or other person is kind to us. Rather than feeling soothed by them, we'll re-experience the anger or anxiety because those are the feelings we associate with people being close, or with people who were supposed to be kind but weren't. We all know people like this: when you're kind and loving towards them, they pull away as if it's a threat to them.

These individuals and others have a misunderstanding of compassion. Compassion isn't about becoming less focused or less able but about becoming *refocused* and *more able*. If you think of people who are seen as very compassionate, such as Buddha, Christ, Nightingale, Gandhi and Mandela, you'd hardly call them under-achievers. Indeed, compassionate people can often be inspired to work for a cause. Developing self-compassion, therefore, is not simply a case of sitting around contemplating one's navel or just having nice thoughts about oneself. Developing self-compassion can be hard work and can inspire us to hard work. Some Buddhist meditators will get up at four or five in the morning to practise. (Don't worry! I won't be suggesting that here!) The compassionate mind is also focused on developing compassion for others.

So, sometimes, the journey into self-compassion can alert us to the fact that we might need to do psychological work with another person, such as a counsellor or a psychotherapist – the kinds of self-guiding exercises that we will work through together in this book are, of course, no substitute for professional therapy. So self-compassion turns out to be a bit more tricky than it looks at first glance. On one level, we can recognize that being compassionate to others and ourselves can be helpful, but on another, we can have all kinds of reasons not to be compassionate.

We cannot leave these problems with becoming more compassionate and self-compassionate without making clear the importance of social context. For example, a recent BBC investigation into knife-carrying gangs in London revealed that many of them came from families that didn't care about them, and without being in a gang and engaging in drug trafficking, they felt their lives would be in serious danger. The ideas of compassion and self-compassion were totally irrelevant to their lives, which were dominated by survival and protecting themselves. The programme revealed lives of immense cruelty, where punishments could include being burned with cigarettes or even being killed. The effects of taking drugs would also increase violence and block compassion.

Evolutionary psychologists, too, have shown that individuals develop strategies and phenotypes that fit their social niche. Distrust, exploitation and cruelty are, throughout the world, common traits that people can develop in these kinds of poor and drug-infested environments. It's ridiculous to blame individuals now that we know how our minds/brains are shaped by genes and cultures. Although I personally doubt reincarnation, there's one idea that I think is helpful. As we drive quickly past the impoverished areas of our cities, in our flash cars, complaining about too much tax, we should give a thought that perhaps, in our next incarnation, we might be living there. It's extraordinary to think that just round the corner from us are places where the candle of compassion has yet to be lit but is urgently required.

The compassionate mind

Why do we call this approach a compassionate *mind* approach rather than just a compassion approach? First, it's a term that has been used many times in various spiritual traditions. More importantly, however, it helps us to focus on the fact that our minds work in terms of patterns. If you access one pattern, you'll make another less easy to generate. If you're very anxious, this can block (patterns for) feelings of calm; if you're very angry, this can block (patterns for) feelings of kindness. Different patterns in our brain turn different systems on and off. You can't feel relaxed and frightened or angry and loving at the same time. You can switch between them, of course, but you can't feel them simultaneously. One pattern negates another.

As we will explore in Chapter 6, when you're focused on compassion, your mind will be organized in a certain way, creating certain patterns of activation within your billions of brain cells. You'll be attending to the distress or needs of others; you'll want to alleviate that distress or help them fulfil their needs, and watch them grow and flourish. In addition, you'll be open to developing empathy and understanding for them. Your behaviour will be orientated towards doing things for them, your thoughts will be on them and what you can provide for them, you'll have feelings of concern, warmth and/or generosity. When you develop *self-compassion*, you'll be applying these talents and skills to yourself. Your thoughts, attitudes and feelings for yourself will include caring, supporting and encouraging rather than criticizing or loathing (*see* Chapters 8 and 9). So developing a compassionate mind is a way of trying to create certain *patterns* in our brains that organize our motives, emotions and thoughts in ways that are conducive for our own and other people's well-being.

Conclusion

We are in a new, exciting and challenging time in our history. The scientific study of the human mind has revealed much about the sources of happiness and unhappiness and various states of well-being. It turns out that, while access to various comforts and technologies (rain-proof homes, central heating, comfortable beds, microwaves, flat-screen TVs, hand-made guitars) give us a buzz of pleasure, the more secure sources of well-being and happiness, not to mention sustainability on a global scale, arise from how we come to understand and relate to *our own minds* and those of others. Compassionate relationships with ourselves and others are a wellspring of happiness and health. Research has shown that if we can cultivate self-compassion, kindness and gentleness, based on a *clear understanding of how our minds work,* we can equip ourselves to create happiness for ourselves and others. I can't promise you that God will love you or that, by opening your heart to the cosmos, the cosmos will make you rich or famous, nor free you from life's adversities and painful tragedies nor from the destiny that awaits us all (sorry). However, you may find that, by trying out some of the ideas in this book, you will become more at peace with yourself and find your own route to happiness and – who knows? – maybe new ways of thinking about spiritual and existential questions.

The next four chapters explore the scientific foundation for our training in compassion. We are going to look deeply into just where our minds came from, how they work, and the nature of compassion.

3 Placing Ourselves in the Flow of Life

The last two chapters indicated that, without training our minds, we may not have the control over them we would like. This means that, in many ways, much of what goes on in our minds is actually not our fault – or even our intention. This was a fundamental insight of the Buddha nearly 3,000 years ago. In fact, it is now fairly well accepted that the kind of person we are emerges from the interaction of two major controlling processes that we as individuals have absolutely no control over: our genes and our early environment. It is the interaction of these that brings us into existence and gives us our experience of 'being oneself'. Understanding this fact about our own personhood and life has huge implications for how we come to see ourselves, our journey into compassion, our path to well-being and fulfilment and, for those interested, our spiritual journey.

When we fully realize how and why we did not design much of what goes on in our minds, *we can then take responsibility* in new ways and learn how to live in and work with such a mind. This may seem odd but it's not really so strange. After all, you didn't build your physical body – your genes did – but learning how your body works means that you can train it to be toned and fit, working on different muscle groups or your cardiovascular system and eating a balanced diet. Two hundred years ago, people didn't realize that lack of vitamin C caused scurvy; now we do and so can prevent it by eating fruit. As we learn more about our brains and minds, we are coming to realize that they too need certain types of 'input' to function well. As we will see, compassion is like a multivitamin for the mind. In the centuries to come, a better understanding of the kinds of inputs and social relationships that 'feed' and 'nurture' the brain is needed, along with political courage to advance a mentally healthy society.

So before we explore how to train our minds and work through some 'brain training' exercises, we need to capture the right spirit of non-blame and kindness. We need to really grasp why we are not to blame for much of what goes on in our minds, and why developing compassion is the road to a better-regulated mind. We can start by thinking about one of the challenges we met in the first chapter: how we became aware that we exist and that *we have a mind*. It was all rather odd, wasn't it? Well, it was for me.

My personal emergence

Like me, you probably haven't much idea of how you got here. We just suddenly find ourselves in the world, don't we? The journey into awareness and that 'we exist' begins slowly. Since all journeys into self-awareness are similar, let me share with you how it happened for me.

Sometime in late 1950, my parents engaged in a reproductive act. The reason they did this was because of an evolved mutation billions of years in the distant past. Originally living organisms procreated via cell division – basically they reproduced by just splitting in half. Male and female differences did not exist. Then a chance mutation resulted in organisms discovering that combining their DNA with another of their own kind introduced genetic variation that was conducive to their survival. Procreation via sex was an evolved invention – not that my parents ever bothered about that, of course. They were just happy to enjoy the pleasures of a process that had started off billions of years before. Anyhow, within a few hours a sperm and an egg had fused together, setting in motion a sequence of extraordinary complexity. Millions of sperm tried to reach the egg and merge with it – any one of them might have led to me being slightly different. I find that a fascinating thought. I wonder if there had been one for not losing one's hair with age?

Once one sperm had penetrated the egg, the race was over and all the other millions of sperm were done for. My genetic pattern was now decided, and under the instructions of the genes in the winning sperm and those in the egg of that month, my basic biological form started to unfold. Slowly limbs and internal organs grew and then my brain, with special cells called neurons connecting themselves into complex patterns. Like ants building an ant hill, emergence arises from the collective actions and interaction of the 'builders' – which, in our case, are our genes. There is no overall designer or supervisor. Following the basic instruction of the genes for our species, I was designed to become a human rather than, say, a fish or a rabbit. I can't tell you how pleased I am about that. Anyway, according to the genetic instructions for my species, and the specific ones from my parents, after nine months a series of changes occurred in my mother's womb and then there I was, pink, crying and probably very confused. The environment of the womb and the hormones circulating around me affected my development and which of my genes got turned on and off. Amazing that – genes can actually get turned on and off by external factors, including the hormonal environment of the womb.

Now that I had arrived, the connections between neurons in my baby brain, which were to become a source of so much of what I would be capable of thinking, feeling and doing, were rather limited, as was my ability to have any sense of being a self. But this was going to change rapidly because, under genetic guidance and external stimulation, my brain would be making hundreds of thousands of connections a day. Some neurons would form into complex networks and others would actually die if not stimulated and used. 'Neurons that fire together wire together' and this is how experience begins to develop the patterns that can emerge within the brain. These patterns of interconnections are what make up 'me'.

But let's just stop here a moment and consider the implications. Obviously I had no say in the genes I have. I did not choose to be this species or even this sex. I did not choose the colour of my eyes or the shape of my ears. I had no say in whether I had genes that would increase my vulnerability to certain diseases, or whether I would get fat or stay slim, or be more or less prone to anxiety or depression. I certainly did not choose the kinds of emotions my brain would be able to create – my capacity for love, anger, fear, disgust and so on were just built for me. I had no say in whether I had the potential to be an Olympic runner or to be musically talented – which I am not! Given that I wanted to be a rock guitarist, that was a bit of a disappointment. The fact that I would be able to learn and use a language and be able to read, imagine and create – all these would depend on the brain that had been built for me. I chose none of it.

However, it is not just my genes that I did not choose. Nor did I have any say about when or where I would be born, arriving in this culture at this time to these parents. If I had been born 2,000 years ago into, say, Roman culture, to parents who had high status or were slaves, then my sense of myself would have been entirely different to what it is now. The experience of being born into a loving household or a stressed and abusive one would actually affect how my brain matured and the types of connections that were made between my neurons. It is not just my 'values' that would be shaped in a certain way by my relationships with others (e.g. my parents), but my actual brain, from where my thoughts, feelings and desires flow, is sculpted by my relationships.[1] If I'd been unlucky enough to have been born into, say, an old-style orphanage where infants were left in cots all day and there was little care or interaction, then all the potential that lies inside me, which could have been sculpted by love and kindness feeding my brain, would simply have withered away. I would have suffered intellectual losses and decline. My brain wouldn't have anything like the connections that it does today. My potential to become a professor of psychology would have turned to sand. Yet all these things, which were not of my choosing, were going to be powerful shapers of who I would become, of the values I adopted and aspired to and of a sense of myself as a person. So my sense of 'me' emerged from a complex interplay between my genes and my environment. I chose none of it! So it follows that much of what emerges inside me is not of *my* choosing. You can probably also sense that this has profound implications for our compassion to others, and of course, it is exactly the same for you; you chose none of it.

My earliest memories are hazy ones of playing with certain toys and being fascinated by clouds in a blue sky. I must have been two or three years old. I have always loved skies. In the UK, every day a new, ever-changing, pattern of blues, whites, greys and pinks is being created over my head. So at the age of two or so, my brain was developing and I was gradually becoming aware that I was here in the world. I had no memory of anything before my time on Earth, which started in 1951. From now on, my body and brain, with its genetic codes ticking away, would go about developing me. I found that, if I fell over, I would hurt and would cry; I found that I was frightened when Mum told me off – didn't like that. I experienced anger when Sally tried to take away my favourite teddy bear at nursery and I whacked her one. Well, it was just automatic. When Mum said she loved me and held me, I liked that. My brain was building for me a whole suite of feelings and ways of behaving that were at the ready to help me deal with various situations as I moved through life.

From about 11, I started to grow hair in strange places and new feelings emerged in me. Where on earth did they come from? A new cascade of hormones had been released with the onset of adolescence, reorganizing my brain in complex ways. Joe and I got caned for smoking behind the bike sheds and trying to sneak into the girls' shower room – *oops*. Learning point: don't get caught next time. Try as I might, I was often close to bottom of the class but got to be captain of the rugby team. In reality, I had chosen none of these feelings and aspirations – not a single one – they were just happening inside of me. Indeed, all over the world boys of my age were experiencing exactly the same changes inside them, more or less. Although I was taught loads of mathematics, geography, history and how to throw a rugby ball, no one taught me about my brain and my mind – I just had to try to live with it and work out what was going on in me – kind of trial and error. I tried to fall in step with others around me and observed the changes in them too. I knew I wanted to be liked and accepted so that seemed a kind of guide. So I found myself to be a 'string along' kind of person.

When we sit back and ponder how we got here and became who we are, we see that, in many ways, we simply arrived and emerged in the flow of life; each of us is like a little wavelet on a vast sea that rises and falls. For some of us, this is a reasonably pleasant awakening, but for many others, who are born into impoverished, stressed families or experience callousness or abuse, it is not. *This understanding is the first step towards compassionate understanding.* It allows us to see that so much of what we are has, in a way, little to do with personal choice. Therefore it makes little sense to blame ourselves for some of our feelings, motives, desires or abilities or lack of them, or for how things turned out. As I suggest throughout this book, when we give up blaming and condemning ourselves (and others) for things then we are freer to genuinely set sail towards developing the insight, knowledge and understanding we need to take responsibility for ourselves and our actions. Learning and practising compassion will help us feel more content and at peace with ourselves and also more concerned for others. None of us is responsible for having a brain that is capable of feeling great fear, rage or all kinds of sexual desires. Nor are we responsible for having brains that can come to understand that our brains are the products of evolution and upbringing. Our 'new brains/minds', however, can take responsibility to discover this and train themselves.

Of course, when we see that we are all emergent patterns within the flow of life, we realize (as the Dalai Lama so often says): 'We don't want suffering. We all want happiness.' So we can see the other struggling human beings in the world as perhaps less lucky than us. For me, this calls us to open our hearts to those whose emergence was not as fortunate as our own. We open our eyes to the suffering in the world and how people just found themselves in such a life and 'there but by chance go I'.

The paradox

So here is the paradox. Even though I am not responsible for loving chips, red wine and chocolate, if I give in to my desires I get fat and have headaches – dash it! If I stay in bed and don't go to work or go to watch sports instead, I'll be sacked. If I let my aggression take over, I could go to prison.

My wife and I shared a fantasy a while ago. It was a late cold December evening before Christmas, with heavy rain, and the dampness had soaked through to our bones. We were trying to get out of a shopping centre car park. No car would let any others through and there was a big build-up. A couple of people pulled in tight to stop others creeping forward and taking turns to get out. 'Wouldn't it be great to be wealthy,' we thought aloud, 'and just smash right into them and say: "That's what you get for being a selfish arsehole"!'

We can learn to be open and even amused by some of what goes on in our minds once we are honest about it. However, acting out some of our fantasies, being taken over by some of our desires, wants, fears or vengeful feelings, can cause problems – so as we'll see, we can learn to develop a way of becoming aware and honest but equally more in control of some of our feelings and urges. Our actions have consequences, and we as a species can understand that and (sometimes) foresee them. Life is about learning when to act and when not to act on our desires and emotions. This takes us to the heart of compassionate behaviour because it isn't just about acting in kind, warm and friendly ways. It's also about *protecting* ourselves and others from our own destructive desires and actions; it's about being assertive, tolerating discomfort and developing courage – as we'll explore more fully in Chapters 11 and 12.

Let's get back to the wine, chocolate and chips. What is interesting and important is that my genes have built for me a brain that is like none other on Earth – it can understand that drinking too much and eating chips and chocolate are bad for me. Freud called this part of our minds 'the reality principle'. There is no brain other than a human's that can understand such connections – that too much chocolate means weight gain and that's bad for my appearance and health. Great – but once I know this, I can simply be angry and ask: 'Why do the things I love have to be so bad for me?' Another response is to tell myself sternly to be sensible and just stop eating junk and drink less. Good old-fashioned 'grow up and pull yourself together' stuff. Another response is not to think too much about it and just carry on in denial, enjoying the good things of life (often my favoured but not-to-be copied response). I once said to a friend of mine who still smokes a pipe, 'That will make you very unhealthy and you'll die from it.' He responded, 'Of course, but who wants to die healthy – what a waste!' The ways of denial are many.

Another response is to be compassionate to that anger or denial, seeing them as entirely understandable – it is indeed very unfair that I have a brain (not of my design or choosing) that makes me really enjoy and want things that are bad for me (or others). I can learn to be understanding and empathic to my feelings of irritation and loss arising from the fact that I can't have what I want. When I was trying to give up cigarettes, my wife bought me a wonderful book by Richard Klein called *Cigarettes Are Sublime.*[2] It focuses on all the pleasures of smoking – and that giving up will involve quite a major grief process. It was then that I realized that I had neither recognized nor been prepared to face up to or deal with my grief and loss – the loss of the romantic Paul, with the jazz, glass of wine and soft smoke. Smokers will understand this. So it was a sad and compassionate goodbye to smoking – well, okay, if I'm honest, a string of goodbyes. But in the end if I want to stave off health problems, getting fat and having headaches, I haven't much choice but to take control over my pleasures of smoking, eating and drinking. It is *how* I do that that is key. The thing is to cultivate the genuine desire to look after and nurture oneself, with a sense of warmth, kindness and even playfulness and to limit our acting on our desires from a position of kindness and understanding.

We'll see that these are central to compassionate behaviour (*see* Chapters 11 and 12). But note how we can use the same reasoning for much wider issues. We love our cars and flying around the world and the products of our industries – but our planet is changing and dying in the process. It's not the psychology of blame but of trying to develop a genuine desire to nurture and repair that requires our attention. Without it, it's so easy to get stuck in denial or simply respond with an angry 'Why should I?'

These are ideas we will explore in more depth later – but they give you a flavour of the key message: you are not responsible for how your brain works and the kinds of emotions, thoughts and desires that can arise in it. However, once we know this, we can learn to work with the inner processes with which we find ourselves living. We can learn to cultivate certain aspects of our minds such as our compassionate mind, which will help us with other aspects of our mind and promote our well-being. We can also become more aware of how our societies may be stimulating the selfish 'me first' part of ourselves with unrealistic fantasies and desires and setting us up to want more and more and, at the same time, to feel more disappointed and personal failures (*see* Chapter 5).

Emerging from the flow of life

So here we are then – we just find ourselves here. But then so did the universe and so did every living thing that has ever existed. We are all emergent beings. To develop more insight into and understanding of how our minds were designed and why they can be full of difficult feelings such as anxiety, anger, despair and unhelpful or destructive desires, as well as, of course, love and kindness, it's useful to see ourselves clearly as *emergent from the flow of life* on our planet.

Modern research has allowed us to see that we are at a certain point along a road of evolution. These insights have even influenced alcohol advertising. Guinness has a great advert of three men standing drinking in a public house with time running backwards – we see them become apes and then rats and then eventually little newts. The message is: 'Everything comes to those who wait.'

This understanding of how we are, as Darwin brilliantly concluded, emergent from evolution, is now more embedded in our culture than at any other time in history. So we too can turn around and look back over our shoulders and see the road that has been travelled to enable us (and our consciousness) to be here now, with the brains and desires, hopes and fears that we have. In essence, the research of the last 50 years or so enables us to look at a kind of 'video' of life from its earliest beginnings until now. So for a moment let's journey together and imagine that we have travelled back in time, to just before the moment when the first living organisms appear on Earth. This journey is intended to offer insight into the kinds of minds we have and what they were/are designed to do.

The first days

Let's imagine that, like in those TV documentaries, we can watch the evolution of life – from microbes to humans (which took billions of years) – unfold *in one day*. So here we are on a hill, staring out across a sea to a vast blue horizon as a new reddish sun just begins to warm a day on this virgin planet. The water is clear and we can see through it down to the depths. Here we notice small organisms struggling for life around hot vents. They grow and die in their millions, generation upon generation, but slowly new life forms appear, and some are going to be more complex than those before them. Using nothing more than genetic codes and slow mutations, new life forms are evolving and emerging on our planet. They have but two purposes – to survive and reproduce. Some of us today may say that genes are selfish, but such a motive is millions of years in the future. Here the genes are just replicators, builders of systems.

The important point is that genes build bodies that can transport them about. The creation of biological systems that can move with purpose is a profound event in the universe. Along with movement, genes build specialized systems inside bodies for being attracted to and motivated by certain things. From this come systems that evolutionists say 'support the Four Fs': feeding, fighting, fleeing and reproduction. These fan out into motives for *acquiring* and *defending/protecting*. As we'll see in Chapters 4 and 5, major emotional systems underpin these two basic concerns. These simple processes are the basis for the design for all sexually reproducing life. With humans come desires to *acquire* knowledge and understanding and create meaning – but we have jumped ahead of ourselves.

By lunchtime, the sea is teaming with life, large and small. We stop the process and ponder the fact that from nothing came the big bang of the universe. From the atoms and elements that were created then, there is now a code and a patterning of atoms that have become DNA and, from that, the possibility for the evolution of life forms and, from them, the possibility of consciousness. Is this a 'grand or intelligent design' – well not really, only in the fact of the possibilities. Nothing is designing these life forms or any changes to them – they are just emerging over time, playing out a set of laws and processes. Why the universe is such that *these* particular codes and pattern-generating systems have come into existence will be debated long after we are gone. So we can't go into that here. We watchers simply bear witness to the progression and intense struggles of life. We will see species come and go. Remember: nearly 99 per cent of all the species that have ever existed on our planet are extinct now. Even the Neanderthals, which were very similar to us humans, are now long gone with only their bones and artefacts to bear witness to them even having existed at all.

As the day wears on, we see lands rise and fall, forests and deserts come and go, the emergence of life on land, mass extinctions from the ice ages, droughts and meteorites. Life is harsh and relentless. But we also see repeating patterns. We see that many life forms have evolved sensory systems that detect light and sound. We see that many of them have the same basic design of four limbs, a head with eyes and mouth to the front and ears to the side. Many have cardiovascular systems and lungs, and they have to eat other life forms to survive. We can also see the first strategies of life that began in the sea and are now on land in the form of reptiles. We are also beginning to see repeating patterns of behaviour. These are the first basic patterns of evolved minds, which will echo in us, too.

Reptiles, which emerged in the flow of life around 500 million years ago, are basically concerned with eating, gaining and defending their territories and mating – the Four Fs again. They will threaten others who challenge them with displays of stiff limbs and staring. No one taught them that; there is no school for reptilian status or duelling. They are guided via their reptilian brains that contain blueprints for actions and strategies, which are embedded in their genetic codes. Perhaps they would be amused or despairing if they could see the same type of movement in the military goose-step or eye-staring of fighting men, as well as their drive for dominance, possessions and territories. Not much change then! The psychotherapist Carl Jung would come to name these powerful, innate patterns for feeling, thinking and behaviour (e.g. to seek status, control a territory, find a mate) 'archetypes'. Their origins stretch back many millions of years.

Indeed, the famous astronomer, the late Carl Sagan, in his book *The Dragons of Eden* (1977),[3] argued that the reptilian brain is a source for some of our dreams, nightmares and intrusive fantasies. The horror movie storyline of becoming 'beast-like' is the archetypal fear of being taken over by the passions of the reptilian brain – a mind that is predatory, cold and aggressive, the Nazi nightmare. Kent Bailey[4] at

Virginia Commonwealth University studied how old brain patterns could affect us today. He, too, pointed out that it's not that difficult to adopt a reptilian view of the world, focused on impulsive desires, sexual conquests, aggression and enforcement of ownership and control. It's also interesting that we often depict evil in horror movies as reptile-like. A reptile's mind is only interested in power, control, food, sex and personal gain – the life strategies and concerns of the reptiles in their struggle for reproduction and survival. The reptilian mind has no interest in (or ability to recognize or enjoy) family life, love, play, building trusting alliances or having empathy – and that's why it frightens us. These are abilities that will evolve with the mammals. Maybe we allow demons to walk the Earth when we use our new mind abilities to fuel reptilian passions?

The reptiles' strategies and archetypes will not be removed from the genetic code as long as they are successful in passing on genes. There's nothing inherently good or bad about this; it's simply how evolution is. Later life forms will adapt these strategies, mould them and add to them, but they cannot go back to the drawing board and start again; they can't just push the delete button. Change through evolution can only adapt what has gone before. So in one form or another, concern with power, sex, territories and control continues to live in and through us humans. Individuals without at least some interest in acquiring resources, defending them and reproducing would not leave many genes behind. 'Intelligent design', favoured by the creationists, never addresses just how poor and 'cobbled together' the designs of our bodies and minds actually are in many ways, or just how many passions we carry over from earlier evolved life forms. The emergence of consciousness was certainly complex and awe inspiring, but this does not imply good design. It is more like the Guinness advert perhaps. If there is any spiritual lesson to be found in all this, it is precisely the fact that, because our brains and the genes that build us have had such a troubled time getting here, it really is going to be the compassion we can harness for ourselves, others and our planet, directed by our 'new brain/mind' abilities, that will make the difference to the kind of future we now create.

Let's get back to our journey in time. We are still standing on that hill watching this process unfold before us and we can see that, as new life forms begin to evolve on our planet, it was the reptilian strategies (i.e. archetypes) that got them – and eventually us – here. It was the reptiles' struggle for life and evolved solutions that have influenced gene flow. They, and the strategies that they followed, are not 'evil' but are part of the evolution of life and of the minds to come. Harsh, savage and tragic they may be to our minds but they also comprise the foundations of our evolutionary journey.

Around 120 million years ago, a new set of life forms – mammals – emerge in the flow of life. With the mammals come new strategies that go with warm-bloodedness – living in family groups that offer care and protection to offspring and in large groups for general protection. Mammals also form status hierarchies rather than strict territorial ones. In some species, there will be a ruthlessness where only one female is able to breed and she suppresses, chases off or even kills competitors. This is common in meerkats, despite looking so gentle and quaint. So for mammals, sexual competition, driven by the desire to both engage oneself and prevent others from engaging in sex, will texture their lives. Long before humans appear at the very twilight of our day, we will see the working of the archetypes that enable sexual competition, loyalties and betrayals, group living and tribalism, submission to leaders and fear of dominant males, the striving for status and social position, cooperative hunting and working together – all the themes that, when we eventually arrive, are going to play big time in the minds of humans. I find it amazing that so many of the desires that flow through me, and indeed all of us, were designed not only long before me but long before all humans.

The things we want and enjoy doing

So we can see that many of our motives and desires are related to strategies and archetypes that have been doing the rounds for millions of years. But we must be careful here. Although passing genes to the next generation is key to evolution, animals are *not directly* motivated to increase their genes in succeeding generations. This is partly because success at passing on genes is an outcome that no animal could actually calculate. Hence, they are motivated to engage in behaviours such as wanting, looking for and enjoying having sex; wanting and enjoying friends and disliking rejection and exclusion; wanting and enjoying status and disliking being marginalized. At certain times of the year, some animals will be motivated to travel (migrate) or build nests or burrows. When done competently, these tasks contribute to reproductive success and, therefore, in the normal course of events, result in the genes that support those behaviours being passed to the next generation. So we still have those motives ticking away in us to because they have been successful for many millions of years.

However, as I discussed in the last chapter and will again in later ones, we have many other 'new brain/mind' abilities, which include being able to use language and symbols, to think things through, to reason, to reflect, imagine new possibilities and even impossibilities (e.g. science fiction tales). It is partly because of these human-evolved abilities for thinking ahead, being able to stand back from and reflect on what is going on in our minds, and in what we are feeling and doing, that we can do things differently from other living things. Hence humans have potentially great flexibility in *how they enact* different desires and motives. For example, we can desire sex but use contraception; we can separate sexual pleasure from the consequences of the act; or we can choose to make money, acquire status and put off having children altogether or, in the pursuit of 'enlightenment', become celibate. More complex still, we might choose to use or not use contraception according to what the dominant males of our religion say. Also nowadays people might try to stimulate their sexual feelings via the internet with no other person actually being present. The point is then that the desires may not have changed that much over time, but because of our human brains, we can invent thousands of ways to act them out or to refrain from them – which is both a blessing and a curse.

So strategies are like the game plans for life. They're the components of the mind that help direct our attention, feelings, reasoning and behaviour, and they're quick to pick up on certain types of information. Indeed, these strategies and archetypes of our minds can be activated quite fast and become active before we are even aware of them or have thought about what has been stirred up in us. You can flash pictures of naked women at young males so fast that the perception of the images is subliminal and they don't 'know' that they have seen such pictures, yet they respond physiologically. Our guiding strategies and archetypes can also have a seductive quality to them; we just fall in with their feelings and ways of thinking. In this sense, *the archetype or strategy thinks through us*. Knowing this can lead to some very important insights about the whole nature of our minds. For example, religions will often try to get you to identify with a local tribal group or leader. The idea is that everyone who identifies with that god or a religion will become part of one group. The religions that were born in the tribal conflicts of the eastern Mediterranean 2,000 to 3,000 years ago are all like this, and are very different to Buddhism, whose founder was a pampered prince and not under any threat at all.[5] That tribal archetype will inject you with passions and direct your thinking so that you'll follow. It certainly won't advise you of the risks of losing your individuality or the potential tribal violence inherent in becoming an advocate, follower, disciple or devotee. It will simply infuse you with a desire to be tribal, belong, be part of and follow/conform.

So what can we do? Most important, of course, is to stand back from identifying with any archetypal process and first think of ourselves as sentient life forms that owe our current existence, experiences and competencies to the millions of other life forms that have gone before us. We can identify with the flow of life. Next, we can identify with the fact that we are human beings and identify with other humans. We have all 'simply arrived here' and are trying to do the best we can with a brain we neither designed nor, to some degree, understand. We recognize that we have enormous capacities for being benevolent or malevolent, which we need to gain insight into compassionately. Only then should we start to think about ourselves in more local terms, such as our tribe or political group. Our evolved mind will already have been working in the other direction, to stir up strong passions of identification with our local group, and it is understanding how we work against those passions, by identifying ourselves as human beings, that can become key to our actions.

The scripts that your archetypes and social mentalities write for your life

So let's look in more detail at our archetypal mind. It turns out that studies of the mind and brain over the last 50 years or so have shown us that our minds are a very mixed bag of strategies, archetypes, desires, motives, fears, abilities and talents. All these evolved at different times to do different things and they do not always work well together. We have minds capable of understanding that 'we exist' and can explore the nature of the universe; we are capable of great charity, love and kindness but also of rage, violence and torture. We are a rainbow of possibilities. No wonder our minds can seem, at times, confusing, overwhelming and out of control.

People often wonder if there is a 'real self' or a 'real me' among all the aspects of self one does and doesn't like. We sometimes talk about trying to discover the 'true' self. However, this is partly an illusion. There is no 'real self'; there are only states of mind and patterns of consciousness. There is not a single atom in your body that you were born with; in fact, you are constantly changing the physical fabric of your body all the time, including your brain. The experience of yourself as a being emerges from the patterns that are created in your physical brain. If, for some reason, part of your brain is damaged, then your experience of yourself would be very different. These are the paradoxes that modern science is grappling with today. So rather than the 'real self', think of yourself as a pattern of great complexity, a rainbow of many colours, and the point of discovery is not so much finding a particular colour, but rather learning how to blend all the colours. A garden is not just the flowers or the trees or the grass or the soil – it is all these things. So think of yourself as not a single self but as a consciousness that is textured by a multi-faceted, multi-coloured set of possibilities.

Now the idea of archetypes has been around for thousands of years, reaching back to Plato and, much later, to Kant. But probably the name most associated with the idea is Carl Gustav Jung (1875–1961).[6] Jung was the son of a pastor and a contemporary of Freud's. While Freud focused on flows of libidinal energy, Jung suggested that the human mind is made up of a set of special systems that organize our motives, thinking, feelings, fantasies and behaviour around specific themes. He called these 'archetypes'. They evolved, he said, because over time they helped us navigate through the basic tasks of life. These tasks included children seeking out and becoming attached to parents and obtaining care from them, and adults forming relationships with peers, joining and defending groups and group boundaries, becoming sexually interested and engaging in procreation, caring for their offspring, growing old, seeking meaning, becoming wise and coming to terms with death.

Archetypes are like inner guides that orientate us towards certain things and motivate us in certain ways. So Jung thought that there can be many types of archetypes. For example, the *mother archetype* can orientate us towards caring figures and to respond to being cared for (mothered). The sexual archetypes, in the form of the *anima* (in the man) and *animus* (in the woman), provide a sense of the desires and behaviours towards the opposite sex. The *persona* influences our social representations and seeks to keep our reputations clean so that we will find acceptance in our groups. The *shadow* represents those aspects that exclude information from consciousness about our true intents/motives. The *hero archetype* motivates us to take risks, excel in the eyes of others and propel ourselves forwards. This archetype can be linked to social motives such as helping and rescuing others or to more dark motives such as wanting power to control others.

Jung suggested that archetypes can become over- or under-developed in us. To give one clinical example: people with persona archetype inflation organize much of their behaviour around the need for social approval. In consequence, they think only of appearances and current fashions, and can lose a sense of their individuality and their ability to stand up against the crowd. Persona deflation occurs in people who care not at all for what others think and risk being either courageous changers or anti-social. Much depends on the balance of other archetypes within the self and how they blend or conflict with each other.

Because our inner archetypes are designed to do different things and pursue different goals, *they can be in conflict with each other* and this often causes neurosis. Because these are evolved predispositions, they are shared with all human beings and, in this sense, are collective. These innate predispositions are largely unconscious – we just feel them in us, in our caring for others, our desire for sex, our desire for friends and to belong to groups or our desire to destroy our enemies.

Jung also suggested that the way an archetype matures and functions is affected by both our personality (genes) and our experience. For example, although we have an archetype that inspires and guides us towards love and comfort in the arms of our mothers when we are infants, if this relationship does not work, well, we can have a stunted mother archetype. Anthony Stevens[7] refers to this as *thwarted archetypal intent*. In this case, as adults, we might spend a lot of our lives searching for a mother or father figure – trying to find someone who will love and protect us like a parent. Or we can close down our need for care and love completely and shun close caring. Researchers studying these early relationships and what is called 'attachment behaviour' have found that children (and adults) can behave in a number of ways. They can be open to love and care, or anxious about losing the love of others and need reassurance. Alternatively, they can avoid close relationships because they're frightened of or contemptuous and dismissive of closeness.[8]

The hero archetype becomes active with adolescence and the emergence of motives to compete and find one's place in the world – to join a group, gain status and find a mate. This is the time when we start to identify with our heroes (e.g. in sport, rock music or films). They represent high status and we want to follow their actions and even copy them. Like all other archetypes, the hero archetype can develop in different ways. People who are secure may be inspired to achieve realistic goals and enjoy their success, while others will be inspired to become famous or excel in certain ways. However, if the hero archetype is fused with anger or hatred (usually because the person feels marginalized or has a sense of injustice), it can become focused on goals such as vengeance with devastating results. Also because the hero archetype is so open to copying what others do and seeks recognition, it's very easy for dominant members of a group to inspire (young) people for good or bad.[9] The many billions of people who have died fighting for their ideals in wars are testament to both the power of the hero archetype and also the tragic ease with which tribes and other groups identify with it and how leaders can hijack and direct them.

Now archetypes are no more than 'rules of thumb', ideas that are linked to the innate aspects of our minds. Personas, shadows, hero archetypes and so on are just ways of describing and thinking about different aspects of ourselves. In fact, psychologists are constantly debating and researching how best to describe and understand the interactions of what is innate in us and how our innate potential turns into lived experiences. The point here is to think about the ways that archetypal processes *live in all of us* and can be harnessed, often without our full awareness.

The importance of literature as mirrors to ourselves

Jung's friend, the Nobel prize-winning author Hermann Hesse (1877–1962), never really understood what all the controversy over archetypes was about. He said that writers had known about them for centuries, and if they could not 'feel different archetypes within themselves and connect with them', they could not write stories. To be able to write about 'a person in love', 'the fears of the hero', 'the love for a child', 'the pain of grief', the desire for 'savage revenge' and so forth requires you to have some sense of them in yourself. If you have no idea what being in love is like, what wanting to excel feels like, what grief feels like, what wanting to hurt others feels like and so on, you aren't going to write about them convincingly. So don't give up the day job!

In fact, story-telling is an interesting human activity from which we can learn much. For instance, despite thousands of years and many differences in cultural styles and language, from the ancient Egyptians, Greeks, Indians and Chinese, we are able to understand the themes of all the stories that humans have ever written! Whatever the textures of culture, they are *surface* textures that do not cover the *deeper* meanings of human life. Jung noted that, down through the centuries, stories have dealt with the same themes of human life: love and family kinships, honour, tribal loyalties and betrayal, fear and courage, the powerful seeking control over the weak, the trials and journeys of the hero – not forgetting lust and sex. Through these themes, literature gives us a whole new way of thinking about the structure and content of our evolved minds. Christopher Booker[10] wrote a fascinating book that examined the basic plots of stories and human life themes – in his view, there are only seven! They include such things as the trials, tribulations and temptations of a hero's search (popular in films such as *Star Wars* and in Joseph Campbell's book *The Hero with a Thousand Faces*) and individuals 'search for insight, wisdom and meaning, a journey from darkness to enlightenment and wisdom (the story of the inner journey, of the Buddha).

Recently researchers have been looking at how we can be inspired and healed by stories that depict people struggling with life tragedies, difficult feelings and dilemmas, and confronting their 'dark sides' – e.g. Dr Jekyll and Mr Hyde. J.R.R. Tolkien wrote his massive trilogy *The Lord of the Rings* between 1937 and 1949, using fantasy characters and narratives to reflect the way our desires for power and money can consume us and we lose control to them. Clearly, he was reflecting on the Second World War, tribalism and the destruction of the Earth via industrialization – which we now have to face up to very quickly today. Peter Jackson made colourful films of these books. The point is that these life *themes* and scripts are woven through thousands of years of history and give colour and texture to our stories because they are archetypal. If we stand back, we can see very clearly that they operate through us; we are a type of consciousness in which they can flow, witness to the pain, suffering and joys of their enactments.

A couple of cautions, though: as amazing entertainment as *The Lord of the Rings* is, it will lead us astray if we take it literally. First, people will rarely do 'evil' knowingly. The Nazis and Pol Pot never saw themselves as evil, quite the contrary. The Romans never saw their gladiatorial games as evil. The real source of destruction is usually from people who believe they are fighting for *good* causes. Hitler believed that he was creating a more perfect and noble society with more perfect people – and he was a vegetarian because he hated cruelty to animals! It's the individuals who justify their actions in this way who are the most worrying. This is certainly true on the international stage. To my mind, George Bush's refusal to veto the use of such torture techniques as 'water boarding' (immobilizing an individual and pouring water over his or her face to simulate drowning) is an endorsement of cruelty. Such behaviour is concerning, too, because Bush has had all the privileges that come from having had a Western education and human rights. And he professes to be a Christian when it's quite obvious that, if Jesus were here today, he would never endorse torture. Yet in his own heart, Bush believes he's doing good and defending his country. Remember the well-known saying: 'The road to hell is paved with good intentions.' So we have to be careful because we often can't see the archetypes working through us.

The second mistake we can make in fictions like *The Lord of the Rings* is to depict badness as ugly (e.g. the Orcs and the Uruk-hai). It is very common to depict enemies that way. They are also often made to look as if they are deformed and 'diseased', which triggers our archetypal psychology of disgust and fear of what we could become and the desire to eradicate them as a disease. Many tyrants refer to their enemies as infections and vermin and use body metaphors. Hitler certainly did. One's enemies are actually just fellow human beings who got started in the same way as you and I did – they just found themselves here – in that group rather than in this group – and are doing the best they can to make sense of it all, guided by their genes, socially shaped brains, needs and human archetypes. Linking badness with ugliness and disgust is a very old trick, but be careful because it is also a serious illusion. To some people in other cultures, our devouring, polluting and exploiting Western society means that *we* are the equivalent of the Orcs and the Uruk-hai.

So be cautious of evil depicted as creating or even seeking ugliness. Enjoy it in the movies if you wish but do not see it as a reality. In fact, ugliness is often a very unintended consequence. Destructive behaviours are very rarely promoted by people who are trying to create ugliness. For themselves, they would create beauty. The Mafia and other criminals, for example, want the best houses, the finest cars and so forth. Indeed, that is the very nature of the problem, that in seeking the best and the most beautiful, we become greedy. We do not become greedy by seeking the ugly; we do not seek power to make things ugly. Books comprising myths can thus prevent us from seeing that it is our own greed for nice things that can be, for others, a source of injustice and vengeance. By constantly creating these false good/beautiful, bad/ugly distinctions, we are able to turn a blind eye to our own destructiveness, because we think that we are pursuing the pleasant, the beautiful and the good. The compassionate point is to focus on what is common to all of us – which is the struggle we have within our own evolved brains and minds with so many competing urges and feelings. We can open our eyes to the ease with which we can become deluded and not see the realities we are creating around us – through no fault of our own.

Social mentalities

In the 1980s, I blended the concept of archetypes with that of evolutionary psychology to develop an approach to thinking about our minds and social behaviour that I called *social mentality theory*.[11] Social mentalities refer to the way our minds seek out other minds to have different types of interaction with. So, for example, if you want to have a sexual relationship, you need to seek out somebody who has certain characteristics and wants to have such a relationship with you; or if you want to have a close friendship, you must find somebody who will share and interact with you in such a way that together you form and experience the pleasures of friendship. To sum up, a social mentality:

- guides your motives, feelings, attention, thoughts and behaviours towards finding and engaging in certain types of relationships

- helps you recognize when that relationship is occurring for you

- gives you appropriate thoughts and feelings that are conducive to the development and maintenance of that relationship

- gives rise to positive feelings when relationships are working as desired but negative feelings when they don't (e.g. we feel happy when wanted as a friend or lover, but unhappy when we can't create these relationships as desired or if we're rejected by others).

Social mentalities differ from archetypes to the extent that a social mentality attends to, watches out for and tracks what other people are doing, how they're relating to you and how you're relating to them. And, of course, we can have all kinds of fantasies and dreams about other folk and what might be going on in their minds. The 'innate' point is that there are various key roles that we're motivated to *co-create* with others, because over evolutionary time being able to co-create these roles has been good for survival and reproduction. As we will see, social mentalities, like archetypes, have both positive aspects and potentially highly destructive aspects – shadow sides – to them.

Let's look at the most common.

Care-eliciting/seeking

Being protected and cared for gave mammalian infants a huge advantage in the struggle for survival. So much so that today we are born completely helpless, and how our brains mature, how we learn language, how we're able to think like humans, which values we endorse, even whether we live or die – all are hugely affected by the caring we received during our early years. Our brains are highly sensitive to paying attention and responding in multiple ways to the behaviour of others. In particular, the facial expressions and voice tones of the mother have powerful effects on a baby's brain.

When we're born, we seek care by emitting signals – that is, we cry if hurt or hungry, which signals our needs to our mother. The signals (cries) we send out impact on her mind in such a way that she'll provide care. Our brain then picks up the fact that 'care is being given' and we're safe, and we calm down. So the sequence is:

1 feel distressed

2 send a signal (e.g. cry)

3 signal is answered (e.g. mother's cuddle or breast)

4 distress is turned off.

As a result, we have co-created a role. In fact, the interaction between a baby and mother is constantly influencing their minds and physiologies – even the baby's expression of its genes. So when our care-seeking social mentality is operative, we feel a need for some kind of input from others.

As we mature, our needs change and we seek and respond to different types of care and to different signals that indicate we are cared for. So today I no longer respond to being picked up and winded and rarely cry for my dinner or if I am tired and want to be put to bed, but I do feel cared for when people take an interest in me and want to help me, listen to my needs and take them seriously, have friendly voice tones and are affectionate. So being able to feel cared for and to be soothed by the caring behaviours of others, and knowing that there are others around who care about us and our well-being, can be central to feelings of well-being. Later in life, we can take this caring approach to ourselves, and, in fact, this is a first step towards self-compassion – as we'll see in Chapters 8 and 10.

The downside, however, is that we remain dependent and under the influence of powerful others for many years and are therefore incredibly vulnerable to their neglect and abuse and the way they educate us. As I noted in Chapter 2 and will explore again in Chapter 5, the very wiring up of our brains and the pattern of connections that is formed are affected by the quality of early care. This care-seeking social mentality also opens us to certain types of emotional experiences, such as yearning for closeness, to feel cared for and protected. When this social mentality is thwarted, we can experience feelings of aloneness, disconnection, being uncared for and abandoned. At the root of many depressions and anxieties is an inner experience of aloneness and separateness from sources of care, protection, comfort and love.

In addition, to feel protected when we feel insecure or frightened, we can actually be attracted to powerful others and not worry if they're kind or compassionate or not. You see this in intimate relationships, where some women are attracted to very tough men who appear protective and in control of resources, but may not be so kind. We can also see this in groups and even nations that pick tough leaders rather than kind or compassionate ones. Protection and acquiring resources are very key qualities that people look for in their leaders.

Care-giving

Caring for one's offspring and genetic relatives obviously increases the chances of their survival and reproduction. Caring of this type is altruistic and when focused on kin is called *kin-altruism*.[12] For caring to evolve, brain systems also have to evolve that create *motives* and *desires* to be caring of others (and of oneself), as well as the ability to be attentive and sensitive to the needs of others and respond to those needs appropriately. There are a number of different (separate) aspects to caring:

- providing *protection* and / or rescuing from harm

- *provisioning* – offering what is needed for the self or others to prosper, flourish and grow

- offering *emotional support* – comforting and, in humans, validating feelings.

Some psychologists distinguish between *instrumental caring* (which is practical and task-focused) and *emotional caring*. One can be good at one type of caring but not another. So we're lumping together quite a lot of different elements here in this mentality.

However, when the care-giving social mentality is operating through us, it links our attention (e.g. to the needs of others), ways of thinking (e.g. how to be helpful), feelings (e.g. of concern, sympathy, empathy kindness and warmth) and behaviour (e.g. attempting to alleviate suffering or help the other person prosper, flourish and grow). How you feel and what you do will depend on how the other person responds to your efforts. As we will see later, this social mentality is very important for the harnessing of compassion and self-compassion; it patterns our feelings and thoughts and behaviours in a particular way that is different from other social mentalities.

The downside of this social mentality is that it's very easy to limit it: it's much easier to be caring to our intimates than to strangers. We lavish care on our own children, while just a few thousand miles away, children are dying from a lack of clean drinking water. Caring is easily knocked out by other emotions such as stress, fatigue and anger. Moreover, as we'll see in Chapter 6, compassionate caring is actually rather complex and more than just a motivation to be 'nice and caring'. Human caring falters if we don't also have the capacity to tolerate our own and other people's distress – it's easy for us to try to avoid being distressed by the distress of others by closing ourselves off to it. We also need empathy and an understanding of the minds of others. So caring and compassion can be fragile indeed.

Cooperation and group formation

Sharing with others – sometimes referred to as 'reciprocal altruism' – evolved because of the benefits that working together, sharing and cooperation bestowed on participants. For cooperation to evolve, brain systems have to evolve that create *motives* and *desires* to share with others, to form reciprocal alliances, to want to feel part of a group with a sense of belonging, to feel valued and accepted by others. There's no doubt that humans excel at cooperation and have evolved abilities such as language almost certainly as an aid to it. From a very young age, children show themselves able to engage in cooperative play, pretending and sharing fantasies (e.g. cowboys and Indians). For children to play such games, there has to be a 'sharing of minds', a mutual understanding of the world and agreement on who plays what.

All of human culture and science has come about because we're such a cooperative and mutually sharing species. Indeed, so powerful is human sharing that we build and share our knowledge generation on generation – which makes progress possible. Ideas that were in my mind that are now in this book may influence the mind of somebody not yet born who reads this long after I'm a goner. Sharing and wanting to share is fundamental to the very nature of being human.

So cooperative *behaviour* has been hugely advantageous to humans and this is why we enjoy it. We like doing things together, be it putting people on the moon or playing in a local football team or orchestra. A sense of belonging (how we feel and interact with those around us) is important to feeling safe and to our well-being. The cooperative social mentality patterns our brains in particular ways, guiding our motives, feelings, styles of thinking and behaviour. It orients us to attend and think about being with others who are *like us*. As a result, we can identify with large groups of people (most of whom we might never see, let alone meet) if we think they are 'like us'. We seek out others with shared interests precisely to cooperate with them and learn and grow together, to feel part of a community. This is one reason why the internet is such a major development in human communications – because we are passionate sharers, seeking others 'like us'.

The cooperative mentality can orient us to be egalitarian in our ways of thinking. Recent evidence suggests that egalitarian attitudes produce more healthy responses when people are confronted with stressful social encounters than biased, competitive and non-egalitarian attitudes.[13] There's also growing evidence that fostering cooperative attitudes and behaviours in children and adolescents (in contrast to competitive and individualistic ones) promotes positive relationships, improved mental and physical health and higher achievements.[14] In addition, it's increasingly thought that cooperative groups will out-compete competitive/individualistic ones in the long term. In fact, business is finding out that the internet is a good source for problem-solving because people simply like to share their thoughts and ideas for free! It's sad that, in the face of this, governments continue to buy into the business model that competition creates efficiency. Within the NHS, for example, we're increasingly split into small competing groups called 'business units'. Fostering high levels of cooperation would be far better.

Cooperation and sharing is the foundation for a sense of belonging. One of the tragedies of modern Western life is the creation of a group of people called adolescents who are no longer welcomed into the world of adults as they were, say, a hundred years ago or as they still are in other societies through initiation rituals. The ability to identify with Father or Mother and join Father's or Mother's group – for instance, through work – and feeling welcomed into the world of men and women is an increasingly rare event. But being welcomed into the world of adults also comes with the responsibilities and expectations of being in that group.

So, as with many aspects of our evolved minds and bodies, there are downsides to cooperation and group belonging. For humans, groups are a source of our greatest tragedies and traumas. For example, this social mentality orients us to compare ourselves to others in the group in terms of *similarity* and whether we feel that we're insiders, accepted and wanted, or outsiders, unwanted and marginalized. Our mental health services are full of people who feel like outsiders. One suicidal patient told me, 'All my life I never felt I fitted anywhere, like I don't belong. There's no place for me in this world.' One of the issues that therapists are constantly coming up against is people's experience that they don't belong, that they've never felt 'welcomed' in the world of adults and wonder how to earn their place or create that feeling of belonging. These individuals are seeking to have their *contributions* valued, to know that their existence matters to the group.

Another problem is that human sharing evolved in the context of small groups of people familiar with each other, so they were able to keep track of whom they were sharing with and what favours had been given and returned; appreciation and gratitude were also shared. This means that our sharing can have limits, and we have mechanisms in our brains to check out whom we might be sharing with – checks on their similarity to us. Thus humans like many other mammals are highly tribal.

It is this tribalism that can turn itself into the very antithesis of compassion. This is especially true when people take a sense of their self-identity from the group to which they belong and adopt its values. Research has shown that we form feelings of 'in-group' and 'out-group' – 'them' and 'us' – extremely easily, and once we've identified an out-group, they then become the 'not us'. To cut a long story short, we can become extraordinarily contemptuous of, cruel towards, and paranoid about, those we see as belonging to the out-group. We may even see their values and ways of life as potentially contaminating our own and then seek to identify, destroy and eradicate them. Whether you want to see this as an archetype, a social mentality or an evolved mechanism, whether you wish to focus on its genetic or social regulators, the fact is that our tribal psychology, tribal prejudices, tribal expansionism and tribal vengeances have been the source of immense suffering perpetrated by humans against other humans for thousands of years. And, of course, because we know that other groups can be as hateful and as paranoid as we can, we fear them . . . and so continues the cycle, from the drug gangs of Los Angeles to the genocides of the world. Our tribal psychology and fear of other tribes can cause us, in the relevant social context, to see cruelty as a virtue (*see* Chapter 12).

We have sometimes tried to tone down inter-group barbarity with 'codes of honour' and 'codes of the warrior'. The Geneva Convention, international law and conflict resolution are other efforts in this direction, towards which some Western leaders have, sadly, had a very cavalier attitude. Of all the challenges that compassion will face in any new world, one of the toughest will be trying to find ways to tackle tribal psychology. Internationally, that means certain countries giving up some of their power in favour of international law. Personally, it means being very thoughtful about which groups you aspire to and why, and what you're prepared to do to defend them. Sharing traditions and values, generation on generation, can have a very dark side.

Competing, social ranks and hierarchies

Competing for food, nest sites, sexual opportunities and so on are basic life tasks for most species on this planet. For some, the losers and less powerful simply keep out of the way of the more powerful – they use space to reduce and avoid conflicts. However, there are benefits to living in groups, and for those to evolve, there had to be ways to remove the potential for constant fighting. This was achieved with the evolution of psychological mechanisms for submissive behaviour and for dominant animals to accept this behaviour as evidence that their rule is not challenged. The formation of *ranks of social deference* enabled animals to live together without continual warfare. That, in time, would enable greater close proximity and, consequently, the evolution of more cooperative forms of behaviour. So began our *social rank mentality*, which would become a major way of thinking about ourselves and our social relationships and a way for us to organize the distribution of resources.

Our social rank mentality involves concerns with social power, place and control. There are, of course, many ways that we humans rank ourselves – by, say, knowledge, experience, age, authority, tradition, power, talent and beauty. We're a long way from using ranks only to regulate aggression. Indeed, outside criminal groups, most of us have little personal interest in competing using aggression and physical threat. Rather, we want to compete by being seen as talented, desirable and worthy: we study to pass exams, diet to fit into the latest fashions and play rock guitar – all to impress. A pat on the head goes a long way because we feel valued and wanted, and feeling wanted helps us feel safe. Indeed, with regard to cooperating and sharing knowledge, we like a little recognition (status) as well as awareness that we've been helpful.

Competition shows itself in many arenas where we seek to *win* the affection or regard of potential lovers, friends or employers. We want to *win* a place at university, or *win* that research grant. We want to *win* in contexts where others are going after the same things we want; our gain will be another's loss. Although there might not be any aggressive intent here because we're competing to be attractive to others (not threatening them), we can still display irritation, anger and even threats of or actual violence if we feel that the competition has been unfair (because of, say, insider trading or other forms of cheating) or that our 'position', 'status' or 'power' is being threatened. We've all met the benevolent doctor, manager or leader who is sweetness itself until we challenge them. In truth, none of us likes his or her 'position' to be challenged.

So humans can be very social-rank aware and motivated. The social rank mentality turns our attention to our social position in a social hierarchy, to *think* about relationships in terms of hierarchies and social comparisons – strong/powerful *v.* weak/powerless, winner *v.* loser, superior *v.* inferior, dominant *v.* subordinate, leader *v.* follower, controller *v.* controlled – and to *behave* in ways appropriate to hierarchies: competing for status, trying to impress those in powerful positions, submitting, showing deference, subduing subordinates or competitors.

While leadership, respect for authority and expertise, and deference are essential to the smooth running of any group, there are, of course, many downsides to this mentality. Depressed and socially anxious people can be caught in the feelings and thoughts that characterize it, believing that they are of low rank – inferior, inadequate, weak or unworthy compared to others. Narcissistic individuals, on the other hand, are highly competitive, seek high rank, want to impress others and be seen as superior and more entitled than them. Both types can be highly motivated to avoid being seen as inferior in certain ways.[15]

While some narcissistic individuals can also be relatively benevolent and caring, others are not. In fact, we now know that gaining power and social rank effects how we think and pay attention to those around us. Individuals who acquire dominance and power can become less interested in, and rather dismissive of, subordinates. Power really can corrupt because exploiting one's position is a very old evolutionary strategy that is very easy to fall into.[16] And in the face of the power of others, we tend to become very submissive and appeasing – you laugh at your boss's (unfunny) jokes but may not even offer one yourself. Some people who are very rank oriented show what is called the *slime effect*. Pleasant and deferential to those above them, they are bullies to those below. They're often extremely ambitious and navigate themselves into positions of power. When they get there, they can be serious threats to the existence of cooperative and compassionate workplaces and even societies.[17] Less well-studied are those who shun power and rank and may have a contemptuous attitude to those above and a paternalistic attitude to those below them in the pecking order. You sometimes find that people who like to fight for the disadvantaged and seek recognition of their needs are just as interested in fighting authority. All these styles can link with early childhood issues.

So this social mentality involves motives to win competitions and conflicts for resources and social position and to subdue competitors. Western societies have now greatly exaggerated rank difference between humans, dividing them into 'haves', 'have-nots' and 'have-lots', with the 'have-nots' being at a much elevated risk of a range of physical and mental health disorders and of being either a perpetrator or a victim of certain types of crimes. The competitive social mentality will also orient us to think in terms of envy and of undermining other people, because this can advance our own interests. From the world trade talks to street gangs, maintaining one's competitive advantage dominates thinking. The competitive archetype also tends to turn off the patterns in our minds that facilitate caring.[18] We'll explore this more fully in Chapter 4.

Sexualities

In evolution, men and women have followed different sexual strategies. Because men are capable of having literally hundreds of children, leaving their genes behind is related to *access*. If a male is to invest in a female and her offspring, he needs to have some security that the offspring are his own and that he hasn't been cuckolded. For women, however, the task is rather different. They can't be cuckolded, although they are vulnerable to imposed sex – which ranges in degrees of severity. They want genes from men who are good at securing resources, successful in the reproduction game, able to achieve high rank and become attractive and popular, because then their sons will inherit those genes and become like that and thus further spread Mum's genes. However, such men are also likely to cheat and not provide the women with the resources and protection they require. So women need to balance these two choices, and the balance may depend upon their access to their own resources. When they have reduced control of and access to resources, choosing 'honest Joes' may be the better bet; whereas if they have access to high resources themselves, they have greater freedom in their choices – e.g. the choices of female film stars.

These issues of sexualities are hotly debated and not straightforward, but the key thing is the way in which sexuality, the experiences of sexuality, sexual desire and the sexual behaviours of individuals vary according to gender, culture, background, resource access and control.[19] These things pattern our minds in certain ways. Of course, as mentioned previously one may decide to follow a spiritual path and not engage in sexuality at all. This doesn't mean that one loses one's sexual feelings; simply one chooses not to act on them. Also sexual behaviour can be blended with the other social mentalities. So one person can be loving and gentle with his sexual partner, whereas another may use his/her sexuality as a way of dominating, to obtain power and/or control. What is true for most of us, however, is that with the onset of puberty we are going to have to deal with the emergence of sexual feelings that follow certain strategies. These feelings and changes within your body at puberty *happen* to you – you don't *choose* them.

Summary

Looking at social mentalities and archetypes in general, theorists have recognized that 'the innate' is only potential, and that the social world we live in and the relationships that surround us guide and help develop our archetypal potential. Social mentalities are constantly arising and patterning our minds through our *interactions*; they're not just processes that go on autonomously in our own minds. This means our cultures and social structures can activate and pattern our minds, too. So, for example, the kinds of relationships we have with each other and the way we affect each other's minds and bodies will be influenced by the kinds of cultures and societies we live in. In our hurry-hurry, competitive societies, we are going to be interacting and stimulating different patterns in each of us than if we were in slower, more contented societies.

We have to think beyond individuals and individual minds and brains, and think about ourselves as *mutually influencing beings*. So on a simple level, our irritation with each other will raise our stress and increase our vulnerability to a range of health problems and to social discord, while our kindness to each other will lower our stress and impact positively on our well-being and increase our social safeness. At a more complex level, mental illness and criminality are woven from complicated genetic, social mentality and cultural/social interactions. And, of course, at an even higher level, the ways in which our societies operate, seek goods and services, secure trade agreements and enable international companies to extract huge profits from stock markets (and, as the recent crash has shown, exploit them) will greatly affect the lives and pattern the minds of people far away. We are all interconnected minds.

It's clear, however, that we can make choices, too. We can live in a world where we choose to foster our tribal psychology or sit back while it develops in areas of poverty and injustice. We are then faced with angry groups who come after us. We can choose to develop our competitive, 'have to be the best and have the most', 'my interest or my tribe's interests above yours' archetypal side. Or we can choose a compassionate approach that's more thoughtful of others. Ideally, of course, we blend these. We think carefully about our values and try to be the 'best we can be' but, at the same time, not ruthlessly exploitative.

How the brain's strategies and archetypes work

How do all these strategies, archetypes and social mentalities actually work in our brains? Basically, they work by activating different patterns within our brains. In other words, like a Christmas light show, some systems get turned off and some get turned on when we enact a particular pattern of strategies, social mentalities or archetypes. For example, if we want to engage in a compassionate and caring relationship with another person, the brain area that produces our ability to have empathy and understanding for them is turned on. We have feelings of warmth and concern for them; our attention is directed at how we can help them. The brain areas that produce our desires for aggression and to harm them are firmly turned off. If we could look in our brain, we would see various parts lighting up in mosaics of activity.

But supposing that the person we are interacting with is seen as a threat or an enemy? The patterns in our brain will now be quite different. The systems for feeling empathy, care, concern and so forth are firmly turned off; the lights will go out in those brain areas and the systems for feeling anger and the desire to retaliate or hurt the other person or even remove them completely will be turned on. We will see a completely different mosaic.

This insight tells us two important things. First, the social mentalities that are operating in (patterning) our brains have major effects on what we find pleasurable and rewarding in social relationships. Consider how it works. If we're in the caring mentality, caring and helping others and seeing them flourish is rewarding and gives us a warm glow, and their suffering is painful to us. By contrast, if we're in the competitive social mentality, seeing others hurt or do less well than us may be rewarding and seeing them flourish may be painful. We might only feel good if we see them suffer, go under or fall behind. So what we're attracted to and get pleasure from can tell us something about how our minds have been or are being patterned by our archetypes and social mentalities.

We can, of course, also experience the conflicts of mentalities as they compete for expression and control over our actions. This is why we commonly talk in terms of 'a part of me feels this and another part of me feels that': part of me is angry with, say, my wife or child and wants to be critical and accusing, while another part of me wants to be reasonable, kind and gentle. Our background brain state influences which one will get control. If we come home from work stressed and irritated, it may be more of a struggle to express kind and gentle sentiments (so your partner puts a glass of red wine in your hand).

Social mentalities can be blended together. So just as a blend of yellow and blue make green, a blend of caring, cooperating and sexuality gives rise to affectionate and sharing sexual experiences in which partners cherish each other and build a bond through their sharing. Most psychologists believe that the ability to blend mentalities, and our emotions, so that we are flexible and multi-faceted is key to our well-being. We understand that we can love and be angry with somebody, that we can want to be close to others sometimes but also alone occasionally. Individuals who are more black-and-white about things, who find it difficult to cope with ambivalence, blends and conflicts, are more prone to emotional problems.

Archetypes and social mentalities can also take control of groups. As we look back through history, we can see that humans have felt so threatened by other groups, or that some individuals have been so in the grip of their search for power and status, with others falling in behind as loyal (and often fearful or aspiring followers), that the world has suffered great cruelties – from the mass crucifixions of the Romans to the torture chambers and genocide of the Nazis. As I write, a mob in Kenya has just set fire to a church into which families and children had run for protection. In these cases, our abilities to reason and pull back from the wrong we do are lost to the passions and urges of the archetypes. We are literally 'possessed' by them – but are blind to it. It is important to see how easily the archetypes that live through us are 'summoned' by the values and passions of the groups we live in.

Once we know this, we can start to think about how we can recognize different patterns of activation in our brains, and the strategies that might be underpinning them, in order to *refocus our minds*. Do we really want our minds to be taken over by the archetypal in us? Shouldn't we object to how our passions are so easily aroused? To pull back and offer resistance is not going to be easy because the patterns and strategies stir emotions and passion. But there is also choice. Psychologists suggest that the more our 'new brains/minds' are able to think, reflect and understand the emotions and passions flowing through them and stand back from them, the more we'll be able to take control and make conscious choices of what to act out and what not. Indeed, that's the whole premise of psychotherapy on the one hand and meditative practices on the other. They seek to help us become more aware of and familiar with our minds and thus more in control. It's not going to be full control, of course, because all kinds of things can be going on outside our awareness, but it's a step in a useful direction. We'll be exploring this more fully in Chapters 7 and 9.

There's a wonderful story from a tribe of Native Americans: One day, an old chief was walking by the river with his grandson, thinking about what wisdom to impart to the boy. He told him that our minds are like the river: ever flowing. But within the flowing water are different currents, and so it is within our minds. Inside himself, the old chief said, he can sometimes feel two wolves: one is gentle and kind, and is a peace seeker, while the other is angry and aggressive. The grandson looked at the old man in wonder and asked, 'Who will win, Grandfather?' The old chief responded: 'The one that I feed.'

Today we can recognize that there are tragic possibilities for the human mind that arise because of the evolutionary journey our brains have taken, and the way that the brain can turn on and off certain key emotions and motives. Cruelty flourishes because we simply turn off our capacities for compassion. When we do that we are at serious risk of losing balance and handing what is essentially an intelligent and creative mind over to protective but destructive strategies. This is what puts humans at risk, but a risk we can reduce by recognizing that care and compassion are antidotes to fear, anger and the desire to harm and so can help us.

We can also become cruel and callous to ourselves with self-criticism, self-dislike or even self-hatred (all very self-uncompassionate). We think, say things and treat ourselves in nasty ways that we'd never dream of doing to others – especially those we care about. Because we are doing it to ourselves, like bullies who have no one to stop them, we think it's fine to behave this way and may even justify our self-unkindness. So important is this aspect that we'll be exploring it in some detail in Chapters 4 and 10.

Religion and spirituality

Becoming aware of how our motives, feelings and thoughts are actually guided by innate strategies, archetypes and social mentalities can help us reflect on key issues related to religions and spirituality, which many people struggle with today. These are not easy areas of exploration. Many writers have noted that religious beliefs and rituals gain the footholds they do in our minds and cultures because they link up with, and tap into, powerful archetypal and social mentality feelings and yearnings (from our evolved minds) and address deep existential fears of life and death.[20] They can make people feel that they have roots and traditions or that they are being cared about in the universe. With this intensity of emotion, beliefs become heightened, so that people will say things like 'I just feel deep inside me that this true.' One assumes that the Aztecs' belief in the value of their human sacrifices also sprang from such feelings of 'certainty' – so we must be careful here.

It's this 'tapping into the archetypal' that partly gives these beliefs their emotional power over us. Hence, when seen through the lens of the social rank mentality, God can be related to as a *dominant male* who must be obeyed; if not, your disobedience will be punished. In some religions, believers adopt the head-down, submissive posture, unable to look in the eyes of God (eye contact can be taken as threat signal). Humans have turned such bowing of heads into a mark of respect, of course, but the mechanisms seem the same. Even some aspects of Buddhism are prone to this deference psychology.

If rank psychology dominates a person's or a group's orientation and construction of God, the believers can have a fearful relationship with the deity (imagine all kinds of punishments) but may also be deferential, with a desire to impress and prove themselves loyal. They can have a harsh attitude towards subordinates or those who 'fail to understand', and they may want to persecute 'God's enemies' harshly. The focus is on power, compliance and obedience. This is not, as many thinkers have realized, a nice or 'good' God, for he may, as in the Old Testament, simply decide to drown all living things, or may have a passion for killing the children of those he doesn't like, send plagues of frogs or famines, or threaten people with the unconstrained sadism of hell. The only thing you can do is hope that he's on your side. So it's not a good God but a God on your side that's the issue. This is why many people feel that they must maintain a belief that they are chosen, for not to be so is terrifying.

The very thought that God can have favourites should raise worries, though. In fact, these are our projected archetypal themes, our own sadistic desires and fears that we put into the mind of God or gods. These are not new ideas – even the fifth *Star Trek* movie *The Final Frontier* was about how our own projections of God can create horrors. Consider just one. People often wonder why the God of the Old Testament was unkind to and slaughtered the children of his enemies. But it's well known that the males of some species, when taking over a harem, kill the young to bring the females into heat. Human victors throughout the ages have killed the children of the vanquished to halt a genetic line and thus end a threat to the winners' rule. Herod, of course, is famous for it. Why blame God for such motives when it is clearly a genetic strategy?

In complete contrast, love requires eye contact and a dissolving of power issues – just as a mother and baby stare at each other in a gaze of wonder.

The shift from a rank-focused God to a care-giving one is, of course, the transition from the Old to the New Testament. Forgiveness, deep empathy, sorrow and compassion are now seen as characteristics of Jesus (although these, too, are linked to social mentalities). So you can cherry-pick your quotes from all the religious texts and find as many appeals to compassion as you can to holy wars. As a result, many scholars now recognize that, because of our social mentalities, we construct and relate to God through our imagination and archetypal mind.[21] This may help us with certain psychological issues, and as Jung noted, if we activate archetypal processes, they can have enormous emotional power for us. People can find great comfort in their religions and I've known many distressed people with hard lives who have found strength through their beliefs (although I suspect that the kindness of their human priests was also key). Religions have also been a focus for group belonging and cohesion, a source of law and moral thinking, but at the end of the day, they are archetypal and part of the past and of our evolved minds. We can't avoid archetypal feelings, indeed compassion is based on one, but we can become aware of their dark sides. We should also clearly recognize that they have little to tell us about the actual nature of the universe, consciousness, how to heal the sick, life after death or any other important issue of this type.

There are many alternative views that leave open the door to a different type of spirituality, one less prone to the rank and tribal pitfalls. Jung suggested that 'God consciousness' – 'an awakening consciousness in the universe' – requires a sense of partnership and morality, and it's as we wake up to our responsibilities that God consciousness does, too – a theme Jung explored in his book *Answer to Job*. Another idea about spirituality is to imagine ourselves as waves on an ocean. We're not separate from the spiritual domain; we are part of it – something that is reflected in pantheistic beliefs that stretch back thousands of years. Buddhism also has its own unique approach, of course – a reciprocal process in which, as one becomes compassionate and enlightened, one automatically turns to the alleviation of suffering in all living things, through all planes of existence, and becomes part of the community of enlightened beings.

Finally, let me share with you a compassionate insight from modern science. Some people behave cruelly, which traditionally is regarded as worthy of punishment, a sin or resulting in the accumulation of bad karma. But what if they behaved liked that because of their genes or because they had a mental illness or a messed-up frontal cortex due to birth damage, or because their mothers were alcoholics or drug users, or because they were terribly abused as children or lived in appalling social conditions or ate food containing toxins? Then suppose that in 50 years we can fix all that. So as a result of, say, new psychotherapies, changes in social conditions or a few drugs, these individuals are not cruel but kind and so go to heaven, not hell, create good karma, not bad. If it all comes down to social conditions, genes or brain chemistry, then if, say, drugs keep people 'kind' and out of hell, I'm all for the drugs. But just think about the implications – including spiritual ideas that have been with us for so long but whose originators were entirely ignorant of evolution, genes and neurochemistry. If good and bad behaviour really are reflections of innate strategies, chemistry and social conditions, then where does this leave traditional views of sin, karma and punishment? If we have so little choice over who we are and what we become, where does this leave the idea that we have souls that are learning lessons? Hey, give me the drugs, make me feel good about me and others – I want to go to heaven!

It seems to me that the alternative is to become aware of how our new knowledge really does open us up to a whole new compassionate spirituality, freed from the fears and passions scripted by old archetypal forms. It is a massive compassionate challenge, though, because we like feeling special and chosen, loved by the Almighty, or being able to punish 'bad' people. How you think about these issues will influence your approach to compassion. We've only just begun to think about the implications of our new understanding of the influence of genes and of early love on our brains and the power of social context and group influence in shaping what we feel, think and do. We're losing the sense of the individual 'in control' self here. So you see, compassion that is open to our new understanding of brains and minds is not an easy road. It's science and our 'new brains/minds' that are going to help us, once we're motivated by caring and sharing social mentalities.

Selfishness and the compassion archetype and social mentality

Before we leave our evolutionary journey, let's end on the major optimistic note of this book: while many dark and cruel potentials have emerged from the struggle for life and can live in our minds (as so much of our great art and literature has shown), we are also capable of compassion. But compassion, too, is an emergent potential of our minds carved from nature. It is easy to focus on many of the darker archetypes of our minds, and forget that out of that darkness of the struggle for survival and reproduction, out of threat and fear, has emerged our capacity for caring and compassion. If we look at the road to compassion, we can see it begins when sentient beings start to take an interest in and care for their own. We will explore the nature and key elements of compassion in Chapters 5 and 6.

Compassion and selfish genes

Some people may see compassion linked to caring as the result of selfish genes. For example, if you go to the hospital and give birth to a baby, you want to be able to take home, care for and love *your* baby. You would not be happy if all the babies born that day were put into a single room, and then you could choose the one you wanted. Even if someone said to you that, compared to that baby, yours will be slightly less bright, less athletic or subject to more chest infections, you wouldn't be deterred. In fact, if anything it might make you even more affectionate towards your child, because you want to look after your genes. People become hugely distressed if, after some years, it turns out that they didn't take home their own baby from hospital after childbirth. So of course, we have an interest in a whole range of things – types of food, forming friendships, sexual relationships and caring for our own babies – because genes have built our physiologies to have feelings about those things. And they've done this because individuals who were motivated by those feelings left their genes behind.

So we know that caring has certain genetic preferences: it's far easier to care for your own genetic infants and relatives, and also friends, than for strangers. However, it doesn't matter that we recognize that our possibilities for compassion have emerged into the universe simply as a gene-replication strategy. This is a point that Richard Dawkins has written extensively about, including the fact that 'selfish genes' do not necessarily make for selfish people; we can develop insight into our minds, train ourselves and overrule the dictates of genes or selfish strategies.[22] So we needn't get too caught up with the fact that, because the origins of compassion clearly arise from genetic politics, this somehow undermines the feelings, motives or processes of compassion. Because your genes make your eyes capable of seeing certain light frequencies does not negate or belittle your experience of colour. The fact is that we now have the brain systems that make the 'experience' of compassion possible, and that compassion can organize our brain patterns in certain ways. What we need to do is to see how, by working on these brain patterns to harness compassion, we can develop a sense of well-being and purpose. We can use our 'new brains/minds' to train ourselves to have and feel compassion more deeply and for a much wider group of individuals than we may be biologically oriented to. We're not limited by our genes but are given a platform by them.

Indeed, it is the motivational, archetypal and social mentality processes that are helpful to understand. Throughout the world, people want to care for others, to become nurses, doctors, social workers, teachers and alternative therapists. Throughout the world, people put their lives at risk to save others – think about such services as the police, peacekeepers, fire, sea and mountain rescue services. If we take the capitalist view, or look at how our history has been shaped by the darker sides of our nature, clashes of tribes and dominant males, it's easy to forget that, although many of us want to have good lives ourselves, we also want to help and make a difference to others. When we fully acknowledge that we've woken up in a world of beauty but also one where many live in hellish conditions, we can see that there's much we need to do with our science, social policies and legal systems. In the hearts of many is a genuine desire to improve the conditions of humans and, indeed, of all living things.

As for selfishness underpinning compassion, then again the answer is: of course. The Dalai Lama makes this very clear in many of his writings. Not only is compassion good for you because it will help you feel good and organize your mind in such a way that makes it more open to happiness, but it's good for others, too, and being good for others means that we live in a happier world. If you are compassionate to others, they are more likely to be compassionate to you – so, sure, there are an awful lot of personal benefits. To be frank, if self-compassion and compassion for others increased your blood pressure, damaged your immune system, increased your vulnerability to heart disease, strokes, depression and anxiety and made you less fun to be with, I would advise against them. The fact is that it's our stress, striving and competitive social mentalities that are getting us into this kind of trouble – not to mention what we are doing to the world around us – because they have got out of balance. Compassion is our potential antidote.

Conclusion

This chapter has outlined how we all 'simply find ourselves here' with a gene-built brain full of strange and conflicting desires, passions and fears that are often turned on and off by the relationships we find ourselves in. Our minds feel personal to us, so much so that we feel this or that aspect is 'me'. Yet there is nothing we can feel or think (other than creative acts of art or science, maybe) that millions of others have not also felt and thought. The feelings we have are based on our shared programming – our common humanity. All that is 'just you' is your consciousness passing through time, moment to moment.

We've taken a view from the hilltop and watched the unfolding of life and of different desires and motives in the flow of life and in consciousness. We've seen how strategies, archetypes and social mentalities originate, become more complex and are played out, helping genes pass their pattern-building talents through time, for without genes there are no bodies, no life and no change and the universe falls silent. The passions and desires of you and me are all from the flow of life. This knowledge, which is the beginning of insight, enlightenment and wisdom and is founded on basic psychological science, will help us think about the tasks ahead and how we might want to engage with them. It will help us to pull back gradually from 'over-personalizing' our minds and realize that much of what goes on in them is not our fault nor our design. These are the first steps towards us becoming compassionate mind seekers and trainers and thus balancing our minds and taking responsibility for our actions.

In the next chapter, we'll get a better handle on the importance of balance by looking at how evolution has designed our brain with three basic emotion regulation systems that play a vital role in our everyday feelings and mental health.

4 Threat and Self-protection: The good, the bad and the really difficult

It is our emotions that give colour to our lives. They texture all that we do. With emotions, things matter; without them, they may not. Our capacity to feel links us to things we value. Some scientists even believe that our emotions are at the root of consciousness itself. For all their importance, urgencies and pleasures, we must admit that they can be a double-edged sword of delights, happiness and joy but also, of course, of fear, anxiety, frustration and anger. Emotions evolved because they serve various functions, and it is the *functions* of emotions that we're going to look at now. When we understand these and how they are work through us, we will be better placed to work with them for self-compassion and to soothe our minds.

As we touched on in Chapter 2, we can think about our emotions as organized through *three* basic systems.[1] So let's remind ourselves of these systems and then explore in more detail how they work through us. Recall that in Chapter 2 (*see* pp. 21–7), we suggested the following systems:

1 threat and self-protection

2 incentive and resource-seeking

3 soothing and contentment.

If these three systems get out of balance or become patterned in certain ways, we can suffer. In modern society, it's very easy for the threat/self-protection system to become overactive. We might fear losing our jobs or making mistakes at work, or being criticized or rejected by other people, or we may just be time pressured. The stresses and strains of life can lead us to have problems with stress, anxiety and depression. It's also easy to become over-driven, wanting to prove ourselves worthy and 'up to the job', and constantly seek pleasures, more expensive comforts, successes and achievements, and so find it difficult to relax. Whether we want it or not, we can find that life keeps us 'on the go' the whole time – no time to stop. When the incentive/resource-seeking system falters and takes a dive, we might think our chances of success have disappeared, feel burned out, exhausted, defeated and depressed and may give up altogether. The drive and 'fuel' seem to go out of the system.

We will look at each of these systems in turn to help us learn how to recognize them working in and through ourselves and how to bring a better balance of them to our minds. That is what we're after in the next section of the book – learning to balance our minds. This chapter is going to focus on the system of threat/self-protection, a source of many of our unpleasant and, at times, difficult-to-deal-with emotions.

Life is threatening

To start our journey, let's explore where the threat/self-protection system came from and how it is fundamental to all living things. In fact, threats to life have been in existence since the first simple organisms evolved on Earth. Indeed, as we noted in the last chapter, even on such a life-conducive planet as ours, the struggle for life has been so difficult and risky that the vast majority of species that have ever existed are now extinct – over 99 per cent of them.

Take the Neanderthals, a species similar to us humans. They lived in caves in family groups, cared for and played with their children and had their own aspirations for the future. However, they are now long gone, leaving only bones and artefacts as testament to their lives and struggles. It's unclear why they faded away: it's possible that they were squeezed out by us modern humans arriving from the south or they may simply have disappeared through interbreeding with us – it looks as if a gene that supports language, and which may have evolved in them because they were highly cooperative, might have come from them. We await more research. However, the point is that, with our comforts of central heating and supermarket food, it's difficult for us to be in touch with just how tough and threatening life was, and still is in many parts of the world.

There are, of course, different types of threat – predators, lack of food and unclean water, disease-causing microbes, the risk of physical injury, inadequate shelter, losing friends, the hostility of others of one's own species. Animals (including humans) have evolved ways – often called *defensive strategies* – of detecting and dealing with these threats. Some of these strategies are related to basic body functioning – for example, having fur or feathers as insulation from the cold or going into hibernation to conserve energy through the winter are ways of protection from the challenges of climate. Our immune systems are designed to help detect and cope with bacteria and other harmful agents that may get inside the body. Our digestive systems have also been designed to help us expel noxious substances through vomiting and diarrhoea. And as for threats from others, we have developed ways of trying to work out their true feelings and intentions towards us, and avoid them or engage in submissive and appeasing behaviour if they seem more powerful than us.

Anxiety

Our brain is the source of many emotions and ways of thinking that have been designed by evolution to be part of a basic self-protection system. In fact, feeling anxious when facing things that could harm us, with the added desire to run away from or avoid them, is a fundamental self-protection strategy. Different people can develop anxieties about different things. Some become nervous around dogs, others become anxious when meeting new people, still others dread public speaking. Many of the things we get anxious about are things that, over millions of years, have been threats. So we can easily become frightened of snakes or spiders, but not so easily of relatively recently invented electricity, which is much more likely to kill you. Fear of germs and contaminants is also easy to develop. But note that, in the modern age, of course, a fear of spiders or snakes can be quite a drawback since, in the UK or US at least, we only rarely encounter dangerous ones.

We aren't born with these fears, but it seems that there are differences in our (genetic) sensitivities that influence how we attend to them and the ease by which we acquire and intensify a fear of them. Sometimes we can acquire fears simply by watching others appearing frightened. From about nine months, as they become mobile, infants automatically start to become wary of strangers, and this intensifies if parents are, too, with the children picking up cues of 'be anxious in this situation' from their parents.[2] We'll be looking at how to compassionately cope with anxiety in Chapter 11.

Anger

Anger is another key self-protection emotion that we share with other animals.[3] It can be activated if our path to a goal or something else we want is blocked. The most common feeling is frustration, which many animals, including the humble laboratory rat, can suffer from. The more we activate the incentive/resource-seeking system (*see* Chapter 5), with our wants and 'need mores' and with time constraints, the more vulnerable to frustration we become. Frustration and frustrated anger make us put more effort into a task to try and *force* things through. This strategy – 'when all else fails, try brute force' – is a rather old one.

Another form of anger, linked to frustration, is *retaliatory anger*, which is linked to our evolved need to defend our resources, status and social position. If someone challenges us by, say, criticizing our work, we can feel anger and want to retaliate; if someone takes advantage of us, or in some way behaves unfairly, we can feel anger then, too. To feel cheated invariably makes us angry. While protective anxiety makes us disengage – that is, run from or avoid something unpleasant or dangerous or submit to it – with anger, we want to engage *more*, to overcome the obstacle or get the better of the other person. When we feel *retaliatory* anger, we want to make the other person do as we want. Maybe we demand an apology or a submission or want to make them suffer, too. Why? Well, because then we'd feel safer with them; we'd feel in control. What would our world be like if anyone could put us down without our retaliating; what if we had no way to defend ourselves so that others could easily take advantage of us or cheat us with no comeback? What if they felt that they didn't have to be wary of us because we'd never retaliate? Very uncool – evolutionarily speaking! So this response was designed by evolution to protect us. But unless we're cautious, our 'new brains/minds' can be inspired by retaliatory anger and cause terrible suffering in the world. To feel an eruption of retaliatory anger inside ourselves can be very frightening because it has the potential to be powerful and maybe sadistic. Some people experience strong anger, but also fear losing control to it and try to suppress it (as shown to dramatic effect in the film *The Hulk*). But anger is a call to action, a notifier, and requires our attention. This doesn't mean, however, that we simply act out in an aggressive way; instead, we should understand the feeling and then decide what we're going to do with it.

Key concepts of anger

Some time ago, the American behavioural psychologist C.B. Ferster pointed out that, if children are punished for showing anger, they will begin to become anxious about being punished. Over time, that anxiety will become associated with anger until the child doesn't really process anger any longer. Instead, at the very early stages of an anger emotion developing inside them, there is an automatic switch to anxiety. Depressed people often have this kind of difficulty.

In fact, any emotions can become associated and linked together this way. Young children who are punished or shamed for displaying fun or excitement can, as adults, become anxious if 'fun feelings' arise in them. This is called *conditioning* and is one of the most powerful ways we learn and adapt to our environments. Although a staunch behaviourist, Ferster was clear that, because of conditioning, some of our feelings become repressed and we are unconscious of them. The children who are punished for having fun or being happy might start to have uncomfortable (anxious) feelings when they are feeling good, yet not know why.

Cognitive therapist R.L. Leahy has looked at some of the beliefs we have about our emotions and the way they can cause us problems. With anger, the beliefs might include: 'Anger is bad. It is shameful. It is too destructive.

It is too sadistic.' This sort of thinking can result in difficulties with processing anger and the causes of anger.

According to Sigmund Freud, depressed people can feel very angry with others on whom they are dependent, for letting them down or being hurtful to them. However, depressed individuals are also frightened that, if they express their anger, the others will withdraw or hurt them even more, or they will be shamed and be made to feel that they are bad, ungrateful and unpleasant. As a result, because anger is threatening to them, they become unconscious of their anger.[4]

As we touched on in the last chapter, and will explore again in Chapter 10, self-directed anger and contempt can also be serious problems. Just because we're feeling angry at ourselves doesn't mean that we're using different brain systems to those we would if feeling anger on behalf of others. Self-directed anger can, therefore, maintain our threat systems in a state of high arousal and make contentment and soothing very difficult indeed.

Always keep in mind that the defensive emotions of anxiety and anger were not designed to be your enemies or to be bad or evil, but are intended to defend you – their function is self-protection. However, evolution designed them long before the appearance of the thinking and imaginative abilities we now have. Evolution could not foresee what would happen when our 'new' abilities combined with these primitive impulses and defences. The latter can focus and guide our thinking and our intelligence in such a way as to get out of control.

So to work on our anger (or any other threat/self-protection emotion), we must first understand that our threat/self-protection system does not want us to be defenceless. *It may even resist us trying to soothe and calm our anxieties or anger.* I often ask people who have problems with anger: 'What would be your greatest fear in giving up or significantly reducing your anger?' Now sometimes they say, 'I'd love to be like that – that would be great!', but with others, there's an outpouring of fear: 'Others won't listen or respect me. I won't respect myself. I won't be able to defend myself. Others will be able to get away with murder. I'll never be heard. You never get justice if you don't fight for it. I'll have to accept people's bad and inconsiderate behaviour towards me. People mustn't be allowed to get away with things like that. I'd be weak, a wimp and submissive, and I need to show people I matter – wimps are ignored. People deserve my anger. Being angry is the only way people learn.' Yes, the list is a long one and no doubt you can add a few fears of your own. However, basically all these come down to three key ones:

- the fear of being hurt or destroyed

- the fear of having no control over one's life goals, meaning or purpose

- fear of being unwanted, marginalized, ignored, excluded or isolated.

Think just how many problems our inability to control our retaliatory anger causes. There are so many points of conflict and violence in the world because anger, vengeance and fears are constantly activated. Humans (especially males) find this cycle extremely difficult to break free from, not helped, of course, by the West, which is often desperate to sell arms to both sides to make money. It often takes a leader like Gandhi or Mandela to change the system and the pattern.

Disgust and contempt

Another of the major defensive emotions is *disgust*, which is primarily intended to help us detect and stay away from noxious substances. From birth, infants and children will spit out bitter tastes and relish sweet ones. This is because, to humans, a bitter taste is a good guide to possible toxic substances. Humans can feel disgust for (i.e. be repelled by) a range of things, including the behaviour of themselves and others. Here the term *contempt*[5] might be the appropriate one. Researchers think that it is often when the emotions of disgust and contempt are blended with fear and anger that we become capable of terrible things. When we see our enemies as both dangerous and contemptible or as 'infecting our way of life or contaminating our values', this sets in motion the defensive strategies of detect, protect, avoid, subjugate and eradicate. These strategies are very useful when focused on dealing with diseases and genuine contaminants, but when aimed at other humans, they can lead to atrocities and genocide. When we feel disgust at aspects of ourselves, we may also wish to get rid of, purge or otherwise eradicate aspects of ourselves. So disgust is an archetypal process – originally evolved as a basic self-protection strategy – but it can now lead us into serious trouble.

The emotion of disgust comes into play when we think in terms of goodness and badness and wanting to 'purify', 'get rid of' and 'destroy', and has been used in both religious and non-religious ways to attack and annihilate people seen as 'defilers'. Hitler regarded the Jews as an 'infection', and once people use this archetype to view others, we're into 'search/remove/ destroy' territory where our compassion brain systems are turned off.

Listening to our emotions

Each of our emotions comes with (limited) instructions about what to do in certain situations. Think of what happens inside your body when anger flushes through you. What does your body want to do? Your jaw tenses, your muscles tighten, your eyes narrow, the tone of your voice changes, the urge to speak increases. As your anger mounts, your attention might shift to memories: 'And let me tell you something else I'm really annoyed about!' If the anger increases further, the pressure builds and you can feel as if you are about to explode. You might want to raise your voice from just loud to a scream, lash out or hit something or someone. Our anger system is designed to threaten other people who are threatening or blocking us – to make them shape up, back off or do what we want. The point is that your anger, which is you engaging in a self-protection strategy, *exerts increasing control in your mind*, in part because it's designed to do precisely that. If you're tired and at a low ebb, it's even more easily done because your brain will shift to 'hyper-protect' mode and any little thing can throw you into fury, tears or anxiety. So these are good reasons why we need to be aware of our threat-based emotions and stand back from them, behave assertively if we need to but not just act them out. The same thing is true of anxiety. If we always run away when we're anxious, we may not develop the skills we need to be able to cope.

It is, of course, one thing for us to have these feelings as a result of actual encounters with frightening or frustrating things or people. However, because we are a social species that can be easily influenced by the rhetoric and displays of others, leaders can easily summon these emotions in us if we are unaware of them. Indeed, people often talk about wanting leaders to inspire them by stimulating their emotions and passions. But rather than valuing this, I would suggest that we must be cautious about what we let our leaders create in us and not be led blindly by our emotions. Hitler got to power because he was regarded as a very inspiring leader who could generate passion and pride in his audiences. Without this ability he probably would have got nowhere – but it was also his audiences who allowed themselves to be stimulated in this way. Therefore, we need to learn to understand our emotions better as they work in and through us. We will find this so much easier when we give up blaming ourselves for having these feelings and desires and see them as part of how our brains evolved.

So a key point here is: always remember that your threat/self-protection system was designed to protect you (and, yes, protect your genes in the flow of life, if you want to look at it that way). However, these primitive little devices, which have served many species for millions of years, are powerful and now, in the modern world, need our guidance and 'new minds' to contain them.

The fast routes: Better safe than sorry

We have now established that our threat/self-protection system has evolved (with no help from you or me) to have a range of feelings such as fear, anxiety, anger, rage, hatred and contempt. These are natural, basic emotions. Although they can get way out of proportion and be highly damaging, we must not forget their basic function is *protection* – mostly of ourselves but of those we love, too, and other members of our groups. They did not evolve just to give everyone a hard time or set demons to walk the Earth. They are often powerful and easily and quickly activated in us because they were designed to be like that (so that is not our fault).

Also the threat/self-protection system is the first port of call for much incoming information to us. This is because the brain is set up to check things out first and then jump into action to protect us – to see if this event or that situation is okay. If you watch birds eating seeds at a bird feeder, you'll notice that they take a couple of pecks and then look around, constantly checking the area. Our own threat/self-protection systems operate in a similar way, often just ticking away even when we don't notice them. This is why a mother can hear the cries of her baby even when she is sleeping. Protection systems that were slow to react or were too thoughtful didn't do well in evolution: 'Oh, look, there's a lion coming at me . . . Hmm, I wonder if it's hungry or if it has eaten recently . . . Hmm, maybe not . . . Well, he's not looking this way so not so sure . . . what's the best thing to do? Maybe run . . . No, climb that tree . . . Or I could feign dead . . . I think I'll run . . . *ahhhhhhhhh!*' (Sorry – you're done for!)

Another interesting and useful aspect to our threat/self-protection system could be called 'Better safe than sorry'. Basically, if we are in lion country and hear a sound in the bushes, we could assume that the noise is caused by a lion and run before even seeing one. Nine times out of ten, our senses will be wrong – it wasn't a lion in the bushes but a bird. However, this mistake means that, while you might have lost some eating time that you can easily make up later, you are safe, whereas you can't undo a mistake in the opposite direction: underestimating a potential threat and becoming a predator's lunch. The point of this story is quite extraordinary – *your brain is actually designed to make mistakes*! To protect you (and your kin and friends), it will make assumptions rapidly, not caring very much if it's wrong. It can quite naturally overestimate threat and danger, reckoning that it's far better for you to run away from a possible lion ten times, nine of which are unnecessary, than to remain the one time when you really do need to run. The natural tendency to overestimate threat and danger – especially in social situations or between groups ('Don't trust them!') – can, of course, spell real trouble for humans, but it is a natural function of the brain. So again we need to train our brains carefully to offset this tendency. We see this in many films in which the hero is keen to trust the other group (or aliens) and another person (usually someone in the military) wants to take the 'better safe than sorry' option and nuke 'em!

Now this 'jumping to conclusions' and 'assuming the worst' has actually saved many of our ancestors' lives. For example, those who worried about their children when the latter were out of sight, even when there was no need to worry, would also have been there when they *were* needed. So the brain has difficult judgements to make about when to assume threat and when not, when to trust and when not, when to take risks and when not. Sometimes it gets it wrong, and in fact, many problems linked to mental health issues often involve exactly that – the threat/self-protection system becoming overdeveloped, sensitive, biased or confused. When we help people to face their fears in certain ways, we are helping their threat/self-protection systems get back on track. When people learn to expose themselves to the things that frighten them, they are gradually teaching their self-protecting brains that it's actually okay, the feared event that they have been running away from won't really happen, and they can learn to tolerate the anxiety that has previously been intolerable to them – thus also reducing their 'fear of fear' and their anxiety about becoming anxious.

Importantly, too, the brain can get it wrong the other way by not being sensitive enough. Some risks simply stare us in the face but we do little about them or try to ignore them. We know that smoking can harm us but many do it anyway. In groups, we sometimes engage in far riskier behaviour than we would if we were on our own. So there are times when we recognize a threat but, if there's not much emotion in it, we can easily overrule it. In fact, there is a whole range of threats that could wreak havoc but which we ignore. For instance, intellectually we know about climate change, the approaching world water shortages and the many injustices in the world that breed resentment, conflicts and aggression, but they seem too distant from our personal lives to activate our emotions sufficiently for us to take urgent action. It's when a threat triggers a powerful emotion in us that we're more likely to notice and do something about it.

How the threat/self-protection system learns to do its job

Our brain may contain a menu of the ways we might feel and behave in threatening situations (e.g. get angry or become anxious and run away), but it also has to *learn* what is and is not threatening and how to modify the basic patterns that can be created in the brain. Genes build brains that pay attention to certain types of stimuli (e.g. bitter tastes, small, wriggling things, angry or happy faces), but also learn from and are transformed by experience. So the brain learns by laying down memories, which are subtle changes in our brain cells and inter-neuron connections that code for what has happened in the past. That information can be made available to help you detect previously encountered threats, respond to them and devise new actions as new threats arise. These memories can actually affect the whole body, as we will see in a moment.

In fact, research suggests that there are a number of different memory systems for processing threatening events.[6] For example, the part of the brain called the *amygdala* receives information quickly and then makes very quick and crude but important judgements of whether the new information constitutes a threat or not – in other words, it makes survival-relevant judgements. So when we have that rush of fear, anxiety or anger, it is the amygdala firing up, and if we become stressed over days or weeks, it can become even more sensitive ('inflamed' in a way – but only metaphorically). There are also genes that can influence the sensitivity of the amygdala, making some people more vulnerable than others to developing fears and anxieties about various things.

What is very important about this particular brain system is that it lays down codes for *emotional* memories, which operate through body-wide physiological systems. So, for example, suppose you go to a party and have a beer or a glass of wine or eat some seafood, and within a few minutes, this makes you very sick – you know, really multiple-toilet-visiting ill! Both your amygdala and your body will remember this incident with the result that, even though you recovered from it fairly quickly at the time, when you go to another party and someone passes you a beer or a glass of wine or offers you some seafood, just the smell of it (sensory cue) or the sight of it (another sensory cue) will re-create nausea in your body. Such physiological 're-creations', or body memories, of an original state are rooted in the amygdala. These cues don't trigger threat emotions of anxiety or anger but *re*-create the patterns for feeling nausea – the same as you felt when you were ill. So this memory works by recalling and *re*-creating bodily patterns in you.

By contrast, another part of the brain – the *hippocampus* – codes for what has been called 'event memory'. This part of your brain won't create physical feelings to remind you of an unpleasant event in the past but will remind you about facts: where you got sick last time, or that you have drunk a lot of beer in the past but were fine – you were just unlucky that day, so it's okay to drink again. Now if for some reason the hippocampus system doesn't access that information for you, then at the next party, you may feel sick at the smell of beer but won't quite recall why you are feeling this way. Also you won't be able to update your memories with the information now available to you and say, 'That was then, a one-off – this is now,' so allowing yourself to override your feelings with the knowledge that this (new) beer is okay/safe. In other words, your physiological (body) memory dominates.

Okay, you've got the idea. However, many of our self-protection memories operate in this way, through both body/feeling memories and event memories. Things that have made us anxious in the past can be associated with certain cues, and when those cues are present again, our bodies immediately react, producing a flush of anxiety or anger. The problem is that these sorts of memories are about high threat, and as the threat system is activated, integrating new information becomes difficult because this system is designed to turn off reflective thought, jump to conclusions and simply act fast. It also activates the hormone cortisol, which can interfere with the processing of the hippocampus and the frontal cortex, too.

We would rather not have these feelings again, not only because they were very unpleasant but also because we might like to get back to drinking beer or wine or eating seafood. However, such logical desires may not make an impact on the emotional threat/self-protective brain unless we train it. *The body remembers* what happened last time and seeks to remind us and to protect us. Here something rather important happens to the 'better safe than sorry' rule: once something bad has happened, our self-protective brains operate on a principle of fast recall and 'once bitten, twice shy'.

I've used the simple examples of drinking a beer or eating seafood to make a point. But exactly the same process is at work when things make us angry, frightened or depressed – the body can remember and react to those feelings and bodily patterns. This is especially important when it's other people who are the source of our anger, fear or depression.

How other people can shape our self-protective brains

Many of the threats that activate, stimulate and shape our threat/self-protection system come from other people. Indeed it is in our relationships with others that we learn to make sense of, and feel comfortable or frightened with, being around other people. It is other people who also help us to become comfortable with our feelings, to understand them and give meaning to them.

So imagine a young girl who is frequently criticized or hurt by a parent or school bully for certain behaviours or for expressing certain emotions. She may automatically respond to those events by becoming *self-protectively* anxious or avoiding. Later, any event or situation that seems similar or where she risks being bullied, criticized and/or hurt can produce anxiety – and this can be in situations in which the girl, even as an adult, does not want to be anxious. Using the previous example, this is like not wanting to feel sick at a party but your body insists on letting you know about 'what happened before'. So because of our emotional memories that are focused on self-protection, it's very easy for past feelings to intrude into the present. In fact, of course, much of psychotherapy aims to help people with exactly that sort of problem – to aid them in figuring out how the past is intruding into the present and how to let go of past constrictions, fears and soothe body memories.

One self-protective feeling can suppress another

We have spent some time discussing how one way of thinking and feeling can squeeze out another. If we become very angry, it is difficult to feel relaxed or compassionate, for example. In some situations, however, we can actually learn not to be aware of certain emotions.

Suppose that, when a young boy expresses anger, one of his parents punishes him and tells him that he is bad. The boy may come to associate getting angry with being punished. Over time, his brain will try to remind him that expressing anger can lead to punishment, so that, when he starts to feel anger, up pops *self-protective* anxiety. As he grows up, this makes it increasingly difficult for him to process anger or become self-assertive because, when he tries to express anger or be assertive, anxiety appears again as a *normal, natural* self-protective reaction. Remember that, as with the party example, this will be a whole-body reaction. Because the boy can't express anger assertively, it might build up and he may develop an intense fear of his own anger.[7] The more he tries to get rid of it and labels it bad or evil (rather than learning to experience and tolerating it as a normal if unpleasant human emotion), the more difficulties he will get into.

Kay's mother was constantly critical and unkind, and in her mind, Kay had often wanted her mother dead. However, she had been brought up with religious views about such feelings and thought herself 'wicked' and feared God's punishment for having such a desire. The compassion approach would, of course, be to acknowledge and accept these desires fully, understand them as perfectly natural if unpleasant and sad (one would like to have had a loving mother that one didn't want to kill off). They became easier to work with once Kay gave up being self-condemning because of them. Obviously this isn't an invitation to act them out – that way leads to prison, of course! So we have to learn how to work with strong emotions compassionately, recognizing that we didn't design them, choose them or ask for them to be shaped in the way they are, but also not to be simply passive in the face of them or blindly act them out.

We can think about all kinds of emotions and behaviours like this. Suppose a child seeks affection from a parent but is rejected or hurt. What do you think the child will come to feel when they experience urges to express affection? The self-protective brain will automatically remind them that, the last time they sought affection, they got punished or were pushed away. And remember, these memories are played out automatically without thought, within our *bodily feelings*. So when such a person experiences a slight feeling inside of wanting to be close to others and feel cared for, what will emerge immediately in its wake is anxiety and the desire to close down all feeling. Such a person may not even be fully aware of what is happening inside them; it is done automatically. The understandable consequence may be that the person backs off from seeking affection and is unable to learn how to look for, respond to or express it; they simply cut themselves off from that system. Or sometimes people want to be close to others and experience affection, but as they draw close, their anxiety increases and they pull away. This difficulty – being a bit of an emotional yo-yo – is because of different emotion systems responding to different things.

Another complication occurs when a parent is sometimes kind but at other times very critical and harsh. The child's emotional brain now really struggles because they cannot predict what they should do. Should they try to get close to the parent and seek comfort or should they keep away? The problem is, if they keep away they may be safe but they will also feel very lonely and isolated. The threat/self-protection system may also produce anger towards the parent who is harsh or rejecting, but to express or acknowledge that might pose another kind of threat – e.g. abandonment for being seen as a bad child.

Now, in these examples we can see that the self-protective brain is trying to control what the child feels and what they express. Unfortunately, this may be a direct contradiction of what they *need* to express and feel. As we grow up, we must be able to experience and understand emotions and allow other people to help us to accept and comprehend them. How can we do that if we don't express them to some degree and learn from that experience? It's like trying to learn to ride a bicycle but never getting on one. Emotions can be difficult and tricky things. In trying to protect ourselves from expressing emotions that could get us into trouble, we may actually end up not being able to develop sufficient understanding of our emotions to be able to work with them.

We also know that all these things interact with a child's basic genetic make-up. Some children are genetically more vulnerable to responding to elevated threat with feelings of anxiety, anger or shut down. Others appear to be more resilient to harshness in early life – though the reasons for that are complex. Keep in mind, then, that children do not choose their reactions and ways of coping – rather these are emerging inside them as their brains try to pattern themselves to cope as best they can.

The compassion approach is always to recognize that the very experience of emotion is an evolutionary design (not our fault), and so by learning (as best we can) to understand the depths, textures and nature of our emotions, we will be able to cope with them. Imagine that you are riding a powerful stallion (your emotions). Without guidance, education and graded practice, such a horse will rush off in all directions, throwing you, its rider. But with understanding, kindness, gentleness and training, it may allow its power to be put at your disposal. Trying to beat it into submission, suppress it, tie it down or ignore its power will not help you.

When the threat/self-protection system is in conflict with itself

Through our threat/self-protection system, we have a number of alternative ways of defending ourselves (or others we care about) to choose from. We can, for example, run away *or* fight. But *these are exact opposites* – you can't run and fight at the same time! So an important complication we have to contend with is how our threat/self-protection system can generate different and conflicting types of defensive responses.

Imagine that you have slaved over a piece of work and your boss criticizes it. You might be inundated with many different emotions. You might feel angry, thinking, 'How dare you! I bet you haven't even read it carefully, you ----!' (choose your own label). You might be anxious: 'Oh, gosh, does he/she think I'm no good at my job?' You might feel like crying: 'I've put so much work into this. It really is so unfair.' Depending on your reaction, you might want to: bop your boss on the nose; run from the room; hand in your notice; grab back the assignment and promise to work all night to make it better; cry and hope the boss will feel sorry for you rather than angry.

You can imagine how hard it is if your threat/self-protection system is throwing up all these options and you're having to focus on some and not others. And, of course, the choosing process is rushing through your head and body very quickly. You want to keep your poise and find a way to get through this. For some people, though, this range of conflicting feelings and potential actions is rather overwhelming. They may cry or run away or lose their temper even if they don't want to. Or more commonly, even if they cope with the situation very well and maintain their cool, rather than being pleased about that and marvelling at their skilled management of a difficult situation, afterwards they ruminate on their anger or their lack of assertiveness and feel even worse. They spend a sleepless night thinking about how to get their own back or wondering how they could have let their boss get away with that. Or if they're self-blamers and conflict-avoiders, they dwell on about how useless they are and, of course, they now see that their work is of little value.

The point is, however, that these emotional conflicts are not our fault because our minds are designed to do just this. So if people try to tell you that you need to be assertive and know your own mind, the answer is: 'Sure, but I have three or four different minds all struggling to be heard!' It is important to learn how to appreciate the way that you're able to cope rather than mull over what you would like to have done.

Conflicts blow fuses

It is easy for our brains to become confused when we have different things we want to do or achieve. For instance, you dislike your job but need the money, or you're unhappy in a relationship but not sure if you should leave because there are children to consider. These quite normal conflicts of life can none the less be very stressful.

The plots of many good sci-fi movies involve a robot faced with two incompatible situations. For example, it may be programmed with the absolute rule that it must never kill a human, but then one day, in order to save the lives of some humans, it has to, say, kill a tyrant. So smoke rises from its back panel, it shrieks, 'Does not compute! Does not compute!' and it blows up – leaving the humans it was supposed to save in the hands of the tyrant. Many years ago, researchers looked at these kinds of conflicts in rats. A rat was trained to run a maze for food if a red circle appeared above the maze entrance. If a blue square appeared, this meant that the rat would encounter an electric shock within the maze and so it should be avoided. All went well while there were clear red circles and blue squares. But then the researchers created a purple ellipse. The poor rat – now terribly confused because it couldn't decide whether to run for the food or avoid the shock – showed high levels of fear, disorganized behaviour and confusion. This became known as 'experimental neurosis' and demonstrated how our brains can become very distressed and aroused in high-conflict situations where there are incompatible alternatives.[8]

The point is that our threat/self-protection system has been designed along fairly simple lines to detect threats and protect us. However, given our 'new minds', our capacity for thinking, reflecting and ruminating and our desire for self-preservation and to impress and influence others, the system can cause all kinds of problems if we are not careful. We may even end up hating the feelings that it generates inside us – which, of course, usually only makes things worse.

Depression and threat

We know that about a quarter of us will suffer from depression at some time in our lives and many of us will occasionally experience very low moods. People often ask me how depression, which feels so awful and can be devastating, can possibly be linked to self-protection. Well, it is and here's how.

Humans, like other mammals, have evolved to have a need for others to care for them as infants and children. For many mammals, including humans, separation from the mother puts juveniles at risk from a variety of dangers. While she is present, she signals safeness and access to a source of support. She also provides food and comfort and will help the infant calm down if it is anxious and upset. So she regulates her infant's threat/stress system with soothing and care because the infant cannot do this for itself. In fact, we now know that these interactions impact on a wide variety of physiological systems and affect an infant's maturation, including the way in which the brain wires itself.

In the mother's absence, the world becomes threatening and the child shows a *protest-despair* reaction, which is part of a normal, evolved protection strategy. Protest involves distress, anxiety, crying and seeking to connect again with the mother. The infant is programmed to engage in urgent searching and to signal/communicate distress (e.g. distress calling and crying) to elicit help, protection and support via reunion with a caring 'other' – that is, the signal is designed to impact on others. This may be called *yearning*. This protection 'protest' strategy can be turned off when the infant is soothed or the mother herself arrives.

Things may not turn out so well, however. Suppose the efforts expended by crying and searching do not result in the return of the mother or in soothing signals from her. This is potentially very dangerous. For most mammals, a distressed/searching young individual on its own is in danger of attracting predators or of becoming lost and/or exhausted and starved. In such contexts, sitting tight and waiting for the parent to return may be the best protection strategy for survival. *Despair* is a form of behavioural deactivation when protest does not work. Positive emotions and feelings of confidence and the desire to explore, search and seek out must be toned down because this aspect of the protection strategy is designed to stop the individual signalling and moving about in the environment when to do so is dangerous. It is saying: 'Go to the back of the cave and stay there.' Extraordinary but true: ancestors of ours who in certain conditions got somewhat depressed and 'dropped out' for a while may have survived better than those who carried on regardless.

There are, in fact, many life events and situations, such as major defeats and setbacks or being bullied or rejected, that make our brain want to go into 'back of the cave' self-protect mode. It *feels* terrible because this self-protection strategy works by turning off our positive emotions and making us focus on bad things. It evolved long before we humans came along, able to think about ourselves and our futures. And it evolved long before we developed self-consciousness or self-awareness, which allows us to realize how unpleasant these feelings 'feel'. Depression will make them worse, leading us to think we're failures and that the future is dark and hopeless. And at root of this is a primitive protection 'keep out of the way' strategy! Now some people have a genetic sensitivity to this strategy, which can make it easier to turn it on and may make it more intense, while for many of us, it's activated by life stresses.

When activated in a self-aware species like us, protest/despair 'brain states' can fuel feelings of being cut off from others, alone and vulnerable. Sometimes depressed people say that they feel that there's a barrier between themselves and other people; they feel totally disconnected from the social world as if in a dream – a sensation that might indicate problems in a particular type of social positive emotion system. They may ruminate on these feelings, try to work out why they feel like this, blame themselves, feel more inferior, become convinced that others don't care about them or that they wish to exclude them, and then feel even more disconnected. Sadly this is another example of our 'new brains/minds', which have self-awareness, actually driving us further into depression. If people with mild/moderate depression can look inwards and think about their lives and what may be causing the depression and then do something about it, the depression may well have served a useful purpose. But some depressions lock people into negative spirals of thinking and withdrawal from the world, unable to work on their life difficulties at all.

Now the reason we might feel bad, can't sleep, have lost interest in food or sex and so forth is because our brains have switched into a specific defensive self-protect pattern. We don't feel bad only because of our thoughts. Had evolution not plumbed this kind of defensive pattern into us, we wouldn't experience it. Our thoughts might trigger, accentuate or maintain this 'hunker down' protection strategy, but such strategies, with their patterns of motivations, emotions and behaviours, are part of evolved brain design. Moreover, they can generate such painful *archetypal* feelings that we can feel as if our very lives can be in danger and we are beyond help – out of reach, completely lost. Helping depressed people realize that these frightening feelings are also innate and archetypal (and may be linked to early memories) can help to ground them and lead them away from self-blaming and self-condemning.

Another natural regulator of positive emotion is *defeat*. If they suffer serious defeats or their coping behaviours are blocked, many animals show a reduction in positive emotions and depressive behaviour, and defeated animals also lose status. It's interesting, therefore, that depressed people will often see themselves as being of very low status, inferior, worthless and inadequate. This suggests that part of their depression involves this defeat/lowly status defensive strategy. It is the strategy that is creating these thoughts in the depressed person's mind, and of course, they may be echoes of parents who once said unkind things to them. Helping depressed people stand back from their self-devaluing thoughts and feelings, see them as part of our human heritage, and treat them with kindness and compassion can be helpful.[9]

Trapped in our threat/self-protection systems

We can sometimes become caught in the urgencies of our threat/self-protection emotions and can't calm them down even when there is good reason to. Consider people who have a problem with panic attacks: even when they have a lot of evidence that the sensations in their chests are due to, say, heartburn and are not the first signs of a heart attack, they can't be reassured and remain very panicky. Or think about obsessional difficulties. Even though people may know logically that cleaning is not really going to save them from germs, they can't stop cleaning because the anxiety becomes too great if they do. And while the socially anxious may know that other people are basically friendly, they still feel anxious about doing something that might invite criticism or ridicule. So they stay indoors, mulling over their loneliness.

These are situations when the poor old threat/self-protection system is playing to the 'better safe than sorry' rule and the person can't override it. The feelings created by the threat (e.g. anxiety) become so powerful that one has to act on them. This is why modern therapists try to help people experience these feelings and practise overruling them by changing their thinking and behaviour. Research has shown that exposure to anxiety – that is, facing up to it – is often important in overcoming it. Clearly, this is done in a measured and appropriate way and not just by overwhelming the person with what makes them anxious. Instead, we try to 're-educate' the threat/self-protection system. The compassionate approach builds on these well-established principles, simply adding to the mix the creation of an inner sense of kindness, support and encouragement when doing the 're-education'. When focusing on coping with difficult feelings like anxiety, we can offer ourselves encouragement and support and practise talking to ourselves in the warm voice. This pulls our attention into a different emotion system, which will help to calm our anxiety. We'll be looking at this again in later chapters.

Sometimes people have learned to be frightened but have forgotten the reasons behind it. For example, take Kim, who had panic attacks about having a coronary. She 'sort of remembered' that a beloved uncle had dropped dead at a family party when she was young – but none of the details. She connected his death to her fear only in so far as she worried about a genetic vulnerability. Encouraged by her therapist to find out more about this event, she spoke to her mother (whose brother Kim's uncle had been). She found that her mother had never wanted to discuss the tragedy because of her own unresolved grief and guilt: they had been drunk at the party and all had been having a great time when the uncle suddenly dropped to the ground. There had been a lot of confusion; some of the guests had thought that he was just very drunk but then others had realized that something more serious had happened and panicked. Her mother was unclear if the person who had phoned for an ambulance had given clear instructions, but in any case, the ambulance had got lost. For some years afterwards, Kim's mother had been deeply affected by her brother's death at that party, and she probably still was. Kim came to recognize that her panic attacks were associated with a lot of other fears: 'Have a good time and something bad can happen out of the blue; people may want to help me, but will not be able to; if I die, my children will be thrown into profound grief and there will be no one to look after them.' There was also her unresolved grief at becoming aware of how her uncle's death had affected her mother – she now realized that she had lost part of her mother that night because of her mother's grief and withdrawal into herself. Working on the meaning of the *physical* sensations in her chest helped Kim, but it was also necessary to work on the other connected *fear* and *sadness*.

The point I'm making here is that the reason some people can get stuck in the threat/self-protection system and not be able to settle it down may be because there are sets of interconnected frightening themes or memories at play. Notice that, once we understood Kim, we were much less likely to see her fear as a 'pathology' or 'illness' in the medical sense, or that it was just about her being irrational or having faulty thinking. Notice, too, that your understanding will naturally pull you into a position of compassionate feeling, where the focus is on seeing clearly how and why the threat/self-protection system is playing up (i.e. only doing its best) and exploring how to reassure it and settle it.

Entrapments and blocks

Finally, we should note that our threat/self-protection system was designed long ago along fairly simplistic lines. It wasn't designed in or for the modern world. It's simple: something threatens you, you run away and avoid it; if you're blocked, you get angry and push at whatever is in your way or hit it. Humans, however, often can't do that. As Freud pointed out, people need to inhibit their impulses for all kinds for reasons, but there is a different aspect here, too. People who are being bullied are often trapped in schools, homes or offices with the bullies. We're not free-ranging monkeys who can stay on the edges of the group and keep our distance. We can become very stressed by having to work to keep paying our mortgages even though we hate our jobs. This *entrapment* is probably one of the greatest sources of modern stress: having to stay in environments and situations we don't like because we lack the resources to leave, can't see any alternatives or the ones that do exist seem worse than the entrapment itself. In these cases, the impulses and motives in our brains for avoidance and escape can be very highly aroused but are constantly being thwarted, leading to serious stress.

If you talk with depressed people for any length of time, you'll also find that many of them, but by no means all, have a lot of anger – something we've already discussed (*see* pp. 126–30). The point about blocked anger is that it is another aroused but blocked-up defence. So when our desire to escape is highly aroused or we're very angry but we can't express or act on it, it's like a car revving away in neutral – it gradually overheats.[10]

The point is that our old emotional brain was designed to work in a world in which we would be able to distance ourselves from others, and in which relationships would not be so entrapping and complex. However, in our modern societies, we now have complex relationships that, in many ways, curtail our freedom to come and go. There's nothing in nature like the Western human family trapped in a house, perhaps with frustrated and aggressive parents. They cannot separate easily and their children aren't free to get away. This is one reason why abuse is so easy and so common.

We're also trapped by our lifestyles and our need to work even as we crave freedom. Animals live in the world of the senses, of 'just being under the sky' – work demands and deadlines are, of course, unknown to them. We live in a world of deadlines and of having to get on with others even if we don't like them. It's not surprising that our poor eons-old threat/self-protection system is bursting at the seams. What help it and soothe it are positive supportive relationships and kindness. If we're going to live in a modern world that can be quite suffocating, we probably need to develop a lot more compassion.

Conclusion

Taking all these things together, we can see that our threat/self-protection system is, on one level, simple with basic emotions and tendencies towards action, but on another level, it's rather complex. Some of our emotions will conflict with each other for expression, and we can become frightened of them or lose control of them. The desire to run away or act assertively can get blocked and, instead, we ruminate. So what started off as fairly minimal defences in the flow of life have become convoluted and tricky things in the human mind.

However, compassionate understanding of these difficulties can move us forward considerably. Remember it's not your fault if you have these difficulties – they're the result of one of evolution's little quirks. In the next chapter, we will explore the two basic positive emotion regulation systems and then think about how all three systems fit together.

5 The Pleasures and Contentments of Life: The two types of good feelings and your compassionate mind

As we saw in the last chapter, the threat/self-protection system is central to the survival of life, including ourselves, but it can really give us a hard time. However, although we are motivated to avoid threats and unpleasant things, and our threat/self-protection system is the first port of call for most incoming information, much of our lives is also spent pursuing things that we think will give us pleasure and make us happy.

Our minds are full of hopes, goals and ambitions. So we seek out certain types of food or sexual experiences, new jobs, new cars, new relationships and new challenges. We prefer to be with people who like and appreciate us rather than those who do not. When things are going well and we are moving towards what we want, the brain gives us a boost of certain chemicals such as dopamine – this is its way of letting us know that we are on track to prosper, which usually has been good for our genes. Feeling good ripples through our consciousness. These are the urges and feelings of the incentive/resource-seeking system. (We examined this in Chapter 2, so you might want to have a look at that model again – *see* pp. 21–7.)[1]

The Puritans were fearful of pursuing such feel-good pleasures in case they led them into temptation. It is sometimes said that the Buddha was also rather down on such desires and on having fun and that he suggested that what would make us truly happy would be the elimination of desire. That does for me then – I rather like my pleasures! I mean, no more Merlot?! However, thankfully that's not what he said at all. Desire is very important to life. Without it, we'd do nothing – 'couldn't be bothered', as they say. We'd gradually starve and humans as a species would die out.

No, actually one problem with desires is that, if anything, we don't actually enjoy them enough! Take eating. If you're like me, maybe at the end of a hard, busy week you'll decide to go out for a meal – let's say a curry. Great, looking forward to it. But despite enjoying talking to my wife Jean, I get a little irritated when it takes overlong for the food to arrive. Then it comes and in a flash it's gone. I've eaten so fast that I now feel bloated. Jean gives me a gentle 'I told you so' knowing glance. How much better it would have been to have taken it easy, enjoyed just being together with my beloved, eating each mouthful slowly, being 'mindful' of all the textures and flavours, paying better attention to my body and stopping before becoming bloated! So I actually need to learn to *savour* and experience the pleasure of eating what the chef has created from the various life forms that have given their lives for me.

Mark Epstein, a psychotherapist and Buddhist, has written a lovely book called *Open to Desire* about desire in Buddhism.[2] He draws attention to the difference between savouring/appreciating something and actively trying to enhance it. He tells a story about when, as a young man more than 20 years earlier, he was in a serious relationship and he and his partner were keen to use a drug that was supposed to enhance their sexual enjoyment of each other, taking them to new delights and heights. They planned to use this on a holiday to Jamaica that they had really been looking forward to for some time. Unfortunately, on their arrival in Jamaica, the anticipated beautiful hotel overlooking a beach turned out to be a pokey room overlooking a garage. Still there was the drug. Sadly, that did little except make them very sick and bring both of them out in an irritating rash, thus making sex impossible. So much for heightening desire!

The point of this story is that, rather than savouring each other, the pursuit of enhancement had led to disappointment. We can overdevelop and expect too much from our desires and then feel let down. Think about the last time you did something that you really enjoyed. It may have felt good, but it probably didn't last that long because those kinds of pleasures usually don't. In fact, desires *always* come to an end. How many times have we thought to ourselves that the anticipation has been better than the actual experience? And sometimes experiences speed by so fast that we are constantly on the lookout for the next one because we haven't learned how to savour 'what just is'. Recollect the last time you satisfied a desire by, say, going out for a lovely meal or having a good holiday or sexual experience. Afterwards, it simply faded, didn't it? You might have had a burst of pleasure but then your life and emotions settled down again.

Vajrayana Buddhism, also referred to as the *tantric tradition*, is sometimes regarded as a third school of Buddhism alongside Theravada (mindfulness focused) and Mahayana (compassion focused). This tantric approach invites people to recognize that their sense of 'self ' is just a pattern, and they can discover this more fully by deliberately practising being different patterns by imagining becoming a different type of person or identifying with a deity and/or engaging in rituals. (We'll explore this in more detail in Chapter 8.) The idea is to see that the ego is just a pattern in consciousness, and what we take to be 'ourselves', the 'me-ness of me' or our egos, are actually like the wavelets on an ocean. This school of Buddhism encourages exploration of core elements of experience by being fully *in* the experience, and this includes being *fully* in one's pleasures.

Many people in the West first come across Vajrayana Buddhism by hearing about tantric sex. (Well, you have to start somewhere.) The reason for mentioning this is to highlight that what people find in this form of intimate activity is a completely different approach to pleasure and sex than usually seen in Western sexual behaviour. Our commercialization of sex has led us to focus on our incentive/resource-seeking system and try to intensify the 'experience' of sex via a sex-toyed, every-orifice-snake-oiled-having-taken-your-Viagra-first approach (and don't ask about the raspberry jelly – that was a mistake). In the West, the focus is on the orgasm and the fulfilment of desire. Every day my email box is sprinkled with invitations and offers to grow my reproductive organ by two inches (if I took up all these offers, by now it would be on the floor!). There are drugs that will allow me to make love all night, and to become a prince of delight (I rather like the last idea actually). This, of course, is the 'more and more' approach to sexuality. And because we are creative and explorative, which is what makes us human, we don't want to do the same things over and over.

By contrast, tantric sex, where the orgasm is irrelevant or can even be unhelpful, is about focusing, savouring, learning and being fully mindful. One learns to be 'in the moment' of sexual arousal rather than for it to be merely a stage on the way to orgasm. Tantric sex focuses not so much on personal pleasure and desire as on the communication and exploration of each person involved, the mutuality and interconnectedness of the experience, the attention paid to subtle feelings in one's body, seen as energies. It's not so much desire but *how we pursue desire* that's the issue.

Buddhist psychologies are based on what is called 'the middle way'. Pleasure is not renounced but engaged with in certain 'skilful' ways. Pleasure and desire come and go, all things are impermanent, including our relationships and our own lives. If we base our happiness only on operating from our incentive system and fulfilling our desires, life will be a roller coaster ride of short-lasting pleasures, striving, seeking, frustration, wanting more and better, with increasing efforts to control our own lives and those of others to give us the next fix of pleasure. These kinds of pleasures are dependent on the world and other people giving us something in some way. In addition, we'll always be running away from the ultimate reality of the impermanence of our lives and the suffering in the world; we're trying to lose ourselves and forget this reality by indulging in pleasure. And in some ways, more importantly, this pleasure detracts from reflection, exploration, gaining insight into and experiences of the very nature of our minds. Moreover, as we will see shortly, there are different types of positive feelings that are based on contentment, non-striving, being mindful and living-in-the-moment. These feelings are also stimulated by focusing our lives around compassion and kindness.

The incentive/resource-seeking system

Buddhist psychologies are oriented to explore the mind from within the framework of one's own consciousness. Western science, however, allows us to explore it from the outside, with regard to evolved brain systems and with research. When we do this, we can see that desires are controlled by the incentive/resource-seeking system, which is partly regulated by a chemical in our brains called *dopamine*. We need to look at this system and how it is activated in our lives in the West because, like the threat/self-protection system, it can also cause us a lot of problems – not least because it also underpins greed ('want more') and the turning away from compassion.

As discussed briefly in Chapter 2, the incentive/resource-seeking system is involved in pursuing and getting a buzz from our achievements and access to resources – including the flush of early romantic love. This system helps to give us feelings of drive and excitement and a 'hyped-up' sense of pleasure. When people take drugs such as amphetamine or cocaine, they're trying to simulate this 'hyping themselves up' by giving themselves energy and excitement. It's also the system that's stimulated when we win something. Notice what happens when one team scores a goal: that team's supporters will jump up, throwing their arms up in their air. When we have a success, we often want to celebrate – that's the effect of dopamine. Think what would happen if you found out that you were a lottery winner and had become a millionaire overnight: you'd be so excited that you'd become agitated, it's doubtful that you'd get a peaceful night's sleep for quite a while and you'd be busy making plans about what to do next. In six months or a year, though, your level of happiness probably wouldn't be any greater than it was the day before you won – this is what research has shown. Some lottery winners can actually become *more unhappy* because they've lost the social networks and contacts that they have developed over years.

Excitement can also become somewhat addictive. For example, some researchers are concerned that children's use of video games, particularly those that involve aggression, may be overstimulating the dopamine drive system. Each time the children score or make a hit, their brains may be receiving little bursts of dopamine that stimulate both the incentive/resource-seeking and the threat/self-protection systems – after all, these games are *deliberately* designed to be tense and stimulating and to have this kind of impact on our children's brains. The problem is that, if you overstimulate these systems, what happens when you withdraw the stimulant? Well, some people can end up being easily bored, needing constant excitement to produce energy, and can become agitated and anxious if they don't get their 'fix'. Indeed research is showing that some people are becoming increasingly addicted to computer games. This need to give ourselves constant buzzes of excitement can also be a cause of an addiction to internet pornography. So it's not just the games that we should worry about, but what we're allowing commercial games publishers to do to our brains and those of our children.[3]

The basic human trait to want 'more and better' has been a fantastic asset to us and helped get us out of caves and become the dominant species that we are. However, in today's world, it can become a serious problem for us. This is because we're clever enough to discover new ways to satisfy our desires but not clever enough to resist doing so easily. Take high-fat or sweet foods. We don't, as our ancestors did, have to work hard to find them and then enjoy them only occasionally; we just go to the supermarket and buy as much as we want. For millions of years, it was the environment and scarcity that kept desires in check but not today. So, through no fault of our own, we are confronted with obesity, tooth decay and rising rates of diabetes.[4]

Indeed, we can even apply this attitude to ourselves. We can feel dissatisfied with ourselves and want to be better (brighter, thinner, more popular, less anxious or depressed), feeling frustrated, disappointed or even hating ourselves if we are not. We look at others and think, 'Why can't I be like that?' Without care, it's easy for our desiring – and our system – to get out of balance. For instance, take people who suffer from the eating disorder anorexia. They can feel bad about themselves, which means that the threat emotions of anger, anxiety and/or disgust are active and focused on the self. They may compare themselves with skinny, computer-enhanced supermodels (high-status figures) and want to be like them, so they set themselves the task of losing weight and controlling their desire for food. To get on the scales and see the pounds coming off gives them a buzz of pride and success – it's a real achievement. This helps them temporarily feel better because the incentive/resource-seeking system blocks out the unpleasant feelings from the threat/self-protection system. They can also feel in control. Some come to believe that they are winning some kind of competition and become addicted to exercising and starving themselves. To stop doing those things feels like a betrayal of their goals when they've nothing else to give them good feelings – and that's frightening and depressing. Losing that feeling of control can also activate a very strong sense of self-criticism and even self-hatred, which is rooted in the rage and fear of disappointment (*see* pp. 309–12). Indeed, this negative experience of the self, and the inability to feel kindness, gentleness and loving acceptance towards it, partly fuels the disorder. Now eating disorders are complex, of course, but this description does reflect aspects of how we can get caught by the drive, need or even preoccupation/ obsession to achieve something and experience the buzz of success and then the fear and come-down if the weight is regained.

The human brain is set up to want 'more and better', to improve things. However, think about what happens when this brain meets our capitalistic society, which is based on actually *stimulating our wants and dissatisfactions*. Advertisements openly say, 'Why be happy with X when – for a bit more money – you can have Y?' or 'Why settle for that job when – for a bit more work or effort – you can have this one?' Without constantly striving for more, we would not keep our businesses going. Striving is built into the fabric of everyday life. From our first day at school, we are taught *not to be content* but constantly to strive to better ourselves. I don't remember anyone ever mentioning to me the importance of savouring things and learning *contentment*. Well, that's not entirely true. I do recall my grandmother saying once: 'Try to enjoy each day as it is, Paul, for they all soon pass away.' Only now, at nearly 60 years old, do I begin to understand this. I'm a very slow learner.

Choice

We are surrounded by firms and businesses showing us how we can have 'more and better' by offering us more choice. That sounds like a good thing, doesn't it? And if balanced, it is. But researchers have pointed out that more choice can also lead to higher expectations and more doubt, disappointment and even dissatisfaction with oneself.[5] Suppose I want a car and there's only one choice. Well, I've worked hard to get one and I'm pleased with what I get. But suppose there are 100 different types of cars to choose from. I'm not sure now which is best (and, of course, I'll want the best for my money). So I make my choice. If it's not exactly as I'd like, then I start thinking that maybe I made the wrong choice, that another car would have been better: 'Oh, gosh, maybe I was too hasty. Maybe I should have tried out some more.' I'm now not only dissatisfied with my car but also a bit self-critical and dissatisfied with myself! Then it turns out that the car has a little fault and has to go back to the dealer. My friend says, 'Oh, I bought *this* other model and never had any problems with it. Why didn't you buy one like mine?' My first thought is: 'Please lie down and let me run over you!'

Having some choice over whom we marry is also a good thing, right? Well, again, a lot depends on how in balance this is with our other systems. We no longer live in small hunter-gatherer groups. Today, thanks to modern media, we can compare our choice of mate against millions of others. If we're able to savour relationships and explore them and have a real sense of *being* with another person, we'll be well placed to work through the inevitable conflicts that we'll encounter. But if our orientation is more self-focused and we are just thinking about how our partners can make *us* happy or fulfil *our* desires, then we're turning our partners into cars and worry about having made the right choice and that there might be a better model out there – why did I choose this one?

We're not helped by myths about soul mates and ideas that somewhere there is some*one* just right for you. Fact is, at one level, we are all soul mates, and there are thousands of people in the world with whom you could have excellent relationships if only you were to meet them all – but you can't. Of course, you'll be more in tune with some people than with others. Whether you find somebody sexy or not may depend on their pheromones and body odours! Yep, sexual desire is linked to smell. So there you are – your soul mate has to smell and look right. Ideally, after the first flush of passion and desire, which wane after the first few years, people grow together because of the way they *work* together and build positives into their lives. So while all of us will have an archetypal 'ideal' mate (always sexy, attractive, admiring, fun, adoring, kind and helpful – never critical, grumpy or farty), we need to be cautious with how these fantasies play out in our minds and lives.

Modern business life wants us to focus on the half empty, so that we will be dissatisfied and want more and better. However, if we apply this orientation to our relationships, we'll want to get more and more out of our partners. If we're not careful, we'll focus on the way they can make us unhappy and we'll miss the happiness that comes from appreciating people as they are, *building* friendships and learning together how difficult our thoughts and emotions can be, upsetting and forgiving, liking and disliking – all in the tumble drier of real relationships. Of course, this is not to deny in any way that some people are better off out of their relationships than in them.

There's another problem with choice that's been highlighted by the existential writers, who are concerned with the creation of meaning and how we come to terms with death and loneliness. They think choice is important because it relates to our ability to live authentically.[6] Here is the difficulty that they have pointed out: You go to a restaurant. If you choose the fish on the menu, then all possibility of enjoying other dishes literally 'dies' for you. Those dishes become the unlived and the unexperienced. If you choose to follow this career rather than those other possible ones, all the other lives that would have resulted from those other careers can no longer be lived and they are dead to you. Every day of our lives, say the existentialists, we're making choices about what will come into existence for us and what will not. Sometimes it is a small decision, sometimes much bigger.

Coming to terms with the process of choice – that is, what things to allow to remain unlived and unexperienced or dead to us – touches us in a deeper way. It's about letting go of what could have been and living in the moment – in this 'now' with this choice. What can help us is how we create meaning from the choices we've made rather than wondering about or regretting those that we didn't choose. Whatever choices we make, our psychology is actually the same: how to make the best of this choice, savour it, commit ourselves to it, work with it through the difficult times and the good times – and make new choices if we need to. These ideas have been explored in various films such as the 2004 American movie *The Butterfly Effect*, which looks at what might happen if someone could go back in time and make different choices. The result would, of course, be entirely unpredictable. You don't like your job so you decide to go back in time and not go for the interview. Now that you have a free morning, you wander over to a coffee shop and get knocked over by the No. 42 bus from Scunthorpe! Ah, well, better try again.

Maybe it's better to come to terms with the fact that we live lives of multiple possibilities, encountering multiple forks in the road, and by choosing some things, other things and possibilities fade away. We can only live in the now. If we do this, we'll slowly switch away from the content of our lives to becoming more conscious of consciousness itself.

Competing and striving

The incentive system is highly involved in the *competitive social mentality* that we explored on pp. 107–10. Research suggests that it's linked to desires for and concerns with status and social standing. In animals, it is linked to and helps regulate dominant and submissive behaviour. We can learn to spot when our incentive-linked competitive social mentality has come into play because of how we're thinking. For example, we see others who challenge us in negative, low-rank terms ('the idiot', 'the dumbo'). We become more interested in winning points than in understanding and gaining clarity (academics can be like this too), and we get a 'buzz' from winning something we value. When our competitive mentality is active, we're highly focused on comparing ourselves with others and worrying whether we match up or if we have negative assets that make us inferior: will others see *us* as subordinate to them, as idiots and dumbos or inadequate and not worth bothering with? If we fail, we think of ourselves as inadequate and inferior, becoming shame-prone and self-critical (*see* Chapter 10). The drive to avoid inferiority (which is not the same as the drive for superiority) can lurk behind many of our motives. The more unsafe and uncertain people are in their social relationships, the more they think of themselves and others in terms of competition and social rank (powerful/weak, inferior/superior, dominant/subordinate) and feel *driven* to try to prove themselves, with fears that other people are criticizing, rejecting or ignoring them.

Life has a habit of moving the goal posts, doesn't it? At least as far as our need to move up the social scale and our desire for pleasure are concerned. We'll just have become happy with one achievement and then, in no time, we feel the need to achieve or have something else, something better. Or within just a few months of getting that promotion we've been hoping for, we'll start looking for another in order to climb further up the ladder. Now, of course, at one level this is what makes us human. This is why we have cultures and science, because we constantly want to improve on what has gone before. But once again, a lot depends on where we focus that improvement. There's a huge difference between improving medical techniques to combat disease and building better cluster bombs and anti-personnel mines. Some of our desires will, if fulfilled, cause harm to others, and these desires can have a passion behind them that makes them difficult to contain.

Another set of desires can be focused on one's self as a person. We can want to become a certain kind of person, to follow a particular career, to identify with or belong to a special group, and we want others to see us in a particular way, with a particular reputation and status. Once again, our desires can inspire us and lead to great effort and dedication. But if we aren't able to achieve these goals, they can quickly turn into a nightmare of self-dislike and a sense of failure. In my research department, we have been looking at people who feel that they need to strive and prove themselves, who are under pressure to 'keep up' and show that they are as competent and able as others around them.[7] They have a constant eye on what others are doing and compare themselves (usually unfavourably) with them. They can feel that life is just rushing them along, but if they contemplate stopping, 'getting off the train', they feel threatened and have a sense that they are failing and inferior and are missing out and being left behind. So they have to keep going and keep up, otherwise their threat/self-protection system starts warning them about possible losses and threats. As you can imagine, these individuals are more vulnerable than most to becoming stressed out, burnt out and depressed. As one person said to me, 'I keep on the go because I need to succeed. I don't want to be a nobody and an under-achiever.'

Striving perfectionists are also vulnerable to stress and depression. Now there are two different types of perfectionists. One sort obsessively concentrates on detail, focusing on high standards for the sake of them – and we can all be like that about some things. You'd certainly want your brain surgeon to be like that. The other type, however, can seem like that – and, to the person concerned, can feel like that – but underneath the perfection-seeking is driven by fears of rejection and failure. In consequence, when these folk don't do something well, make mistakes or fail altogether, they can fear rejection and launch really quite savage attacks on themselves.[8] Some perfectionists are trying to find ways to head off threats of criticism or rejection because they've experienced them so often in childhood. Many famous people have revealed that, because they've had unhappy childhoods, they always feel that they have to prove themselves. Here the threat and incentive systems have joined forces. So what desires we have, the purpose of them, how we set about trying to satisfy them and how we feel and treat ourselves if we don't get what we want or think we need – are all important to our well-being.

Social pressures and comparisons

Many commentators worry that our children are growing up too fast. However, as far as our commercial world and capitalist businesses are concerned, they can't grow up fast enough. Children are targeted as consumers as soon as they begin to watch television and express their choices and demands to their parents. As they move on to school, the competitive atmosphere there reflects the pressures on teachers, because schools now have targets. So children grow up in an environment in which everyone is seeking the 'competitive edge' and so stimulating that competitive social mentality in us. They know that they're being constantly assessed to see if they measure up – are they good enough for this school, for the A class or D class, to get on the football team? – and test results are constantly being pushed under their noses. Learning isn't fun; it's all about how they're going to stand in comparison with others in the competitions of life. This is all a long way from our hunter-gatherer lifestyles, when it was automatic for children to be accepted and initiated at certain ages. No schools and no exams and no being forced to think of oneself in comparison to others or 'Where will I fit in tomorrow or when I grow up?'

As we emerge into the world of work, we cannot look forward to secure employment any more but perhaps to multiple changes of job because the business model demands mobility and flexibility regardless of how well this fits with what our minds and our mental health require. We no longer live in a world where we can work with our friends to build our own mud huts and go hunting together. Survival and the ability to progress in life depends not on mutual cooperation but on the competitive edge. To be able to earn enough to buy our beloved comforts, keep paying the mortgage and so on, we have to compete with others who are trying to secure the same things. The drive to have the competitive edge links directly to the incentive/resource-seeking system itself: we feel good and pleased when we do well compared to others. But it can also feed the threat/self-protection system because we become anxious, depressed and feel like failures if we believe that we're losers in the social competitions of life.

This can have a negative effect on our attitudes towards others and towards ourselves because, from school through to later life, we're encouraged to compare ourselves with each other – am I doing as well as him or her? When I was at school, I was usually around the bottom of the class, so some of the comparisons I made were to see if I could avoid being in the last three. There would be a glow of relief when I succeeded and a few others were placed even lower than me: 'Great, I'm not bottom this term!' School had done its job. I felt good knowing I was better than others. But that meant that I felt not so good the times when I was actually bottom – usually it was languages, at which I was truly awful.

Social comparison can influence our feelings and make us unhappy in other ways, too, by feeding into us the desire to want 'more and better'. For example, imagine you're happy taking two weeks' holiday. Then you discover that people in another firm doing exactly the same work get six weeks. Nothing has changed except your comparison, but you'll no longer be happy with just two weeks' holiday.

And, of course, some of our comparisons are also desperate because we have to compete for jobs or contracts in order to be able to maintain our mortgage payments and other obligations. Not only do we live in a society where we're encouraged to compare ourselves with others but there are few domains of life that our comparisons do not reach. People can compare themselves negatively in terms of body size (feeling fatter than others), intellectual ability (feeling dumber), attractiveness (feeling uglier), achievement (feeling a failure), marketable skills (feeling less employable), the types of emotions they have (bad emotions and fantasies), lovability (feeling less desirable and wanted) and so on. Although social comparison is something all animals do to a degree (this is how they work out whom to choose as sexual mates and whom to fight or avoid to propel themselves up the ranks), in humans, social comparison can turn us away from learning how to be content and at peace with ourselves, and it can turn our attitude towards ourselves into disappointment, anger or even self-hatred: 'Why can't I be/look/feel like him/her?' Kindness and self-compassion, which together form the best basis for coping with life's hardships, have vanished. All we're left with is the disappointment and threats of the outside world and our own negative feelings for ourselves on the inside. Feeling inferior and marginalized in the outside world and having an inner voice of criticism and put-down means that we're caught in a pincer movement. Nothing supports us or provides us with kindness and support – no wonder we feel bad.

Learning how to fail

Western society runs on hyping up people's urges to achieve and fuelling open competition with others, and is rather contemptuous of those who are less interested or able to achieve. Even worse, very few schools teach children perhaps one of the most important lessons in life – *how to fail*. However, every psychological study of enhancing success that I know of actually says that, if you want to help children and adults succeed and be confident, then *focus on their efforts, not their results*. Yet capitalism has no interest in effort, only in results. In fact, in sport and many other areas of life, the message is: 'Who remembers who came second?' The other day, I heard a new one: 'The person who came in second is the first loser.' Of course, most of us come second or lower! But even if you do well today, you may not do so well tomorrow, so success is often only temporary. It turns out that focusing on effort and learning how to fail are actually the secrets to success. The moment we are no longer frightened of failure and can face it openly as something to learn from, we'll be free to succeed.

How much and how often does our fear of failure stop us in our tracks? Our fears prevent us from doing things in so many ways, don't they? Developing a compassionate attitude towards failure does not mean signing up to passive resignation but to cultivating a determination based on openness to learning and to being supportive and encouraging of effort.

In every aspect of our society, we are increasingly focusing on results and not effort. Governments everywhere (and various media columnists) completely misunderstand this aspect of our psychology, with rather serious consequences. When you only focus on results, you invite people to cheat, commonly out of fear. As a result, for instance, few people today fully believe government statistics because they know the way that the figures are massaged.

The other problem is that targets keep moving. Those of us in employment are now given job plans and personal performance reviews that are wrapped up in the language of 'wanting to be helpful' but, in fact, ensure that we stay on an upward curve. So, if you meet your targets this year, you can be sure that they'll be increased next year. Some businesses and government departments apparently believe in the concept of constant change. The idea here is that you must not let systems settle down and become organized because then people become self-satisfied and inefficient. So here in the NHS, we are constantly reorganizing – and reorganizing the reorganizing – in order to meet targets that change year on year.

Not only do these methods play havoc with our minds, morale and ability to develop cooperative working relationships (which are actually the gold dust of well-run organizations as well as of mental well-being), they are not very efficient either. Many commentators now recognize that the striving for results and the neglect of process, structure, and integrated frameworks have cost the NHS and other organizations very dearly. It doesn't really matter whether you're managing a football team, a company or a country – managers who are only results-focused rather than effort- and process-focused and who can't inspire people to do their best, end up wasting money and not getting the desired outcomes. An inspired, dedicated, cooperative 'all for one and one for all' team of the lesser talented is likely to beat one made up of those who are more gifted but are treated as marketable objects and don't cooperate.

The point of mentioning all this is for us to keep in mind that our personal psychologies are rooted in the psychologies of our social and working lives. It's very easy for us to absorb values from the media, attitudes that are pervading our working lives, and not appreciate their negative effects on our minds and relationships. So we can end up with overstimulated incentive systems in our own personal goal seeking and lose focus on many other facets of our lives. We look for the competitive edge at the expense of support, cooperation and integration.

Thwarted drives and desires

Let's get back to the personal and our own individual minds. Stop and think for a minute about what happens when your incentive/resource-seeking system is thwarted. Say you're driving to work and thinking about what lies ahead of you. The traffic is really bad today and you're going to be late. That will set you back on a number of tasks you wanted to get done, or you will miss a particular meeting and look bad. You frantically run through all the short cuts you've discovered on your route to work, but there are too many road works today to take advantage of them.

You arrive at work flustered and snappy. Someone brings you a coffee and you nod your thanks. Two minutes later, you turn around, knocking the coffee all over the report you've just finished. 'Why did they have to put it there?' you think, while at the same time knowing that the accident happened because you weren't careful because you're stressed. By the time you get home, you feel as frazzled as a burnt sausage and as much use. And you have discovered that thwarting your incentive/resource-seeking system automatically activates your threat/self-protection one.

Most of the things that wind us up have something to do with the thwarting of everyday plans, which, in turn, are linked to more complex networks of plans. Getting to work on time is important because you want to do a good job, and you want do a good job to keep your job or get promotion, and you want that for status, to pay the mortgage and to buy a few more of life's comforts. Of course, you'll be working too hard to enjoy them, but let's not think about that. Then your babysitter lets you down; you get sick before a major holiday; the money you saved for the holiday is needed instead to pay for an unexpected car repair. Or you are confronted with the very major stresses of disease, death and injury. 'Why me?' is not far from your thoughts. The point is that being thwarted is inevitable for all of us. We are constantly faced with minor hassles and stresses, but if we can train our minds for compassion in the heat of frustration, we'll find ways of working with those difficulties instead of having tantrums or panics so often.

The consequences of desires

We also need to look more deeply into the consequences of *how* we try to satisfy our desires. The Buddha pointed out that, while desires are not harmful in themselves, it is our attachment to them, our need for them, our addiction to them, our feeling of 'must have them', and our sense of frustration and deprivation if we can't have what we want – all these do the damage. He also said that the satisfaction of drives, even if they appear successful, may not be without cost somewhere else in the system; without careful thinking about how we fulfil them, they can become very harmful.

For example, we have just commemorated the 200th anniversary of the ending of the British slave trade. This was a classic example of where, in order to fulfil the desires of some people, millions of others suffered terribly. But, although we are now appalled by slavery, millions of people are *still* trapped in a form of it today as bonded labour. As consumers, we are beginning to think more about where our food and clothes come from to fulfil our desires, and some of what we have discovered is very disturbing.[9] A compassionate approach to life, therefore, asks us to be more responsible in how we satisfy our drives. Having desires and drives are part of being human and this includes, of course, selfishness desires; compassion asks us, not to blame ourselves for having them, but rather to think about the consequences of fulfilling them.

Simply saying 'no' to our desires can be problematic – that's obvious in the case of people with actual addictions. However, modern research has noted another problem with desire: when it's aroused, it can give our thinking a narrowed tunnel vision with a limited focus. We can want something so much that we don't stop to think in detail about its effects or the trouble it can cause. Addicted people don't think about the harm they are doing to themselves or others. We buy our clothes and food and don't think too much about what might be going on to bring these to us so relatively cheaply. Men surf the internet for pornography but don't stop to wonder if the women they're looking at have been trafficked ... and what if one of them was their own daughter? Big businesses take over smaller ones and don't worry about throwing people out of work. Much of what we desire is written in our genes, in broad brushstrokes at least, but that doesn't mean that we have to act them out. The desires for sex, fame, fortune and the nice things of life are millions of years old – they work through us; it is up to us, though, if we want to run mindlessly down the road after them.

So the incentive/resource-seeking system influences all aspects of our lives and feelings. It is essential to us in many ways, because it inspires and rewards our efforts. But it is also potentially problematic because it can be quite shallow, is designed to be rarely satisfied and leads us to pursue both benevolent and malevolent goals. Through it, we can also become frustrated with ourselves and self-critical if we fail to achieve the things we want or reach our self-imposed standards. The Buddha's idea here was to follow the middle way/path and try to achieve balance. It's when we become overly attached and addicted to our desires that we get in trouble because our desires now control us, we don't control them. The Dalai Lama has often pointed out that just because he's a Buddhist doesn't mean that he doesn't have sexual desires or feel anger or get anxious and want to avoid things. It's not that he's stopped having human feelings. It's more that he has trained his mind to be able to notice these feelings and then make choices about how he thinks about his own feelings and the actions that will follow his experience of them.

Zen perfectionism

In Zen, we put our attention completely and mindfully into an activity. Whether making a cup of tea or painting a masterpiece, we seek to do it to the best of our ability, to seek perfection in the activity. This has nothing whatsoever to do with making ourselves feel better.

So keep in mind that the approach in this book is not against achieving and trying. There are many times in life when achievements add to the pleasures of life and can be savoured. Keen gardeners derive great joy from watching their gardens bloom, musicians from mastering difficult pieces of music, and do-it-yourself-ers from a newly decorated room. It's also important to try to improve ourselves. Indeed, the whole point of compassionate mind training is to put effort and energy into training our minds in a particular way. The issue, therefore, is about balance and about understanding the shadow side of the drive and achievement-seeking parts of us. As many psychologists now point out, we can learn to enjoy our achievements *for themselves* and not because they make us feel better or superior as persons, or because they stave off feelings of inferiority or envy. We *can* learn to cope with setbacks with relatively low frustration, and we *don't* have to turn desires into 'musts' and 'have-tos'. Even though we'll all fall for this sometimes, when balanced with the soothing/contentment system, our achievements will not over-inflate our egos and our failures will not deflate them.

Appreciation

A key message of many of the new approaches in psychology and spiritual practice is the importance of learning to appreciate and generate feelings of joy through experience 'in the moment'. How many of us really stop and look at the beauty of the sky and its ever-changing patterns or the beauty of flowers or trees in the park or spend time really exploring the tastes, smells and feel of things? How many of us actually experience joy in our ability to see or to hear or focus on the pleasure of seeing and hearing, knowing that there are some people who have been robbed of these senses? Our hurry-hurry lives narrow down into tunnels of greyness with just the odd glimpse or impression of wonders. But if you think about it, you are a consciousness passing through time. We only exist in *this* moment. We do not yet exist in the moment to come and we no longer exist in the moment just gone; only in *this one right now* do we truly exist. Yet our 'new minds' can be so distracted that we don't fully exist here either.

There's a rather far-fetched story that shows how appreciation can help us even in moments of stress and tragedy. It goes like this: A Buddhist master was walking along a cliff when a gust of wind blew him off. As he fell, realizing that his life was about to end, he saw a strawberry growing wild on the cliff face. He plucked it as he shot by, noticing its beauty, its redness and, as he ate it, its sweet taste. The wonder of the strawberry was with him at his death. This is, of course, just a story – if this were really to happen to us, we'd probably scream some rather serious four-letter words and certainly not notice any ******* strawberries. But that's the point, of course.

The soothing/contentment system

We now come to an emotion regulation system that's going to be the focus for much of the rest of this book. It's the soothing/contentment system that helps to balance the other two systems, of threat and desire, and it's a major source of our feelings of well-being and connectedness.[10]

Now it's clear that animals (including ourselves) aren't always just running away from threats or rushing around doing things like eating, having sex or advancing their careers (though, looking at us humans, you'd sometimes be hard pressed to think of what else we do). Animals are also able to take time out, to be in a state of satisfaction and contentment. At times when they don't need to avoid threats and dangers and have had enough to eat, they can 'chill out'. Indeed being able to 'chill' and have 'out time' because all systems are satisfied is linked to important reparative changes in the body. Now it used to be thought that these states of mind were simply the result of the threat system being on low volume or toned down; thus, if we weren't threatened, we were relaxed. But recent research has shown that this is only half of the story. In fact, contentment can accompany *very profound, positive feelings* that are not just low threat feelings. (Indeed having low threat feelings without positive feelings can lead to boredom.)

So there is now evidence that we have a special soothing/contentment system in our brains that enables us to have a sense of well-being and of being at peace. This system uses natural chemicals in the brain called *endorphins* and *opiates*. Indeed, when people take manufactured opiates like heroin, they can experience a general sense of well-being. They don't become charged up, excited and want to party or agitated or aggressive as can happen with the dopamine that stimulates the drive/excitement system. So if you want to have the experience of happiness and approach it purely from a mechanical, physiological point of view, then this is the system that you would be aiming to work on and develop. It encourages you to enjoy and savour what you have as opposed to seeking more and more. We will be looking at this in some of the exercises in the next section of this book. Don't be tempted to go the artificial route, though, and try heroin. The come-down is terrible and the risk of addiction is great. Much better to learn how to enhance this system in your own brain by doing certain types of exercises and trying to adopt a certain lifestyle.

One of the aims of compassionate mind training is to help us create brain states conducive to a calm and content mind. Research has shown that this sort of mind, at peace with itself, is also one that can think clearly and develop new insights and feelings about the nature of self and relationships to others. This is because a content mind is not dominated by any particular archetype or feeling, and therefore it's 'free' to explore in an unfettered way.

Soothing, contentment and affection

Now, as mentioned in Chapters 3 and 4, evolution tends to conserve things that have developed through it and, if necessary, adapt them and put them to new uses. The soothing / contentment system, which produces feelings of peacefulness, safeness and quiescence, was adapted to function in a very new way with the arrival of warm-blooded mammals – to become the system through which the calming and soothing effects of caring, love and affection would work. To help it perform these functions, evolution came up with some new hormones, including vasopressin and oxytocin, the latter being especially important for feelings of closeness to others and for a sense of safeness and well-being. One of the most important discoveries in the last few years has been that the soothing / contentment system has played a huge role in the development of mammalian caring and attachment behaviour.[11]

So let's think about the evolution of caring behaviour for a moment. Caring originally evolved because of the (genetic) benefits it conveyed to those expressing it. Caring helped your offspring and genetic relatives to survive and reproduce, and caring and helping others also helped you develop helpful alliances and friendships, called *altruism* in evolutionary psychology. Here, however, we're interested in how caring actually works in our brains and is linked to compassion. So basically we're looking more deeply into the caring social mentalities that we discussed on pages 103–4.

Caring for, and looking after, one's offspring became a highly successful strategy and has undergone considerable evolutionary change and development over millions of years.[12] We can easily see the benefits. For a contrast, just look at turtles. These reptiles lay hundreds of eggs and then leave their offspring to survive as best they can when they hatch. Their species only survives because of the huge number of eggs they produce, 98 per cent of which will not make it into breeding adulthood – instead, they will be lunch for sharks, foxes or birds or die from other tragedies long before that. When you look at it like this, the turtles' life is a kind of hell – definitely no Garden of Eden! There is a spiritual message here, if you like: don't reincarnate as a turtle. The more serious message is, of course, the coming into the world of caring motives, feelings and behaviour.

The arrival of the mammals was the start of the evolution of a very major strategy/archetype/social mentality that would eventually blossom to become the foundation for compassion. Mammals care for their young; they take an interest in them to promote their welfare. With caring behaviour, they're able to protect their young from threats such as predators and provide a secure base from which they can explore and return. Of course, when caring first appeared on our planet, it was rather mechanical, operating on the basis of black-and-white rules such as: 'Feed those in the nest.' There will be conflicts of interest between parent and infant, and some parents won't be very caring, but this shouldn't obscure a recognition of this fundamental evolutionary leap forward to a mind that can be oriented towards and respond to distress calls from others and provide things to help others flourish.[13]

By the time we get to primates and humans, this caring relationship and social mentality has evolved into a complex set of desires and competencies whereby parents not only protect their infants but their affectionate behaviour actually affects how the brains of their infants will mature. In addition, of course, human parents are vitally important for teaching and mentoring their children through life.[14] We'll return to this caring strategy later because, as I've said, it's a foundation for our capacity for compassion – that is, our ability to take an interest in the welfare of others and be distressed by their distress, combined with a desire to relieve it. We'll also see how we can develop the 'compassion brain pattern' and direct it at ourselves so that our very sense of self (and brain) becomes organized around the compassion archetype and care-giving social mentality.[15] And the reasons for doing this are because it's good for our physical health, fosters feelings of well-being and inner peacefulness, and helps us create positive, non-aggressive relationships with others.

So the mammalian mother is able to provide food, comfort and warmth to her infant and, in doing so, also calms it and gives it a sense of safeness. If the young mammal is threatened, it will run back to its mother, and her presence will soothe the child and reinstigate the feelings of safeness. Once safe and calmed, the child will be able to play and explore again. If this relationship goes well, for the rest of the child's life it will associate contentment and well-being with feelings of acceptance and affection from others.

Most parents will know that, as well as protecting their offspring, one of the most important roles they play is helping to regulate their children's emotions. One way they'll do this is by stroking and holding. In fact, when frightened, all monkeys seek physical comfort and hold on to their mothers or, if they're adults, to each other. To mammals, physical comfort is a key soothing stimulus that the brain needs to regulate its threat/self-protection system, because comfort calms down the threat/self-protection emotions.

Robert Sapolsky,[16] professor of neurology and neurological sciences at Stanford University in California, has spent years chasing, hiding from and studying monkeys in the savannahs of Africa, and has discovered a great deal about how various hormones affect behaviour in the wild groups. He has made clear – along with many others – that the attachment (caring) relationship we and other mammals have with our parents, the way they are able to soothe and calm us, is vital to the way our brains develop and are able to regulate the emotions of incentive and threat. Touch is a key regulator, in part because it stimulates the opiates and the soothing system. In 1994, Sapolsky observed that:

> Touch is one of the central experiences of an infant, whether rodent, primate, or human. We readily think of stressors as consisting of various unpleasant things that can be done to an organism. Sometimes a stressor can be the *failure* to provide something to an organism, and the absence of touch is seemingly one of the most marked of developmental stressors that we can suffer.

Another important researcher, Tiffany Field[16] at the University of Miami, has spent a long time looking at the effect of touch on our stress hormones, our moods and our general state of well-being. She and her colleagues have shown, for example, that babies born prematurely will develop better if touched and stroked rather than left alone. 'Love matters,' to use

Sue Gerhardt's words – and it matters a lot.[18] Notice, too, how kindness from others is often referred to as touch – 'I was *touched* by your kindness' or 'I was *touched* by your concern/thoughtfulness.' It is tragic that our terror of paedophilia has led to teachers not being allowed touch or hold distressed children, and to a situation where sun cream can only be sprayed, not rubbed, on them. Such prohibitions could only have been made by people who haven't the faintest idea of how our psychology works, what happens in our brains when we are distressed, and what we need from others by way of comfort. There is increasing evidence that young children may find nurseries more stressful than has previously been recognized, and one possible reason for this, which needs to be explored, is whether or not these children are getting enough *physical* affection. This is a very serious and urgent research question.

Basically the soothing system is alert to signals of being cared for by others and that others are being helpful and supportive (rather than cold, critical or rejecting) – this indicates that we're safe. Hence, the way parents and others in authority talk to and show an interest in children, the voice tones and facial expressions that they use, the way they share positive feelings, the way they validate and explore what the children are feeling – all these signals convey to children that they are loved and valued. To the brain, this is very good news indeed (because the world is a potentially hostile place without this safeness). The soothing system is therefore able to signal to the threat system: 'It's okay here. We're cared for and safe.'

These experiences have a profound effect on developing children's brains in certain ways. Caring experiences affect the way that emotion regulation systems are wired up for later life and how positive emotions are stimulated.[19] These caring behaviours also enable children to lay down emotional memories that then become a resource for later life; they also have a profound effect on how the three emotion regulation systems are balanced. There is a now a lot of evidence that, if we experience caring in childhood, it helps us to deal with the various ups and down of life – it's one of the things that makes us resilient to stress. Having current support and caring relationships is another, and being able to treat ourselves kindly rather than harshly is yet another.

Emotional memories and our sense of self

Early experiences with our parents and others stimulate different emotions and combinations of emotions that become associated with our sense of self and our sense of what others are like. This is how it works.

Consider how a child experiences the *emotions of others* in an interaction and how these become the foundations for how one feels about oneself. Being able to say to yourself, 'I'm a lovable, competent person' is really shorthand for: 'In my memory systems are many emotionally textured experiences of having elicited *positive emotions* in others and of being treated in a loving way and as competent – therefore I'm lovable.' Suppose parents are often angry with their young daughter. She develops a sense of self in which others don't see her positively, which is shorthand for: 'In my memory systems are emotionally textured experiences of having elicited *anger* in others and of being treated as bad – therefore I'm bad and others are potentially hostile.' Suppose parents always sneer at or withdraw their love and turn away from their young son. It's not anger that's internalized here but contempt or loss. The boy may develop a sense of self in which he feels others see him as someone to turn away from and believe he's unlovable and reject him, which is shorthand for: 'In my memory systems are emotionally textured experiences of having elicited *withdrawal* in others and of being treated as undesirable – therefore I'm undesirable and others find me undesirable and reject me.' Consider the child who has been sexually abused. This can become: 'In my memory systems are emotionally textured experiences of *fear and disgust* – therefore I'm disgusting and bad and others only get close to me to abuse me.'

Which of these children chose to have their particular sense of self? None of them – it was all created in them via interactions with others. If you're like me and would like to have more control over what you feel about yourself, maybe we both need to recognize that, by sticking with the sense of self that *we have been given*, we're not learning how to break free of our conditioning and flourish.

Note as well that what the human brain will do is to put a *label* on each of these complex feelings. The problem is that the label might not be very accurate but only the nearest approximation of what we feel. For example, people can experience the pain of having a sense of separation from others, which might be linked to emotional memories of others not being there for them. The closest label that matches this feeling and this sense of self is: 'I'm alone and thus unwanted.' But the label is wrong. The reality is that perhaps the parent did love/want the child in their own limited way but was depressed and very withdrawn, and this is why those emotional memories exist within the son or daughter's self. This is about loss and sadness, *not* being unwanted.

Children, using their innate strategies, will try to optimize care and investments in time and energy, usually employing a mixture of coercion, tears and tantrums (to satisfy drives and wants) and behaviours that inspire affection (e.g. smiling and trying to be helpful and compliant). Generating positive feelings in the mind of the (m)other about the self and seeing them displayed on her face and in her voice is a key strategy for securing resources and care and thus is crucial to the building of the security/safeness of the self – it soothes us. For instance, imagine Sue, a three-year-old, drawing a picture. When finished, she proudly holds it up for Mum's approval/admiration. Mum responds by kneeling down and, displaying a positive facial expression and voice tone of pleasure, says, 'Wow, that's wonderful. What a clever girl!' Now, in this encounter, Sue experiences a display of positive feelings and affection in her mother that she attributes to what she (Sue) has done. So Sue learns that she can create positive feelings in the minds of others and this indicates that others are positively disposed towards her and will care and help her – in other words, she is safe. But very crucially, too, Sue also has emotions in herself about herself *generated directly via her mother's verbal and nonverbal behaviour.* That is, the mother's behaviour activates inside Sue certain physiological patterns that give rise to good self-feelings – she feels good about herself.

The linkage of positive feelings to the self is clearly a physiological and whole-body effect. You would be right to say: 'But isn't that sense of doing well linked to the incentive/resource-seeking system?' Yes, but keep in mind that these are interacting systems; here we are making the point that, when we feel that we exist positively in the minds of others, this helps us to feel safe and content. We will use this in our imagery exercises on pages 256–61.

But suppose Sue's mother had responded with: 'Oh, no, not another of those drawings – they're all over the house making such a mess!' Or suppose the mother had said dismissively with a blank face: 'Sure, very good. Look, I'm busy right now. Why don't you go and watch TV?' Clearly, Sue is unlikely to have good feelings generated in her about herself. Her head may drop and she may move away in disappointment and/or shame. Feelings of shame (e.g. heart sink, self-consciousness) are generated automatically by the mother's annoyance or dismissiveness, triggering Sue's threat/self-protection system and reducing her positive feelings. Moreover, these bad feelings may be associated with displays of abilities such as drawing, and thus become a shameful memory that can become a script for later experiences in life, such as not trying to draw because of feelings (arising from this memory) of not doing it very well. It's important to note that these 'feeling communications' have whole-body effects and lay down the feeling regulation patterns for the sense of self. They can form the underlying textures for subsequent self-criticism, as we will see in Chapter 10. Some children become so desperate to get feedback and an assurance that they exist positively in the minds of their parents (despite the latter's criticism, emotional distance or even abuse) that they become hard-driven and/or self-critical perfectionists.

Saying such things as 'That's good, dear' while being simultaneously dismissive or showing via nonverbal communication a distinct lack of interest can be quite confusing to children. Indeed, receiving different messages via different channels can lead people to doubt verbal content and reject it – 'You're only saying that.' Humans, of course, are far more interested in working out people's *feelings* about them rather than just relying on what they say. This, of course, raises crucial issues about nonverbal communication and how you monitor and read facial expressions and styles when people talk to you. Some just seem to give off a sense of contempt while others appear to be really engaged with you, even though they can *say* similar things. So pay attention to your nonverbal communication, your smiling and your engagement with others.

Feeling safe by creating positive feelings in the minds of others

We now know that, although humans can be extremely cruel to each other, the desire to feel valued, cared for and cared about is one of the most powerful of human drives. When we satisfy that drive, we can feel soothed and content, safe and at peace. This is because caring for each other is what has helped us survive numerous setbacks. At one time during the last ice age, we humans may have been down to as few as 700 individuals worldwide, and we only got through because we are a highly social, cooperative species that cares for each other.

This is easily demonstrated. Think about your friends, lovers, parents and co-workers. Now you have a choice. You can either be seen as powerful and threatening so that they will do what you tell them out of fear, or you can be a positive person in their minds, someone they love and care for and about. Which are you going for? Chances are, you'll want to feel valued, loved and cared about. And of course, we understand this and play the game. If you go to a friend's house for a meal, you say, 'Thanks for that lovely meal,' not 'Thanks for the meal – I've had better, I've had worse. Yours was perfectly okay, an average meal.' Or to a new lover you care for: 'Your lovemaking is fine – I've had better, I've had worse. Yours was perfectly okay, average.' As the friend who cooked the meal or the new lover, we want to hear that the meal was great and enjoyable and that our lovemaking was super and real cool (or should I say 'hot'?)!

Now this is not about being deceitful or not giving people helpful or accurate feedback, or always telling children that they're wonderful so that they never learn to cope with criticism or setbacks. The point is that, as humans, we feel safe when we have created positive feelings in people's minds about us and they care about us, and we feel more secure in supportive predictable networks. We spend much of our time thinking about other people's feelings towards us – in fact, our brains have specific areas for thinking about what others are thinking – and trying to earn other people's approval, appreciation and respect and be accepted in our group. So if you think about how you would like your friends, lovers, parents and co-workers to see you, the answer will mainly be for them to value you and see you as desirable, helpful, talented and able. If you can create these sorts of feelings in the minds of others, three things will happen. First, the world will be safe and you will know that these people won't attack or reject you because they value you. Second, with them you'll be able to create meaningful roles for mutual support, sexual relationships and/or sharing. And third, receiving signals from others that they value and care for you will have direct effects on your body and on your soothing/contentment system.

Let's look at what happens if the opposite occurs. To be seen as undesirable, unhelpful, untalented and unable risks us losing all the benefits outlined above and, as such, is a major threat. There's now very good evidence that critical relationships, in which people (adults or children) are labelled in this way, greatly elevates the risk of anxiety and depressive disorders, even if the labels carry no direct physical threat. Also, *to believe* that we are seen in this way, even if we aren't, can be as bad as actually being seen like this – and becoming self-critical is also strongly linked to depression. So important is our social need to feel safe, accepted and valued by others that people will risk serious injury or even their own lives to avoid shame and exclusion. This is why shame (related to feeling unattractive to others and looked down on) can be a major threat to anxious and depressed people. Basically, criticism and shame activate threat systems and cut us off from sources of soothing and emotion regulation.[20] Given that you feel a lot better if people are kind and positive towards you, so that you feel safe with them and know that they will help you if you need them to, and given that you also know that other people have exactly the same needs as you, then it makes sense that compassion and kindness should be at the centre of our relationships and engagement with the world. In this way, *we co-regulate each other's brains and brain states*, which give rise to experiences in consciousness. To put this another way: *experiences in consciousness are co-constructed by our relationships with each other*.

From caring to compassion

Compassion arises from the balance of the three emotion systems. In particular, it operates through the care-giving social mentality that orients us to focus on alleviating distress and promoting flourishing. We now know that this social mentality has evolved with, and is linked to, the soothing/contentment system. It's underpinned by the release of natural hormones in the brain such as the opiates and oxytocin.[21] When our brains are in a caring mentality pattern, this brings on line certain feelings and ways of thinking and certain behaviour – e.g. concern and kindness for others and working for their welfare. However, it's a brain pattern and so the feelings and behaviour it supports and encourages can be lost when either the incentive/resource-seeking system or the threat/self-protection system becomes dominant and regulates feeling and thinking. By learning compassion, we learn how to activate a particular state of mind and brain pattern in us associated with caring and nurturing that have soothing qualities. We can learn certain exercises that will stimulate this system, a kind of physiotherapy for the mind.[22] In the next chapter, we're going to look in detail at the basic attributes of compassion and the skills that can be developed to promote it.

Conclusion

So there we have it. Ticking away in our brain, evolution has given us three basic systems that give rise to many of our feelings and brain states. The archetypes that we discussed in Chapter 3 have to operate through these systems, too – well, actually, everything we do and think has to, more or less.

Keep in mind that these basic emotion systems for protecting us, for making us want and want to do certain things, and for contentedness and soothing, are part of an evolved design. They operate in us as clusters of neurons in our brains. A lot of the time, we're not even conscious of them; rather, we just feel their effects rippling through our consciousness.[23] Our consciousness usually just goes with the flow. But then that's where we came in, isn't it, in the opening paragraphs of Chapter 2? However, going with the flow and just riding along on the rapids and eddies of our minds, as these systems in our brains shift this way and that, isn't always a lot of fun.

Fostering compassion and kindness in ourselves and for others is the way to develop feelings of contentment and well-being and soothes both the threat/self-protection and the incentive/resource-seeking systems. To choose to deliberately foster these brain patterns in ourselves is the path of compassionate mind training. As we'll see, there are many tasks along the way, such as: learning how to pay attention to what goes on in our minds (mindfulness) and how to refocus our attention to appreciate and savour things; how to be curious about our feelings rather than be frightened of them or in denial about them; and, most of all, learning how to be kind – which lies at the heart of compassion. Developing these qualities will texture and colour your consciousness – and may well change your brain.[24]

6 Compassion in the Context of Old and New Brains and Minds

Our ability to imagine and fantasize is very much part of our 'new brain/mind'. This ability can have a powerful influence on our emotions and on how we experience ourselves and others. This chapter is going to explore the power of imagination and fantasy and how they work in and on our brain. We'll visit the way in which self-criticism and self-compassion can have different effects on our brain and then look in detail at the various qualities and aspects of compassion itself. Its power in our lives comes from how we focus our minds, how we attend, think and imagine and fantasize compassion.

Using the imagination

Let's start with our imagination – one of the most important qualities of our 'new brain/mind' and one that has enabled us to develop science and culture. Imagination allows us to 'create worlds in our head', to pretend and consider multiple possibilities – 'I wonder what would happen if I did this or that...' A capacity for imagination plays an extremely important role in our lives and cultures. In his book *Stumbling on Happiness*, Daniel Gilbert (no relation) looks at research on the nature of the imagination and how it can also be a source of trouble.[1] I touched on this in Chapter 2, where I noted that fantasies can become unrealistic and we can imagine dangers that don't exist or desires that are impossible to fulfil, leading to disappointment or frustration. We can lose ability to enjoy 'what is' because it doesn't match up to our fantasies of what life should be like.

Humans live in two related but very different worlds. The first is the world as directly experienced, which comes to us through our senses of sight, hearing, smell, taste and touch – we can call this the world 'as is'. The other world is the one that is imagined, thought about and created in our heads. However, both worlds are creations of our brains.

Our senses, which evolved over million of years, are our link to both the outside world and the world of our minds. Our experience of the external world has its genesis in the brain. To demonstrate this, let's take a journey together. Suppose we're walking in the countryside on a bright spring morning. We breathe deeply of the fresh crisp air and feel the tingle of a cool breeze on our faces and hands. The air has a slightly muddy, rich smell about it. Looking up, we see the crisp blue sky interrupted by white hazy clouds. Walking down an unpaved lane, we can see that the farm fields are green and that the brown trees are just starting to bud. As we walk on, we see some wild daffodils and bluebells. If this countryside is unfamiliar to you, then think about walking somewhere you know. For example, if you walk by the sea on a hot day, the sky may be a white-blue stretching far to the horizon, and you can smell the sea and feel the sand under your feet and the warmth of the breeze on your face.

But are you seeing something that is actually out there? Well, yes and no. We are actually seeing the colours of the sky, grass, leaves, sea, sand – and beach balls – because our eyes are absorbing and reflecting different light frequencies. In fact, overhead there is actually only the blackness of space. There is no blue, white, green or brown 'out there'. It's our brain that gives us the experience of blueness, greenness and brownness by how it processes those light frequencies. Of course, some people are colour blind so they can't actually 'see' or 'experience' certain colours. What also struck me when I found out about this was that the variations in the light frequencies that give rise to the experience of, say, blue, green or red are extremely tiny – actually measured in millionths of millimetres. The key message then is that the brain is constantly picking up energy frequencies that are coming to it in the form of light or sound and turning them into 'experiences'. If we had different brains, our 'experience' of the universe would be different. This experience will also, of course, be textured by our feelings and the whole process of being conscious and aware.

However, as fascinating as this is to think about (the mind boggles at the possibilities for experience in alien brains), we are going to leave the world of experience as created and constructed from actual sensory information and consider the world of imagination. Think for a moment about what happened in your mind when you read the words above about taking a walk in the countryside or by the sea. You could close your eyes and imagine a walk on a spring day – one might have flashed into your mind as you read the journey I described. So you read words on a page and your mind created a bit of video for you in your head. It might be only fleeting and impressionistic but it would be there. Not only do our brains create conscious experiences from actual sensory information, but through our imagination, we can create imagined worlds. Another important aspect of the pictures of that spring walk created by your inner mind is that you will have textured them with your own memories.

I can write words that, years later, through my readers' imaginations, create pictures in their minds. Well, this is what all good authors do – when reading old books, we're inhabiting the imagined worlds of writers who may have died hundreds of years before.

Creative thinking and imaging

Imagination is far more than a passive process; it's creative and dynamic. Animals can be frightened and upset by things that happen to them, but they don't dwell on what it means to be upset. They aren't able to ponder how the universe came into being or about their personal futures or the meaning of their lives, or whether they are lovable or not. They don't worry about job interviews or how they're going to pay the mortgage. Our ability to think about the world we live in, to have self-awareness, to reflect on ourselves, our life goals and relationships with others, to plan things in our heads and be creative is a source of much of what makes us human. It's the reason why we have culture, science and fashion shows. We can change what happens in our heads. For example, we can create a scene and imagine what would happen if A or B or C occurred.

We can also plan, conceptualize and anticipate, and we can run lots of different video-like simulations in our minds. In our imagination, we might picture dating a certain person, what he or she might say, what we would say back, what he or she would say back to us, and on and on until the alcohol takes over. Or we can anticipate the fun of a holiday, what we'll definitely do, what we'd like to do, what we don't want to happen. We can think about our plans to achieve things and how to avoid failure – for instance, the acclaim and life change that would occur if we were to pass an exam and the lost opportunities if we fail. We are now a long way from the world 'as is' and deep in the world of imagination.

The upsides and downsides of imagination

Many researchers think that it was the evolution of our ability to imagine in creative ways that gave us the advantages that led to us becoming the dominant species. For the first time, a life form – us – was not constrained by what its genes directed it to do. We humans can improve on our genes because we can imagine better solutions. Bees, birds and beavers will build the same types of living quarters (hives, nests and dams) for generation after generation – indeed, for thousands of years – because they are primarily reliant on the knowledge stored in their genes that tells them 'how to do', aided by a little observation of others and learning on the job. But humans have gone from mud huts to skyscrapers, from stick fires to central heating, from walking on the savannah to flying to the moon. The evolution of a mind that can 'imagine' and go beyond what is 'there' has had a phenomenal impact on the face of the Earth. We are approaching a technology through which we will even be able to change our genes.

The upsides to our imaginations are many. They not only enable us to be creative and have foresight, but as we will see in a moment, they can enable us to stimulate our physiological systems as well. However, like so much in evolution the upsides are often matched with downsides. It is often our imaginations that can make us unhappy or anxious. They can become trapped in and by memories of what happened to us in the past. If, for example, we had a rather unhappy childhood, it may be very difficult to imagine that we can ever find a loving relationship or that we can ever be successful. More commonly, if we've had a lot of difficulties in the past, then because the brain will try to protect us, our imaginations will focus on threat – e.g. 'You'd better remember this and you'd better remember that' (images of the past come to mind) and 'Don't let your guard down.'

Because we can imagine, we can also *ruminate*. Now there are different types of rumination. One is related to trying to solve problems. We'll turn a puzzle over and over in our minds as we try to sleep and sometimes a solution will just be there when we wake up and we have one of those *ahhh* moments. However, in another form of rumination, we are upset and go over and over things that have made us unhappy, anxious or angry. A sad example is what happens when someone we love dies. It's very hard not to imagine them and not to dwell on what life might have been like if they were still alive with us. Or suppose someone has really upset you, taken advantage or treated you unfairly. You can find yourself going over and over in your mind how unfair they've been and how you might be able to get your own back. Being creative, you might think up some pretty scary stuff.

So our imaginations can keep our minds *turned towards our suffering*. Walking down the street, an aggressive-looking youth seems to purposely bump into you. The actual pain of the bump lasts about a minute or two, but the pain caused by focusing on your anger and thinking 'If only I was 20 years younger' and 'What's the world coming to?' can last much longer. It's often ruminations like this that take us to live in the very places that cause most pain. Although it can be difficult to lift ourselves from rumination, because our emotions can be very strong magnets or whirlpools that pull us in, we can also recognize that we don't want to live in and dwell on the unhappy, the angry or the vengeful. We can work to steer a course away from those places, not to deny them but simply not to sit in them.

How our thoughts and imagination affect our brains

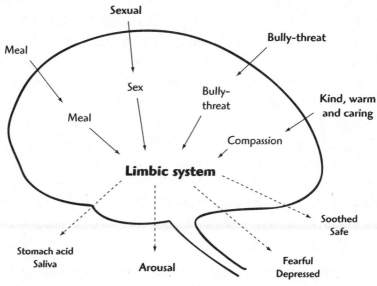

Diagram 2: How thoughts and imagery affect our brains and bodies

Our thoughts, imagination and memories can have powerful effects on systems in our brains. Look at Diagram 2, which shows how external things and your imagination of external things can work in very similar ways on your body. In the middle of the diagram, you see the term *limbic system*. This is an umbrella term for a number of important brain systems (such as the amygdala, pituitary and hypothalamus) that regulate our desires, feelings and various bodily functions. Let's see how our imagination alone can actually activate these brain systems.

Say you're very hungry and a lovely meal appears in front of you. What happens in your body? What you've seen (and probably smelled) will stimulate an area of your brain that will send messages to your body so that your mouth will start to water, your gastric acids will get going and your stomach will rumble. However, supposing you're very hungry and you close your eyes and just *imagine* a wonderful meal. What happens in your body then? Spend a moment to really think about that. Well, the images that you *deliberately create in your mind* can also send messages to the same part of your brain that then sends messages to your body so that your mouth will water and your gastric juices will again get going. But remember: this time, there is no meal, it's only an image that you've created in your mind, yet it's capable of stimulating physiological systems in your body that make your saliva and stomach acids flow. Take a moment to think about that.

Okay, let's look at another example, something that all of us have come across. Say you see something sexy on TV, which stimulates an area of your brain that affects your body, leading to arousal. But equally, of course, even if you're alone, you can just imagine something sexy and *that* can affect your body. The reason for this is that the image alone can stimulate physiological systems in an area of the brain called the pituitary, which will release hormones into your body.

So the point of all this is that images are very powerful ways of stimulating our brains and our bodies. Spend a moment and really think about that, because this insight will link to other ideas to come. The images that you deliberately create in your mind will stimulate your physiology and body systems. (Incidentally, be sure you don't get meals and sex mixed up as did Hannibal Lecter!)

Let's turn this around and think of a more negative example. Imagine if someone is bullying you – always pointing out and dwelling on your mistakes or things that you're unhappy with, or telling you that you're no good and there's no point in you trying anything, or being angry with you – all this will affect your stress systems and the level of the stress hormone cortisol in your body will increase. How do you feel when people criticize you? How does it feel in your body? Spend a moment thinking about this. Their unpleasantness probably makes you feel anxious, upset and unhappy because the threat/self-protection system in your brain has been triggered. If the criticism is harsh and constant, it may make you feel depressed. You wouldn't be surprised by that. However, the point is: *our own thoughts and imaginations can do the same.*

So if you're constantly putting *yourself* down, this can also activate your stress systems and trigger the emotional system in your brain that leads to you feeling anxious, angry and down. That's right – our own thoughts can affect parts of our brain that give rise to stressful and unpleasant feelings. They can certainly tone down positive feelings. If we develop a self-critical style, we will be constantly stimulating our threat/self-protection system and will understandably feel continually under threat! This is no different from saying that sexual thoughts and feelings will stimulate your sexual system or that the thoughts of a lovely meal will stimulate your digestive system. In fact, with other researchers at the universities of Aston and Glasgow, my colleagues and I are currently scanning people's brains to see what happens when they're told to be self-critical or self-compassionate. So far, it's clear that these ways of thinking about ourselves stimulate different brain areas.

Now there are many reasons why we might become self-critical. In Chapter 10, I'm going to explore in detail shame in self-criticism and what to do about it using a compassion approach. Briefly we can note here that we may become self-critical because others have been critical of us in the past and we simply take their views as accurate. We don't stop to think whether they were genuinely interested in our welfare and really cared and wanted to help us – in fact, they may just have been rather stressed and irritable people who were critical of everyone. We just went along with their criticism of us – as one often does as a child – and never stopped to think if they were being accurate or reasonable. Or it may be that we've been trying very hard to reach a certain standard, achieve something or present ourselves in a certain way. Or bad things may have happened that we feel we can't recover from and we've been damaged, and we may hate ourselves for it. When things don't work out as we'd like, this can frighten us because we might think that we've let ourselves down or that others will reject us. In our frustration, we then criticize and take our feelings out on ourselves. While understandable, these ways of treating ourselves are themselves damaging, because we're then giving ourselves negative signals that will affect our brains detrimentally.

Self-soothing through compassion

In the normal course of events, we feel soothed when others are kind and understanding, supportive and encouraging. Our brains can respond to that kind of behaviour from others. In terms of social mentality theory, kindness emerged with the evolution of altruism and especially with the caring-giving social mentalities (*see* pp. 103–4). So suppose that, when things are hard for you and you're struggling, there's someone who cares about you, understands how hard it is and encourages you with warmth and genuine care. How does that feel? Spend some time thinking about this. Notice how your brain and care-receiving mentality are able to respond to these signals with soothing.

Now turn your thoughts to what happens when you're struggling to learn a new skill and other people seem to be getting the hang of it easier than you. Awareness that others are doing better than you could activate your competitive and rank-focused mentalities. You then notice that you're comparing yourself with them. You might then force yourself to do better or drop out, or you might simply accept that others are better at that particular task and just carry on as best you can.

What if you have a teacher who's very gentle and warm, pays careful attention to your difficulties, helps you see what you do right and how you can build on those good things. Compare this teacher to one who's clearly irritated with you, makes you feel you're holding up the class and focuses on your deficits. It's fairly obvious that you're going to prefer, and indeed will do much better with, the first teacher. Notice how the first teacher's behaviour will calm you but the other teacher's will further activate your stress, competitive mentality and rank-focused feelings of being inferior.

Let's use this insight to see that we can also treat and relate to *ourselves* with kindness or irritation, which will stimulate different social mentalities in us, too. We can be kind and soothing, or we can be critical and put ourselves down, making us feel inferior to others. So in exactly the same way that imagining a meal can stimulate sensations and feelings in our bodies linked to eating, our own thoughts and images might be able to stimulate our inner caring mentalities and brain systems that lead to soothing. If we can learn to be kind and relate to *ourselves* with a caring mentality – to send ourselves helpful messages when things are hard for us – we're more likely to stimulate those parts of our brain that respond to kindness. This will help us cope with stress and setbacks.[2] If you develop an inner relationship with yourself based on the competitive mentality of striving and needing to succeed, achieve, and control or impress other people, then you might feel good if things are going well but depressed (and inferior or a loser) if you fail. The caring mentality, however, steps in precisely when things aren't going so well, to encourage, support and soothe. So self-directed caring, understanding and encouraging, kind and supportive thinking and feeling are what we're trying to create in our minds.

Training our minds in compassion

So it's a two-way street. Our imaginations, thoughts and reflections can stimulate systems in our brains, and our emotion regulation systems can direct our thoughts and imaginations. Given this, it's not difficult to understand the benefits of compassion and kindness. We also know that wanting to associate with others who are helpful is probably part of our innate heritage because helpful and compassionate people are good for our survival and genes. Indeed, so important is kindness to humans that, even from a young age, we're very attentive and sensitive to those who show it. For example, Professor Kiley Hamlin of Yale University showed six- to ten-month-old babies a figure struggling to get up a hill. Then he showed them a toy that tried to help the figure and one that pushed the figure down again. The babies much preferred to play with the toy that was depicted as being helpful – and that's at less than a year old![3]

Yet despite stating the obvious, that kindness is good for us and we seek it out, we all suffer from a lack of it[4] – not least the poor of the world, the starving, those caught up in wars and conflicts, those trapped in violent relationships, those lost to the ravages of mental illness, the sick and the dying. In our hearts, we know life is harsh and that all of us are in need of considerably more kindness and active acts of compassion that we receive now. We can also appreciate that many of our friends and intimates – and we ourselves – can suffer from a lack of *self*-compassion. And of course, we need to respect and nurture our environments that we have so exploited, polluted and destroyed.

Being sensitive, caring and compassionate isn't easy because we have so many other pushes and pulls on us. Evolutionists tell us that kindness and caring are expensive resources to dispense, and so we reserve them mostly (with some exceptions) for our kin, lovers and friends. As for self-kindness, consider what it takes to be kind to yourself when things go wrong or people criticize you. We become angry at or disappointed in ourselves, and we may replay in our minds the criticisms of others or the errors we've made. Out of frustration or fear, kindness and forgiveness might be in short supply.

There are many books on the market that focus on the value of compassion as a way of finding happiness. However, compassion can assist us with many aspects of our lives, not just happiness. It can help us to cope with failure, to take risks, to practise and deal with our failures on the path to competence, to deal with criticism and conflicts, to develop more harmonious relationships. It can become a focus for our self-identity, something to strive for and work at. It can help us to link to a caring/soothing aspect of our mind, and to face and cope with life's tragedies. In recognizing that we live in a sea of suffering, we can find meaning and purpose if we dedicate ourselves to bringing compassion into the world. And it can help us to develop wisdom so that we can step back from vengeful, fearful and aggressive solutions to problems and seek instead fairness, justice and kindness for all of us in a world of limited resources.[5]

The elements of a compassionate mind

Okay, we've now arrived at the point where we can start to think about *what compassion is* and how we can develop it. We've established that it evolved and emerged out of caring – that is, a care-providing social mentality and basic archetype. This archetype, when present in interactions in which we're being mutually caring of each other, can help us feel soothed and safe and can influence how our bodies work. When we're in kind relationships rather than critical ones, the levels of our stress hormones are lower and our feel-good brain chemicals higher and our immune systems are more robust. The same is true when we treat *ourselves* with compassion rather than criticism.

Compassion is also a major pattern generator in our brains – it harnesses certain motives and competencies and organizes them in certain ways, ways that are very conducive to our minds' and bodies' experience of well-being.[6] But we need to focus and train the brain to develop our compassion abilities to reap these rewards.

Now there are many different definitions of compassion and the elements that go into it. The Buddha and his followers recognized that we need to train our minds in many different ways. He talked about the eightfold path:

- *right view* – linked to developing clear insight into the true causes of suffering linked to attachments and craving

- *right concentration* – linked to focused attention as a form of mindfulness and compassion

- *right intention* – linked to the motivation for caring

- *right speech* – linked to interpersonal relating, saying kind rather than hurtful things

- *right action* – linked to behaviour that tries to heal rather than destroy

- *right livelihood* – linked to choice of career and how one conducts oneself at work

- *right efforts* – linked to the need to practise with effort/dedication

- *right mindfulness* – linked to paying attention 'in the moment' in a compassionate way.

We'll be seeing some of these again in new contexts below.

Kristin Neff has been at the forefront of developing the concept of self-compassion and you can find references to all her work – along with some questionnaires you can fill in to look at your own levels of self-compassion – on her *Self-Compassion* website <www.self-compassion.org>. Kristin focuses on three major dimensions:

- *kindness* – understanding one's difficulties and being kind and warm in the face of failure or setbacks rather than harshly judgemental and self-critical

- *common humanity* – seeing one's experiences as part of the human condition rather than as personal, isolating and shaming

- *mindful acceptance* – awareness and acceptance of painful thoughts and feelings rather than over-identifying with them.

My own thinking is based on an evolutionary neuroscience approach, and it changes as our understanding and knowledge change. Just as the Dalai Lama says that his basic religion is kindness, a neuroscience approach also places kindness high on the basic attributes of compassion and well-being. In my approach, our capacity for compassion evolved out of the capacity for altruism and caring behaviour. Compassion can be defined as behaviour that aims to nurture, look after, teach, guide, mentor, soothe, protect, offer feelings of acceptance and belonging – in order to benefit another person.[7] Such behaviour requires a number of different competencies and attributes, which can be linked together as a *compassion circle* (*see* Diagram 3). These interconnected elements enhance each other, and all are infused with basic warmth, rather than, say, cold detachment. There is an inner ring of *attributes* and an outer one of *skills*. The outer ring contains the 'how to's' for the inner ring. So we can learn to direct our attention compassionately, to think and reason compassionately, to feel compassionately, to behave compassionately, to generate compassionate images and imaginings, and to work on creating a bodily sense of compassion. Don't worry if this seems a bit complex. It will become clearer as we move along.

Compassion circles are something that we can choose to develop in our relationships with other people, but importantly also in our relationship with ourselves. This is because compassion is made up of many interacting elements. When active, it patterns our whole mind; thus, it's called the *compassionate mind*. When we train our minds for compassion, this is called *compassionate mind training*. We'll now move around the circle and explore each of the compassion attributes.

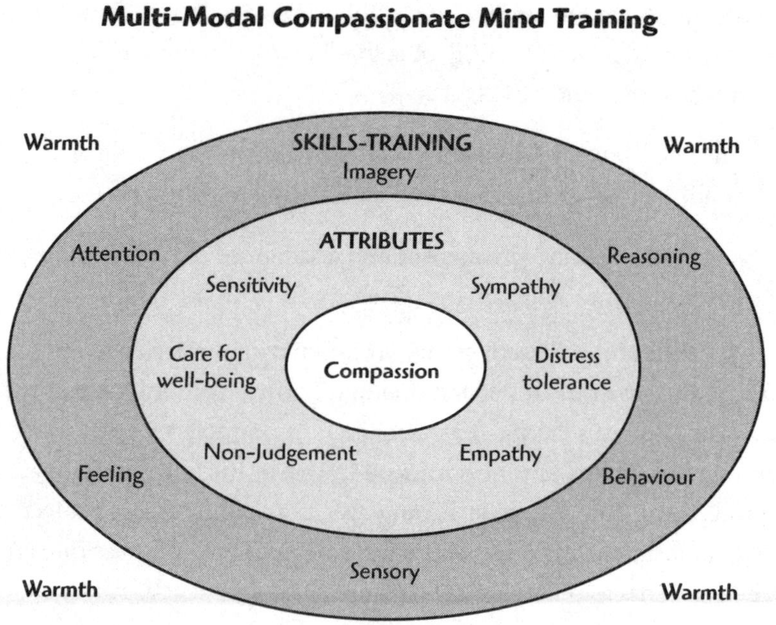

Multi-Modal Compassionate Mind Training

Diagram 3: The compassion circle: key attributes of compassion (inner ring) and the skills needed to develop them (outer ring)

Care for well-being

Motives and desires to be caring, supportive and helpful are at the root of compassion. Caring for yourself and others involves harnessing a desire and motivation to take a genuine interest in caring for and about others (and yourself) when in distress *and* to promote their well-being.[8] In Buddhist psychology, the desire is to alleviate suffering, but it must be done 'skilfully' with knowledge of the causes of suffering and with efforts to acquire the means to help.[9] In fact, humans can work out how to care for and nurture many things – from one's own children to the family pet, plants and even the family car. Of course, we understand that caring that's directed towards living things and those with sentient minds is different to caring for inanimate objects, but the desire to 'look after' runs through them all. Sometimes our caring is coloured by our also wanting appreciation from others or to be cared for in return – in fact, it usually is; that's only human. Much of what we do is for mixed reasons, so don't try to work out if your emotions are uncoloured by selfish desires; just go with the flow on this one. One clearly selfish desire is 'I like to feel I'm a caring person' as it aids our sense of self. I personally get a lift from being helpful. However, as I will continually emphasize, it's the combination and integration of *all the compassion qualities* – that is, the pattern – that's important. In Chapter 8, we'll look at some imagery exercises in which we'll generate feelings of compassion for others.

When compassion is directed at the self, we become focused on desires to care for, nurture and support ourselves to promote our well-being and flourish. People from harsh and shaming backgrounds can be very unclear about being motivated and working to care for, nurture and look after themselves. They may be caring of other people or able to defend themselves or focused on 'achieving' things or winning social approval or self-promotion – but genuine care and concern for their own well-being is different. In fact, as mentioned in Chapter 2, they may see this motivation as selfish, self-indulgent or even a weakness. Some will have beliefs such as 'You should always put others first.' It is, therefore, important to think about what 'caring for one's well-being' means. One of the exercises on pages 243–5 will address this.

One approach is to take a very practical look at this in terms of your brain systems and how to balance them and see that, like getting physically fit, it's not about 'deserving' but about mind training. So we can think about developing self-compassion as a kind of physiotherapy for the mind.

Sensitivity towards distress and need

Being sensitive to other people's distress means that we're able to pick up on it and attend to it. Obviously if we're rushed or busy, this can get brushed aside. But we can at least decide if we'd like to train our minds to be sensitive or insensitive – that is a choice.

In fact, I've worked with a variety of people who felt that they needed to train themselves to be *insensitive*; otherwise they couldn't make difficult decisions. This isn't as strange or as heartless as it might seem. A business executive told me how he had to be relatively insensitive and harden himself to suffering when making employees redundant. If he hadn't done that, his firm would have collapsed and everyone would have lost their jobs. A more extreme example is army training, which teaches soldiers how to become able to kill. In the normal course of events, humans don't actually like killing other people, and so without this training, soldiers might hesitate too much and put themselves and others at risk. Of course, if we train our soldiers' minds in this way, we shouldn't be surprised when some of them act cruelly. Sadly, too, when some return damaged from war, their trauma is usually not only due to the violence that was done to them, but also to the violence that they did to others. There's no good and bad here, just complex brain states that are emerging as a result of the person's personality, background and training, current social contexts, patterns of fear and vengeance and so forth.

Some people think that the best way to get through life is to be insensitive to one's own pain, to block it out and just get on with the job, develop a hard skin. To be compassionate is to be respectful of this process of trying to become 'hard-nosed' and 'thick-skinned', to acknowledge that we're all trying to get through life as best we can. For some people, however, these tactics can lead to mental health problems or a certain callousness that can spell trouble for others. Training our minds to be more in tune with ourselves – our upsets, feelings and needs – is usually more helpful to us.

Developing self-awareness, openness and sensitivity for our distress and needs means learning to be more attentive to the changes in our physical feelings and emotions and to our thoughts. This may reveal that, at times, we experience certain small cues or feelings in our bodies that trigger avoidance or defensive strategies rather than processing those feelings. For example, when Kirsten criticized Alan, he'd go straight to anger, bypassing feelings of confusion, shame, hurt, upset, fear of rejection and the reactivation of memories of rejection from his childhood. Anger eliminated the need to process all that distress. 'Learning to be sensitive to one's distress' would, for Alan, mean slowing down, stepping back and seeing what was behind the anger. Basically angry people are easily threatened people, and some use drugs or alcohol as a distraction from painful feelings and memories. When you discuss change with them, they'll sometimes say that 'sensitive to one's own distress' is the last thing they want to become; they want to get rid of the distress, not embrace it.

Becoming sensitive to what upsets us can also mean working out what is really bothering us: what the key fear or threat is, what the major issues in our minds really are. This argument you're having with your partner about forgetting your birthday – is it really about that or is it because you think he/she doesn't care about you? That anger you felt when your colleague criticized your work – is it really about the work or is it that you just don't like him? Or are you actually angry because you lack confidence in your work, too, or because you're just over-stressed and any small thing will set you off? Are you disappointed in, or angry with, your colleague because he reminds you of your father who criticized you? Being sensitive to ourselves means learning to be curious and interested in why we react as we do.

One of the things that psychological therapies can help with is giving you the space to think these issues through. But as long as our fears are not so great, we can learn to do this for ourselves by becoming *mindful* and *observant*. We can learn to put our feelings into words and also to write about them – e.g. write letters to ourselves about the situations we find ourselves in. We'll be looking at this later. I think it's always easier to face up to our fears and needs if we're clear in our minds that many of our feelings of distress aren't experienced by ourselves alone but are shared with other human beings the planet over. Indeed our vulnerabilities and need for love, care, affection and respect are what make us human.

Sympathy

This is the ability to be emotionally moved by the pain of others. We go to a sad movie and cry in our popcorn. In fact, we have special neurons in our brains called *mirror neurons* that enable us to feel things just by watching someone else experience them. The neurons that fire up when we ourselves feel disgust, fear, anger or joy can also fire up when seeing these emotions in others. Some researchers believe that this is the basis of sympathy (the ability to feel for others) and empathy (the ability to understand others).

These begin very early in life – for instance, in a nursery if one baby becomes distressed and cries, others may well do, too.[10]

How prepared we are *to allow* ourselves to be emotionally moved can be crucial to how we understand things. In 1995, the BBC ran a series of documentaries to commemorate the fiftieth anniversary of the ending of the Second World War. I had, of course, seen many documentaries on the Holocaust and concentration camps and thought that I understood how awful the latter were. However, one two-hour programme, with a soundtrack of Gorecki's Third Symphony, was different. I started watching it because, well, I thought I ought to, being sort of respectful, I guess. To be honest, I would rather have watched the cricket. In this documentary, however, the music paced the words. It started with a slow train ride along snow-covered tracks to desolate buildings filmed in black and white. It then went into detail about individual lives, reading from letters hidden in mattresses and from graffiti on walls, written by frail and dying hands. One was from a mother in despair at what had happened to her daughter and hoping that heaven would reunite them. Voices overlaid pictures of forlorn rooms where the experiments in the camps had taken place. Thoughts and images of how I would have borne that if it had happened to my wife and children were painful and unbearable. For the first time, I wept. In fact, I was so distressed that I was tempted to turn off the programme.

I was glad I didn't. In the discussion that followed, people expressed the usual simplistic ideas about good and evil, but then one person pointed out that this had little to do with good and evil and everything to do with our brains, what they are capable of and the social contexts that pattern them – that we must give up believing that we have full control over our minds when history shows time and again that we don't – it's an illusion – in groups, we can do all sorts of terrible things.[11] That sentiment is the road to compassion. My understanding of the pure despair in this tragedy and my realization of what we are up against from our evolved minds, and how we can be so easily led by our 'old brain/mind' passions, gave me new insights and greatly affected me.

What about developing *self*-focused sympathy for our own distress? How does that differ from self-pity? Well, self-compassion means we are moved by the painful things that we've experienced; we're emotionally open to our suffering. Self-pity has nothing to do with compassion because it involves elements of contempt and overly identifying with a sense of being a victim and/or a sense of angry injustice: we may see ourselves as 'poor pathetic me' or become angrily tearful, complaining about unfairness. This isn't sympathy with one's own distress. To have sympathy is to be genuinely moved by, for example, how awful it is to feel depressed or how frightening it was when, as a child, your mother threatened to abandon you or your father was drunk or beat you or you were bullied at school or always felt the odd one out. This doesn't mean that you just dwell on how bad it is or was in an unhelpful way, but rather how you could develop compassionate understanding for your pain. It also helps us to reflect on the fact that we did get through these things and that sometimes we have more courage and endurance then we think we have.

People may say that they've been able to 'intellectually' recognize how difficult things were for them – as children or when they went through a divorce or when struggling with loneliness while bringing up children as a single parent – but they never really had much sympathy for or felt any kindness towards themselves for having had those experiences. They had spent so much time 'holding themselves together', 'protecting themselves' or 'keeping going' that they'd never really had a chance to process those experiences and the pain they'd been in. This style of coping can, in one way, be quite compassionate in that it's what was needed at that moment, given possibilities and resources. It helps greatly, though, if someone who cares for you can provide a safe environment and offer kindness and support. This is what being a human being is about – helping and understanding the feelings and minds of each other. No other animal can match these abilities. When it comes to ourselves, sympathy is the ability to recognize our pain without minimizing, denying or dissociating from it; it means that, when opportunities arise, we can if necessary work with the pain and share it with others.

For instance, consider Christine, a woman I worked with who had had a difficult background and had learned 'not to feel things'. When her mother died, Christine noticed that other people at the funeral were very sad, but she felt somewhat empty and cut off and rather contemptuous of their crying and 'not being in control of themselves'. Therapy involved her re-engagement with her own feelings, and during that journey, she began to contact the pain she had felt earlier in her life due to her mother's distancing of herself due to depression and drinking. She also grieved for the mother who might have been, the one who was wanted, as well as her real mother who had died. Mixed with the profound grief was, of course, rage and anger, too. After years of medication for depression, Christine now felt that she had regained the ability to feel and to feel alive, even though this was, at times, desperately painful.

Having sympathy for ourselves begins the process of acknowledging pain associated with bad memories, difficult times and basic fears – and being genuinely moved by them. Many of us face our lives' tragedies in different ways as best we can. Sometimes it's a case of just keeping our heads down and keeping going, but it's important to recognize what we can lose by doing this, that we can be putting some of our feeling systems on hold. I should also add here that research is beginning to show us that people who come from difficult backgrounds and suspend their feelings like this, who avoid intimate feelings in some way, are potentially very damaging to all of us, particularly if they get into positions of power. And these types may often seek power to compensate for their emotional detachment.[12]

Distress tolerance and acceptance

Sensitivity and sympathy towards distress operate together and are key components for a crucial element of compassion: *distress tolerance*. However, it's important that we bring the feelings of kindness and warmth to tolerance so that it's *compassionate tolerance* that is the focus.

Linked with but not identical to acceptance, tolerance is the ability to stay with emotions as they happen. We might learn to tolerate something in order to change – e.g. tolerate the pain of training in order to get fit. Acceptance can involve tolerance, but it's also a deep philosophical orientation to one's difficulties. It's a coming to terms, 'letting it be', not fighting or struggling any longer. This is quite different to defeated resignation or enforced, resentful giving-up. Our relationships with other people can be important to how we become tolerant of painful experiences and feelings. It's often easer to tolerate things if we feel supported. Even death may be easier to face within the context of love than if we are alone. But there is a similarity with our relationship with ourselves – the kinder and more compassionate we are with ourselves, the more we can develop the courage to tolerate difficult things.

Both tolerance and acceptance are totally different from submissive resignation. In that, you feel that you have to give in to the inevitable, and you're defeated and powerless to do anything else. This is often associated with feelings of hopelessness or resentment. The spirit of acceptance is in coming to terms with a situation without these feelings.

The importance of learning tolerance for painful feelings is fairly clear. However, it's perhaps surprising to discover that some people also need to learn to tolerate and savour *positive* emotions. For some people, enjoyment for its own sake can feel wrong. Some depressed people develop a 'taboo on pleasure' or certain types of it – a trait for which the Puritans were noted. Some people can't tolerate feeling happy or contented because this triggers fears that they'll let their guard down and something bad will happen; or because they feel it's self-indulgent and they don't deserve it; or because feeling happy might conflict with their self-identity – as someone said to me: 'I'm just not a happy person, that's just not me.'

One individual may feel that they shouldn't be happy about, say, a holiday in case it goes wrong and then they'd have to cope with their anger and disappointment. Another may have been told repeatedly as a child not to get overexcited because they did 'silly things'; as a result, feelings of excitement often triggered caution and a fear of 'losing control' or of doing something that would make them feel ashamed. Still another may believe that being happy and dedicating one's life to happiness when the world is experiencing such suffering is immoral. And yet another person didn't want others to see them happy because they might take advantage of them or stop caring about them. Finally, a person might think that being happy would mean giving up what they consider to be justifiable anger and forgetting the injustices of the past and their desire for revenge. They need to keep reminding others (and themselves) how bad things have been for them, hoping for recognition or rescue. The recognition they seek often never comes so they remain in this position of avoiding happiness. And, as we saw in the last chapter, some individuals believe that to become 'enlightened' means to give up pleasure.

Sexual feelings are also another major area where shame-prone people can have a range of blocks to allowing themselves to feel and explore a *variety* of sexual pleasures. They may have religious beliefs that stop them, or bad memories, or a fear of losing control.

Now these fears of enjoying pleasures, while understandable, can put our three emotion regulation systems out of balance. So we might try a few things, a kind of experiment, exposing ourselves to learning how to stay with, and tolerate, *positive* feelings. Of course, you might say, 'some feelings might feel good to you but they make me anxious and feel bad to me.' So if you want to leave a situation like that, that's fair enough. But what would it be like if you could enjoy various positive feelings, for example like those that make you feel as if you don't have a care in the world? A simple question we might put to you is: 'What would be your greatest fear in becoming really happy (or sexual), really letting yourself go?' If we sit and think about what our greatest fear is in allowing ourselves to experience pleasure, happiness and contentment, we might come up with some very interesting ideas. But remember that, in compassion work, it's important to keep this questioning at the level of curiosity and not become self-attacking.

Empathy

This consists of both an emotional component and the ability to 'understand' and have insight into why we feel what we feel or why we think and react in the way that we do.[13] Empathy begins with an open-minded curiosity and a genuine desire to know and discover. If you have little interest in these things, it's difficult to develop some aspects of empathy. Empathy also requires us to stay in touch with our own and other people's feelings – hence the value of distress tolerance.

We bring our knowledge and personal experiences to empathy. Our understanding about why we think feel and behave as we do, and why others think, feel and behave as they do, rests on the things that we know about ourselves and other people. If we know someone is having a hard time in life, then if they're snappy with us we understand why and don't take it personally. Developing our empathy and understanding of our own difficulties (why me, why now?) aids us in being able to become sensitive, sympathetic and tolerant of our feelings and difficulties. This empathic understanding is personal (linking into one's early history) but also *trans*personal – that is, it involves understanding the innate nature of some of our protection strategies (fears and angers) and our wants and desires and common humanity.

Compassionate empathy enables us to use the knowledge that we all 'just arrived here' and are struggling to control a brain we never designed, which was put together over many millions of years, and some hairy, scary feelings and desires. This kind of compassionate empathy leads naturally to the next key element of compassion – non-judgement (*see below*).

As we saw in Chapter 3 (pp. 56–7), some researchers believe empathy is a dimension of personality and is intuitive. It's also been said that empathy can be used for very negative ends. The non-empathic torturer puts a gun to your head, whereas the empathic one puts it to your child's. Such an act requires clear insight into the fact that our minds are more likely to be influenced by a threat to a child than a threat to ourselves. Some psychopaths can be quite empathic and understand how to manipulate people because they seem to have an intuitive sense of people. This is why we have to think of compassion as an integrated *set* of talents and not as a single process. It's how these abilities, outlined in the compassion circle, work together. Having a few of them on their own doesn't necessarily lead to compassion. And if any one of those abilities are lost, then compassion can struggle.

However, empathy is complex because there are clearly both intuitive and non-intuitive aspects to it. We must make intuitive assumptions about the minds of others – if we couldn't do that, it would seem as if we were confronting aliens. True empathy, though, is an act of imagination. We have to imagine what it would be like to be in the minds of others, to walk in their shoes. We have to consider their background and how it would have impinged on them / us; we have to consider their context – that is, their fears, desires, hopes and wishes.

So, for example, if I'm working with a man who has an aggressive background and *is* aggressive, empathy towards him won't involve just thinking about one specific event when his aggression was apparent. I'd have to try to imagine the kind of person I would have been if my own father had been as brutal as this man's had been. And how do you imagine what it's like to have a different genetically influenced temperament or frontal cortex? In fact, it's very difficult to think about people being shaped by genes and contexts that are different to your own experience.

This is what makes empathy so different from sympathy. Sympathy is an automatic reaction; we are moved and feel according to how the other person expresses themselves. In empathy, we have to work hard, to get to know and understand the other. To see empathy as purely intuitive and automatic or linked to personality is only half the story. Also, of course, you have to be motivated to do this; if you have no interest in trying to understand the mind of someone else, empathy stops before it starts. Hence one of the biggest problems when we deal with people who are seen as enemies is the lack of empathic thinking on our part, or if it does take place, it's only used to try to work out what the others might do, so that we can find them or defeat them.

Looking back in history, we can see that people were fascinated by cruelty (e.g. the Roman games) and were all too prepared to use violence and torture as solutions to social problems and conflicts. If we lack empathy, we can't imagine ourselves as them – for instance, enjoying the games. Therefore, our ancestors become alien to us and we fail to recognize that their minds were the same as ours and that, in similar circumstances, ours could become like theirs again.

Thus empathy requires of us a courageous step, to visit those places in our own minds where the fascination with cruelty and the potential for sadistic retribution and other unkind behaviour resides. Jung called this 'visiting the shadow'. He suggested that those individuals who did not know or come to terms with their own shadows were most likely to see only bad things in others. For such people, the bad, disgusting and horrible are 'in the other', never in the self, or if they are, they must be disowned. The fact is that all of us have been genetically built in the same way with the same potentials, more or less. None of us chose how our brains are constructed, so in one way, we don't need to blame ourselves for our shadows, and because of this, we can now visit and take responsibility for them.

Self-empathy has the same focus. We have to suspend our judgement and work at trying to truly understand why we feel what we feel, what the historical influences on us have been to give us these values, these thoughts, these emotional dispositions, these attitudes about and towards ourselves. If we're dissatisfied with ourselves, if we're critical, we can ask, 'Where has all that come from? How did I learn to be self-critical? Is my self-criticism related to competing – a mentality – and trying to achieve and impress others?' To be self-empathic is not to accept things at face value but to insist on a deeper understanding of ourselves. It's hard work and, of course, is exactly the process of psychotherapy. Via the empathy of the therapist, the patient develops self-empathy and becomes more knowing and understanding of the self and more compassionate about accepting or changing. Here is another area where compassion requires courage, because discovering the origins of pain or anger or the nature of our shadows is not the easiest thing to do.

Non-judgement

Last but not least, we come to the ability to be non-judgemental – that is, to engage with the complexities of other people's and our own emotions and lives without condemning them. As previously noted, developing empathy, especially how we humans have been created through our genes and environments, can help non-judgement. We realize that, had we been born in Rome 2,000 years ago, we might be happily looking forward to the games this Saturday and watching people kill each other and children being chased down by lions, followed by a nice meal and getting laid at Marcus's orgy.

So social contexts have an impact on our values and states of mind. The latter also impact on our values and behaviour. We know, for example, that people can become trapped in mental states of depression, fear, paranoia or vengeance, propelled along by powerful emotions that shape their experience of the world. Indeed, such states can direct their thoughts and behaviour, even though these individuals didn't design those emotions or dispositions. Clearly how much we understand this will impact on our judgements and desires to condemn.

We must be clear that non-judgement is not non-preference; it doesn't mean that everything is acceptable. Many Buddhists pursue non-judgement as a value but clearly would like the world to be a more spiritual and compassionate place and will work for that goal. So we can make a distinction between preference, which encourages energy, strong, dedicated commitment and hope for how we would like something to be, and condemnation of error, which encourages anger and contempt.

To be non-*self*-judgemental is not to say that we do not have preferences or values or are not open and dedicated to self-correction (*see* p. 322), but rather it is the giving up of self-attacking and condemning that's the issue here. You see, the problem is that criticism and condemning come with a set of feelings, too, usually ones of anger, frustration or contempt. Mindfulness, which we'll explore later, is often regarded as a helpful way of becoming more aware of our feelings and thoughts and non-judgemental in our awareness.

Warmth

This is the emotional quality of gentleness and kindness that operates through all of the above. Warmth is a difficult quality to accurately define, but it involves being non-threatening while having a caring orientation. Commonly, experiences of warmth are notable for their nonverbal communication and interpersonal manner. People who are viewed as warm are usually seen as safe and non-threatening but not dull or passive – they have a calming impact on the minds of others. Feeling threatened or frustrated commonly turns off warmth.

Self-warmth may develop from genuine sympathy for your own distress and a gentleness towards your own needs. It's not, however, to be confused with self-centredness or a feeling that you're following your own agenda. It arises from enabling yourself to feel compassion from the inside. In the exercises in later chapters, we'll be looking at how to develop warmth as an emotion and a feeling for the self.

The skills of compassion

We can now touch on the outer circle of compassion and think about some of the *skills* involved. As shown on Diagram 3 (*see* p. 194), they comprise learning to:

- direct our attention

- think and reason

- behave

- sensory focus

- feel

- use imagery

– all in a compassionate and helpful way. And we do all these things with feelings of warmth, support and kindness.

Compassionate *attention* is all about learning to pick out and focus on the helpful. You make a joke at a party and most people seem amused except one person. Do you focus on the majority or the one who seemed bored by your joke? When something negative happens or you're unhappy with yourself, do you focus on your upset or anger with yourself or do you acknowledge it but then redirect your attention to something that's helpful, perhaps memories of past successes or kindnesses from others? So learning to become more mindful (*see* Chapter 7) or bring to mind helpful memories or a helpful focus are part of compassionate attention (*see* Chapters 8 and 9).

In compassionate *reasoning and thinking*, we train our minds to focus on reasoning and thinking about others, ourselves, our relationships and the situations in which we find ourselves in a helpful way. When we ruminate on our anxiety, disappointment or anger, this is only going to lock these feelings in. So can we practise deliberately choosing to refocus our reasoning helpfully – to ask ourselves the question: 'What's a helpful way for me to think about this problem, situation or difficulty?' Imagine reasoning it through with a friend, or having a dialogue with someone else who is compassionate (or even, as we'll explore in Chapter 8, your compassionate image), or talking to someone else who has been through this difficulty too, or maybe writing a letter as if you were writing to someone else with this difficulty (*see* Chapter 10). Thinking things through compassionately is being honest about what we feel, which at times can be difficult, painful or even aggressive feelings and dilemmas. That takes us to the importance of trying to develop self-honesty and emotional tolerance. However, we have to acknowledge that this will only ever be partial honesty because we are not fully conscious of some of our motives – so we can only do the best we can. But at least we can try to have a compassionate, 'what would be helpful here' focus to our thoughts.

To *behave* compassionately means behaving in ways that you identify will be helpful to you in your suffering and will move you forward on your life's journey, and this behaviour can be directed towards others, too. Now sometimes compassionate behaviour can mean being nice to ourselves, recognizing that we need a holiday, to take time out, a bit of pampering or the support of others or just to treat ourselves kindly. But it can also require *courage* to do things that may be blocking us. Sometimes compassionate behaviour is about doing things we don't want to do, such as taking a stand despite wanting to avoid confrontation because of depression, anxiety or prejudice (*see* Chapters 11 and 12). It's compassionate because, although taking what might seem an easier path in the short term (e.g. avoiding doing anything) might give us temporary relief, it doesn't take us anywhere (*see* Chapter 11).

Genuine compassionate helpfulness is never submissive nor does it mean simply giving in to what other people want, only to leave us feeling resentful or very needy for their approval. It's difficult to act compassionately from a position of fear or weakness. So sometimes we have to learn assertiveness to stand up to others and say: 'No.' So the compassionate person has to be wise, thoughtful, curious and open but also at times require courage – and we can all struggle with these.

Table 1: Compassionate attributes and skills

Compassionate attributes and skills are used to counteract the feelings, styles of thinking and behaviour that can arise from our threat/self-protection system, such as anxiety, anger and depression. We can also use them to develop new ways of experiencing the world and ourselves.

Compassionate attributes	Compassionate skills
• Motivation to be more caring of the self and others.	• Deliberately focusing our attention on things that are helpful and bring a balanced perspective.
• Sensitivity to the feelings and needs of the self and others.	• Mindful attention (*see* Chapter 7) and using it to bring to mind helpful compassionate memories, images and/or a sense of self (*see* Chapter 8).
• Sympathy, being open and able to be moved, and emotionally in tune with our feelings, distress and needs and those of others.	
• The ability to tolerate rather than avoid difficult feelings, memories or situations.	• Thinking and reasoning, using our rational minds, looking at the evidence and bringing a balanced perspective.
• An empathic understanding of how our mind works, why we feel what we feel, how our thoughts are as they are – and the same for others.	• Writing down and reflecting on our styles of thinking and reasoning (*see* Chapters 9 and 10).
• An accepting, non-condemning, and non-submissive orientation towards ourselves and others.	• Planning and engaging in behaviour that acts to relieve distress and moves us (and others) forward to our (or their) life goals – to flourish (*see* Chapter 11).

Each of these skills, along with compassionate imagery, feeling and sensory focusing, are outlined in later chapters. The key issue is learning to focus on what is helpful to you (or others), but not in a selfish 'me, just me' way, because you'll find that that's not helpful and other people will lose interest in you. With genuine compassionate helpfulness, we think about other people as well as ourselves

Table 1 summarizes the compassion attributes and skills. You'll find some overlap with the Buddhist eight-fold path (*see* p. 192) but also some differences. Notice that different skills can help develop different abilities (and vice versa). For example, with more compassionate attention and thinking, we might increase our feelings and motivations to be caring; or practising compassionate attention and thinking might increase our empathy and reduce our condemning tendencies.

Shame, guilt and justice

There are three key elements that we need to consider in our analysis of compassion. If we are to move to a compassionate society and sense of self, how we deal with these will be important. In Chapter 2, we saw how complex our moral thinking is because there is sometimes a trade-off between considerations of justice and of compassion. It's very clear that at times we do things that are harmful to other people and to ourselves. It's useful, therefore, to get a view on this from a compassionate perspective. Compassion is not about simply forgiving and saying things don't matter, because clearly causing harm matters a great deal.

Shame and guilt

A distinction that can be helpful here is between *shame* and *guilt* – people often get these two confused. When we feel shame, our attention is on ourselves and how others might see us – i.e. think badly of us. In shame, we feel exposed and think that there's something wrong or flawed about us. We feel anxious, depressed and our hearts sink. We put our heads down and avoid the gaze of others, covering up the things we feel ashamed about. If we become shameful to ourselves, we do this by being self-critical and contemptuous of ourselves. Shame is, therefore, about threats and attacks and how bad or inadequate we feel we are; it's about judging and being judged. Sometimes, of course, if people make us feel like this, we can have anger and rages as defences. You probably know people like this – any criticism sends them off into a rage and a torrent of self-justification. Because shame can be about blame and punishment, people will naturally try to avoid it.

Now guilt is very different. When we feel guilty, we're able to be open about the things we might have done: 'Oh, gosh, did I do *that* – I'm really sorry!' Our facial expressions and feelings are quite different – no head down or hiding away here. Our feelings are of wanting to repair, to reach out, whereas in shame we want to pull away or attack. In addition, guilt tends to focus on specific events and behaviour – 'I feel guilty because I did that or thought this' – whereas shame is focused on feelings about our very selves such as being inadequate, flawed or unattractive. Finally, guilt can arise where there are conflicts over things that we want to have or want to do but where this might harm others, where one person's gain is another's loss. However, if we become too concerned about hurting or upsetting others and not balancing that against our own needs, we can become submissive and that isn't compassionate. Compassion is not about avoiding all conflicts; it's more about the way in which we engage in differences and conflict.

To clarify this distinction, consider the reactions of two men, John and Tom, who are both having affairs. When their respective wives discover their infidelity John thinks, 'Oh, dear, my wife will give me a hard time now. Maybe she won't love me so much. Suppose she tells our friends? How will I face them? I think I'd better hide from them for a while. I'll be nice so my wife will like me again.' John's focus is not at all on the harm, pain and hurt he's caused his wife but only on himself. His main concern is the damage that the discovery has caused him. His feelings are *shame*-based.

Tom, however, feels terribly sad for the hurt he's caused his wife and the damage to their relationship. He recognizes how bad he would feel if the situation were reversed and feels remorse (empathy). Tom may also worry about his wife loving him less and what his friends might think of him if they found out, but principally he's focused on the harm he's done and the hurt he's caused. His feelings are *guilt*-based.

Guilt feelings are often related to fear and sadness. When we have done something that has hurt or caused harm to someone, there can be feelings of sorrow and these, in turn, are linked to feelings of remorse and regret. It is these feelings that make us want to put things right. So, for example, John may not feel that much sorrow for what he's done because he's focused purely on the damage to him of the discovery. Tom, however, feels deep sorrow at seeing his wife so hurt.

The American psychologist Martin Hoffman[14] sees guilt as related to sympathy and empathy. Adult guilt, therefore, is linked to compassion and a desire to care for others. If we don't care about others, why would we be bothered with guilt? You don't need to care for others to feel ashamed but you do to feel guilt. Indeed, one of the reasons we can behave so badly and hurtfully towards others is because we neither have sympathy for nor care for them. So we can easily turn off our compassion qualities but still feel shame. These distinctions are incredibly important because governments and other agencies may believe that shaming and punishing people is the only way to change people's behaviour. In fact, more than a hundred years ago the behaviourists said that that was a bad idea because people will try to avoid punishment but not necessarily engage in the behaviour you want them to adopt. And they learn that instilling fear and punishment gives you power – you've just got to be the one with the power!

What societies need are not people who are frightened of being caught and shamed and so will work out how not to be caught, but people who have been trained to be empathic, have a sense of guilt and be self-regulated from the inside by compassion and empathy. Of course, we need punishments, deterrents and prisons – compassion is not naive about this – but there are compassionate ways by which we can move towards a more just society, one that also promotes and encourages moral development. This society is based on compassion training in schools, work places and systems of restorative justice. Despite evidence that compassion works, governments are worried that people won't agree to these approaches because they want punishment and to be seen as tough and dominant. Compassion also directs our attention to the costs and complexity of prevention in providing care and support to those vulnerable to 'going off the rails'. Deterrents just rely on the fear of being caught; they don't retrain, re-educate, heal or help people flourish.

Types of justice

Although considerations of justice and compassion can conflict (*see* pp. 67–71), it's difficult to think about how we could have a compassionate society that is unjust. But what do we mean by justice, and how should we deal with individuals who break the rules or are harmful to society? This raises a very important distinction about the type or types of justice we want and which elements of our minds fuel different types of justice-seeking.

An important distinction here is between *retributive* justice and *restorative* justice. Retributive justice focuses on condemning, blaming and punishing. The focus is on shaming, fear, causing some kind of physical pain and/or curtailing movement/freedom, and deterrence; it's intended to make the perpetrator suffer in some way. In restorative justice, however, the emphasis is far less on making the perpetrator suffer and more on trying to create healing and change in both perpetrator and victim. They are brought together and directly confronted with the pain of the other. Rather than shame emotions, which can turn to self-justification, anger or denial of the seriousness of what has been done, the focus is on developing mutual empathy: in the perpetrator, a sense of remorse, sadness and guilt; in the victim, movement towards forgiveness and acceptance. These differences are outlined in Table 2.

It is harnessing these feelings and processes that has been behind the endeavours of the Truth and Reconciliation Commission in South Africa. To have gone down the shame, blame, retaliation and persecution route there could have risked a bloodbath. There's increasing evidence that,

Table 2: Retributive and restorative justice

Retributive justice (shame-focused)	Restorative justice (guilt-focused)
Victims/or courts:	*Victims/or courts:*
• Anger	• Complex emotions of anger, sadness, fear and vulnerability
• Blaming	• Making clear the pain that has been caused
• Shaming	
• Condemning	• Needing to understand
• Persecuting/punishing	• Trying to depersonalize
• Vengeance/retribution	• Possibility of forgiveness
• Retaliation.	• Non-retaliatory.
Responses in perpetrators are defensive, self-focused and threat-linked:	*Responses in perpetrators are more open and other-focused:*
• Depressed, fear, anxious	• Sorrow, regret
• Self- and shame-focused (bad self)	• Guilt for one's behaviour
• Punishment-focused	• Empathic awareness of harm done
or	• Taking responsibility
• Dissociated	• Repairing.
• Other-blaming, aggressive, defiant	
• Feigning regret as socially expected.	

on the whole, in restorative justice both victims and perpetrators gain from the experience, with the added bonus of lower reoffending rates. So compassion is not about letting anyone off the hook or avoiding acknowledging the harm we do – very much the opposite. It's about taking responsibility *in a specific way* based on caring for and about others – rather than just being focused on our own sense of self and self-identity. A Google search of 'restorative justice' will take you to many interesting documents on the issue – see, for example, *Restorative Justice: The Evidence* <www.esmeefairbairn.org.uk/docs/RJ_full_report.pdf>.

Currently the UK government is intent on locking up more and more people and building more (mega)prisons. Anyone who knows anything about crime will tell you that many of these individuals are struggling with learning difficulties and mental health problems and/or come from harsh, critical or abusive backgrounds, including having been in care. We need to decide if we want to treat people with these kinds of problems like this and, indeed, what kind of society we want:

- one that is focused on retribution, that will vote for people who spout the rhetoric of 'a need for more punishment' because of their own fears and desire for retribution – and that is in the face of the evidence that these approaches don't work well, are costly and don't get at the roots of offending. Do we really want to keep building prisons and paying the earth to lock people up?

- one with politicians who really understand that a lot of crime results from social and psychological issues and that it requires social and psychological solutions, not least compassion, caring and engaging in the tough task of adequate, preventive policing, working in schools and deprived communities and helping people feel valued members of their community. That's before we get into good sex education to reduce the incidence of unwanted pregnancies and emotional support for struggling parents.

The situation is actually even more complex. It's increasingly recognized that some individuals may have a genetic vulnerability to acquiring traits that increase their risk of committing crimes. Genes don't 'cause' crime but they can increase a person's risk of acting in certain ways if he/she grows up in certain backgrounds or social conditions (e.g. with low affection and/or deprived). It's very unclear how these individual differences should be handled in a fair and just system.

We know from history that crime can excite us to sadistic retaliation. Burning, drowning, stoning, crucifixion, hanging-drawing-and-quartering, electrocution, branding, torture, amputation – these are just some of the ways our ancestors have dealt with those who have committed crimes. Executions were also witnessed by thousands of people, and indeed it was very important in previous centuries that justice was *seen* to be done. Of course, people also commonly demanded public executions and would riot if robbed of such spectacles – it's believed that Pontius Pilate wanted to free Jesus but the crowd demanded his crucifixion. The social acceptance of sadist punishment as both a solution and a deterrent, as useless as they turned out to be in preventing crime, still exists in a some countries! So compassionate thinking has quite a hill to climb when it comes to how the human brain deals with its lawbreakers, cheats and dangerous individuals. Indeed when you realize that the ending of the slave trade occurred only two centuries ago and that prison reform and the Geneva Convention on the treatment of prisoners of war are even more recent, you can see that, in the West, compassion is a relatively new concept and one that is still extremely fragile in the face of 'old brain/mind' passions for vengeance.

So, to get back to our compassion circle, the issue of judgement and non-judgement in compassion is complex. Non-judgement can't be non-preference, it can't be about avoiding the complexities of thinking about justice or the realities of harmful behaviour and crime. None the less, when compassion does begin to enter our consciousness and we take it seriously as a way of dealing with these problems, we can come up with very different solutions. The British ended the slave trade because it was inhumane, they ended hanging because it was inhumane, they ended the practice of sending children down mines, up chimneys and into factories because it was inhumane. This is just the start of a compassionate awakening, perhaps. The way we criminalize and treat some people, and especially the young, from deprived backgrounds is inhumane and unhelpful.

Conclusion

Building on previous chapters, this one has explored the nature of compassion. We have seen that there are different ideas about compassion; the one that we are following here is based on an evolutionary and neuroscientific view, and these ideas are developing all the time. One of the major points was to look at the way in which we think and imagine, and show how that links to underlying physiological processes. We've demonstrated that what we think can affect our physiology – just by imagining a meal or something sexy, we can stimulate physiological systems in our brains and bodies. Therefore, creating negative thoughts and images can clearly have a physiological impact. Anger at others and self-criticism are common problems that deprive many people of happiness and a sense of well-being and purpose. The ease by which such things can be aroused can be linked to painful past memories and experiences. Self-criticism and shame also maintain our sense of threat by stimulating the threat/self-protection system.

Another key element of compassion is the recognition that it operates in and through social relationships. People often respond to the environments that they are in; indeed, we know that some environments inhibit compassion a great deal.[15] Compassion is difficult and complex. Not only do we need much more research on how to promote it and its effects on well-being, but we're going to need compassion training in many areas of life – in schools, families and places of work. We've all woken up in a harsh world of short lives. Some will look for solace in a God (or gods) who is supposed to have created it; others think that we need to look to ourselves and each other. So armed with insight into how our brains and minds work, we can now move to exercises to help us develop a compassionate mind.

Part II
Building the Compassionate Self

Skills and exercises

7 Mindful Preparations on the Road to Compassion

We've now arrived at the work and exercises part of our exploration together. Sometimes people find it really helpful to keep a folder or a journal in which to write their reflections on different exercises, the thoughts they've had during the day or notes on the ways in which they might have responded to things differently, or even on the changes in their dreams. It's like a personal log. You can also gather other things along the way – relevant pictures, poems, articles – and place them in your journal.

Reflective writing can be very helpful in helping us to clarify our thoughts and insights. You'll find that there will be some days when you'll enjoy writing in your journal and other times when you'll skip it. This, of course, is only a suggestion, although I'll be inviting you to use your journal in different ways as we go along.

First steps: Mindfulness

Of all the skills that will help you in your development of compassion towards yourself and others, becoming 'mindful' is one of the most valuable. Basically 'mindfulness' is learning how to pay attention in the present moment without evaluation or judgement; it's using your conscious awareness and directing your attention to observe and *only* observe. We want to create a new relationship between the 'old brain/ mind', with its sensing, feeling, desires, archetypes and 'me wants', and the 'new brain/mind' of self-awareness and reasoning. Buddhism has, of course, been developing these 'techniques' for mindfulness for thousands of years. In the notes to this chapter, I've suggested some books, websites and CDs that that you might like to explore for developing your understanding and practice.[1]

There are different aspects to mindfulness. Sometimes it can happen automatically. Have you ever been simply struck by the beauty of a sunset or a piece of music, or become completely absorbed playing a game with others? In those moments, you lost your sense of yourself and were just *in the flow of the moment* – no judgement, just being and experiencing. This is not something that you can *make* happen. Rather it's like sleep: you can create the conditions for sleep but the moment you start worrying about it – 'Am I going to sleep now?' – it's lost. However, this is only one aspect to mindfulness – it's just as easy to get into the flow of anxiety or of anger and allow yourself to be whipped up in fear or anger, too. So mindfulness is not mindlessness in that sense; it's a type of 'clear' awareness.

As I've noted before, many of the great teachers of meditation have pointed out that we only exist in *this moment* – each of us is a 'point of consciousness' passing through time. Our consciousness doesn't exist in the moment just gone or in the moment yet to arrive. Mindfulness brings us fully alive to the *now* of our conscious existence, the only place we actually exist! If you're materialistic, you might say that your brain is generating patterns that give you consciousness of this moment of time. If you have more of a spiritual view, you might say that your brain is creating patterns in consciousness and time. Scientists and philosophers have debated this at great length.

The point is that we can be so lost in our hopes or fears about tomorrow or our regrets of yesterday that we miss the moment *now* – we live in a remembered or imagined world, not in the world of *right now*. Of course, sometimes it's very important to reflect back and project forward, but when we do this, we want to do it purposely rather than just being automatically dragged there by fear or anger or strong desires.

Mindfulness also means becoming more aware and more *in* your experience, paying attention to the details of the world you exist in *now* and your inner feelings and thoughts as they emerge in your mind. How many of us, for example, when anxious or angry, actually stop and pay attention to where this feeling is in our bodies, to what our voice sounds like, to the part of our mind that is now issuing the instructions to our thoughts and bodies, to our primary thoughts and fears. How often do we stand back and practise observing what is actually happening in our minds? Mostly we don't; our archetypes and brain patterns just 'do their own thing'.

Mindfulness means learning how to change this being caught in the 'automatic-ness' of the 'old mind' by applying the art of non-resistance rather than forcing. Effort is important to the extent of putting time aside to practise and enabling and allowing things to occur. Mindfulness is about deliberately using one's attention to create brain states in which patterns in our brains can be stimulated and networks of brain cells can be developed that are conducive to calming the mind and developing soothing compassion.

So mindfulness is a way of understanding 'attention'. You can choose to give your attention a particular location. For example, if I ask you to concentrate and 'attend' to the big toe on your left foot, you will suddenly have sensations from that part of the body. If I now switch your attention to the top of your head, you will experience different sensations. So our attention can be thought of as a spotlight that moves around. It is learning how to be *in* that mechanism, *in* the attention, that is key to mindfulness.

Mindfulness is also about clarity of observation. For instance, suppose you're going to eat an apple. How would you do this mindfully? First, look at the apple and note all of its colours and textures, and hold it in your hand and feel the quality of its skin. Don't rush – spend time just observing. When your mind wanders from your focus on the apple (as it most likely will), gently bring your focus back to it. In this exploration, you're not judging the apple; you're simply exploring its properties. Then take a knife and peel or cut into it. Once again, notice the effect that you have on the apple, the colour and texture of the fruit beneath the skin. Take time to really observe. Next, take a bite of the apple: now focus on your sense of taste and what the apple feels like in your mouth. Next, chew slowly, feeling the texture in your mouth, noticing how the juice is stimulating your salivary glands and how the saliva feels in your mouth. Really focus on the taste. As you chew, notice how the apple becomes mushier. As you swallow, pay attention to the sensations of swallowing.

So you have explored the apple visually, by touch and feel, by smell and texture and by taste. If you had dropped the apple, you would have been able to hear what it sounded like – but you don't need to do that today! In this interaction, there's *no judgement*; there's only *your experience of your interaction* with the apple. This is mindful attention – being in the activity rather than distracted from it by other thoughts, and exploring all aspects of the activity to the full.

If you performed this activity – biting into an apple – without mindfulness, your mind would undoubtedly have wandered: 'This isn't a good apple – where did I buy it? I ought to eat more fruit. Actually I don't like apples … Oh, damn, I just cut my finger!' In mindfulness, we learn to notice the distraction – the wandering off of thoughts – and gently and kindly bring our minds back on task and into focus.

Mindfulness is important because most of our lives are spent doing one thing and thinking about something else and we're never fully in the moment. Our minds are constantly distracted. Take driving, for example. We can get home and realize that we can't actually remember how we got there, because our minds were full of 101 other things. If something unexpected happened – say, a group of naked motorbike riders flashed past us – our attention would have been awakened, or if the driver in front of us suddenly put on their brake lights, our attention would have been focused again. But this is not an example of savouring the moment – it's about being brought to alertness for a specific reason. Mindfulness is about being in the moment.

Learning how to breathe

We're now going to use the same idea of mindfully peeling and eating an apple, but this time concentrate on our breathing. This will become a central focus around which we will do some compassion-focused exercises later. The most important thing here is simply to practise breathing without worrying if you're doing it correctly. These thoughts are common and understandable, but distractions. If they arise in your mind, simply notice them, call them your 'judging and evaluative thoughts', *smile compassionately* to yourself and bring your attention back to the task.

Seeking out experienced teachers is very helpful, some would say essential, for more advanced development of this technique.

Okay, to start with, find a place where you can sit comfortably and won't be disturbed. Keeping your back straight, place both feet flat on the floor about shoulder width apart and rest your hands comfortably on your knees or in your lap. If you're sitting on the floor or on a small meditation stool, you may like to have your legs crossed. Try and find a position that's comfortable for you but don't slouch – your back should be straight. Sometimes lying flat on the floor can be helpful if that's the most comfortable position for you to start your work. The idea is not to relax so much that you become sleepy but to develop a certain type of alert focus and awareness.

Now just gently focus on your breathing. Breathe through your nose, and as you breathe in, let the air reach down to your diaphragm – that's just at the bottom of your rib cage, in the upside-down 'V'. Place a hand on your diaphragm with the thumb pointing upwards and notice how your hand lifts and falls with your breath. Feel your diaphragm (i.e. the area just below your ribs) move as you breathe in and out. Do this for a few breaths until you feel comfortable with it and it seems natural and easy to you.

Next, place your hands on either side of your rib cage. This is slightly more awkward because your elbows will be pointing outwards. Now breathe gently. Notice how your rib cage expands out against your hands, your lungs acting like bellows. This is the movement of the breathing you're interested in – you feel your lungs expanding around you. So basically you want a breath to come in and down while expanding your rib cage at the sides. Your breathing should feel comfortable to you and not forced. As a rough guide, it's about three seconds on the in-breath, a slight pause, then three seconds on the out-breath. But you must find the *rhythm that suits you*. As you practise, try to replenish the air in your lungs but not in a forced way.

Exercise: Mindful breathing

Now just notice your breathing and experiment with it. Breathe a little faster or a little slower until you find a pattern that, for you, seems to be your own *soothing rhythm*, which feels natural to you. As you engage with it, you'll feel your body slowing down. It's as if you're checking into and linking up with the rhythm. You're letting your body set the rhythm, breathe for you, and you're paying attention to it. Rest your eyes so that they're looking down at an angle of about 45 degrees. You may wish to close them but be careful – you may become very sleepy. Now spend 30 seconds or so focusing on your breathing, just noticing the breath coming through your nose, down into your diaphragm, your diaphragm lifting, your ribs gently expanding sideways, and then the air moving out, through your nose. You can check on this by, first, putting a hand on your diaphragm and feeling it lifting and falling with your breathing. Next, put your hands on each side of your lower ribs and feel them being pushed apart as you breathe. Notice the difference. It's an 'all-round experience' of the breath coming into your lungs and expanding them. Notice the sensations in your body as the air flows in and out through your nose. Just focus on that for 30 seconds (longer if you like) and sense a slight slowing of your breathing . . . Feel your body slowing down as you find and slip into your soothing rhythm.

The important thing is to find your own rhythm rather than impose one. As for a focus for your attention, once you're comfortable with your breathing, you can bring your attention to the inside of the tip of your nose. Try it and see how useful it is as a focal point for you.

Now some people can find these first stages quite anxiety-provoking and don't actually like them. If that's true for you, don't worry – we can do the compassion exercises in later chapters without doing this mindful breathing now. However, it would be useful to practise, so even if you do only a few seconds at first and then gradually expand over the next few weeks, that would be good, too. It may be the sensations arising from focusing on the body that are difficult – so it's often helpful just to practise gently and get comfortable with these feelings.

Assuming all went well, what did you notice during the breathing exercise? You might have been aware of how your body responds to the breathing, with feelings of slowing and being slightly heavier, and of how your chair is holding you up. You may also have noticed that, although it was only 30 seconds or so, your mind wandered. You may have had thoughts like 'What's this about? Will this help me? Did I do my job correctly yesterday? Where did that pain in my leg come from?' If you practise breathing for any length of time, distracting discomforts are very common. Your attention may have been drawn to the sound of letters being pushed through the letterbox, the traffic outside or whatever. The point is that our minds are very unruly, and the more you practise this breathing exercise and the longer you extend it, the more you'll notice how much your mind simply bops about all over the place. When you first do this kind of mindful breathing and focusing, it can be quite surprising just how much your mind does shift from one thing to another. This is all very normal, natural and to be expected.

So we need to train the mind, and the only thing that is important in this training is *not to try to create anything*. You are *not* trying to create a state of relaxation. You are *not* trying to force your mind to clear itself of thoughts – which is impossible anyway. All you are doing is *allowing* yourself to playfully and gently notice when your mind wanders and then, with kindness and gentleness, bring your attention back into focus on your breathing. That's it: *notice* and *return*. Notice the distractions and return your attention to your breathing. Notice how often your judging mind tries to get in on the act with thoughts like 'Am I doing this right? Is this helping me? Am I relaxed now?' Just notice these thoughts and then return your attention to the breath. In other words, this exercise is simply one in which you're learning to focus your attention. *You're not trying to achieve anything.* If you have a hundred thoughts, or a thousand thoughts, it doesn't matter. All that does matter is that you notice them and then, to the best of your ability, with gentleness and kindness, bring your attention back to your breathing.

Now if you practise 'notice and return', 'notice and return', 'notice and return', with gentleness and kindness you may find that your mind will bounce around less and less. It may become easier. Remember: *you're not trying to relax*. All you're doing in this exercise is noticing that your mind is wandering and then returning it to focus on your breathing. So it is *notice* and *return*. Each time your mind wanders, that's fine, don't get angry with it, just kindly bring it back to the focus of your breathing. It can also help if you allow yourself to smile when you notice your wandering mind. Develop an attitude of gentleness and kindness towards it.

You can do this exercise at any time, such as when waiting for or sitting on a bus or a train or in the bath. Later you might decide to develop your practice and put special time aside for mindfulness work. You might choose to just sit quietly practising this mindfulness exercise. Indeed, you may find it helpful to put aside time to practise two or three times a week and do this exercise for five minutes, then ten minutes, building up to however long you can manage and is comfortable and seems useful to you. You might find it helps to join a group to learn more about it.

So this exercise of mindfulness is just about allowing yourself some time to focus on your breathing and for your mind to come back to that single focus. You may be surprised at how much of a grasshopper mind you have (mine is more like a kangaroo), but at all times, try your best not to condemn its wandering; always be gentle, always be kind. Just notice and return. If you have thoughts telling you that you're not doing it right or that it can't work for you, then note these thoughts as typical intrusions and return your attention to your breathing and the airflow at the tip of your nose.

Some people like to have a focal point such as a candle or a flower. Again the issue here is learning how to focus your attention, allowing various thoughts, reflections, concerns, worries and so forth to be there but not your focus. Another variation is to have a mantra – that is, a word or phrase that you can use to focus on in your mind. Some people think you need to be given your mantra, whereas others believe that you can choose your own, such as PEACE, CALM or LOVE.[2]

Applying the principle of mindfulness

Now you can use mindfulness in many different ways. For example, while eating, you might practise really focusing your attention on the taste and texture of the food or, while out walking, really focus on your stride:[3] notice how your feet lift and fall in coordinated action; how a foot lands from heel to toe as it hits the ground; how your arms move and your breathing flows with the action. In mindfulness, you can focus on the thought: 'I am walking.'

A nice mindful practice is mindfulness in the bath. Often when we relax in the bath, we allow our mind to wander all over the place. However, practise a soothing breathing rhythm and also attend to the experience of being in the warm water. Feel how your weight is different. Explore how, from your toes to your head, the warm water is caressing your body. Try to notice and explore every detail of the sensory experience. These exercises can be enhanced if you allow yourself a gentle, compassionate facial expression.

You may wish to be in the moment in a different way by paying attention to your senses. So while you're out walking, direct your attention and notice the sky – keep your focus there. Notice its changing colour from the horizon to overhead, or the rushing of the clouds or their shapes or how the light catches different aspects of them. Or notice the trees with their different shapes, textures, leaf colours, and the feel and taste of the air itself. Again, if the mind wanders, just gently bring it back. Seeing colours, hearing sounds and sensing the air that we are surrounded by can become new experiences for you, focused as you are on what is around you *in this moment*.

When we get depressed, worried or preoccupied, we can withdraw from the world of the senses and from being fully 'in this moment' and instead become focused on our thoughts about tomorrow or yesterday or our feelings of heaviness or the butterflies and anxiety or dread. We won't be living in the present moment but somewhere else. When we're on automatic pilot, we're lost to our thoughts and may hardly notice the outside world. There's evidence that learning to be mindful can help depression because it lifts us away from overfocusing on the negative and gives the brain a chance to rest from being bombarded by negative thoughts.[4]

People who want to use mindfulness as a way to bring them more fully alive in the present moment or help them with painful feelings can practise mindfulness every day using the 'sitting and breathing' exercise or combining mindfulness with yoga. It can be useful to go to a mindfulness or meditation centre, which will bring you in contact with like-minded others and where you will find someone who can guide you in your mindful practice.

Allowing ourselves to relax

We can now move to another exercise using 'notice and return', but this time we are going to focus on allowing ourselves to relax. I'm going to talk about letting tension go, and by this I mean trying not to see tension as a bad thing or your enemy that you have to get rid of, but rather as an understandable way your body has used to try to protect itself by making itself tense and ready for action. We need to be gentle and help our bodies understand that they don't need to be like this right now. So as we let go of our tension, it's like giving the body permission to relax – for which it is grateful.[5]

Exercise: Mindful relaxing

Once again, take up the sitting or lying-down position that suits you and then focus on your breathing until you click into, find or sense the rhythm that feels most comfortable and soothing to you. If that seems hard, don't worry, just breathe in as comfortable a way as you're able. Spend about 30 seconds finding your rhythm – longer if you wish. When you've done that, focus on your legs. Notice how they feel for a moment. Now imagine that all the tension in your legs is flowing down through your legs and down into the floor and away. Let it go on its way.

So, as you breathe in, just note any tension and then, as you breathe out, imagine the tension flowing down through your legs and out through the floor. Imagine your legs *feeling pleased and grateful* that they can let go. Imagine your legs smiling back at you. Sometimes people find it helpful if they slightly tense their muscles as they breathe in and then relax as they breathe out. (You can try that with each of the muscle groups, which we will be going through.) Just spend 30 seconds now letting that tension go with kindness . . .

Now focus on your body and sense the tension in it from your shoulders down to your trunk. Again, as you breathe out, just imagine the tension leaving this part of your body, going down through your legs, down through the floor and away. If it helps, gently tense your stomach and back muscles as you breathe in and then relax as you breathe out. In a way, it can be like imagining emptying a vessel of the tension that's now running through your legs and down through the floor . . . Your body is grateful and you feel kindly towards it. Feel its pleasure.

Now focus on the tips of your fingers and up through your wrists, forearms, elbows, upper arms and shoulders. Imagine that the tension that was there can be released – that you can let go of it. Gently let the tension go so that it can run off down through your body, down through your legs and out through the floor and away – free.

Now imagine the tension that sits in your head and in your neck. It has been your alert system and it would like to be released now – to take a rest. So again, as you breathe out, just imagine it running down through your body, down through your legs and down through the floor and out . . .

So now we can focus on your whole body. Each time you breathe out, focus on the keyword RELAX. Just imagine your body becoming more relaxed . . . Okay, spend a minute or so doing this.

You can end this exercise by taking a deeper breath, moving around a little and stretching out your arms at right angles to your body. Note how your body feels and how gently grateful it is to you for spending time trying to let go of tension. Spend a moment really trying to experience the idea of your body being grateful to you for spending time with it. When you're ready, get up and carry on with your day.

You can practise this exercise as often as you find helpful. It can help with sleep, too. Remember that, if your mind wanders when you do it, you should just gently bring it back to the task at hand – with a slight, knowing, compassionate smile.

The idea is that, as you sit there, allowing yourself to focus on your breathing, you become more relaxed as you become increasingly familiar with your body and more aware of where tension resides in it. Gradually, you may come to think of your body as a friend and take an interest in it and in how you can nurture it, care for it and help it relax. Tension isn't your enemy, to be got rid of. It only arose as a form of protection and to prepare your body for action – so it's actually grateful for its release from your body. It's like telling an army that the battle is over and they can all go home. So focus on the feeling of *gratitude* in your body that comes from doing these exercises.

Variations

Now there are many variations on this basic exercise, and it's up to you how you go about exploring different relaxation exercises and finding the ones that work for you or that you like best. The one that I've given you is fairly standard and helps some people. The idea is to do the practice and then see what happens.

Relaxing through activity

Sometimes people notice that relaxing produces unpleasant feelings in their bodies that are associated with negative emotions, or they find that relaxing actually makes them feel more anxious. This isn't uncommon. In addition, when we're in certain mind/brain states, relaxing might be a bit tough.

If I'm very uptight or agitated about something, what works for me is focusing on soothing breathing along with *some physical activity*. So I might try to focus my mind on the here and now and engage in soothing breathing but also carry out a physical activity such as cycling, digging the garden, taking a walk, doing the dishes (okay, emptying the dish washer) or playing my guitar.

Sensory focusing

When Sue Procter, clinical manager for one of our day services, and I ran a group for people with mental health difficulties, they found mindfulness and relaxing hard to do at first.[6] So we brainstormed the issue together. The people in the group felt that, if they had something they could focus their attention on, other than their breathing and bodies, this might help to get them started.

So together we came up with tennis balls to focus on. Each member of the group would engage in a soothing breathing rhythm and mindful attention but focus on holding a tennis ball, exploring its textures and the way it felt in the hand. And, yes, it made for some very amusing comments: 'Hold on to your balls – we're going mindful!' The point here is that, if you find the breathing focus tricky, don't worry – some people do. So just try to loosen your body as best you can and focus your attention on something else. Later you may find the breathing bit gets easier.

Grounding

In many parts of the world, people use things like worry beads to focus on; they are smooth to the touch and can be run through the fingers. When I lived in Dubai in the late 1960s, I was struck by how many people used worry beads with the very clear understanding that they were intended to help them focus their attention and stay calm.

Sometimes people do like to 'ground' their practice by using a memory trigger. You can do this in a number of ways. One is to find a smooth, semi-precious stone or just one from a beach that you like the look and feel of. As you do your relaxation exercises, hold the stone gently in your hand. Just feel it as you breathe. This will help you link the feeling of your stone to your state of relaxation. Then, later, if you're feeling tense you can just breathe in your usual soothing, rhythmic way while holding your stone, to help ground you slightly. We're going to use the same idea when we look at compassionate imagery in the next chapter.

Another grounding method is to use smell. Some people like to associate relaxation and calm with a scent of some kind. These are all sorts of smells and scents associated with relaxing, such as lavender, and scented oils are now also available at many chemists. If you find one that suits you, you can carry it with you so that, if you want to relax, you can do your breathing exercises while simultaneously using your smell/scent. Psychologists suggest that we can help ourselves to trigger new states of mind if we use multiple senses, such as attention, smell and/or touch, to do so.

As with all the exercises in this book, once you understand the principles of what you're trying to achieve, look to your own feelings and experience to guide you. Try out different things and see what works for you. You have intuitive wisdom; you just need to listen to it.

Keep in mind that these ways of being with your body can also be used when you're active. So while you're doing the washing-up or ironing, you can practise relaxing rather than being on automatic pilot and dwelling on your difficulties. Developing a relaxed body is a way of being kind and gentle to it and nurturing it.

Bringing relaxation into everyday life – the chill-out

Being alone

It's often useful to recognize that, although caring relationships are vital for us, at times it's important to be alone. This can be hard in modern society, with houses designed as small boxes and weather that can trap us inside. By contrast, for million of years we wouldn't have needed to wander far before we were away from others.

Aloneness by choice is, of course, very different to loneliness, which we do not choose. If possible, try to get some time alone. I have known women who feel guilty about telling their families that they need chill-out alone time. One said that, even when she went to take a bath, it wasn't long before voices would call to her: 'Where are you? Where did you put my shirt? Mum, have you seen my homework?'

Try to explain to your family and friends that we all need time to ourselves, just to chill out, become focused and able to relax without having to think about others – and that doesn't mean that you dislike being with people. The point is to put time aside to be alone and think about how to use that time to *nurture and nourish* yourself.

Chill out in your mind

If you're busy, just small chill-outs can be helpful. Keep in mind that what you're trying to do is stimulate brain patterns. Say you get a phone call and someone says something to upset you. Just stop for moment and focus on your breathing. Notice the feelings rippling through your body. As we noted in Chapter 4, there might be a number of different and conflicting ones. Try putting them into words: 'Right now my body is feeling tense. I have this tension and butterflies in my stomach, my face is tense. My mind is leaping from one angry or upset thought to another. Okay, just for a moment let's find that soothing rhythm and stick with that for awhile. My "old brain" will be rushing along as it always does, but I'm just going to be with my soothing rhythm for a moment and watch my thoughts and feelings go by.' Practising in this way can be very helpful. Later we'll be adding compassionate imagery to this work.

Mindfulness in sex

Although it's extremely helpful to set aside time that you can dedicate to mindful practice, it's also useful to bring it into key activities in all facets of your life. Mindfulness can help you enjoy the small things more, to savour your pleasures. One of these, of course, is your sexual enjoyment. Learning to be mindful means that you learn to pay attention to the pleasures of giving and the pleasures you are receiving. By being in the moment, with the feelings as they unfold, we change our orientation from results (racing to or having to have an orgasm) to 'experience in this moment'. This is the basis of tantric sex, and if mindfulness approaches to sex appeal to you, this may be something that you would like to explore in more detail.

Sorry, folks, that's it from me – you'll have to explore this particular pleasure elsewhere! I note it here to highlight how important it is for mindfulness to become a *way of being* in many of the things that we do regularly, not just an activity to be practised at certain times.

Exercise: Becoming an alien for a day

Here's a rather nice, playful exercise – becoming an alien for a day. Try and see if it creates a special type of mindfulness for you and gives you new feelings about being alive.

Imagine that you come from a very different planet, maybe where there is little light and the sky is dark, and you're visiting Earth for the first time. You're fascinated by everything you see and sense – by the sky and its ever-changing patterns, the smell and feel of the air, the sounds around you, the colours of the trees and grass. Allow yourself to be amazed and fascinated by the greenness of living plants. The idea is to begin playfully to experience the world anew, to bring a freshness to your perceptions and senses.

I once read some funny graffiti. Someone had written, 'Is there any intelligent life on this planet?' – clearly they were moaning about some of the silly things that people do. Underneath someone had written: 'Yes, but I'm only visiting.'

Exercises: The art of appreciation

If we can direct our attention to where we want it to be, to the top of our head or to a big toe or to the plants sitting on the windowsill, why not use this ability to stimulate some of our positive emotions. There's an old saying about a glass being seen either as half full or as half empty. When feeling depressed, we see it as half empty; when we feel good, the glass is half full. We know that our moods shift our attention. The glass is the same whatever – it doesn't change, only our feelings towards it and perceptions of it do. But we can practise learning to shift our attention to the things that we appreciate, that stimulate pleasure and other nice feelings in us; we can practise directing our attention to the half full bit of the glass. Here's how.

Each day when you wake up, focus on the things that you like or give you just a smidgen of pleasure. For example, you may like being in a warm bed. So rather than focusing on how having to get out of bed is annoying, smile to yourself at the enjoyment you've had in being comfortable and warm and how, in just 16 hours or so, you can return there. Think about how you'll enjoy taking a shower, drinking your first cup of tea, tasting your breakfast or looking at the paper. When you make your tea and toast, try doing it mindfully. Pay attention to the water, that life-giving fluid, and how the hot water on your tea bag gradually produces a swirl of brown liquid. As for your toast, focus on the taste and feel. Imagine that you're an ant crawling over your toast – it would be a lunar landscape. When was the last time you really tasted fresh toast and butter – I mean, *really* tasted it? Are you aware of what the air of a new spring day *really* smells like? Do you ever take time to really breathe it, notice it and appreciate it? If we're honest, we're so preoccupied thinking ahead to all the issues of the day that all these simple pleasures simply pass us by.

Even when doing something as mundane as the washing-up, notice the warm feeling of the water and the bubbles and the way in which you can almost see rainbows in them. As a child, I was fascinated by the colours you could see in soapy bubbles. We lose our fascination for these everyday things because we, as a species, easily get used to things and always want something new. We're also always thinking about so many other things, one of which is how it's such a drag to have to do the washing-up when we're tired and we want to do so much else – get back to that warm bed for one. But learning to *notice*, to feel and to see, can stimulate our brains in new ways.

Do you take time to appreciate what people do for you? Choose a day and spend time focusing only on the things that you like and appreciate in people, letting go of the things that you don't like. Think about how all of us are so dependent on each other. People have been up since about four o'clock in the morning so that we can have fresh milk, bread and newspapers. And every day they do the same. What about the people you work with – what are their good points? How often do you really focus on those? How often do you make a point of telling them that you appreciate them?

What you're doing in these exercises is practising overruling your threat/self-protection system, which is determined to focus you on the glass as half empty. Its job is to warn you that you might run out of water or to make you exclaim: 'Hey, what happened to the other half? Some bugger drank it!' It's what it's designed to do, and you could let it do that. But let's start to take control of our feelings and *deliberately* use our attention to practise stimulating emotion systems that give rise to brain patterns that create good feelings. Appreciation is one way of practising doing this.

Now the key thing is the *spirit of kindness and playfulness* embodied in this exercise. When we do appreciation work, it's very easy for us to think how lucky we are compared to so many people in the world, who may be starving or lack basic comforts. We have warm beds, nice food, nice cars and so on. If we have anything more than an earth floor under our feet, we are in the top 50 per cent of the world's population. If we have a house with a roof, we're in the top 20 per cent. Few of us in the West go to bed hungry at a risk of our lives.

However, that kind of thinking is actually not helpful to you in this exercise, though it can be useful for developing a moral conscience. The reason we have to be careful with this way of thinking is that it is negatively focused and, I'm afraid, is part of our threat/self-protection system. There will be a tinge of *feeling bad* at not appreciating things; there will be the feeling that we *ought to* or *should* enjoy things more. The problem is that we can never feel really good if what we feel is accompanied by 'ought' or 'should'. Genuine appreciation is learning to take joyful pleasure; it's not about 'ought' or 'should' feelings. Your brain is more likely to develop joyful pleasure capacities if you choose to train it and direct its attention; you can help your 'new brain/mind' to gain more control over your 'old brain/mind'.

Revisiting mindfulness

So mindfulness has many aspects to it. It can be a form of observing and focusing the attention on specific things, like the in-flowing and out-flowing of breath, a mantra of OM or PEACE, a focus on a candle or a plant or closely observing a common activity such as walking or washing-up. These forms of attentiveness are designed to help us become aware of how the mind tries to pull our attention away from the focus in *this moment*. By training the attention to return in a gentle and calm way to the focus, the mind gradually settles. When it settles or begins to experience 'settled-ness', we become more conscious of simply being conscious and aware. We reside in the 'consciousness of consciousness', and as a result, the mind experiences itself in a slightly different way.

Mindfulness can also be used to direct attention to specific elements and aspects of our lives. We take control over what we attend to rather than allowing our attention to be directed by whatever emotions happen to be activated at the time. So much of our lives are lived on automatic pilot; we're just floating along on the currents of feeling and shifting brain states as we engage in everyday life. But suppose we actually chose to refocus our attention in a way that *we* want to. Suppose we practise having a fresh focus to our attention through imagining ourselves as aliens, or we practise focusing and attending to things we enjoy, like and appreciate. In this way, we can start to take control over the patterns we want to be created in our brains. This is one of the most exciting and important understandings of modern psychology.

Brain changing

As we've already noted, different styles of attention stimulate different patterns in the brain. This is no different from being aware that, if you focus on sexual things, you will stimulate your pituitary and so create changes in your body. What is fascinating, though, is that, if we use our attention to stimulate patterns in the brain, the brain will rewire itself. We already know that 'neurons that fire together wire together' – the process is very subtle and takes time, but it puts you back in control.

In the next chapter, we're going to focus on imagery more specifically. When working with imagery, it does help for us to be mindful, having learned to be gentle and notice when our minds have gone off-task and how to bring them back in a compassionate way. These are the secrets of mindfulness.

Sadness

Although I hope you will enjoy and have some fun with these exercises and develop a new fascination for your mind and being in the world, you should be aware that, in becoming mindful, previously unaddressed issues may surface. Sometimes when people practise mindfulness, they can become sad and at times tearful because they're now open to these sorts of difficulties. Once the mind stops rushing from thing to thing, it can begin to experience the more subtle levels of itself. For instance, Jennifer discovered that working with a compassionate form of mindfulness made her feel sad, and she came to realize that she was in touch with a memory of the death of her mother five years earlier. In her heart, she knew that she'd been avoiding grieving, almost as if, if she didn't grieve, then maybe her mother had not really died.

So if you have sad or anxious feelings arising during your mindfulness work, try and stay with them: be mindful of them and observant, maybe write about them in your journal. If you have friends or a partner with whom you can discuss your feelings, then do so. If, however, these feelings become a block and you'd like to find a way to deal with them, you may want to find a mindfulness or meditation teacher or a therapist to work with and share your experiences. If sadness is key for you, you might find *The Mindful Way Through Depression: Freeing yourself from chronic unhappiness* by Mark Williams and his colleagues very helpful.[7]

The point is that there's nothing wrong with you or with your mindfulness if you find that distressing feelings are bubbling up; this may simply be an indication that there are things you could address and perhaps it would be a good idea to obtain the help of others at this time in your life.

Conclusion

This chapter has guided us through some ideas on mindfulness, on developing a soothing breathing rhythm, on ways to think about and engage with relaxation, and on the importance of giving yourself space to practise. In our busy lives, this is not always easy and so we have to grab slices of time to spend on ourselves when we can. The key, however, is to seize every opportunity just to gently engage in soothing breathing and practise mindfulness. You could even try it while commuting to work because it's better for you to be doing those exercises than for your mind to be focusing on how irritated you are about traffic jams or late trains. It's all about bringing this attitude into every facet of our lives.

However, to develop mindfulness in such a way that you begin to understand the nature of your mind and develop insights into it, you'll need to give yourself space and time. Of course, you know perfectly well that, just as you need to do it to be physically fit or to learn how to play a musical instrument really well, you'll need to put time aside to practise. Sitting with one's thoughts and feelings and simply observing them usually results in us initially becoming aware of a rush of thoughts and concerns and multiple worries and desires, but gradually they subside. We shouldn't be surprised by that because, until you start this practice, these aspects of your mind will have been going full tilt and you will have become very skilled at generating a whole range of thoughts and feelings that all push for your attention.

Also keep in mind that it is best to practise when things are calm for you, don't just try using these skills to calm you when you're distressed. Practise when calm and develop your skills first.

There is nothing hard about being mindful because there is *nothing to achieve* in the doing of it. But there is nothing easy about mindfulness either. When we let go of trying to 'make something happen' and just be in the moment as observers, we become observers of the most extraordinary thing – namely, consciousness itself. To become fully conscious of consciousness, of being conscious and aware of being aware, can be fascinating. So have fun, explore different facets of mindful meditation and maybe make it part of your life. As I've indicated, however, I hope you'll also feel able to reach out and find a group in your area that can help you in your explorations.

8 Compassionate Mind Training through Imagery

Cast your mind back to Chapter 6 and recall the discussion about how thoughts and images can affect our brains and bodies. Take another look at Diagram 2 (p. 186). Remember how we explored the way imagining a meal in all its detail can stimulate stomach acids and saliva, or how focusing on our hot sexual fantasies can cause changes in our bodies? Well, we can use this basic principle to help us develop compassionate patterns in our brains, too. Compassion-focused exercises, linked to imagery, thinking and behaviour (what I call the 'compassion skills' – *see* pp. 207–10), have been key to Buddhist practice for a long time. Those who focus on mindfulness have a slightly different tradition than those who focus on compassion, but most practitioners believe that they are like two wings of a bird and fly together.[1]

We've seen that much of what goes on in our minds is non-rational to an extent and also isn't our fault – we're built like this. However, we also want and need to get more control over our minds. It would help if we could develop our ability to be self-soothing. It will not protect us from the pains and tragedies of life, but it can help us to deal with them in different ways. So let's now move on to specific exercises, keeping in mind that we're practising trying to stimulate certain kinds of feelings, sensations and mind–body states within us.

With all these exercises, some people can experience shimmers of self-focused kindness and warmth quite quickly, whereas others have more difficulty. If at first you get little from these exercises, try not to worry as things can take time to get going. Also, there are many exercises in this book, some of which might suit you better than others. Consider Kim who practised some compassionate imagery most days but didn't get much out of it. None the less she kept putting time aside daily to try it. Still not much happened. Then one day someone was kind to her and she experienced this warm flush of feeling and felt a smile spread across her face, just as she had been practising with her imagery. She suddenly realized that she was indeed beginning to feel more warmth in her life. So sometimes you just have to hang in there.

We're going to look at various types of exercises. Some will focus on generating compassionate feelings from *memory*. Others will concentrate on creating these feelings from *desires* and *fantasies*.

The compassionate desire to be happy

Exercise: Exploring the desire to be at peace

In this first exercise, we'll explore your desire to be at peace with yourself. This is what you do. First, engage in a soothing, *mindful* breathing rhythm for about a minute. Adopt a relaxed posture. If you wish, work through your body, relaxing from your feet upwards while staying alert. Then make a half-smile, noticing how your facial muscles create a gentle, compassionate expression. Again, spend about a minute on this. Now allow your attention to come back to yourself. In Buddhist practice, there's a focused exercise that is linked to developing *loving kindness for the self* – a friendly, caring motivation to be free from suffering. You imagine your heart area opening up and you gently repeat: 'May I be well. May I be happy. May I be free from suffering.' You imagine these phrases going into your heart area repeatedly.

Here's an adaptation of that basic exercise:

- Recognize yourself as a being created in the flow of life; like all of us, you've just found yourself here.

- Now consider your deep and true desire to be at peace with yourself and have a kind and contented mind.

- Focus on your desire to be free from suffering and in a state where you'll experience full well-being.

- Become familiar with what that desire feels like.

- Focus on what it feels like to know within yourself that there's a part of you that understands the struggles of the flow of life and *really* wants peaceful contentment.

- Be clear to yourself that this part of you is *wise* and *caring*; it's not the part that feels exhausted and thinks, 'Oh yeah, anything for a rest – I'm knackered.' The part that really wants peaceful contentment may recognize how tired you are but *that* part isn't tired.

Try and spend as long as you can focusing on these. After you've practised for as long as is comfortable, write down any thoughts you've had in your compassionate journey notebook (*see* p. 221). Writing is useful for reflection and can also act as a memory or journey trail for you. What you might find interesting is whether you noticed any resistance to the idea of really wanting to be content and at peace – any thoughts that this is difficult to achieve or even that you don't deserve to be peaceful, or fears of being peaceful, for example that you might miss out on other life opportunities or let your guard down. At this point, just note them with interest. Also jot down what it feels like to think that there's a part of you that genuinely desires a state of well-being for yourself.

Exercise: Experiencing peaceful joyfulness

In the next imagery exercise, which you might want to try a few days later, imagine yourself experiencing a certain *peaceful joyfulness* – that is, not just being content and at peace but feeling more joyful and happy. This joyful feeling also links with our drive and energizing system. Happiness of this type relates to a slightly different balance or pattern of interactions between the drive/excitement and soothing/contentment systems than that which operates with contented peacefulness.

It's very useful to be aware of the kinds of thoughts that emerge during these exercises. When your mind wanders, just gently bring it back on task.

For me, focusing on peacefulness and joyfulness enabled me to understand that there's a certain restlessness within me. I found the exercise more difficult than I'd imagined I would. I became aware that I had thoughts about not becoming *too* peaceful, content or joyful because of a feeling in the back of my mind that there was always more to do. It was strange but I suddenly became aware that I was slightly uncomfortable with the idea of peaceful joyfulness. Would you believe it? I noticed feelings and thoughts that seem to be telling me: 'It's all right for you having peaceful joyfulness. What about those other poor souls?' Dear, oh, dear. And, yes, that does link to various issues in my background and – who knows? – maybe even to my genes. Of course, the important thing here is to stay compassionate, to smile to yourself, to be grateful for your discovery and to think about how you want to deal with it.

These exercises can be useful in themselves for stimulating brain patterns within us, but they can also be valuable because they illuminate interesting thoughts that may be blocking our path to personal well-being and developing self-compassion. So to deeply, truly and fully *want* ourselves to be at peace or happy may not be as straightforward as it looks. Strange that, isn't it? People I've worked with have noticed that they had thoughts like 'If I become content, I'll miss out on things and fall behind' or 'I might be peaceful but life won't be much fun' – which, of course, would then lead to them not feeling content. The interesting thing here is the *fear* of contentment. It's important not to worry about that but to be grateful that you have discovered it in yourself and then think about how you would like to move forward on these issues.

One of the things you might do is consider the feelings and meaning of contentment itself. 'Contentment' might actually involve a degree of striving towards a goal or a commitment to a cause or to finding a meaningful way of life. The Dalai Lama has been deeply committed to flying around the world to try to increase compassion in the world – but is also very content and at peace within himself. So we're talking about inner states of mind here. It's not so much that we need to find contentment outside our goals, but we should be wary of making contentment *conditional* on achieving them: 'I can *only* be content if I succeed at X or Y.' So creating states of contentment within ourselves is not the death of our commitment to a cause or to our pursuit of meaning or knowledge. These can be most interesting meditations and reflections. What in life do you value and want to commit yourself to?

Using imagery

We are now going to use our imagination and deliberately try to create different types of imagery. A word of caution here, however. For most people, such images are not sharp photographs in the mind; rather, if we get anything at all, it's fleeting impressions of things. If you think about those meal or sexual fantasy examples again, the images you created then were more impressionistic than vivid. So it will be the same when we come up with compassionate imagery and explore feeling compassion by revisiting it in memories.

The key things are the *feelings* that the imagery generates within you. I've done compassionate imagery where some people never really see any clear images, but it was the sense and feeling of compassion that were important. Also, some individuals find imagining sounds and voice tones easier than creating visual images. In fact, one of the reasons why religions often have icons, such as of Jesus or the Buddha, is because, with the icon that you can see and/or hold, you have a ready-made image and don't have to create one yourself. So in the practice that follows, be kind and gentle and accept that what may be coming to your mind is fairly impressionistic rather than clear and vivid.

Exercises: Using memory to create compassionate feelings

We are now going to switch from exercises exploring emotions and desires to be happy, and try to create compassionate feelings by using memory. Here's a useful exercise to try.

As with all these exercises, sit comfortably with a good straight posture, engage with your soothing breathing rhythm for a short while and then engage with the exercise when you feel you can attend to it. Start by trying to recall someone who was caring, kind and warm towards you. Try to imagine a specific event and then focus on the *details* of that – what was happening? Don't pick something that was very distressing for you because then your attention will be focused on the upset caused by the difficulties that you experienced. The purpose of this exercise is to recall how you felt when you experienced the kindness of another. So focus on the kind person's facial expressions, his/her voice tones and general manner. Focus on as much *specific detail* that you remember as you can. What feelings were being directed at you? Could you sense those coming from the kind person? Explore your feelings about receiving kindness. Can you sense them in your body? You're exploring from memory feelings of kindness and compassion *flowing into* yourself. When you've finished, you may want to note down your thoughts and feelings in your journal – maybe note the memory itself and what it felt like going into it again.

Our next memory exercise is to focus on compassion as 'arising within the self' and *flowing out*. Recall a time or times when you have felt kind, warm and caring towards another person (an adult or child or even towards an animal) who was in some distress. Again, don't recall times when you were trying to help others in major distress because of problems, traumas or accidents, or if you had heightened anxious and 'need to rescue' feelings. If you do, you might be reminded of feeling alarmed and unsure whether you could help that individual or becoming upset by their upset. It's not the 'distress of the other' that we want to bring to mind; rather, the focus should be on your feelings of warmth, understanding and kindness. So it's better to start with gentle(ish) feelings of wanting others to experience well-being. It is the warmth and kindness that is *flowing from you* to the other person that is important here.

So, again, engage your soothing breathing rhythm, close your eyes or look down and really try to bring a memory to mind in all its *sensory* details. What was happening? If you could see yourself, how would you look? How were you feeling? What's the tone of your voice? What expressions are on your face? Notice if anything happens to your feelings or bodily senses. No worries if nothing does – it's just interesting to notice if something does happen. Recognize these memories and what it *feels* like when you focus on warmth and kindness for others. Again, jot down your reflections in your journal. Which exercise did you find easier – compassion flowing in or compassion flowing out?

Exercises: The desire for others to be happy

So far we have reflected on our feelings when we recalled being kind to another adult, child or animal in the past, but you can extend this in an imagery exercise to the here and now. Imagine directing kindness towards people you care about. Bring them to mind, see their faces and how they move, what it is you love about them, remembering that in mental imagery you usually only get fleeting impressions, not clear pictures. Now explore the feelings emerging from this desire for them to be happy, peaceful and content. You might repeat in your mind the Buddhist statements: 'May you be well. May you be happy. May you be free from suffering.' They, like you, have simply found themselves here in this world and are doing the best they can. Sometimes this realization might make you sad because you're actually rather worried about them. Or it might make you tearful as your emotions overflow with the desire for good things to happen to them. Or perhaps you just experience a gentle sense of warmth for them. Note these experiences; you can later reflect on them as stimulating specific brain patterns within you. Keep in mind that thinking of them as brain patterns is not in any way to reduce these feelings or explain them away. They are important, meaningful experiences in the flow of life.

Now our feelings are likely to be strongest towards those we are attached to, have shared our lives with and are genetically related to. None the less, it's useful to begin to widen the circle of people to whom you direct compassionate feelings. First, imagine directing towards your friends your desire for them to be happy, content, peaceful and free from suffering. See them in your mind's eye as best you can. Imagine that you truly wish for their contentedness and happiness. Don't rush through this – allow time for things to emerge in your mind. See your friends actually smiling and becoming happy and free from suffering.

When you're ready to move on, focus on people you don't know very well and, as before, think about your desire for them to be peaceful, content and happy. They, too, have just found themselves here and want to be happy and free from suffering. Then you can imagine directing kindness towards all your neighbours and those in your local area (okay, yes, and to your local football team, who you hope will do well today). Keep extending this desire for others to be content, peaceful and happy to your city, to your country and to the world. You'll end up wishing for all living things in the flow of life to flourish and be free from suffering. You can extend this through time so that your desire for warmth, contentment and peacefulness is not just for people and things living now but for all living things to come in the future. In studies of the effects on brain physiology of having compassion for others, this was the exercise used where an 'unconditional feeling of loving-kindness and compassion pervades the whole mind as a way of being with no other consideration or discursive thoughts'.[2]

At some point, you may realize that, by extending your desire for others to be content, peaceful and happy, you're going to have to include people you don't particularly like, those who have done you harm and even your enemies. Although it's a bit trickier, extending your desire for contentment, peace and happiness to these people can be a very useful exercise if you've built up to it. You have to remember that none of us has chosen to be here in this life, nor did we choose the genes that we were born with or the archetypes that can so easily set one against another, or the conditioning we were given. We're all actors in the flow of life. We hurt each other because we're ignorant and because it's so difficult for us to be truly and fully in control of our own minds.

Buddhists sometimes talk about the 'eradication of hatred' from within ourselves. But 'eradication' is a word linked to hate itself, indicating that one 'hates' hate. In compassionate mind training, we approach nothing with the attitude of eradication. Rather we approach it from the position of understanding, compassion and transcendence. Transcendence is quite different to eradication – it's about moving beyond or 'no longer being influenced by', rather than destroying or 'getting rid of'.

I should repeat here that, in Buddhist practice, a major idea is: 'May I and others be free from suffering.' Sometimes the focus can be on 'May I bear my suffering' or 'May I have compassion for my suffering.' I've found that my patients sometimes find that this is easier for them to do and helps them develop courage to face difficult things. The key thing is to listen to your own inner wisdom and see what resonates for you.

The music of compassion and the role of sadness

Some imagery practice and meditations can also be practised with chants, songs, music or drums or bells – i.e. facilitated through the use of sound.[3] We know that music can be extremely powerful in evoking feelings. That's why, in many films, the moods and feelings of certain scenes are accentuated by the soundtrack. Music can connect us to and stimulate emotions that we may have to struggle to gain contact with in other ways. You may want to explore different pieces of music for yourself and see which helps you reach feelings of compassion towards yourself, towards others and indeed towards the world.

Sometimes this sort of music can be tinged with sadness. There are various aspects of Sufi music that are designed to create within the listener a sense of yearning, an awareness of separation. I still remember when I lived in Dubai in the 1960s and heard the *muezzins* calling the faithful to prayer from minarets around the city as the sky turned pink with a new dawn – it was powerfully emotive. These songs and music are also designed to be heard in groups so that they produce a sense of connectedness with the experience. For me, the first track on Hans Zimmer's soundtrack CD for the 2003 film *The Last Samurai* captures something sad and spiritual in this tradition and offers a powerful, nonverbal sense of compassion.

Music can help us experience feelings with complex textures and mixtures that aren't easily described in words. Indeed, it often speaks to our pain and suffering and helps us induce, communicate and share this with others. Musical traditions such as Spanish Flamenco and Portuguese Fado are designed to touch the pathos in us. And as I mentioned in the last chapter, Gorecki's Third Symphony was written as a testament to the suffering of the last century.

It's interesting, therefore, to reflect that, when we focus on a desire for others to be happy, there can be also an element of sharing in 'the tears of the world' – that is, we're moved by the suffering of the world and have sympathy with and are emotionally moved by the suffering of life.

Importantly, some types of sadness are not anti-compassion feelings – quite the opposite, in fact. It can open us up to a sense of connectedness

– we are all in the same flow of life, subject to the same tragedies, wanting somehow to find connection and liberation from suffering. Indeed, in compassion-focused therapy sadness can be a very important feeling state. So compassion is not just about 'happiness' but about connectedness, sympathy and empathy and tolerating and sharing emotions (*see* p. 194).

However, there are so many textures to compassion that other kinds of music can generate different types of feelings. For example, some people may prefer music that resembles the sound of running water, or is mystical or has a certain joyousness to it or a calming, soothing quality. It can be interesting to search out pieces of music and notice how they stimulate different feelings in you.

Exercise: The compassionate self

The tantric schools of Buddhism believe that the seeds of many different 'selves' are in each of us, and it's what we choose to feed and nurture through commitment and practice that's key to our development. Our Buddha nature is already in us, waiting for the 'mental watering' that will enable it to grow.

This next exercise has some resonance with that view. However, I got into it in an unusual way. In the 1970s, psychiatrist Bill Hughes, an academic tutor interested in the arts, brought us young psychologists and psycho-analysts in training together with some actors. The two groups began to explore different methods of achieving empathy. When asked how we'd understand depression and anxiety, the actors were highly focused *creating the feelings inside themselves* – actually trying to become and feel like a depressed or anxious person. They spoke of how they'd focus on facial expressions, body postures, tones of voice and inner feelings. We psychologists, on the other hand, wanted to understand these emotional states from the outside looking in, to think about the symptoms of an anxious or depressed person and make a diagnosis or problem list. However, we were encouraged to do some acting and imagine being anxious or depressed ourselves – really get into the role! It was fascinating training and encouraged me to practise trying to create states of mind in myself. Sadly, 'acting training' to teach health professionals and therapists is not used these days. I learned a lot from it, though, including the ideas behind this exercise.

So if you've ever fancied being an actor or even a Hollywood star, now's your chance – well, at least to practise in your own home. This next exercise is about getting into a role from the inside and involves us practising the body postures and body states of compassion.

Basically you're going to *get into the role* of a wise, compassionate person, as if you're an actor who, in order to convince your audience, has to live this part from the inside. To do that, you must really get in touch with what it is to be *that person*. Just as a good actor studies the individual whom they're going to portray and tries to re-create the role within themselves, you're going to do the same – you're going to become the perfect, ideal, compassionate person. Now you may have an individual in mind; you might decide that you want to become like the Buddha or someone whom you consider your compassionate ideal. The idea is not to become *them* as such but to use them as a guide or inspiration for you to become the most compassionate that you can. There are many texts that discuss doing this.[4]

Here's what to do. First, stand loosely and relaxed, looking down or to where your vision is most comfortable. Adopt a soothing breathing rhythm for 30 seconds or so. Allow your body to relax and go as loose as it is able. Now, for a moment, imagine that *you* are a deeply compassionate and wise person. Think of the *ideal* qualities that you would like to have as a compassionate person. These might include: deep kindness, warmth, gentleness, being difficult to provoke, a sense of having 'been there' and gaining wisdom as a result. It doesn't matter if you actually have these qualities or not, because you're focusing on *imagining* and *thinking* about what it would be like to have them, what they are and your desire to develop them. So think about your age and appearance, your facial expressions and posture, your inner emotions of, say, gentleness. Now, like an actor about to take on a part, feel yourself *become* these.

Try to allow your facial expressions to be gentle and *compassionate*; allow yourself a slight, gentle smile. Think about the idea that you are a wise person who has seen much in life. When you speak, think about the tone of your voice. Think about what it's like to be a forgiving person who doesn't bear grudges. Think about the qualities that you really value in compassion and imagine having them. Allow yourself to become this person. Spend as long as is comfortable practising this role, and try and do it seriously but also playfully. With this exercise, it can be interesting to notice how it affects your body, including your posture, breathing rate and so forth. Do you notice your muscles becoming tense or more relaxed and softer? Are there any areas of your body that feel warm?

You can practise this at any time of the day (or night) if you wish. As you move around in your life, imagine being (and becoming) this compassionate person. To begin with, it may feel a bit artificial but it can also be great fun. Do be cautious, though. I remember, one morning before work, doing my compassion practice while slowly walking, focusing on all the qualities that I'd like to have for the day ahead, keeping my attention to the present moment – and I got quite carried away. Then I remembered that I'd left the porridge boiling away, rushed back to check it and fell flat over a footstool. So do be careful!

Over subsequent weeks, you can practise your focus on becoming compassionate by re-creating compassionate body postures, facial expressions and voice tones. All these are designed to help you think about and focus on becoming self-compassionate and exploring how that affects your feelings and body. Keep in mind that you're in *training*, learning to cope with the frustrations and anxieties of life.

Compassion fantasies and imagery

Imagery has been employed by many Western psychological therapies for quite a few decades.[5] How it's used varies. It can help people with things they are frightened of – i.e. phobias. For instance, people who are scared of spiders might begin their therapy by *imagining* a spider, then drawing one, moving on to touching a toy one, then a dead one, then a real one.

Imagery is also employed to help people mentally go over things that have been traumatic for them and so face them rather than avoid thinking about or feeling them. If they avoid such memories and fear, they can suffer flashbacks and various other kinds of symptoms. Athletes, too, use a lot of imagery in their training – for example, imagining over and over again playing the right shot – and imagery can also help us develop confidence and to stimulate arousal (e.g. sexual arousal).

In fact, imagery has been carefully researched and its use is now regarded as a more powerful way to produce change in certain feeling states and situations than talking or 'thinking' methods.

Exercise: Finding your safe place

Before we engage in specific compassion exercises that are designed for self-soothing, it can be quite useful to practise 'safe place' imagery. First, go through the brief relaxation exercise that we tried in Chapter 7 (*see* pp. 230–4). Then allow your mind to focus on a place that gives you a feeling of *safeness, calm* and *contentment*. This place may vary from day to day; you don't always have to have the same one, although sticking with one place can be helpful.

Your place might be a beautiful wood where the leaves of the trees dance gently in the breeze, and powerful shafts of light illuminate the ground. Try to feel the wind gently brushing your face and get a sense of the light dancing in front of you. Hear the rustle of the trees, and smell the woodiness and sweetness of the air. Or your place may be a beautiful beach with a shining blue sea stretching to the horizon where it meets the crystal blue sky. Underfoot is soft, fine, white sand that's silky to the touch. You can hear the gentle hushing of the waves on the shore. Try and feel the sun on your face, sense the light dancing in diamonds on the water, feel the soft sand under your feet as your toes dig into it and feel a light breeze delicately touching your face. Or your safe place might be by a log fire, where you can hear the crackle of the burning wood and smell the smoke. The technique here is to try to compile as much sensory detail of your image as you can.

Now this is your own, unique safe place. You can add to the feelings by imagining that this place really *welcomes* you and *enjoys* you being here. So focus on a sense of belonging here because it is your own, unique place. A feeling of being welcomed can be very useful in this kind of imagery. You can practise any time – for instance, while waiting for a bus or lying in the bath or in bed. Again, people vary on how easy they find this exercise.

Now when you become stressed or upset, you can practise a soothing breathing rhythm for a few minutes and then take yourself to this place in your mind, allowing yourself to settle down and give yourself some chill-out time. Remember to work through all the senses in your imagery.

Compassion–focused imagery

There are now many studies in which researchers have taken pictures of the brain as people were asked to perform different tasks, including imagining things. We now know that, if I were to ask you to imagine being angry or happy or sexual or anxious, different patterns would light up in your brain. Compassion-focused imagery and practice can also affect various brain pathways.[6] It's not just your brain, though: Atkinson and McCraty[7] explored the impact that anger imagery and compassionate imagery had on the body's immune system by measuring a substance in the body called secretory immunoglobulin A (s-IgA). Anger imagery had a negative effect on s-IgA, while compassionate imagery increased it. Therefore, among the many things that compassionate imagery might do is alter the body's neurophysiological systems positively.

Compassionate imagery is well established in Buddhism and other religious traditions, which use it to put adherents into certain mental states. There are a variety of rituals and meditative practices that are designed to help participants tune in to and feel compassion.[8] For example, a set of Buddhist ones consists of a series of steps, each of which is a focus for practice. The steps are: imagining a certain type of Buddha; imagining the Buddha harnessing the compassion in the universe; imagining the Buddha directing that compassion energy to you and what that feels like (i.e. being given and receiving compassion unconditionally); imagining the Buddha merging with you and you feeling the nature of compassion; imagining being full of compassion (being a compassion Buddha yourself); and then imagining giving compassion to all living things in the universe.

There is no single compassion Buddha image; instead a variety of them have been developed for compassionate imagery practices. They each have a different function, being used to inspire and develop spiritual awareness but also to calm people when distressed.[9] In Buddhist practice, the initiate focuses on certain images or figures. These are viewed as having developed, in themselves the refined qualities of compassion. At one time, they were just ordinary humans and didn't have these qualities, but with experience, insight and practice, they developed them and can now understand what a struggle it is to be human, as well as the road to compassion. These images are called the *compassion bodhisattvas* (*bodhi* means 'awakening' or 'enlightenment' and *sattva* is a sentient self-aware being). The *bodhisattva* of compassion appears in different forms in different traditions. In Tibet, he is called Chenrezig but is also known as Avalokiteshvara. The *bodhisattvas* of compassion can be meditated on in many male and female forms (e.g. for their qualities of wisdom or kindness), the idea being to awaken these aspects of one's own self – what is called 'archetypal awakening'.[10]

Imagining your ideal 'compassionate other'

The usual way we experience compassion is, of course, through the kindness of others. Compassion usually flows in and through relationships. So we can practise stimulating and activating our systems that react to social safeness and 'feeling cared for' with a soothing response, by using our imaginations and relating to 'compassionate others'. Just as we can imagine ideal meals or ideal sexual partners who can stimulate our bodies in specific ways (*see* p. 186), so we can create inner images that can stimulate the soothing system. The idea here is to play with, create, discover, build and develop compassionate imagery.

So let's think about how we might create a compassionate image that we can relate to and use to stimulate our compassion and inner soothing. When using *fantasy images*, we'll focus on our *ideal compassionate image* and how to converse with him, her or it. So when you think of compassion, what kinds of images come to mind? What colours are associated with compassion for you? Which sounds and textures? Take a moment to just chill out and think about all this.

To develop a compassionate image, you want to do more than just focus on its soothing qualities. Try to imagine it having four basic qualities:

1 *A wise mind.* It understands what it means to be a human being, to struggle, to suffer, to have rage, to have desires, to feel joy. It understands the creation of mind – with all its complex feelings, strategies and archetypes, all of which can conflict – as part of the flow of life, but it knows how to cope with these.

2 *Strength and fortitude.* It can endure and tolerate, and also has the strength to defend and protect if necessary.

3 *Great warmth and kindness.* This radiates from and around the image. In some Buddhist practices, the initiate imagines the compassion Buddha sending compassion to them in the form of energy.

4 *Non-judgemental.* Our compassionate image is never condemning, judging or critical. This doesn't mean that it doesn't have desires or preferences; indeed its main desire is for your well-being and flourishing.

Okay, so we've got some key qualities that we're going to build into our compassionate image. The idea here is to create one that is *unique* and *special* to you. The image is yours and yours alone. Some people like to use religious images – for example, of the Buddha or Christ. If these are helpful, then by all means use them, but for our specific compassion exercises here, it's better to create a new image from scratch, one that will suit you exactly.

There are two reasons why you should do this. First, the idea of it being an 'ideal' means that it is ideal to *you* (it may not be ideal to anyone else). So you should give it every quality that's important to you, just as if you were trying to come up with your ideal house, meal or car – you'd give it everything that you wanted and wouldn't hold back. So it is with your ideal compassionate image: you imagine it to have every aspect of compassion that is important to you. Second, my colleagues and I find that if people use religious images such as Christ, there can be associations that are not helpful, such as the worry that Christ would be rather 'down' on sin, whereas the compassionate image is never judgemental or punitive in any way.

Exercise: Building a compassionate image

Find somewhere to sit comfortably, where you won't be disturbed. Decide if you want to play a CD of chants or other music or, say, turn on a water feature or some other sensory aspect in the room. Later, you may not want these additions, but they can be helpful to start with, to create the right mood. Sit with your eyes looking down or closed, and engage in a soothing breathing rhythm. When you feel that your body is now into the rhythm of breathing, start to imagine your ideal of compassion. Bring a compassionate expression to your face with a slight, gentle smile and consider the following: If you could design for yourself your ideal 'compassionate other' (which may or may not be human), what qualities would they have? What would they look like? If you're struggling, try this exploration: If you could design the ideal 'compassionate other' for a child, what qualities would they have? How would they change as the child grows and what would they be like when the child is an adult?

On pages 259–60, you'll find a worksheet that can help guide you. Read through the instructions on it, then engage in a soothing breathing rhythm for 30 seconds and allow your image to come. The idea is to do it mindfully so, if your mind wanders, just bring it back into focus. Try to go into as much sensory detail as you can. For example, think about how old the image is, its gender, what its eyes look like, whether you can see them smiling. Do you have a sense of their hair style and colour, their clothes and posture? Next, focus on the tone of their voice: if they communicate with you, what would their compassionate tone sound like? If there are any other sensory qualities that you would like your compassionate image to have, bring them into your exercise.

One person I worked with didn't bring to mind a person but a tall, leafy tree. That became her compassion image – a wise tree. It had been there for a long time and she felt that she could snuggle into its branches and be protected. Another person had an image of a Buddha dressed as an Earth goddess, and felt that it was both male and female in its essence. She never saw this image clearly, but it conveyed a sense of nurturing and great warmth to her and she'd focus on it when she was distressed.

Worksheet 1: Building a compassionate image

This exercise is intended to help you build a compassionate image for you to work with and develop key areas of your mind. You can have more than one image if you wish, and they may well change over time. Whatever image comes to mind or you choose to work with, remember that it's your creation and therefore your own personal ideal: what you would really like from feeling cared for and cared about, understood, supported and encouraged.

In this practice, it's important that you try to give your image certain qualities, including:

- wisdom
- strength
- warmth
- non-judgement.

So as you deal with each box below, think about these qualities and imagine what they would look, sound and feel like.

If possible, begin by focusing on your breathing, finding your soothing rhythm and making a half smile. Then let images emerge in your mind as best you can. Don't try too hard – if nothing comes into your mind or it wanders, just gently bring it back to your breathing and practise compassionate accepting.

Here are some questions that might help you:

- Would you want your caring/nurturing image to feel/look/seem:
  - old or young?
  - male or female?
  - human or non-human (e.g. an animal, sea or light)?
- What colours and sounds are associated with the qualities of wisdom, strength, warmth and non-judgement? (Indeed if you only have a sense of a compassion colour surrounding you that feels warm and caring, that's a good start. Remember your colour and image have compassion for you.)

Worksheet 1 *continued*

How would you like your ideal caring/compassionate image to look – that is, what visual qualities should it have?

How would you like your ideal caring/compassionate image to sound (e.g. voice tone)?

What other sensory qualities does your ideal caring/ compassionate image have?

How would you like your ideal caring/compassionate image to relate to you?

How would you like to relate to your ideal caring/ compassionate image?

Think about how you would like your image to relate to you. Some people would like their compassionate images to appear older and wiser and very protective – for instance, the woman who thought of the tree was focused on protection. Other people like imagining being cared for or about. One person wanted her image to truly understand how painful and difficult certain aspects of her life had been and still were. A compassionate image can also give you the feeling that you are an important, valued member of a team or community. This can be quite useful in helping you think about feelings of belonging and how you are in relation to others pursuing similar goals. You might also think about how you would like to relate to your image, how you would like to speak to it, the kinds of things you would want to communicate to it.

It can sometimes be useful to experiment with different *genders* for your image. If yours tends to be female, then imagine an ideal compassionate male image and vice versa. Sometimes if we have negative feelings towards one or other gender, this exercise can be helpful, but it can also bring up great resistance – so only explore if it is helpful. You can have more than one image; indeed, you may find that your image changes with your mood. You may have both male and female images that bring different kinds of compassion to you, or images which blend both genders.

Difficulties finding an image?

If, over time, you find that you're struggling to create a visual image, it may be that sounds can help you. Try focusing on the sound of a compassionate voice. Is it male or female, softly spoken or powerful?

Another thing you can try is to search magazines for pictures of compassionate faces and then use what you find as a template to get started on your imagery. Research has shown that, if people practise focusing on pictures of smiling faces, they gradually train their brains to pick up on these cues, which can have an impact on their self-esteem.[11]

Some people are not so keen on creating their own 'ideal'; rather they want a real someone who wants to be compassionate to them. A man I worked with said, 'I guess in a thousand years we may be able to build robots that look, feel and sound like humans and can be extremely compassionate. However, I'm not sure that would work for me.' He wanted to experience compassion but from someone who wanted to relate to him, not an ideal that he had created himself. To get over this barrier, we built into his imagery the fact that his compassionate image wanted to relate to him but needed 'to be tuned in to'.

Some people – e.g. those who have been abused or have had difficult childhoods – can find *human* images too threatening, so they may prefer having as their compassionate image a stallion, an eagle, a mountain, a tree and the like. These are fine provided that they are imagined as having human-like minds. The only slight problem with them is that they generally can't produce a smiling compassionate face. To imagine compassionate expressions on the face of the 'other' can be very helpful because the amygdala and other parts of our brain respond to facial expressions.

One more thought: when people think about their compassionate image and its wisdom, they usually like it to have gained its wisdom by having been through the kinds of things they have – thus they feel a *kinship* with it. This can be an important experience. *Bodhisattvas* are indeed like this: they have been fully human and subject to the same passions and desires, mistakes and regrets as all of us, but through their training, study and practice, they have gained insight and developed compassion – compassion that has emerged from struggle.[12]

The exact relationship people have with their images can vary. For example, some like to imagine their images as almost parental and obtain a sense of being cared about and nurtured as if by a loving mother or father. Others like to regard their images more as guides or gurus who don't nurture them like a parent but lead them; still others like to imagine their images as companions or inner helpers. A variation of this imagery work can be to imagine that the universe is full of *bodhisattvas* at different levels of enlightenment. You can then imagine that you are linked into the community of individuals who are seeking to bring compassion to the harshness of the flow of life.

Exercise: Heart focusing

Some people like to imagine the kindness and warmth of their compassionate images being focused as a kind of energy. One method of working with images that uses this approach is called HeartMath.[13] The group of researchers involved in this have been studying a physiological process called *heart-rate variability*. This is different to the heart rate itself, which is the number of times the heart beats in a minute. Heart-rate variability, on the other hand, measures the difference in the time *between* heartbeats, which varies by milliseconds and reflects the relative balance between the sympathetic and parasympathetic nervous systems. If the time between beats is nearly always the same, you have a low heart-rate variability, but generally a higher heart-rate variability is preferable because it represents a good integration and balance of the two nervous systems. Indeed this balance has been linked to our ability to be flexible and self-soothing.[14] New research suggests that there are various mechanisms in the heart that feed back to the brain, and by focusing on changing heart-rate variability, we can have an impact on our feelings.

People can be trained to improve their heart-rate variability in various ways.[15] One is through focusing on affection and kindness, as these experiences affect heart-rate variability. The researchers suggest imagining kindness and compassion being directed at your heart and expanding into your chest and then throughout your whole body. So when you're engaging with your compassionate image, or using your memories of compassion, imagine compassion flowing into you via your heart and that you can feel the warmth of it in your chest.

A very interesting exercise is to take your right hand and place it about an inch away from your chest over your heart – close to your chest but not touching. Imagine compassion flowing into you and into this area through your hand. Notice if you feel any heat there. Maintain a soothing breathing rhythm as you do this exercise. Sometimes people like to associate a colour with compassion, so you can also imagine a colour of compassion flowing into your heart area and soothing and healing you.

Exercise: Compassion for our distress and threat feelings

As we have seen, our threat/self-protection system, which gives us feelings of anger, anxiety, disgust and other unpleasant things, can get very worked up.

If you've experienced difficult feelings or become upset about something, here's an exercise that can be helpful. Sit quietly in a chair or in your compassion posture, engage in your soothing breathing rhythm and then focus on becoming a compassionate self. Imagine that you *are* a deeply compassionate person, never condemning and possessing wisdom and great warmth. Now imagine that the angry, anxious or upset part of you is in front of you as the deeply compassionate you. Look at your facial expressions and behaviour. Imagine what that part of you is feeling and thinking. Now simply send compassion to that part of yourself. Try to really feel compassion for it. Don't try to change anything – just sit looking at that part and feel compassion. You recognize these emotions are from the threat system and are related to fears and upsets. If you practise holding your compassionate position and looking at your upset, anxious or angry self, you may notice that different feelings and thoughts come to mind that are helpful to you. Give it a try and see how you do.

You can do exactly the same exercise as above but imagine being with your compassionate image. Together you can send compassion to your anxious, angry or upset self. Again practise and see how this works for you. If feelings that seem condemning, patronizing or dismissive of the anxious, angry or upset part creep in, then just notice them and return your attention to as full a compassionate, kind and understanding focus as you can.

Grounding

We can use our compassion and imagery to try to stimulate certain patterns in our brain and create brain states that will help us. Sometimes this helps us think things through in a kind and supportive way or do things that we find difficult. For example, suppose you have a difficult phone call to make. Engage in a soothing breathing rhythm and spend a few moments imagining your safe place or your compassionate image and how it is offering support to you. Then, from that state of mind, make your phone call. It's not magic, but it might give you a bit of a helping hand.

As we've already noted many societies use 'worry beads' that are gently run through the fingers as a way of soothing the self. So you might want to use beads like this or, say, a smooth stone or other object that feels soothing in your hand and hold it while doing your imagination exercises. This is called 'grounding'. Carry the beads, stone or whatever in your pocket, and when you need to, you can run the beads through your fingers or hold the stone and this will link you to your image and the feelings that you have been practising.

Deborah Lee[16] worked with someone who found it useful to associate a specific brand of hand cream that had a particular smell with compassion images. It reminded her of a very caring grandmother. Smelling it could reinstate her feelings of being cared for, so she practised her image as a meditation on its own and also with the hand cream on, and when distressed, she would use them together. The use of scents and smells to affect feelings is, of course, very common in many societies. For example, many spiritual rituals involve the use of incense. Smells are also good because they have direct access to the emotional brain. Aromatherapists can advise you on the scents and smells that are believed to have soothing qualities and you may want to pick a scent in that way.

In various spiritual traditions, imagery exercise are associated with other sensory triggers and processes called *mudras* and *mantras*.[17] *Mudras* are gestures, body postures and hand movements associated with particular aspects of feelings or themes, such as wisdom, strength and kindness. So, for example, if you practise your compassionate imagery sitting in a traditional meditative style – that is, sitting cross-legged – or, what I sometimes find more comfortable, sitting in a chair, you may want to rest your hands in your lap with each index finger and thumb touching. By adopting this posture whenever you're doing the compassionate imagery exercises, you'll later be able to re-create the same sensations simply by breathing and having the tips of your index fingers and thumbs touching.

So, for example, you might have been practising your compassionate imagery at home in the morning, then set off for work. While you are waiting for a train, you engage in a soothing breathing rhythm, hold your fingers in the same way and bring to mind your compassionate image. Don't forget the relaxed posture and compassionate facial expression. You can imagine radiating compassion to all around you on the station – those who are also caught up in the great flow of life and everyday hustle-bustle even though they may not want to be there either. Which of your fingers your thumbs touch can have different meanings. If you're interested, you can look up *mudras* on the internet and read all about them. Have some fun.

Flow-of-life imagery

There are a number of other soothing and compassionate imagery exercises that you may be interested in trying that are about the flow of life and which can offer an experience of *connectedness* and *acceptance*.

Exercise: Connecting with the flow of life

Decide if your preferred link is with the sea, sky or mountains. Which do you feel you have most affinity to? Choose that one. Okay, for the purposes of this exercise, let's assume that you have chosen the sea. However, this imagery exercise would be exactly the same if you had chosen a mountain or the sky or some other aspect. Clearly, if you don't like the water, you'll choose another image.

First, engage in a soothing breathing rhythm as best you can, while looking down or closing your eyes. Now imagine that the sea is in front of you and that it is beautifully blue, warm and calm, lapping on to a white, silky, sandy shore. Imagine that you're standing in the water, which is just lapping gently at your feet. In this imagery, it's very useful to pay as much attention to as many of your senses as you can. So, for example, imagine a slight warm breeze gently caressing your face, the smell of the sea, the sound of the waves lapping on the beach, the sparkling diamonds on the surface of the water, the sun warming your body. This sensory focusing helps to create the experience that you want.

When you've been through each of your senses and you've some 'feel' for the image, you can now engage in the 'connectedness' part.

As you look out over the sea to the horizon, imagine that this sea, which has been here for eons, is a source of life. Indeed, all life on this planet began here, millions of years ago. This sea has seen many things in the history of life, has been witness to countless species evolving and decaying, and knows many things. Many battles have been fought within it and on its surface. Now imagine that the sea completely accepts you, that it knows all about your struggles and pain, that it recognizes you as a mindful living being in the flow of life. Allow yourself to feel connected to the sea, to its power and wisdom that have total acceptance of you. Try to build a sense of connectedness, of being welcomed by something old and wise.

Some people like to modify this image in all kinds of ways. For example, some imagine that the sea is very cleansing and simply washes away difficult thoughts or feelings. Others think of the sea as very soothing; they can float in it and it holds them up. Again the key thing with this type of imagery work is to experiment and find what is of value to you. Sometimes I imagine a grey sky, huge purple thunderclouds and a strong wind. Odd, I know, but for me sometimes that is rather soothing as well as invigorating; it connects me to the power of life somehow. So do experiment for yourself.

In many ways, you're doing what all novelists do – creating scenes and characters in your mind. The only difference here is that you're doing this mindfully and exploring the impact on you from a soothing, connecting, compassionate point of view. If you happen across images that don't work for you, just drop them. If you know that your images change with, say, your menstrual cycle or some other physical cycle, go with the flow, provided it seems to connect with your inner feelings of warmth and compassion, which are able to soothe you.

Ultimately some people may find that they are attracted to the more traditional spiritual traditions and want their images to be of the Buddha or some other icon. The point about all this is not to get lost in complexity but to recognize the primary spirit and purpose, which is to help you stimulate patterns of activity in your mind that give you access to and help you to develop a compassionate, soothing mind. This takes practice; it takes time to recognize and work with a mind that is like a grasshopper. However, if you stick with it, you may find that it's useful to you, and you may discover that you have indeed trained your mind for compassion.

Conclusion

In Chapter 6, we explored the amazing power of the imagination. So much of what goes on in our minds is our own creation; even what we see and hear is, in a way, created by our brains. However, we live in a hurry-hurry world where so much is created *for* us and thrown *at* us that we don't often have an opportunity to sit back and decide which patterns *we ourselves* actually want to create in our brains. But if we can learn to self-soothe and create compassionate brain states, we may feel a lot better and will probably be better partners, friends and colleagues.

You know quite well, of course, that whether you are learning a new musical instrument, sport or foreign language or even if you are just getting fit, the more time you dedicate to it, the better. You would not expect to be good at any of these things at first – practice is the key.

You have to decide how you want to practise these compassionate imagery exercises. If you can find, say, half an hour to be alone every couple of days or so, that would be very helpful, but finding time is not always easy. Even if you only have a chance to practise these things in the bath or just before you go to sleep, that's better than not practising at all. And, of course, remember always to be compassionate about the practice that you have done and not critical of what you haven't managed to do.

When you practise, it's useful to keep a journal, making notes of your observations. I want to encourage you to do these exercises *mindfully*, and not feel that you are forcing or pushing yourself. At the same time, make a mental note to be curious and observant and, above all, have fun.

9 Compassionate Thinking

As we've already seen, our 'new brains/minds' are fantastic in many ways. With them, we can plan, anticipate, predict, imagine and fantasize. We have the intelligence and ability to think in ways that enable us to understand and gain insight into how the world, and we ourselves, work and function. Be they atoms, universes, our bodies or minds or even the family car, we can understand that it's the relationships between different constituent elements that bring them into being – that is, we're able to grasp the idea that things *emerge because of relationships*. Genes build our cells, our cells build our bodies and brains, our brains give rise to our minds and our minds build social relationships and our cultures. Then we also find that our cultural and social relationships affect our minds, which in turn affect our brains and bodies and even gene expression. We're able to understand how we get sick (e.g. because of bacteria, viruses or social conditions) and how we can heal ourselves. Our 'new brains/minds' give us an awareness that we are 'alive', that we exist, that we have desires, wants and hopes. We can learn amazing things such as a complex language and how to drive a car, cook pizzas, build nuclear reactors, play the piano (think of a Rachmaninov concerto, which requires all sorts of extraordinary fine motor skills and complex feats of memory) – and play and watch cricket over five days!

We can understand our minds and the minds of others as no other species has done in all the billions of years that life has existed on this planet. We're able to work out why people might be feeling good or bad, and what we can do to help them, and what we can do to prevent bad things happening to them and to ourselves in the future. Our 'new brains/minds' can enable us to be compassionate in extraordinary and far-sighted ways. We can share and pool what we know to the point where we can accumulate knowledge and develop sciences and technologies generation upon generation. Because of our 'new brains/minds' and their ability to communicate, we may one day live *Star Trek*-like lives. (Actually I've decided to put off my next reincarnation until then.) And who knows? – we might be the only ones in the universe who have minds like ours (although as a Trekkie, I doubt it).

However, as with many things in evolution, there's often a catch, a dark side. The dark side is that these talents can also drive us slightly (or, indeed, very) crazy. It's one of nature's little unplanned glitches. The way our 'new brains/minds' get used, and the problems they're given to work on (especially those urges, wants, fears and prejudices of our 'old brains/minds') can spell serious trouble to us personally and for us as a species. The way we think about ourselves, other people and the future can fuel anxiety, depression, paranoia and violence. We can use our 'new brain/mind' competencies to create weapons of mass destruction, to torture others and to be extraordinarily cruel. And when it comes to thinking about ourselves, our life situations, our relationships, our futures and the meaning of our lives – well, our 'new brain/mind' competencies can so stimulate 'old brain/mind' fears and other emotions and motivations that we can become very disturbed.

Actually this isn't a new idea. We've known for rather a long time that we can drive ourselves crazy with our 'new brain/mind' capacities for thinking and reasoning. This was basically the message of the Buddha, of course, though he used the word 'suffer' rather than the term 'drive ourselves crazy'. The Buddha was very clear that, without training our minds, we're in danger of being controlled by our passions, desires and fears. He outlined a series of steps in this training that requires us to: (1) pay attention and become more aware and mindful of how our minds are being used (*see* Chapter 5), and (2) follow the 'eight-fold path', which we discussed in Chapter 6 (*see* p. 192).

The Stoic philosophers of ancient Greece, more than 2,000 years ago, also noted that, if emotions and passions are given free rein, without the constraints of reason, chaos can follow. They advocated training the mind to observe and reason carefully. Rationality and being prepared to debate and examine one's premises and beliefs critically were, they believed, the essence of the noble and worthy life. A life lived just on the whim of whatever emotions or moods hold us in any moment was not, they thought, worth much and was vulnerable to going off the rails. Reason should be the master of the emotions. Humans have the ability to stand to one side of or against emotions – to not act out of fear, rage, lust or prejudice.

So the problem of how we use our 'new brain/mind' ability to regulate some of our 'old brain/mind' passions is something that has preoccupied human thought for many, many centuries and in many cultures.

As we have seen, thinking and reasoning are major skills of the compassionate mind (*see* pp. 207–10). There's more to compassionate thinking than 'mindfulness' or just cold rationality, of course, but we're not going to get very far along the road to compassion unless we address our styles of thinking and reasoning.

Constructing reality versus information processing

The concerns about our minds, which reach back thousands of years, were to take on a new twist in the mid-twentieth century. During the 1950s and 1960s, as science and scientific methods became increasingly popular, psychologists started talking about how humans develop 'theories' about the world and, like scientists, operate (i.e. live their lives) according to these theories – and beliefs – about themselves and their relationships in the world. A key player in this was the psychologist George Kelly (1905–67). His major contribution was to show that we *construct* models of the world from our knowledge, beliefs and social relationships. So, for example, a person who studies the weather will experience rain on their wedding day as an irritating result of precipitation in the Atlantic, whereas a very religious individual might think it was a bad omen from God. Or one person might see Jane's behaviour as evidence that she is bad and selfish, while another might see her as fragile and vulnerable.

Kelly pointed out a number of implications about the *active constructive processes* in our experience of the world:

1 People form their constructions using basic *dimensions* of judgements, constructs and values (e.g. good/bad, nice/nasty, attractive/unattractive, complex/simple, hard/easy).

2 There can be very many alternative constructions of the same event.

3 Alternative constructions cannot be simply defined as 'right' or 'wrong'.

4 Our constructions can have major consequences because we tend to behave on them.

5 Unlike scientists, we humans tend to try to confirm our beliefs rather than pick holes in them because, if we were always trying to disprove what we believe in, life would become almost impossible. In fact, people will hold to constructions even in the face of evidence that they're wrong because to change can destabilize a sense of self or meaning.

6 Psychotherapies should help people recognize the reality of 'alternative constructions' and help them explore the ones that are more conducive to their health and well-being. Therapists can support people as they embark on this potentially destabilizing process of literally 'changing their minds'.

7 We form relationships on the basis of our constructions and beliefs (e.g. in the existence of a God or in political values) and then talk to each other to reinforce rather than 'deconstruct' them. People may root their self-identities in their 'cultural traditions' and the constructions of their ancestors, even if their ancestors had no access to today's knowledge and even if holding to traditional beliefs is very harmful. The passion to belong and have a sense of self-identity linked to kin groups powerfully underpins our constructions. People will also support beliefs and social constructions held by groups even if they know they're wrong, for fear of being shamed or harmed by breaking ranks. So people can have both private and public constructions.

The point here is that any neat separation of reason and emotion (with one regulating the other) must recognize that our thinking emerges with and from our constructions. These in turn are often located within society, serving our needs for belonging and feeling connected, and to make life meaningful rather than meaningless. (Note that, for Kelly, both connectedness/disconnectedness and meaningful/meaningless could be salient constructs for a person.)

Kelly's highly influential work helped the development of a new approach to psychology and psychotherapy called *constructivism*. However, at the same time, other psychologists took a very different approach to how the human brain thinks and reasons. They began to compare it to a computer and talked about *information processing* in it – very much a computer age concept. The problem with this idea, however, is that it's very imprecise. For example, the computer I'm typing this book on processes information, and so does my DNA and my immune system. But I don't think you can say that any of those have thoughts or beliefs. And thoughts and beliefs are not only about information processing.

Simultaneously, among all the excitement of trying to work out how humans 'construct' their realities and 'process information', psychotherapy was diversifying into even more new schools. Some forms moved further away from Freud's belief that neurosis was due to unconscious conflicts and blocked libidinal energies. Rather, some therapists started to focus on the fact that much of people's distress was rooted in their *flow of ongoing thinking*.

For instance, in the 1960s Professor Aaron Beck, a psychiatrist and psychoanalyst at the University of Pennsylvania, noticed that, when one of his patients was relating a sexual dream, she became increasingly anxious.[1] Now standard psychodynamic ideas of the time suggested that her anxiety would be related to the sexual content and forbidden desires. However, when Beck asked her, 'What's going through your mind?', he found that her anxiety related not to the dream but to something completely different: she'd thought that Beck was bored with her, that he must have heard all this many times before and would soon ask her to leave therapy. Beck became increasingly interested in the different *self-evaluative streams of thought* that run through the mind. He noticed that they can often occur alongside other thoughts and actions. For example, while an actor is trying to remember his lines and do a good performance on stage, another stream of self-evaluative thoughts might be going through his mind: 'How am I doing? Do the audience like my performance? Mmmm, they seem very quiet today – gosh, the way I just did that line wasn't good . . .' And, of course, other, fear-linked thoughts could intrude in our actor's mind, such as: 'Did I forget to turn off the gas? I must remember to call home and see how Mother is . . .' The more anxiety there is in his streams of thought, the more the thoughts could disrupt his performance.

Beck also realized that, while the thoughts that come into our minds can be automatically focused on many things, in people with anger, anxiety and depression, the themes are threats and losses. Beck called these *automatic thoughts* because that's precisely what they are: they just pop into our minds without very much reflection. Each emotion and mood has its own type of automatic thoughts, which in turn play with the abilities of our 'new brains/minds', amplifying and accentuating our emotions and moods. We can become more anxious, angry and depressed by what we think about and dwell on – what our 'new brains/minds' focus on. For example, in anxiety our thoughts focus on harms. People who have panic attacks can become afraid that their increasing heart rate indicates that they're suffering a heart attack. Now, of course, that construction is scary so they become more anxious. Socially anxious (shy) people focus on thoughts about doing things that others will find silly or boring, and as a result, they fear rejection, over-monitor their behaviour and become even more anxious. In anger, our thoughts focus on transgressions: 'This shouldn't happen. They shouldn't do that – I'll teach them.' And in depression, our thoughts focus on our being trapped, inferior and losers and that little will change in our lives.

Automatic thoughts can, of course, be linked to underlying, earlier developed fears. For example, children who have been rejected may quickly experience automatic thoughts telling them that people are likely to reject them.

Changing our thinking to change our minds

Aaron Beck was very influenced by George Kelly, but he was less concerned with theory; rather, his focus was on therapy. So what would happen, he wondered, if we were to focus on those streams of thought and try and help people to stand back from them and look at them more objectively? Let's forget about Freudian concerns with unconscious conflicts, repressed hostilities, Oedipal desires, oral, anal and phallic stages, and, instead, let's bring automatic thoughts to the forefront, explore them in detail and see where they lead. Then once we've clarified our thoughts and where they're going to take us to, we can see if they're reasonable and accurate and, if not, learn to generate some more reasonable alternatives. The point here is: Just because you think something or feel strongly about it or feel it to be true in your bones, don't assume it *is* true. In a constructivist approach, we learn to construct different versions of events and possibilities. This became known as *cognitive therapy*.

In the 1970s, cognitive therapists linked up with behavioural therapists who focus on helping people change by confronting their fears and altering their actual behaviours. So, for example, they encourage agoraphobic people to face and learn to tolerate their anxiety and leave their homes. The behaviourists' motto is: 'We learn and become confident from the doing.' In fact, some behaviour therapists think that over-focusing on our thoughts rather than our behaviour is a bit of a red herring. This marriage of the two therapies (not always a happy one) was to give rise to a hybrid school of therapy that is now cognitive behaviour therapy (CBT).

Living up the road from Aaron Beck was the New York psychologist Albert Ellis.[2] He had come to the same conclusion, that our on-going thoughts and interpretations about things can cause us to have serious emotional problems. In his view, you can help people by helping them to recognize that, while we're *biologically set up to be irrational*, we can train ourselves to be more rational. This approach is now known as *rational emotive behaviour therapy*. Ellis took his inspiration from the Stoic philosophers of ancient Greece who, as we've seen, suggested that humans are above animals because humans have the ability to reason. Moreover, reason should be the basis of our lives and should be used to regulate our more irrational passions. Ellis also, like the behaviourists, advocated the importance of directly changing behaviour to something more rational and goal enhancing.

Ellis focused on different aspects of our thinking from Beck. He noted, as had the German psychoanalyst Karen Horney in the 1940s,[3] that humans can be tyrannized by their own thinking in terms of 'oughts', 'shoulds' and 'musts'.[4] For example, someone might have the belief 'I *have* to do well – I couldn't stand it if I failed' or 'I *must* make John/Sue love me – I couldn't bear it if he/she doesn't.' If you have these kinds of beliefs, you can see that you've already decided on the impossibility of coping with some of life's difficulties. The trick, of course, is to turn 'musts' and 'shoulds' into preferences (i.e. 'I'd prefer to do well'), and to recognize that many of the things we see as catastrophes are not – certainly when compared to other suffering in the world. So we need to learn to keep our perspective and balance and discover how we can cope with losses and disappointments rather than indoctrinating ourselves with thoughts that we can't. No one says that this will be easy to do, but learning how to cope is going to be more difficult if we have 'must have', 'impossible to bear' and 'got to' beliefs. Such beliefs are a denial of the realities of life that, as we saw in Chapter 1, are as much about suffering and tragedy as they are about other things. And, yes, the Buddha said very similar things, too.

These ideas appealed to psychologists and their research skills and they conducted a lot of research on the CBT models. Today the early cognitive and rationality-based approaches can seem rather simplistic and out of date with modern scientific understanding of how our brains actually work, but because they are therapy-focused, they've developed into a multitude of ways to engage with people's fears, worries and depressions. They teach people how to:

- pay attention to their thoughts in order to 'catch' them

- stand back and reflect on their thoughts and feelings and think about alternatives

- test out ideas about themselves and others

- face up to things and change behaviour that they often would rather not.

The UK government's National Institute for Health and Clinical Excellence (NICE), which looks into the effectiveness of therapies, has suggested that these types of therapy have a reasonable evidence base.[5] This has been a somewhat controversial assertion because other types may be helpful, too; there are major (often heated) debates as to whether there's enough evidence to say one way or the other. Let's just say that, like all such approaches, CBT has its strengths and its weaknesses, and many critiques of CBT are based on very simplistic views of the therapy.

Thinking about what goes on in our minds

It may seem that, with the above discussion of various schools of therapy, we've drifted away from compassionate thinking. But this isn't really the case because, you see, the essence of the CBT and constructivist approaches is that our lives and minds are constantly confronting us with difficult things. You may have suffered some setbacks, loss, trauma or grief, and while you can't avoid the pain of those, your suffering can be far worse if you interpret and think about these upsets in certain kinds of ways. For instance, let's say that you've gone through the break-up of a valued relationship. You might be able to reflect that this was because of conflicts within the relationship that you may have contributed to, but it was mainly a two-party problem. If, on the other hand, you feel that you're totally to blame or that you're unlovable and will never have a loving relationship again, this focus of your thinking could drive you further into despondency.

Many automatic thoughts are not only reactions to anything specific. Our thinking can be affected by quite a number of things, including our current physical brain states and states of mind, and emotions, thoughts and sensations can seem to pop out of nowhere. It is sometimes said that men have intrusive thoughts about sex up to 30 times a day. I don't recall that myself, sadly – but maybe I'm just too old and the testosterone is on the wane. For the most part, such intrusions are not regarded as problematic but natural. However, it turns out that the way we interpret those intrusions – the emotions, bodily sensations, thoughts, images and fantasies that buzz about in our heads all the time – can affect our mental states. For example, we might notice our hearts beating in what we feel is a slightly odd pattern. This is a 'sensory' intrusion and is not uncommon. However, some people can become alarmed by this and believe that it indicates a problem with their hearts and that they are about to die. This, in turn, produces panic, which, of course, accelerates the heart rate, adding to the panic – and very unpleasant it is, too. These people then develop the belief that they mustn't do anything that could tax their hearts, constantly monitor them, and begin to do less and their lives shrink around them. In fact, exercise is good for the heart. As we discussed in Chapter 5, what can be fuelling thoughts and intrusions linked to panic may be quite complex, but the focus and real driver in the here and now can be the *interpretation* of sensory cues – for instance, that we are about to die.

Some thought and fantasy intrusions are extremely unpleasant. For instance, some people have very unpleasant images popping into their minds – of stabbing people or pushing them under trains or of jumping off high buildings. Or sexual fantasies might come unbidden into their minds. These are sometimes collectively called *obsessional contrast thinking* because they're in contrast to people's usual thoughts and wishes. Again they are not uncommon, but our interpretation of what it means to have these types of thoughts can make us very anxious and even depressed. Most of us are able to dismiss them, but some people dwell on them. One person who had an image of carrying out a certain sex act was so shocked by that fantasy that they concluded that the devil was putting things in their mind. You can imagine how terrifying their life became: the more they tried not to have that fantasy, the stronger it got and so the more terrified they became of being possessed. That, sadly, turned into a very serious mental illness. Although the psychology behind these experiences is, of course, complex – for example, since childhood this person had had very strong religious beliefs and a great fear of the devil – the point here is to note how the *interpretation* of what's going on in our minds can cause us to have serious difficulties. If we can learn that much of what goes on is related to our evolved brains, and sometimes it is quite strange stuff, we may be spared some pain. The story again is that our 'old brains' can throw up some very odd or unpleasant feelings, fantasies and thoughts. People with obsessional disorders can become very frightened of those experiences. On the other hand, writers of horror novels are only too delighted to have these fantasies so that they can sell books based on them.

It is common for us to have negative thoughts about our emotions. We might think that certain ones, such as anger towards people we love or wanting to run away from our families to get some respite, indicate that there's something wrong with us or that we're bad in some way. We may think to ourselves, 'I shouldn't have felt that' or 'I shouldn't desire that,' and then we try to block out those emotions or desires. Of course, they're emanating from our 'old brain/mind' and simply telling ourselves to stop feeling or thinking these things, or that we mustn't think or feel them, isn't going to work. We have to approach them compassionately, recognizing that our brains provide us with a whole array of complex feelings, fantasies and desires that we never created and may not want. The thoughts and feelings may be just odd things in the mind or they may be telling us to pay attention to things in new ways. When we feel angry with those we love, it could be because we're tired and in an irritable mood and therefore need to be more mindful of our feelings. However, it might also be because our anger is genuine and it might be helpful to address key issues with them. Therefore to help ourselves, we need to work *with* these feelings and understand them rather than simply trying to get rid of them.

We also know that our emotions can be very 'sticky' as far as our thoughts are concerned. Like magnets, they seem to pull our minds to them, and we find ourselves *dwelling* and *ruminating* on things that we are anxious, angry or depressed about. There's now a lot of evidence that ruminating on negative and unhappy subjects does us very little good. As I've already said, our thoughts and images can powerfully stimulate our bodies and the way they work – you only have to think about sexual imagery to see that. So think what we're doing to our brains when our minds go over and over things that we're angry, frightened or sad about. We're repeatedly stimulating the brain systems responsible for these negative thoughts and feeling, which isn't conducive to our well-being or our happiness.

East meets West

In 1993, Marsha Linehan published a very influential book entitled *Dialectical Behaviour Therapy (DBT)*, which offered a radical integration of Zen Buddhist ideas and behaviour therapy. Linehan pointed out that many approaches to therapy focused mostly on change and creating alternatives. However, for people who have difficult emotions, learning how to tolerate them and accept feelings is often as important as trying to change them. This was the dialectical aspect; working through the dilemmas arising from change versus acceptance or from focusing on self versus focusing on others. Linehan also introduced Buddhist concepts of mindfulness (*see* Chapter 7) into her therapy as ways of learning to be present to one's emotions rather than avoid them.

Another psychologist, Stephen Hayes, also developed a therapy that integrated various aspects of Buddhism and behaviour therapy, which became known as *acceptance commitment therapy* (ACT). Hayes, too, pointed out that a lot of people's difficulties occur because they try to avoid painful feelings (a situation called *experiential avoidance*); acceptance of emotions thus becomes a key process in therapy. In addition, what helps us to navigate through our difficulties is having goals and values that make our lives meaningful. Sometimes patients lose their goals and values and begin to drift. ACT can help them think about and discover key new ones in themselves, which will provide the basis of a commitment for change. Both DBT and ACT now have impressive and growing evidence to support them.

During the 1990s, two Oxford psychologists, Mark Williams and John Teasdale, along with the Canadian psychologist Zindel Segal, linked up with Jon Kabit-Zinn. Now Jon was a medical doctor who had introduced the practice of mindfulness to his patients who had chronic, often painful physical conditions that medicine could do little for. Many found new ways of coping and living with their conditions through Jon's 'mindful' teaching. The question was: could mindfulness also help depression? Following carefully controlled studies, the data look very promising. If people could learn how to 'be with' their depressing feelings and thoughts mindfully rather than being dragged into them or trying to run away from them, this could be helpful indeed. Williams, Teasdale, Segal and Kabit-Zinn have now published a self-help book with a CD on this method called *The Mindful Way through Depression: Freeing yourself from chronic unhappiness*.

In 2005, the European Association for Cognitive and Behaviour Psychotherapy met in Sweden. One of the highlights of that conference was a meeting between Aaron Beck and the Dalai Lama. This had been on the cards for some time because psychologists had increasingly recognized that some of the principles and ways of working in the newer therapies were very similar to what Buddhists (and indeed other healing traditions) had been proposing for many centuries. The Buddha said: 'Via our thoughts we create the world,' and his eight-fold path, which we discussed on page 192, is a well-worked-out approach to the problems of our 'new brains/minds'. The union of Eastern and Western psychologies and interventions has been one of the most important recent developments in psychotherapeutic practice. What is vital to both is the recognition that our minds are far from easy to understand or cope with and that we need clarity of insight and training. This is one of the most profound and challenging messages of the twenty-first century.

So we can look back through the ages and see that many philosophers and thinkers on the human condition have come to the same conclusions – that as fantastic and liberating as our 'new brains/minds' are, they're also a major source of problems. As we saw at the beginning of this chapter, evolution has given us minds that are extraordinary – and for all we know, there may be no other minds in the universe like ours. But – and this is a very big 'but' – evolution hasn't taught us how to use them appropriately because it simply can't do that. Only the 'new brain/mind' itself, which is capable of reflecting on itself, can develop insight into the positive and negative outcomes of how it expresses itself. This is a major point of wisdom – that the 'new brain/mind' must use its own talents to understand the 'old brain/mind' in detail and work with it to promote our personal welfare and that of the rest of humanity. That means finding ways to cope with the archetypal and social mentalities discussed in Chapter 3.

So there's the challenge for humans: can we use our 'new brain/minds' to recognize them as both a gift and a potential destroyer if not handled with care, wisdom and training? Despite the efforts of Buddhism and the Stoic philosophers, we live in an age where we're only just beginning to understand this. The Western capitalist model has very little interest in whether you understand your mind. It will train you in the skills necessary to make you into a contributor towards profit-seeking goals. There's no conspiracy here; this is simply the way it is because we've allowed this model to emerge in our pursuit of comfort and pleasures. And, of course, you know what I'm going to say: this isn't our fault. I like my comforts and pleasures, too – and yes, I buy a weekly lottery ticket. None the less, what can we now do?

Taking responsibility

The old psychodynamic schools of therapy implied that, through insight and making unconscious conflicts conscious, we could find happiness and morality. Now, although it's true that there are times when we do need to become more conscious of, and work through, our defences of denial, projection, dissociation and repression, or come to terms with that part of us that is looking for the loving parent we never found in childhood, it's also now realized that a lot of what we need to do to help ourselves is simply hard work. Having insight is just not enough. This is absolutely not our fault: it's because of the way our brains were designed.

So make no mistake – being human comes with some wonderful abilities and talents, an awareness of being alive, the joy of life and pleasure (yes, the ability to partake of red wine on warm evenings at sunset did come to mind). But we also carry a great burden because it's only ourselves who can look at our brains and recognize what we need to do to train them. It is only ourselves who can understand how our social relationships shape us and therefore think more carefully about what kinds of social influence we encourage (or turn a blind eye to). It's at this point that we can utilize much of the wisdom in recently developed psychotherapies as well as the insights of Buddhism and other traditions. So the question is: how can we learn to think compassionately?

Mind training in thinking

Exercise: Attending to and monitoring your mind

When we train our minds, one of the first things we need to do is to *attend to and monitor* what is going on in them.[6] This is actually easier said than done. Cognitive behaviour therapists teach us how to pay attention to the thoughts that emerge in our minds and note how they're often linked to feelings. These thoughts are windows that allow us to see how we're creating meaning in our minds, and thus it can be useful to look in these windows in more detail. To do this, I'm going to use an exercise that we'll utilize as the basis of others throughout the rest of the chapter.

Suppose you're expecting a phone call from a friend who said they would ring at, say, 10 p.m. You wait in but the call doesn't materialize. You may find yourself feeling various things such as anxiety, anger, sadness or not much at all. Cognitive behaviour therapists would advise you to pay attention to the thoughts and interpretations that are going through your mind, and ask yourself some questions. The first one is very straightforward: 'What's going through my mind? What am I actually thinking about this event?' The idea here is to stop and pay attention to what is in your mind. It's not until we deliberately stop and do this that we realize how often we don't actually know our thoughts in detail – we just let our minds wander all over the place. Sometimes it can be helpful to write down your thoughts because this will help you to slow and 'catch' them. That may sound odd or a bit tedious, but sometimes thoughts are rather hazy and in the background, and it isn't until we focus on them that they become clearer. Give it a go and see how you get on.

When we write down what we're thinking, we can see that different kinds of thoughts and interpretations are associated with different emotions. For instance, if your primary feeling about your friend not ringing is anxiety, you may be thinking about whether something has happened to them. Once your mind is on that emotional train of thought, all kinds of possible scenarios might pop into your mind – your friend could have been in a car accident, or they might have had an argument with their partner and forgot all about their promise to ring you. If you note this pull on your thoughts and images, you could then try and reassure yourself by creating some alternative thoughts and explanations, such as perhaps your friend's mobile phone battery has run out.

Suppose that the lack of a phone call irritates you. Here your thoughts may be about feeling that your friend has forgotten you and that they could have made more of an effort. If the 'friend' happens to be a new boyfriend or girlfriend, you might have various scenes popping into your mind of them being at a bar or party having a good time and simply forgetting all about you. You might then sail away on your emotion of anger, thinking up all kinds of things that you're going to say to them the next time you meet. Whether or not you do is another matter, but think what you've done to your brain by running those thoughts and the scenes over and over in it! Do you really want to live in that place? What would your greatest fear be of giving up your tendency for angry or vengeful thinking? Would it make you feel powerless?

If your emotion is one of sadness, then when you stop and look in detail at your thoughts, you might find that they're focused on the idea that perhaps your friend doesn't care that much about you and they're not bothered enough to ensure that they phone when they said they would. As you think this, you may begin to remember other times when you felt rather rejected – come to think of it, maybe you've never felt popular and now you focus on how lonely you feel right now. In this way, the tide of emotion is gradually pulling you deeper into the sea of sadness. It's as if the sirens are singing to you, but it's not your fault because this is what emotions do and were designed to do.

Psychologists will also suggest that different people will make different constructions and interpret the same events differently because of a number of interacting processes. These include:

- *Genetics.* Evidence now suggests that genes do a play a role in the ease by which some of our emotions can be aroused.

- *Background experiences.* Taking the example of the friend not ringing, if important people in your life have had accidents, that could prime that interpretation in you. If, on the other hand, the same people have simply forgotten and ignored you in the past, that may prime anger. And, of course, if you've often felt rather shy and ignored by people, that may prime sadness. Basically we tend to view the present through the eyes of the past.

- *Current stresses.* If you've been very irritated all day by people not doing what they said they'd do, the lack of a phone call will simply fit in with what's been going on that day. So your current brain state can influence your constructions and interpretations.

Exercise: Behind the scenes

Most psychotherapists suggest that our threat-focused feelings of anger or anxiety can point to more complicated and perhaps more important threats and concerns. So what do you think might be the underlying threat of someone who becomes anxious about a phone call that hasn't come? Before reading on think about that. Make a few notes in your journal.

One possibility is a fear that something bad has happened to the person who should have rung and, if that's true, then they won't be there for you any longer. Or it might be that you think something has happened to the friend and are fretting over what to do next – should you phone them?

What do you think might be the underlying threat for someone who becomes angry and irritable? Again, before reading on, think about that question. For this person, it may be a fear that they can't control others or that others are fickle. A sense of being out of control can induce some individuals to use anger to keep other people toeing the line. And, of course, the underlying fear of the sad person can be of loneliness and not being valued or wanted.

When we chase many of our automatic thoughts down, they often turn out to be focused on just a few key fears. These can be fears to our *physical being* in the form of injury or hurt, and fears of harm to those we love. A second set of fears relates to our control and ability to secure and reach our goals. A third set, which comprise the ones that most commonly preoccupy people, are related to self and social fears – of being shamed, criticized, devalued, rejected, marginalized and left unwanted. Sometimes we can look into our fears by creating a mental image of them. So you can ask yourself, 'If I could see myself in the feared state, what would be happening around me? What would I look like? What would be going on?'

Now we can call these fears *archetypal* because they're shared by just about every human being on the planet. Some people, however, have backgrounds or genetic profiles that make it easier for them to cope with such fears, while for others, these fears can be quite pronounced.

Self-monitoring

So far we have established some key points. First, our thinking can easily head off in all directions when confronted with various life events, and very often we find ourselves simply going along those paths. Our emotions can be like whirlpools pulling us in or a tide on which we drift away. We find it difficult to stand back and think about what is the underlying fear that may be driving these emotions or whether our thoughts are fair and reasonable. However, if we want our 'new brains' to do some work and not simply be passive passengers or collaborators on the charging train of emotion, then learning to monitor ourselves by paying attention, standing back and reflecting are key skills that we need to develop.

Exercise: Paying attention

The first skill we need is: learning to pay attention to the flow of feelings and thoughts in our minds, to recognize when we have flashes of feeling or when our mood shifts in a certain way. There are many ways you can do this. Here are some suggestions:

- You could write on your left thumb the word 'ATTENTION' as a prompt. This will help you remember that, if your emotions become too upsetting, you should pay attention to your thoughts and their inner meanings and implications. This technique can also be useful in developing mindfulness (*see* Chapter 7) because it will remind you just to take a moment and reflect on the buzz of different thoughts and feelings going on in your mind and then bring your attention back to the present moment.

- You can carry some cards or a notebook in your pocket or handbag to write down your thoughts. If you choose cards, it can be quite nice to look for postcards that have pictures on the front that you like – a relaxing mountain scene, a bluebell wood or maybe the smiling face of Buddha.

- You could speak your thoughts into a small dictaphone.

Whether you are writing or talking, take note of your thoughts and feelings and describe them. Imagine that you're a television reporter, one step back from the action but observing and reporting it. For example, using the non-phoning friend example again: 'Right now I'm feeling slightly anxious, there's a tension in my stomach and my body feels fidgety. My thoughts are being pulled towards the possibility that something might have happened to my friend. I feel the urge to phone up or go and check that things are okay. The odd image of an accident has popped into my mind.'

This exercise can help guide your attention to your experience *in the moment*. You become aware of your bodily feelings and emotions, your thoughts, the implications of your thoughts, and then the images or fantasies popping into your head. As you focus your attention, you could also become aware just how active your brain is in different moods and states or when focusing on different types of social relationships.

Exercise: Compassionate mindfulness

If we practise mindfulness, we'll learn to become *observers* of bodily processes, feelings and thoughts. In mindfulness, we don't try to change thoughts, but rather are curious and fascinated about their emergence and the relationship we have with them. The more we give voice to our thoughts, images, emotions and urges, the easier mindfulness can become. This is why it's useful to articulate and verbalize thoughts such as 'Now I'm experiencing the urge to phone my friend.'

When we do things compassionately, we always try to inject them with feelings of *kindness, warmth* and *gentleness*. So we don't want to monitor our thoughts coldly or hostilely but in a gentle, caring way. It's useful to focus on our emotional orientation and try to create as much warmth as possible. This can give a different 'feel' to monitoring our thoughts, emotions and fantasies.

One way to do this is to imagine that you're describing your thoughts and feelings to a very good friend, a therapist (imagined or real) or your ideal compassionate image, see pages 258–62. Imagine that your compassionately imagined friend, therapist or image is very interested in what's going on in your mind. And they're unshockable: they know that there's nothing you as a human being can think or feel that other human beings have not thought or felt at some point in the history of the species.

So your task is to describe your thoughts, feelings and fantasies as clearly and in as much detail as you can. You're not trying to explain *why* you're feeling or thinking like this or to justify it or be ashamed of it, but rather explain just exactly *what* it is you're feeling and thinking. Keep in mind that your compassionately imagined friend, therapist or image has a genuine concern and interest in hearing what you have to say. Some people can find this a very moving experience, depending on what they are describing. Clearly you should use this exercise in the spirit in which it is written – as something to help you and not overwhelm you.

Exercise: Compassionate writing

Sometimes you may want to spend more time helping yourself to *understand* your feelings and how they're related to various themes in your life. In fact, there's now good evidence that writing things down and expressing your feelings in this way can be very helpful.[7]

You might want to write down your thoughts in the form of a letter or a short paragraph. Depending on what you're feeling, it might look something like this:

The anxious scenario

My friend didn't phone me tonight and I stayed in waiting. I feel rather anxious about that because he/she is usually reliable. I can't help wondering if something might have happened. I guess my fear is that something bad might have happened and whether or not I should check up. Thinking about it, I suppose it reminds me of many years ago when we were waiting for my sister to come home, and then found out that she had been beaten up by a school bully. Also I come from a family that was always worried about 'things happening' to us. So I guess it's very understandable why my mind goes off into these anxieties.

The angry scenario

My friend didn't phone me tonight and I stayed in waiting. I feel rather annoyed about that. I can't help wondering if something more important caught his/her attention. I guess my fear is that others tend to rate me quite low on their list of priorities; I simply don't matter enough to them. Thinking about it reminds me of how it was at home. Mum and Dad were always so busy with their lives, and although they weren't unkind to us, we often were pretty low on their list. So I guess it's very understandable why my mind goes off into these anger scenes because I feel I've always had to fight for attention.

The sad scenario

I was really hoping my friend would phone because I'm feeling lonely and I wanted to talk to him/her. I guess part of me thinks that I may not be important to people. I suppose I am a bit boring really – I never have anything exciting to say and nothing exciting ever happens to me. I'm also always waiting for other people. I never go out and make things happen. It's just the way I am, I guess.

When you monitor and attend to your thinking in this way, remember to try to do it in a *kind, gentle* way that is reflective. If you return to the compassion circle on page 194 and the table on page 214, you can see how what you've just done above fits:

- By spending some time on yourself to work out what is in your mind, you are motivated by a genuine wish to be *caring* of yourself.

- You are learning to be *sensitive* to what you feel and think. You aren't trying to deny, avoid, explain it away or tell yourself that you're silly to think this.

- You have *sympathy* for what you feel because it's distressing not to receive a phone call and be upset about it.

- Staying with your thoughts and feelings, writing them down and thinking about them honestly, you're learning how to *tolerate* your thoughts and feelings and any distress you may be experiencing.

- By giving yourself some space to really think what your feelings are about, you're developing understanding of and *empathy* for yourself.

- By doing this exercise in a mindful way, you are being open, gentle, kind and focused on the activity in a curious yet *non-judgemental* or critical way.

We'll look at writing to ourselves again in Chapter 10 when we explore compassionate letter writing.

The different parts of us

If you're anything like me, it's very rare to have only one stream of thoughts, feelings or fantasies. Typically I have many, which bob about all over the place. I'm quite capable of doing the angry, anxious and sad routines all at the same time. So you can have different thoughts and feelings to the same events. In this situation, it's useful to tell yourself: 'Part of me thinks and feels this . . . or that . . . and part of me thinks or feels this . . .' If you practise this, you may begin to recognize that you may have a dominant stream of thoughts and feelings but running alongside that can be other streams. Sometimes, if we're very caught up in an experience, we lose sight of the *mixed parts of ourselves*. We only hear one internal voice. For example, when some of my depressed patients are in conflict with other people, they can be so used to attending to their own *anxious* feelings and thoughts that they don't notice their feelings and thoughts of *anger*. But remember, from our discussion of the threat / self-protection system (in Chapter 4), that when this system is confronted by a threat, such as somebody criticizing us, it's likely to fire off a lot of different feelings and thoughts because it can't always immediately decide on one course of action. It will also tend to quieten the voice from the more positive emotion systems.

We can also be affected by different competing concerns, by what we actually think, feel or do, by what we'd *like* to think, feel or do, by what we believe we *should* think, feel and do, and by what we feel we're *able* to think, feel and do. We can also notice what we feel held back from thinking or doing. For example, if your boss criticizes you, you may feel angry, but because you don't want to lose your job, you hold on to your anger; then, later, when you're at home and thinking it over, you feel cross with yourself for not being assertive. So the thing to do is to stand back from these inner conflicts, note them and see them as quite normal, competing tendencies within your own mind. Come to terms with the realities of your situation: maybe it's difficult to be assertive in the way that you would like or fantasize; or maybe you need to go to assertiveness lessons; or maybe you need to accept that your submissive way of dealing with things is actually quite effective in that it gets you what you want. Learn to value the way that you have coped even if it's not your ideal.

Learning how to balance our thoughts

Cognitive behaviour therapists used to talk about 'distorted thoughts' or 'faulty thinking'. However, skilled therapists rarely use that sort of language now because it doesn't help and can make us feel worse.

Of course, if I get myself into a state, part of me knows that I'm being irrational and biased – but I claim my human right to be irrational and biased from time to time, so let's be clear about this: we are by nature often irrational. Much of what we do and much that gives us pleasure in life is deeply irrational. Falling in love, having children (which now costs the earth) and driving in a Grand Prix (risking life and limb) are all irrational – and watching cricket for five days as I would love to do is deeply, deeply irrational (especially given the England team at the moment). And many of the things that soothe and comfort us are not based on logic but on kindness.

So the question is: What type of thinking are we dealing with? Is it threat-focused or more caring-focused? Is it helpful or unhelpful? Does our thinking cause our moods to worsen and us to become more distressed, or can we step to one side, balance our thoughts and thus bring more soothing to the situation?

We can focus on thought-balancing, recognizing that we can have many mixed thoughts and that our emotion systems are like whirlpools that pull us, sometimes inappropriately, towards them. So it's useful to create another, counterbalancing force to the thoughts, fears and concerns of the threat/self-protection system. We can create this by our ability to stand back and focus on kindness and gentleness and on supportive, helpful and encouraging thoughts. A way to think about this is that you're literally taking your thinking, self-aware mind (or 'new brain/mind') out of the focus of the threat system and deliberately concentrating on compassion, kindness and support. It is those qualities you want to guide your thinking.

Many thinkers and researchers – among them Buddhists, Stoic philosophers (both ancient and modern), therapists and psychologists who study moods and emotions – have offered a lot of wisdom to help us balance our thoughts. None of them suggests that it's easy, but if we *practise*, we can gain benefits. So what we're going to do now is to go through a series of stages of using the compassionate approach, and the first thing we must do is acknowledge when we're hurting.

Exercise: Validating our feelings

I'm going to stay with the simple example of the friend who was supposed to call and didn't, but of course, you can apply these principles to many situations. If we're compassionate to our feelings, we'll be able to say that the anxiety/anger/sadness we're experiencing is very understandable. We might have insight into recognizing why we tend to have those kinds of thoughts and feelings. Moreover we'll be able to be kind, recognizing that it can be distressing for us not to have received the phone call we were expecting. This is called *validating* or *emphasizing* with our feelings and is a very important skill to learn. Some of us will have come from backgrounds in which our parents told us that our feelings were wrong, silly, pathetic, stupid, bad, excessive, weak – and that's just for starters! We may have grown up unsure about which feelings are appropriate. Indeed, many of my patients are often concerned with trying not to feel what they feel. They *invalidate* themselves with thoughts like 'I shouldn't be feeling this' rather than accepting and understanding themselves.

So your first compassionate task is to note that whatever you feel is okay. It may not be desirable, it may be unpleasant, you may know that you mustn't act out your feelings and, in a short while, you may actually discover that you don't need to feel like this, but you shouldn't in any way feel ashamed of what you feel. I can assure you that, in the course of my life, I've had some real panics, tantrums, sadnesses and other excessive feelings. In fact, I'm a born-again neurotic!

So before we begin to look at the evidence and alternatives for our thinking, let's make a slight modification to the monitoring exercise we did above. This exercise starts with the idea that 'It's understandable that I feel like this because . . .' Now write down the reasons why you feel as you do. You can write them on a nice postcard or imagine explaining them to a friend, to someone else you like and trust or to your compassionate image. Learn to *validate* your feelings and not just push them away. Imagine your compassionate friend or image being perfectly understanding and accepting of what you feel right now, in this moment or because of this or that event.

When you feel that you can accept your thoughts and feelings for what they are 'in this moment' and that you're not ashamed of them, that as a human being you demand the right to be as irrational as the rest of us (and, in any case, your thoughts and feelings may be not so irrational), you might want to explore the next set of exercises.

Before doing so, however, keep in mind a vital aspect on which the whole of the compassion approach is based – that life can be tragic, with much pain, disappointment, frustration and sorrow. Sometimes accepting painful realities and states of mind is very hard. For example, no one wants to accept being severely depressed, and yet it is only when we have unashamedly accepted our depression as a brain state that has emerged in us, through no fault of our own, that we can begin to take steps to change that brain state. If we are ashamed of it or feel it's a weakness, we fight within ourselves and we may even avoid seeking help. Disorders such as severe depression are about our brain states and we need to be quite practical about that if we're going to change them through psychological therapies, medications and other solutions.

Generating alternatives

Key to the CBT approach is to look at our thoughts and emotions as theories, or as one construction, experience or viewpoint created by the brain from among many possibilities. We've seen that the threat/self-protection system operates on a 'better safe than sorry' principle and therefore it will pull us towards threat-focused thinking.

The idea is to learn to generate alternatives because we *understand* that these will balance our minds and help us to flourish, grow, prosper and develop wisdom. We don't want to be caught up in 'old brain/mind' passions and emotions. We want to be able to choose how and which emotions texture our lives.

So we generate alternatives by asking our 'new brains/minds' to do some work by considering some questions. Below, we'll examine which to ask. Spend some time thinking about each one and perhaps write down some answers. If it helps, you can imagine your compassionate image, imaginary friend, or ideal compassionate therapist asking the questions. The important point here is for you to hear the question in your mind as a gentle, kind and genuinely compassionate inquiry aimed at helping you. The emotional tone is very important in these exercises. If you also adopt a compassionate facial expression with a gentle smile and take a few soothing breaths, this can help you create that tone.

You might notice that, as you try to answer some of these questions and think about them in reasonable ways, another part of your mind is coming up with 'Yes but . . .' thoughts. That's not at all uncommon. You might find that the emotion associated with these thoughts is fear or irritation, but for the moment, just notice the thoughts and bring yourself back mindfully to the task at hand.

We'll stay with the example of the friend who didn't phone, simply because this offers consistency and it's the process rather than the details that's important here. Now keep in mind that, to work with your thoughts, you'll first validate your feelings in the ways we've already suggested.

So let's think of how we can stand back and get a more balanced view that will help calm down our threat/self-protection system, which, remember, is one of our aims. Let's see if we can get our 'new brain/mind' abilities in on the action. Imagine that it was your friend who hadn't rung, and ask yourself the following questions or think about the statements.

Exercise: Thinking about the facts

- How would I typically see this situation if I weren't stressed, anxious, depressed, irritable, upset or uptight, or if I was happy and relaxed – that is, if I was in a different state of mind?

- Although as a human I have many textures of feeling that are important for my well-being and protection, it's not helpful for people to rely too much on their feelings to give accurate views of the world. So in what way might my feelings not be accurate today?

- Although I can utilize the past, what evidence do I have from what's happened before to support my view 'in this moment' for *this* event?

- What other possible reasons could there be for my friend not phoning? Are any of them a more reasonable or likely explanation than my feared ones?

- How will I feel about this event in three weeks, three months or six months? Will I even remember it? If it passes so rapidly, what will make it go away even quicker now?

Exercise: Thinking about the background rules we're operating

- Let's assume the worst for a moment: perhaps my friend *did* forget me. Am I telling myself that this is awful and totally unacceptable and I can't stand it? Is that reasonable? I've had setbacks like this before and come through them. They're part of life and I certainly wouldn't be the first person in the world to have an experience like this.

- Have I slipped a clause or rule (or two) into my thoughts about life? Am I insisting on something like 'People *must*' or 'People *must not*', rather than accepting people as fallible human beings, different to me and with their own desires and ways of living in the world? Maybe I just flip into this idea of 'musts' and 'have tos' when I get anxious, in which case I can think about why I'm so anxious and whether I need to be.

- Have rules like 'People should *never* let me down' or 'People should *never* forget about me' become background rules in my life? Have I ever explained my rules to others? If I haven't, would they accept them? Well, probably not, actually, because they're not very reasonable rules to force people to abide by, if I'm honest.

Exercise: Balancing my strengths and abilities

- I've coped with these kinds of events in the past – many times, in fact – and I can again. They're painful but part of life's ups and downs.

- Maybe I am underestimating my ability to cope with these events. Perhaps I'm reacting out of habit, and when I give myself a moment to chill out about them, I'll be able to work out how I'm going to cope.

Exercise: Thinking about what's supportive

- If I were advising and supporting a friend in the same situation, what might I say and how might I feel about the support I'm giving?

- If I had a friend with me right now, what would I like them to say? What would be the most helpful thing for that friend to focus on?

Exercise: Taking an empathic stance

- My friend who hasn't phoned is a different person to me, with different genes and a different background, and therefore has (slightly) different values and rules to mine. For a moment, let me imagine what might be going on with him/her and this phone call. What do I notice when I think from *his/her* point of view, inside *his/her* mind, about making or not making the phone call?

- If I recognize that perhaps my friend wouldn't be so bothered about not ringing, could it be that this is just his/her style and is not about me specifically?

Exercise: Noticing blocks

- What holds me back from really taking on board my own wisdom and understanding that things are not quite as I'm telling myself they are?

- If I've always seen myself as an anxious person, or someone who reacts to events like this in ways like this, is there a part of me that's worried about changing? Is a part of me nervous about what kind of person I might be if I chilled out?

Okay, enough questions – these are meant as gentle enquiries to help you stand back and not assume that the thoughts and feelings flowing through your mind are accurate. It's this ability to question and not take things for granted that's so important as a first step in balancing our minds. I like these kinds of questions because sometimes, in the back of my own mind,

I know that some of my feelings are irrational, and that there can be an almost inner resistance to being rational. However, if I gently and kindly question myself, this helps.

This can, however, also take you into slightly more complex territory. For example, one person I worked with who had a lot of anger that got in the way of her developing harmonious relationships with others recognized that, actually, she didn't want to be rational and give up her anger because, as she said, 'Anger gives me power.' Moreover, she had a strong belief that, if people are thoughtless (by her definition), they *should* be punished in some way. So even though her anger was upsetting her and causing problems in her relationships, she was too frightened to give it up. So sometimes we have to take seriously the fact that we've *locked out* our wisdom and logic because we haven't really got to the source of our difficulty.

Compassionate skills

You may recall from Chapters 6 and 8 that we distinguished between compassionate abilities and compassionate skills. Compassionate skills focus on compassionate attention, thinking/reasoning, behaviour and feeling.

When you focus your attention on, say, memories of coping or other times that your friend hasn't phoned and it's been fine, or that you have other friends who phone when they say they will, or who enjoy your company – indeed any such elements that you experience as useful – that's *compassionate* attention. The aim of this is to deliberately focus on the helpful. The key is to bring these strongly to mind, breathe in a soothing rhythm way and *hold* those memories in mind, letting them work in you.

When you focus your reasoning and thinking with the clear aim of being helpful and caring – for example, opening yourself up to the recognition of our common humanity, that other people have these difficulties – and when you seriously say to yourself, 'What will be the most helpful and compassionate way for me to think about this?', you're engaging in compassionate thinking. Again, spend time 'being with your thoughts and feelings' with kindness – feel them.

Compassionate behaviour consists of deciding what's the most helpful and compassionate thing to do in a given situation. It may involve accepting your feelings and just being mindful of them without doing anything, or it might entail engaging in a self-soothing act. Compassionate behaviour might also require you to be not submissive but open about your feelings to your friend, not saying you weren't hurt by their forgetfulness if you were. It may require courage or forgiveness. There are no recipes: all we can do is to try to work out what is compassionate behaviour in a particular situation. It's the effort and focus that are important.

Exercise: Focusing on emotion

When it comes to thinking and generating alternative thoughts and ideas (i.e. compassionate thinking/reasoning), these can be written down as a series of ideas. For example, suppose we think about the anxious thoughts that could follow that phone call that didn't come. They could be something along these lines:

- It's understandable that I'm feeling upset, but it might still be helpful if I could stand back for a moment and see if I can explore some alternative ideas and constructions. Those would help me cope now.

- Hmmm. This isn't the first time my friend hasn't kept a promise to ring.

- The most likely explanation is that something else did crop up but nothing major.

- He/she is a bit like this with other people so it's not a personal rejection of me.

- I remember that we've had good times together and I can bring those to mind.

- I've had anxieties like this before, and 99 times out of 100, they've come to nothing.

Now you may be able to come up with a number of other alternatives. The main criterion is whether you *experience* them as helpful and this means that you have to give them time to filter in by sitting and really focusing on them. Let them be in your mind and really imagine them being true for you. How does that feel?

Try this as an experiment. Close your eyes for a moment, take a few soothing breaths and let your body go loose. Then, as you breathe in, focus on your compassionate image or your compassionate self (as in Chapter 8). Allow that feeling to build inside of you. When you've done that and you feel in contact with your compassionate mind, open your eyes and read your alternative thoughts again, but this time don't worry too much whether you believe them or not, or whether they're accurate. Just focus on the warmth, kindness and understanding you can put into them. Read them and hear them in your mind in as warm and encouraging a way as you can.

Did you notice anything arising from this exercise? Did you notice that, when you focused on a kind *emotion* when reading your alternative thoughts, they felt slightly different? Indeed, sometimes people say that this makes them even more believable! Isn't that strange? We focus on the emotion of kindness and support in the alternatives and somehow enable them to be more believable and acceptable.

You don't have to do battle with yourself to try and convince yourself of the logic. In fact, if you do that, the exercise probably won't work. What you should try to do is recognize that life can be painful and difficult and we all get worried about things, but we can also develop kindness, support and encouragement for ourselves and gain a different perspective from that. If those understanding, wise, kind and gentle tones get going for you, you're likely to feel different.

There is a variation on this that some people prefer. As before, engage in a soothing breathing rhythm and then focus on your compassionate image or compassionate self. From that viewpoint and position, you can actually generate alternatives in a warm and compassionate way. You can imagine what your compassionate side says about support for this upsetting situation. If you're keeping track of your alternative thoughts, this method will counterbalance some of the anxious or stressful ones. Write down your thoughts as if the compassionate part of you is doing it. In this way, you'll be using your compassionate mind to link with your 'new brain/mind' to come up with alternatives for you.

Some other ways of working on compassionate thinking

With all ways of working with your thinking, remember that we're all caught up in the flow of life, like corks bouncing on the sea, and we're simply trying to do the best we can to go through life balancing our feelings and harnessing compassion. So I hope that one of the principles that you've picked up in this book is the importance of experimenting and working out what works best for *you*. Below are some variations on the same theme as above.

Exercise: Writing down your thoughts

One variation is to actually write down your thinking and make yourself spell out alternative ideas. I go into this in a lot more detail in my book and CD *Overcoming Depression*.[8] Because writing actively engages a different part of the mind from that used when speaking or internally thinking, people do find writing down alternative thoughts extremely helpful.

You can do this quite easily by making two columns. In one column, write down your distressing thoughts and your key fears; in the other, set about trying to balance those with alternatives. Keep your written-down thoughts and alternatives in a folder so that you can look back over them later.

Remember, too, that you can write down alternative thoughts on the pleasant postcards that you may be carrying around with you.

Exercise: The mirror

If you don't faint at the prospect of looking at yourself in a mirror, this could be quite a powerful and helpful exercise. Stand in front of a mirror and imagine yourself as your compassionate person (*see* pp. 251–4).

Imagine having all the qualities of deep compassion. Create a gentle facial expression (but don't make it a sickly smile because then you won't feel it's genuine). Now look at yourself in the mirror and tell your image your alternative, helpful, soothing thoughts. Try and express as much kind feeling as you can to the person you see in the mirror.

Treat this as an experiment. Some people find it quite a moving experience, while others don't find it helpful. Only explore things that you'll find helpful or that you think are likely to prove helpful if you stick with them and practise.

Exercise: Two chairs

As I have said, there are usually many different parts to ourselves, with different points of view, and this is because we have different processing systems in our brains. The threat/self-protection system is one of three important emotional players in our brains. It usually gets incoming information first and it has only two purposes: to detect threat and generate protective responses. This system has no other way of thinking, which is why we need to bring in another, our soothing system, which will help to bring about a more balanced approach.

Now one way you can help this balance to develop is to allow the two systems to talk to each other. Place two chairs so that they are facing each other. Sit in one and speak your distressing or worrying thoughts aloud, focusing on your key concerns. Don't get too deep into your feelings, which will just make you distressed; you're more interested in what your thoughts are actually about. When you feel that you've given your threat side an opportunity to voice its concerns, get out of that chair, walk around for a few moments, engage in a soothing breathing rhythm and take on a compassion posture – including facial expressions and tone of voice – to become your own compassion person (*see* pp. 251–4).

Now sit in the other chair, facing the one you left earlier. Talk kindly and gently to your anxious self from the position of your compassionate self. You may wish to start with something like this (using the non-phoning friend example):

Hello, Anxious Side/Self. [*Try and put warmth into this.*] It's very understandable why this has worried you. It's upsetting that your friend didn't phone and it reminds you of people forgetting you in the past. I remember this, too, but also the fact that you did cope with those feelings and events and that you came through them. So maybe you have more courage than you're giving yourself credit for. In your heart, you know that these feelings will settle down in a few days and that the chances are that nothing has happened to your friend . . .

Now that's just to get you started. You'll probably be far more creative because you'll know the kinds of messages that you'll find helpful. One thing to be cautious about, though, is giving yourself instructions or advice. Saying 'You should' or 'You don't need to feel this or that' might not be helpful and could actually invalidate your anxious side. To get away from this, really imagine that you're talking to an anxious individual.

It's a good idea to spend more of your time in the compassion chair speaking your thoughts out loud, hearing them spoken, building on them, learning to feel them as you speak. This will get you into the practice of delivering – in an ordered and articulate way – your compassionate way of thinking about and dealing with things.

Another thing to consider is whether you use the language of 'we' and 'our'. Because the compassion self is part of you and not separate, it can be useful to phrase things as 'It's upsetting that *our* friend didn't phone' and 'We might have more courage' and so on. You may sound a bit like Gollum out of *The Lord of the Rings* ('We wants it, we needs it – must have the precious!'), but experiment with it and see if this helps you. The use of 'we' is to emphasize kinship rather than separateness of the compassionate part of you. You might just use 'I' in all cases, e.g. 'I feel . . . '

Developing compassionate coping-in-the-moment

Situations and events can trigger thoughts and feelings throughout the day, and it's very easy for us to swing out of balance into distress states. To learn how to cope-in-the-moment, we have to pay attention to any distressing feelings or thoughts as they emerge. So we need to recognize these stressful feelings and thoughts and use them as cues to make a sincere effort to get back into balance. Here are some of the steps you can try for coping-in-the-moment. Let's imagine that something has upset you.

1 A good first step is to pull your attention back into *observing* your thoughts, feelings and bodily states 'in the moment'. You may want to describe them – turning them into words can put a bit of space between you and them.

2 Try to consciously slow down your body and mind by engaging in a soothing breathing rhythm and focusing on the posture of your body. Allow yourself to have a slight smile and consciously let your muscles go loose. Imagine yourself taking on a compassionate stance and becoming the compassion person described on pages 251–4.

3 Now shift your attention to your soothing/contentment system. You can do this in a number of ways. As you breathe, you may want to shift your attention to your calm, soothing place (*see* pp. 254–5). See it in front of you and focus on the sensory details – the slight breeze in your hair, the nature of the light, the sounds, the smell. These can help to ground you. The main shift of attention is, however, towards the experience of caring, support and encouragement. Imagine that your own compassionate voice is warm and calming, or imagine a compassionate friend or your compassionate image talking to you and being with you. Focus on the feelings of understanding, warmth, kindness, support and encouragement that you're receiving and taking into yourself.

4 Using this kindness and support, concentrate on helping yourself balance your thoughts by focusing on a different perspective – your coping, your strengths, your courage. What would your compassionate side say that would be helpful? You can also imagine the kinds of support you might offer to a friend in a similar situation to you.

Those who developed the HeartsMath approach (*see* p. 263) also suggest focusing your attention on feeling kindness *physically* coming into your heart. Try putting your hand an inch above your heart and imagine compassion entering there and spreading through your chest and the rest of your body.

In the exercises in this chapter, you've learned how to refocus using your breathing and slowing yourself down, how to refocus your attention by shifting it and your orientation into your soothing system, and how to refocus your thinking into a more objective perspective.

A variation on the attentional focusing that can be helpful is to bring to mind an actual memory of someone who was kind and helpful to you, or an actual event that was similar to the one that you are dealing with now and which you coped with well. The key here is learning how to figuratively step to one side of your threat/self-protection system and refocus yourself from within your positive emotion systems. You can experiment to see what works best for you. You may find that, on different occasions, different things are more effective. So, for example, for one type of event, bringing to mind an actual memory will be helpful, whereas for another type of event, engaging in compassionate dialogue and focusing on compassionate feeling may work better for you.

These approaches will be even more useful if you practise them. Indeed you could try practising the 'compassionate coping-in-the-moment skills' every day. Try to find a situation, no matter how minor, in which you feel a bit distressed, upset or anxious and use your compassionate coping-in-the-moment skills to help you.

Seeking the help of others

It is easy for us to lose perspective, and 'mind balancing' is all about keeping things in perspective. However, there is another important aspect to this.

I've known people try to use self-help approaches for what are really very tough life experiences – the break-up of a relationship, discovering that their partner is having an affair, being bullied at work or at home, a major financial loss, or developing a serious physical illness. If you experience something like this, it's possible, indeed likely, that you'll feel distressed. It's very important to recognize that these sorts of circumstances will sometimes require all your courage and, often, the help of others. So keep in mind that, while this book is designed to be helpful, it can't take away the real pains of life because, as I've said, many people experience tragedies.

The key thing, though, even with a major tragedy, is to try to balance your thinking so that you don't, for example, criticize yourself in such a way that there's no inner support. Basically when life gets tough, what will help you is developing the compassionate approach within yourself.

It may well be that, in the context of certain life experiences, the compassionate approach demands that you reach out for others and seek professional help. Indeed the recognition that 'I need the help of others because my brain state or my distress has become too intense or too difficult to shift' can be a major step on the road to self-compassion.

Compassionate thinking towards others

This chapter has focused primarily on compassionate thinking directed at you. However, it's also extremely helpful to develop compassionate thinking for others. You can do this in many ways. For instance, consider how you would think compassionately about somebody you deeply cared for if they were in distress. How would you help them? What would you want to say to them? What would you want to do? Now you can refocus on your friends with the same orientation, then on your acquaintances, then on strangers and finally on people you don't like or even your enemies. With those last, you will recognize, as the Dalai Lama has frequently pointed out, that none of us would choose the pain of a broken leg, the fear of cancer, the sadness of seeing one's loved ones die, or to be lost in a depression; rather, 'all of us want happiness and none of us wants suffering'. In the context of this book, this is to recognize that: all of us *just find ourselves here* in the flow of life; all of us are very temporary; all of us must come to terms with certain, inevitable pain that we never chose. Therefore we really are all in this boat together.

You may find that harnessing and developing your compassionate thinking for others will also help you, too. For example, if you're having conflicts within your relationship but you'd like it to work, put yourself into a compassionate orientation as you approach those conflicts, in contrast to aggressive anger (and 'I'm going to tell them how rotten they are' thoughts). Try to spend a few moments *imagining that you are them*, thinking and feeling as they do. Try to get a feel for what's going on in their minds. There are also, as we noted in Chapter 7, a variety of mediations that focus on compassion for others.

Remember, as with all compassion-focused work, to prevent this approach becoming a 'should' or an 'ought to' because that's the wrong emotion system to operate from. And if you find it hard to be compassionate to yourself about such compassionate thoughts, that's because *it is very difficult!*

Conclusion

This chapter has looked at one aspect of the compassionate approach to life – our thinking and reasoning. First, we focused on how our 'new mind' abilities of thinking, reasoning, ruminating and predicting can all be caught up and directed by the threat/self-protection system in our 'old brain'. When that happens, we start going round and round in circles, our emotions of anxiety, anger, depression or distress pulling on our thoughts in different directions, and then, as we refocus on those thoughts, we become more distressed. So we simply stop and notice the way that our thoughts, feelings and body states constantly interact. Given this, it becomes possible to engage in the flow of thoughts, becoming more mindfully aware of how our thoughts emerge within us and can be linked to feelings and bodily states. Both this process of becoming *more observant* – of noticing some of our emotional triggers and how our minds work and bodies react – and practising mindfulness can help you. We may become aware, for example, that our moods vary over the course of weeks or months, and that in some mood states, we're more likely to think in certain ways than others. We might notice, say, that when we become stressed we're more irritable than usual and our thoughts are more likely to focus on irritable themes that, in turn, make us even more irritable.

Second, in becoming more mindful we learn to notice our thoughts but treat them more like leaves flowing on the surface of a fast river. Thoughts emerge from the hustle and bustle of our minds, but consciousness and our attending self can stand to one side of them – we can feel the wind and the rain but *we* are not the wind or the rain. So we can observe our thoughts without engaging with them.

Third, compassion-focused approaches build on those basic ideas but also suggest a more 'physiotherapeutic' way of dealing with our threat/self-protection system. This is especially useful for people who find mindfulness difficult or are not used to being compassionate, supportive and kind to themselves. It's then necessary to build 'muscles' for compassion by doing compassion-focused exercises, of which compassionate thinking is one. So in compassion-focused approaches, it's suggested that we can balance our thoughts by literally trying to trigger another emotion system or by simply stepping into another one. We can do this by using our attention, not just to be observant but actually to shift into the soothing system. If we can do that, we can bring our 'new brain/mind' reasoning ability into play by deliberately trying to create compassionate viewpoints and orientation through imagery or 'compassionate being' (*see* Chapter 8). From this position, we're then able to use our wise, logical and reasoning minds to bring balance to our feelings. So in compassion-focused approaches, you're literally trying to stimulate a particular emotion regulation system and then utilize it to direct 'new brain/mind' abilities.

Finally, remember that studies have shown that, if people exercise and repeatedly practise, they'll build up connections in their brains. It's important, therefore, to practise compassionate thinking, even when you're not distressed, because you'll be building up that way of thinking. In a way, it's like getting fit. By exercising, your body gradually becomes more toned and stronger and these qualities are then available when you need to run for the train. If you develop compassionate thinking as a way of life, it will then be available to you when life hits you with something really distressing.

You'll also find that, if you develop and practise compassionate ways of thinking, you'll begin to see the world in a different way. You'll start to see that all of us are caught up in the flow of life and that life is actually more about tragedies than good and evil. You'll become less interested in persecuting others and vengeance and more interested in compassion, fairness and justice. If we could bring compassionate thinking to international conflicts, think what that would do to the world!

10 From Self-criticism to Self-compassion

We can all suffer from a sense of shame. No one goes through life without being criticized, doing things you later regret or having attributes that you'd rather not have. It's part of the human condition. A sense of shame can arise when we think that others might be looking down on us in some way, that they see us as inadequate, inferior or bad, or simply not up to much or not worth bothering with.

We can also have a sense of internal shame when we feel these things about *ourselves*. Commonly our own sense of shame is accompanied by self-criticism and even self-attacking. In fact, shame-based self-criticism and self-attacking are among the most pervasive problems in Western societies and seriously undermine our contentment and well-being. They're the opposite of self-compassion. Rather than feeling support, kindness and enthusiasm for ourselves when things go wrong, we feel anger, disappointment, frustration or even contempt for ourselves. It's these threat-focused feelings, with ourselves as their target, that can keep our threat/self-protection system stirred up.

Look at page 186 and remind yourself how the way you think and feel about yourself can stimulate systems in your brain. So learning to replace shame and self-criticism with compassion and compassionate understanding is important and will help you move forward in life and develop your courage. If you're tackling problems of shame and self-criticism, be they mild or more severe, then never be deluded into thinking that you're alone – these are widespread problems that many humans face in daily life.

As we'll see shortly, there are many triggers for becoming self-critical or even self-disliking, and there are different forms of self-criticism and different situations that can provoke our self-criticism.[1] Let's look at a few.

To get a feel of how self-criticism works, imagine the following:

Scenario 1

You've moved to a new area of the country and are keen to make some friends. So you invite some people over for a meal. You don't know them particularly well but you think that you might get on with them. You spend time thinking about what you're going to cook and you get the ingredients together. Your guests arrive, you give them a few drinks and then you realize that you've forgotten a key ingredient. So you put your glass of wine down on the sideboard and out you dash to buy it. Problem is that, when you get back, you find that you'd forgotten to take some of the saucepans off the heat and they and the food in them are now burned. Looks like it will have to be the local takeaway. What do you think your guests will feel and think about you? What self-judging thoughts and feelings might go through your mind?

Scenario 2

It's going to be a busy day at work. You have some papers that you worked hard on the evening before and are ready to submit them to your team for an important meeting. You're just about to leave home when you get a phone call that requires you to sort through some other papers and organize another dossier to bring into work. You shove everything into your briefcase and set off in heavy traffic, but you're happy because you know that you've completed the assignment. Arriving at work, you open your briefcase only to find that you've brought the wrong documentation and all the work that you'd carefully prepared the night before is still lying on your desk at home. What do you think the others will think and feel about you when they discover that you've not got the important papers for the meeting? What self-judging thoughts and feelings might go through your mind?

Scenario 3

You look at your clothes and see that they're getting a bit scruffy – the time has come to buy some new ones. You go to the shopping mall and find an outfit that really catches your eye. You head off to the changing room and then – 'Oh gosh!' – you discover that you can't fit into any of the clothes. They're the same size you used to buy, of course, but you've expanded! What do you think others will think and feel about you now that you've put on weight? What self-judging thoughts and feelings might go through your mind?

Okay, one last scenario – one especially for the men:

Scenario 4

You've been going out with somebody you really like and the time has arrived for the romantic meal to be followed by a stay-over. The meal is great and, of course, so is the red wine, but you're cautious about how much you drink because of what you hope may follow. You both return to your home, engage in cosy, affectionate romance and then you begin the Full Monty. But slowly, and to your great surprise, you realize that something is happening to your body – or rather it isn't. Old reliable has turned into a sleepy Joe! Your beloved looks rather sad but not critical. What do you think your partner will think and feel about you? What self-judging thoughts and feelings might go through your mind?

So many things in life can stir up self-criticism. To these scenarios can, of course, be added more distressing ones, such as going bankrupt, having an affair, getting drunk and having sex with somebody you regret sleeping with later, lying, cheating and so on. Severe problems with self-criticism and shame can arise from traumas and abuse in childhood, and we might have a sense of shame and self-dislike because of things we know we did not cause, such as a disfigurement. We can also feel reflected shame if, say, a son or daughter is convicted of a crime. In years gone by in the West, and still in many cultures, a woman getting pregnant outside of marriage or having a relationship with someone outside the accepted caste or culture can bring shame to her family – the tragedy of 'honour killing' is an extreme example of this, centring around issues of reflected shame. It sometimes happens that a person wanting to marry someone not chosen by their family isn't ashamed of their choice (because they love their prospective partner) but still feels shamed because of 'bringing shame' to family members.[2]

And when it comes to behaving in ways that are different from what is acceptable to your family, a sense of having betrayed their values or traditions can be a source of shame, even if you know that you've acted reasonably. Karen greatly enjoyed sex with her partner, but she admitted to always having a slight sense of shame about her enthusiasm because her mother, who was very religious, disliked sex and thought it was bad and not something to enjoy. 'I know it's silly,' Karen said, 'but it's kind of like I'm going against her, letting her down somehow. I know she'd disapprove and look down on me – even though I really value my own decisions. God, at my age you'd think I'd have got over that by now, wouldn't you? But I still sense the condemnation – just in the background.'

An inner sense of shame can spoil many aspects of our lives because it causes doubt, self-criticism and inhibition. Remember that one of the reasons why we have these difficulties is because of the way our 'old brains/minds' and 'new brains/minds' interact (see Chapter 2). As a species, we have a sense of self and just about any negative event can be seen to indicate something bad about our selves. This means that, when we have difficulties in our lives or make mistakes, or things don't go as we wish, we always face two potential problems. There is the 'thing itself', be it being overweight, making an error of judgement or finding our bodies don't work as we would like them to. And then there's the experience of our own self: that sense of feeling unwanted, undesired, inferior, a disappointment. We might get over the first problem quite quickly, but the second, involving our sense of our self, can linger and undermine us. Self-compassion helps us to address these problems and to become kinder, more accepting and gentler with ourselves. We must remember that there's no mistake that we can make that millions of others haven't made, too, or any worrying aspect of ourselves that millions of others haven't also worried about. It's all part of the human condition.

Shame and self-criticism

Research has shown that self-criticism is often linked to a concern with what other people think. Therefore when you monitor your self-critical thoughts and feelings, it's useful to remember that there will be *two types of streams of thought*. One of them will focus on what you think is going on in the minds of other people, while the other will focus on your own thoughts and feelings about you as a person.

To help you recognize this, let's use the first scenario above – the one in which you rushed out to buy an ingredient and then all your food got burned.

Looking at both columns of Table 3, you can see that, when we become self-critical, we often assume that others are also critical of and reject us. We make assumptions about what goes on in other people's minds. For example, although those potential friends behaved in an understanding and pleasant way, saying, 'Having a takeaway really doesn't matter at all,' you may worry that they're thinking something very different – that you're incompetent. They might even talk about you behind your back! You see both the outside world and your inner world as critical and condemning, and as a result, you have threat from the inside and threat from the outside and *there's nowhere safe, calming, soothing or kind to go!* You're clearly going to be very stressed and feel quite threatened.

One of the things you can do about this is stand back and recognize your streams of thinking; then try some of the interventions outlined in the previous chapter. So engage in a soothing breathing rhythm, refocus your attention and try to balance these thoughts with some questions, making sure to keep the tone kind and gentle:

- Did anybody really seem that bothered about having to eat a takeaway?

- Did anyone express sympathy and empathy to you about the burned meal?

- Did anyone seem concerned that you might be upset?

- Did people seem to enjoy each other's company?

Table 3: Self-critical thoughts and fears

Column 1	Column 2
How I think others feel and view me	*What I feel and think about myself*
These new people will see that I'm disorganized.	I'm so annoyed with myself for forgetting such a basic ingredient.
They'll not be very impressed with my cooking abilities or my organization.	What's the matter with me? Why can't I get my head in gear?
	The meal I cooked would have been so nice and impressed them.
They'll feel let down at having to eat a takeaway.	I've really let myself down again by being careless and not paying attention.
I've probably blown it with them.	
They'll now always see me as a bit scatty and not take me seriously.	*My key fear is*: I'll not be able to make close friendships with people who respect me. I'll be marginalized and lonely.
My key fear is: I'll not be able to make close friendships with people who respect me.	

- Taking things as a whole, the food was a disappointment, but is it really going to prevent you becoming friends with these people?

- If the roles were reversed and this happened to somebody else, would you reject them?

Run through these questions in your mind, *creating as much warmth, gentleness and kindness as you can,* and concentrate on (compassionately attend to) the positive aspects of people's reactions towards your burned meal. It will, of course, be much easier to focus on any possible negative reactions because that's how your threat/self-protection system works. So if only one person of the ten who were invited seemed a bit put out, you'll focus on that one. However, in compassionate mind training, your attention is concentrated on the other nine, who were generally concerned about you and more interested in the time they were having with you and the other people there, rather than with the burnt meal. If you went to somebody else's house and this happened to them, you'd probably think, 'What a shame. So it's not just me' and maybe even be slightly relieved!

There's also a little problem about trust. People may act nice but do you believe them? And if you're likely to forgive someone else in the same situation but don't think those you invited to your house would do the same to you, why do you assume that it's only you who can be kind and forgiving? And even if they see you as a bit scatty, this may actually endear you to them rather than drive them away – I personally get on well with scatty people. Whether they like you or not is going to depend on how friendly, open and caring you are and whether you have similar interests and values, not whether you burn your cooking. It's our fear of rejection and of being looked down on that really drives this self-criticism, isn't it? If we weren't frightened of these people and did genuinely believe that they weren't that bothered about the meal and even believed that our behaviour endeared us to them, would we be that self-critical? So when we're compassionate, we recognize our underlying fears; that's why in Table 3 I've included a question for you: *'My key fear is . . .'* You can ask this question every time you engage in self-criticism that contains any feeling of anger, contempt or disappointment. Learning to address and be compassionate towards your fears can stop you from beating yourself up.

Shame and disappointment

There's now good evidence that, when we feel shame, it's not so much because we're not meeting our targets or standards but because we think we're moving close to becoming undesired and undesirable in the eyes of others and then in the eyes of ourselves.[3] So we don't say, 'I'm not as thin as I'd like to be'; in shame, we say, 'I'm fat.' We don't say, 'I'm not as good as I'd like to be'; in shame, we say, 'I'm bad/inadequate.' Shame, then, involves feeling close to the self we don't want to be. And we don't want to be that self because it's identified with certain threats, particularly those of rejection, being criticized by others or marginalized or even becoming a source of humour and ridicule. So it's often the threat system that gives us certain feelings that then get labelled in certain ways. Of course, from an evolutionary point of view, if others treat you in a negative way your brain will pick it up as a threat to your very existence.

All the examples we explored above demonstrated disappointment. This is often the result of experiencing threats of becoming the *undesirable self*. Let's take the example of finding that you can't get into the same size of clothes that you used to. Consider Anne. She had an important birthday coming up and had been trying to lose weight to get into a dress she really liked. Unfortunately when the day came and she couldn't get the zip done up comfortably – well, not at all, actually – she sat on the bed and cried and berated herself for being unable to control her diet, not exercising enough and being fat. She now had two problems: (1) not being able to get into the dress, and (2) feeling depressed after beating herself up. Remember what we said about how self-criticism can influence our brain physiology and bodily feelings (*see* p. 186). It's not just the thoughts but the emotions of frustration, anger and contempt that do the damage in self-criticism.[4] Keep in mind, too, that self-criticism is commonly linked to the fear of damaging relationships with others, being seen as silly or inadequate or bad in some way. Anne particularly didn't want other women to notice her weight gain.

One of the things we don't often realize is that, when we're vulnerable to shame and self-criticism, we often have in mind various *ideals* – how we *want to be* and how we definitely *don't want to be*. The difference between the ideal self and the actual self is called the 'disappointment gap'. The closer the 'actual self' is to the 'undesired self', the more vulnerable to shame we can be. You can see this in Table 4. In this example, the 'actual self' seems identical to the self you don't want to be. That's how we experience shame – becoming the 'undesired self'. Many of our efforts to improve ourselves and impress others can actually be fuelled by a fear of becoming or having some of the attributes of the 'undesired self'.

Table 4: Disappointment and shame

Ideal self	Actual self	Undesired self
Slim	Larger size	Larger size
Keeping strictly to diets	Often snacking	Often snacking
Feeling light	Feeling heavy	Feeling heavy
Exercising regularly	Visit the gym only occasionally	Visit the gym only occasionally
	Disappointment gap	Shame vulnerability

As we become more vulnerable to shame, a number of things can happen.

- *Attack self.* Here we may have various thoughts such as 'I should have done better. What's the matter with me? Why am I like this? Why don't I try harder? I'm not good enough.' These are usually not just statements but come with feelings of frustration, anger and sometimes even contempt attached. If you remember the discussion we had on page 186, you can imagine what this is doing to our brains.

- *Attack others.* The disappointment gap can leave us feeling frustrated and then we can be irritable with other people or even attack them. For instance, if we burn the food we made for a party, we might be critical of our partner and say, 'Why couldn't you have reminded me that I needed this ingredient? Why is it always me who has to remember everything?'

- *Give up.* We might have that 'heart-sinking' feeling and then thoughts like: 'There's nothing I can do. I'm always going to make mistakes so there's no point in trying. Things never go right for me. It's all pointless and useless.' So we can feel that we've been defeated and there's nothing to be done other than to give up or resign.

If we stand back and think about them, none of these responses to disappointment is very compassionate. Instead, try focusing on the idea that the key to success (and, indeed, happiness) is the ability to fail and learning how to deal with disappointments. Thus we're well on the road to coping with these kinds of problems. You can't live your life without disappointments, failures, mistakes, setbacks and other human cock-ups. We need to learn how to deal with that little voice in our heads that can be angry, has a good line in four-letter words relating to reproduction, and says: 'I don't want to be kind. I just want to be angry!' The compassionate approach is to accept this anger as an understandable reflection of something we're disappointed about or feel threatened by. At the same time, however, it's about learning to be kind and supportive, acknowledging the disappointment and the threat rather than just sticking with the anger. It's useful, therefore, to speak out loud or write down the following: '*This situation threatens me because . . .'* Then you can think about how to compassionately deal with that threat.

You can mindfully focus on your breathing and recognize the thoughts and feelings travelling in your mind. You can view them as the result of your brain pushing you to feel certain threat emotions, and recognize that underneath the unpleasantness of the emotions is actually a self-protection system that is anxious on your behalf and trying to warn and save you. Remember, it was designed millions of years ago so it's pretty basic and primitive but doing its best. Still it's not the brightest part of you, is it?

The need to be valued by others to value ourselves

In Chapter 5, we spent some time looking at how the feelings we create in the minds of others about ourselves have a major impact on our own personal feelings. Do you recall Sue (pp. 175–6) who did a drawing for her mother and how she felt differently about *herself* according to how her mother reacted? Because our minds are so dependent on the minds of others, we need others to help us learn to attend to the good in ourselves and appreciate the small things we do, not just mega-achievements. Indeed, this attention actually helps us develop positive feelings about ourselves.

How our view of what others think of us shapes our own feelings and judgement about ourselves has been researched by Mark Baldwin and his colleagues at McGill University in Canada.[5] Having asked students to write down some research ideas, Baldwin then subliminally showed them pictures of their professor. One group was flashed a picture of him smiling approvingly; the other was flashed one of him scowling. (By 'subliminally', I mean that the picture was presented so fast that, although the students were aware that they'd seen something, a flash of light, they didn't know that they'd been flashed a picture of a face.) Those who were presented with a smiling face thought their ideas weren't too bad – quite good, in fact. Those who had been shown the scowling face thought their ideas weren't much good. So it turns out that their judgements of *their own ideas* had been primed by whether they had seen an approving or a scowling face. Now, remember, the students didn't actually know they'd seen any pictures of their professor, so this priming was done outside of their conscious awareness.

Mark Baldwin's research revealed something that philosophers have recognized for a long time, that humans will do many things – good and bad – for the sake of recognition and creating positive feelings in the minds of others. At the turn of the last century, the famous American sociologist Charles Horton Cooley (1864–1929) coined the term 'the looking-glass self'. He pointed out that our views of ourselves often depend on how we think others think about us. He suggested that most people don't realize this, but they would quickly do so if, one day, they woke up and found that everybody had become critical and rejecting of them or simply uninterested. Their confidence would soon ebb away and they'd feel miserable. Indeed, we now know that the human mind has evolved to have a keen interest in impressing other people and eliciting care, support, respect, liking and even admiration from them because these things are extremely beneficial to our survival and reproduction (something we explored in Chapter 5). Our sense of security, safeness and well-being is linked to how we think we exist in the minds of others.

In much of the work I do as a therapist, I find that people have often been – consciously and sometimes less consciously – striving to achieve things in life to impress and win the approval of their parents or other people important to them. A key reason for this is because our brains have worked out that, if people value, like and respect us, they're going to be there when we need them. If we feel that we can't win their approval, life is going to be that bit more risky. To help clarify this in your own life, it can sometimes be worth writing a letter to yourself asking whose approval you value most, whom you want to impress, from whom do you want to hear that they value you. Now why would you want these things? What is it that you're really seeking? Sometimes it's particular individuals, such as our parents, or it might be a teacher or friends. For religious people, it could be God – or even the cosmos, if you're a New Ager!

You probably want to feel loved, wanted and that you belong – all basic human wants. However, now perhaps we can recognize that compassion begins at home and that we need to train it in our own minds. So bring your compassionate image to mind, adopt your compassionate facial expression and try to imagine a sense of acceptance and being valued emanating from your image, which is a part of you.

Self-criticism and being devalued

Self-criticism can develop because we've never really felt that we are perceived as good enough in the minds of others, or because we haven't received the kind, positive feelings that we need from others to feel good about ourselves, or because we keep striving, moving the goal posts, becoming disappointed and angry with ourselves rather than learning the art of contentment and rewarding our own efforts. The problem is that humans feel threatened by the possibility of becoming marginalized, excluded or rejected. In fact, our brains are very attentive to that.[6] Our ability to be supportive of and helpful to each other is the upside of evolution. The downside is that we become threatened if we can't create positive feelings in the minds of others, and so fear that the support and care of others may not be there if we need it.

Sources of self-criticism

If you look at how self-criticism affects your brain (*see* pp. 187–8), you'll quickly realize that the self-critic inside you will be continually stimulating your threat/self-protection system (which is, of course, itself a source of stress), constantly giving it little prods with bursts of stress hormones. For the well-practised self-critic, few days pass without them having some negative thought about themselves. In a way, it's like constantly picking at a scab. When you sit back and think about it like this, self-criticism doesn't make a lot of sense, does it? And yet and yet . . .

. . . And yet the funny thing is that people are often quite loath to give it up. So we need to think about this in detail: what is it that makes us self-critical and why are we so hung up on it? Now the sources of self-criticism are not that hard to find. Obvious ones are, of course, things that happened to us in the past. Some people who are self-critical and self-condemning have had parents or teachers who were critical and condemning.

Suzanne, for example, recalls her mother as someone you could 'never please'. She was not abusive, she didn't agree with physical punishment, but boy, she could use the silent treatment. One of life's fault-finders, she was a woman who also saw the 'glass as half empty'. If Suzanne came second in a school test, her mother would ask who came first and what had stopped Suzanne from coming first. Suzanne's achievements were never acknowledged, praised or celebrated. In her mother's view, you shouldn't 'blow your own trumpet', you should 'never be satisfied with where you are' and you should 'never rest on your laurels'. According to Suzanne, 'I can't remember my mother getting excited about anything I did.'

Sonia's mother was similarly difficult. She was always telling her daughter how much harder her life had been, how much tougher she was than Sonia and how easy it was for girls today. So Suzanne and Sonia in different ways had grown up learning *not to pay attention* to the things that they did well, not to be satisfied with or feel good about themselves, but only to focus on the things that they didn't do so well and might have done better, or on how others were always doing better than they were. They had lot of training in feeling that 'others see me as not good enough'.

The problem is, of course, that we can always do better at anything we attempt, and so Suzanne's sense of disappointment and self-criticism of herself was never far away. And do you recall Jack, Jane and Carol, whom we met on pages 73–6. To them, the idea of being self-compassionate, kind and self-appreciating and feeling good about themselves seemed rather odd, like a self-indulgence. Then there's the issue that Sonia and many others have also encountered, which is to really appreciate that their parents were wrong – yet this idea itself can seem wrong, too. Sonia might express it as: 'If I change my values, I'll feel as if I'm betraying Mum and her memory.' It's not so uncommon for people to hold on to values they know are not helpful – out of loyalty.[7] They'll even support leaders they know are disastrous because feeling we belong can seem more important than standing up for ourselves. If we reject the views and values of others – that is, rebel – we can feel disloyal and an outsider.

So you can see that how we think about ourselves and treat ourselves is often linked to how we've been taught. And this happens in so many avenues of life. Women who have been taught that sex is 'bad' or 'disgusting' and 'only for men' or that it's 'shameful' to have 'rude' fantasies may never discover or examine the range and depth of their own sexuality and may self-condemn their own sexual feelings. Their exploration of their own potential and consciousness is constrained. In some social groups that fear homosexuality and so condemn both it and those who practise it, individuals can be plagued with terrible shame for the homosexual feelings they have, even to the point of suicide – and yet, in other societies, homosexuality has been celebrated. You see, shame is very much linked with the social worlds in which we live.

For some people, shameful memories blend into traumatic ones. Tom had an abusive childhood. His father was a bully, and although his mother was caring in her own way, she was quite submissive and somewhat depressed. Tom's father – who probably carried quite a lot of shame in himself that he projected on to Tom – was the kind of man who would turn up at football matches and scream in a very critical way at his son from the touchline. By recalling specific events, Tom gave me an insight into what we can call *shame/trauma memory*. One such event was when his father discovered that Tom was struggling at mathematics and got hold of some of his work, on which he saw some poor marks. Tom remembers his father's face turning red with anger – 'I thought he might explode,' he said. As the father raged, he told Tom that he was 'f——ing lazy and stupid', that there was no reason for him to be getting poor marks, and that, if he didn't improve, there would be serious trouble.

Now let's think about how this all gets laid down in memory. First, there's the emotion emanating from Tom's father, which is anger and aggression. So Tom's brain immediately goes into major threat/self-protect mode because he's under attack from a powerful adult male, although it's unclear if he is going to be hit or injured by the big male. He automatically becomes very frightened and struggles to speak, is rooted to the spot but also desperate to flee. His arousal level is high, and at the same time, he's hearing himself being labelled 'lazy' and 'stupid'. These labels are associated in his mind with things that he has struggled with because, in reality, Tom has tried hard with maths but just can't do it. The level of threat and rage from his father gives him the feeling that he's done something very wrong/bad. His mother, who's frightened of her husband, is nowhere to be seen, and so Tom has an acute sense of being alone with this potentially violent man; there's no one nearby capable of helping or rescuing him. And from what I could learn, Tom's father came from the same sort of background and was regularly beaten – a tragic and dreadful legacy.

So here we have mixed experiences that have become *fused together* in a shame/trauma memory. This fusion comprises:

- a great threat from the outside

- the experience of being labelled

- a sense of ourselves as bad and stupid and of having done something terrible

- a massive burst of inner fear, confusion and feeling 'rooted to the spot', yet also wanting to flee and hide

- an awareness that we're completely alone and there is no rescue.

So you can imagine what happens if Tom gets into situations where he believes that he's made a mistake or isn't good enough and in which authority figures or those he relies on could become critical: *If he feels he's not good enough, he'll feel alone because that's exactly how it was when he was a child.* Indeed, people who have been subjected to shame, especially as children, can have underlying feelings of aloneness – because the shame experience is one of being pushed away as not good enough, unwanted, undesirable, discarded.

Tom recognizes that some of his self-criticism is an echo of his father's voice in his head, some is linked to his own frustration and some is linked to his anxiety: 'Oh, how could I have done that? Now I'm really vulnerable all over again.' Tom could also be seen as a perfectionist, but research has shown that there are different types of perfectionist. One is linked to personal standards, while another is associated with a fear of criticism – people seek perfection to avoid criticism.[8]

One of the problems for people who have experienced powerful shame events is that their memories can be intrusive. For instance, Tom would often have memories of his abusive past – and the feelings they produced – popping into his mind.[9] He was also prone to explosions of anger that then made him ashamed, self-contemptuous and withdrawn.

The bullied becoming the bullies

Some of the children who come from these types of backgrounds, which can involve various degrees and combinations of neglect, control, expectation, abuse and low levels of affection, can go in the opposite direction. Rather than becoming submissive and self-critical, they become bullies themselves and identify with their aggressors, modelling their behaviour on that of their abusers. Children can learn that, if they can threaten other people, those people won't threaten them. The problem with this, of course, is that, in terms of their brain development, all the systems that are important to compassion are not perceived as useful to them – in fact, they could even be unhelpful in developing this particular strategy for survival and self-protection. If other people have hurt and threatened you, they would think, why would you trust them? Why would you want to develop kindness? You must develop your self-protection first. So the social mentalities for compassion are underused and don't develop within the minds of these bullying individuals. Indeed such people can view having compassion for others as a weakness, making them vulnerable.

For them, the drive for power and being in control is a defence against other people controlling them – because they basically don't trust those in authority to love, care and look after them. Men from these backgrounds can regard women as something you can love or want but never as equals, because their mothers were never strong enough to protect them from their hostile fathers. If these damaged people strive for and get into positions of power, the rest of us suffer the consequences. Human history is riddled with them and their ruthless ambition. These individuals are less likely to be self-critical and much more likely to be blaming of others when things go wrong.

What shines through all of these examples is one underlying fear – the fear of disconnection in some way. If we knew fully and completely in our hearts that people will love us whether we succeed or fail, we wouldn't suffer anxieties to this degree. And, of course, it's not just in the home that these problems begin; they can also originate at school, with school bullies. And they're textured by our society, too. You see, the more we have to compete for social position, the more threatened we feel. The days when young boys ended their adolescence by following their fathers into apprenticeships or other work and there was a sense of community and belonging to one's traditional family group are long gone. There's little social continuity now for many of our adolescents. A feeling of alienation, of not really belonging anywhere – neither part of the world of children nor welcomed into the world of adults – haunts many. Because the human brain really doesn't like or do well with this sort of alienation, it reacts with a feeling of threat. And, of course, adolescents compete among themselves over things they believe that they need to own, all of which is driven by the business model of life.

There's also the issue of the sense of aloneness in shame. Since shame can be linked to being pushed away or seen as not worthy of much attention, children who are neglected can often have a sense of shame. It comes from emotional memories of being alone and not being able to influence others to take an interest in us.

From self-criticism to self-compassion

Because self-criticism can arise from a number of sources, one of the things we need to work on now is to identify where ours comes from and what our greatest fears would be in reducing it or even giving it up. We've discussed how self-criticism can be harmful to the brain and how self-compassion is good for it, but even so, you may be somewhat reluctant to give up self-criticism. So here's an exercise to help you.

Exercise: Distinguishing between shame-based self-criticism and compassionate self-correction

Have a pen and paper to hand. Now imagine that, after reading this book, you'll *never* be self-critical again. Close your eyes and really imagine that self-criticism isn't part of your make-up any more. Do spend some time on this. What are the first feelings that flush through you? What are your greatest fears? Now, if you're anything like me and the people I've worked with in the past then, like other human beings, you'll be able to produce all kinds of 'Yes, buts' to giving up self-criticism. These could include: 'Yes, but if I'm not self-critical, I might become lazy, I might not achieve, I might become arrogant and not see my faults, I might become unlikable.' You still believe that your self-criticism is helping you, don't you, at least some bits of it?

Now make two columns on a sheet of paper. Head one of them 'How my self-criticism helps me' and the other 'How my self-criticism hinders me'. Now write down all the advantages of self-criticism in the first column and all the disadvantages in the second one. What you might note when you look at what you've written are reasons why you're holding on to your self-criticism, why you can't give it up. So let's think how to address this with compassion.

First, I want to make a very clear distinction for you between shame-focused self-criticism and compassion-focused self-correction. This distinction is made on the basis of your *feelings*. You see, self-criticism is often accompanied by disappointment, frustration and even contempt, and it is these emotions that are really damaging to you, partly because they are coming from your threat/self-protection system. They stop you from realizing that, actually, you won't become arrogant because you have a *genuine wish* to be caring towards other people, and you won't be lazy because you have a *genuine wish* to achieve things and do well – not because you're going to criticize and kick yourself or be critical. Self-criticism can blind us to the *positive emotions and desires* within us and can fool us into believing that only if we have a stick at our backs will we become half-decent people.

You may remember your parents saying to you: 'Why do I always have to chase you? Why do I have to get angry with you before you'll do anything?' Knowing what I know now, I'd love to go back to adolescence and calmly tell my father: 'Hey, my not doing much isn't unusual. It's because I'm a teenager, created by a set of genes from you and Mum. That means that, at my age, I like to be with my mates, get pissed, sleep all day and play in my rock band at night. There's nothing abnormal about me – it's not my fault! Don't worry, I'll be okay.'

Of course, I recognize now that a lot of my parents' pushing was based on worry because we're in a competitive society and they were afraid that, if I didn't acquire the qualifications to compete, I wouldn't get anywhere in life – I'd not have that competitive edge. It was slightly worrying when, 30 years later, I found myself saying to my children about studying for their exams as well as about the washing-up: 'Why do I always have to chase you? Why do I have to get angry with you before you'll do anything?' Genetic programs are so boringly repetitive, aren't they? But I guess it's a matter of balance. Sometimes a little urgency is helpful, and these parental concerns can also be seen as expressions of caring, provided they're not expressed with hostility or contempt.

However, we still have the problem of what we do with our self-criticism and how we distinguish between it and self-correction. Indeed, when it comes to how we treat ourselves, it's about learning the distinction between shame-focused self-criticism and compassionate self-correction. Understanding these differences can help us deal with shame.

Self-criticism is usually backward-looking and focuses on the things that we've done; it doesn't encourage us for the future. It is normally accompanied by feelings of anger or contempt rather than support and encouragement; it often undermines our confidence rather than inspiring and developing it. Compassionate self-correction, on the other hand, when accompanied by compassionate feelings, can inspire us and help us face mistakes and learn from them. So let's remind ourselves of the qualities of compassion. They include: being motivated by caring and helping; being able to recognize and empathize with distress; fostering feelings of kindness, warmth and support and recognition of distress; developing patience and tolerance; looking at difficulties in order to learn from them and develop wisdom (*see* pp. 195–213).

In Table 5, it's quite easy to see the difference between compassionate self-correction and shame-based self-criticism. You can get the hang of it by imagining a child who is learning a new skill but is struggling and making mistakes. A critical teacher will focus on those mistakes, point out what the child is doing wrong, appear slightly irritated, imply that the child isn't concentrating or could do better if they tried. The basis of that style of teaching is really fear and shame – to make a child frightened or feel bad if they don't

Table 5: Distinguishing between shame-based self-criticism and compassionate self-correction

Shame-based self-attacking	Compassionate self-correction
• Focuses on the desire to condemn and punish • Punishes past errors and is often backward-looking • Is given with anger, frustration contempt, disappointment • Concentrates on deficits and fear of exposure • Focuses on a global sense of self • Includes a high fear of failure • Increases chances of avoidance and withdrawal.	• Focuses on the desire to improve • Emphasizes growth and enhancement • Is forward-looking • Is given with encouragement, support, kindness • Builds on positives (e.g. seeing what you did well and then considering learning points) • Focuses on attributes and specific qualities of self • Emphasizes hope for success • Increases the chances of engaging.
Consider example of critical teacher with a child who is struggling.	Consider example of encouraging, supportive teacher with a child who is struggling.
For transgression	*For transgression*
• Shame, avoidance, fear • Heart sinks, lowered mood • Aggression.	• Guilt, engaging • Sorrow, remorse • Reparation.

do well – and it's a common reason why children fail and give up.[10] Despite this, it was a common approach in teaching in the past – many doctors of my age tell me how consultants used to like to humiliate them when they were medical students, believing that this was good for their education.

We can contrast this with a compassionate teacher who recognizes that learning new skills can be difficult. This teacher acknowledges the struggle in new learning, recognizing that things that are worth learning are often difficult, and focuses on what the child does well and builds on that, praising their efforts, trying to develop a detailed understanding of where the difficulty lies, giving clear and accurate feedback on how to improve performance and providing opportunities for guided practice in a supportive, kind environment where making mistakes is part of the learning process. Now, of course, if the problem is in the child not making an effort, then the focus is on helping them try harder and seeing what the blocks are. It may well be the child's lack of interest, but it could also be their underlying belief that the task will eventually be too difficult and they will fail and be shamed, so why bother?

We can have these kinds of relationships with ourselves, too. Think about whether you have a critical teacher in your head or a compassionate one. If you realize that the way you deal with setbacks and mistakes is rather self-critical, then simply noticing this (without being self-critical!) and making a decision to switch to compassionate self-correction can be helpful and help you start gradually shifting the balance from shame-based self-criticism to compassionate self-correction. Some of my patients tell me that they can't imagine giving up self-criticism completely, so it's all about balancing, step by step, doing the best we can. Indeed, I'm still prone to self-irritation if I forget things.

Self-esteem versus self-criticism

If you're going to train your mind to be compassionate towards yourself and others, it's important to remember to balance the different emotion systems within yourself. Recently there's been a great deal of interest in harnessing self-esteem in children and adults, helping them become optimistic, achieve and persevere. There's a lot of wisdom in that and it seems to be helpful. However, concerns have been raised that self-esteem tends to increase when you're doing well – it focuses on getting ahead of others and is rather self-focused. Self-compassion, on the other hand, concentrates on how we treat ourselves when things are going badly. It teaches us to open our hearts to others and recognize that we're all struggling to avoid suffering and to be happy, that we all just find ourselves here and have been handed a set of genes and life experiences that have shaped our brain. You can see more debates on this on Kristen Neff's website <www.self-compassion.org>.

So self-esteem needs to be balanced with self-compassion, which brings us back to a previous point I've made, that it's so important to work on *how to fail,* how to accept that we may be less than we want to be, in order to free ourselves from that fear and continue on into 'just being.'

Shame and guilt

At the bottom of Table 5, you'll see that I made a distinction between guilt and shame with regard to transgressions – that is, making mistakes, breaking the rules or letting others down – and hurting others. This is important and something we've covered before (*see* pp. 210–13). Shame is really about the negative feelings we have about ourselves and the negative labels we give ourselves, as well as the bad things that other people feel about us. The psychology of guilt, on the other hand, focuses on the *other person.* It's about our behaviour and its impact on *them.* We must move psychologically towards the other person to try to understand their feelings in order to feel guilt and have sympathy and empathy with the hurt or upset of the other. It's not the global sense of the self as good or bad; it's about *specific* behaviour. You can't feel guilt for just having thoughts or feelings unless they result in actual harm. Feelings associated with such thoughts can feel shameful if you think they also reflect badly on you and how you're judging yourself ('I'm bad for thinking or feeling these things'). Guilt is an opening out to others if we've done harmful things to them. It's an important social emotion that helps us build relationships because it makes us think about the harm we do to others – in fact, looked at this way, we could do with more guilt and less shame in our societies!

In everyday life, of course, we usually have various mixtures of shame and guilt because, although they are quite different emotions, they can be activated together. One of the problems with shame and inducing shame in others is that, because shame is threat- and punishment-based and about the self feeling bad and open to rejection, people who feel it can defend themselves by denying that they've done anything wrong, to avoid the bad feelings that shame gives. They simply won't look at their harmful behaviour; they become more focused on defending their self-esteem. It's perhaps a strange thing then that developing compassion makes us more open to our transgressions and more willing to acknowledge when we've hurt others – sometimes purposefully, sometimes inadvertently. It enables us to feel that pain and want to make reparation.

So where does this leave us with regard to self-criticism? It helps us to see that shaming forms of self-criticism are usually not helpful for many reasons: they're punishment-focused and threat-activating. Compassionate self-correction and the desire to improve with encouragement and kindness comprise a different motivational system altogether. Our ability to tolerate guilt, to recognize when we've hurt others, to imagine ourselves in their position and to try to acknowledge and feel the pain we may have caused are important elements in developing compassion. Indeed, in many aspects of life, imagining ourselves in the minds of others and learning what they feel about our actions can be very helpful. Before saying hurtful things to your partner, for example, give a thought to how you would feel if your partner said that to you. This isn't intended to make you feel bad, but to help you with compassionate understanding.

Complications: Self-criticism and the fear of powerful and wanted others

Sometimes when my colleagues and I work with very depressed people who are very self-critical, it quickly becomes obvious that they're harbouring considerable anger that they're frightened of or extremely upset about.

They may behave in very submissive, withdrawn and self-blaming ways, but they clearly have serious conflicts with parents or partners.

Back in the 1880s, the German philosopher Friedrich Nietzsche said, 'No one blames themselves without a secret wish for vengeance.' Freud borrowed this for his theory of depression. He suggested that people become depressed because the anger they feel for others, who have hurt or let them down, is turned inwards. He thought that they couldn't express anger to others because they were dependent on them, and the depressed people were frightened that if they expressed anger, these others would turn against them.[11] If you're desperate to be loved and cared for by someone, you won't express anger towards them; if you did, your own sense being a 'nice and lovable person' could take a bit of a battering. So anger is suppressed because of its effect on the other person and how that makes you feel about yourself.

This strategy of blaming oneself for the bad behaviour of others is actually archetypal and also deeply embedded in many religious beliefs. This is how it works. We know that life has been very difficult for the human race, with diseases, droughts, wars and all kinds of catastrophes and dreadful tragedies befalling us. Then there is the little problem that we all decay and die. So humans, with their 'new minds', have tried to figure out why such awful things might be happening and what they can do about them. Many groups have developed beliefs about powerful deities who cause and control these frightening and tragic events. For example, seafaring peoples created gods of the sea, storms or sharks, but if you live in Tibet, you won't find any gods of the sea. The Greeks had gods of war, love, fertility and so on – all the processes and forces that scare us or are responsible for life's essentials (e.g. fertile lands). In addition, many of the gods worshipped by humans have proven to be pretty scary and fickle. Zeus could be very vindictive, as could the God of the Old Testament. The Aztec gods were none too nice either.

Now, in many societies, people worked out that if deities controlled good and bad things, then they needed to be brought on side, to be appeased, courted and won over. Since it was commonly men in charge of these religions, they thought, 'Hmmm . . . what would I like if I was a god? Aha!

I know – a few virgins perhaps! That's it! We'll send a few virgins to the gods, that's bound to impress them, then they'll be happy with us and be kind and helpful.' It all sounds very logical and reasonable, I guess, when we use projection (i.e. our own minds) to imagine what a god wants and desires. The concept of having to obey, submit and appease or give yourself to those who have power over you would make perfect sense to a human brain that evolved from primates – fear of dominant males is archetypal to primate societies and sexual access an appeasement.

But what happens if you obey, submit and sacrifice your virgins but the storms actually get worse or diseases like typhoid or malaria rip through your group, killing your children and other loved ones? Then you're raided by another tribe. You're a pre-science society so you have no way of understanding that this isn't personal to you; it's simply the flow of life and a consequence of the way malaria and typhoid are carried by mosquitoes and water. As for war, you wouldn't know that potential tribal conflicts are written in our genes and billions will die because of that, because we are easily seduced by tribal-identity stories, myths and heroic quests. So if you're in such a society, all you can do is to refer back to your gods. There's nothing else – no other hope. Now since those gods are powerful and you're weak, you can't be angry with them, because they really could harm you – you have no power over them whatsoever. If, on the other hand, they're not powerful and can't control these fates, they're probably not worth believing in, which takes you back to the fear and meaninglessness of these tragedies in life. Also, even if they might not control/interfere with things on the planet, the gods might still control things after death – so that's a snag! So you make the only 'safe' assumption you can: that for such bad things to have happened you must have done something wrong, you must have sinned and offended the gods, and so you now must submit and sacrifice some more. So even more virgins next year (or maybe the last ones lied about their sex lives!).

This kind of thinking can also lead to a very persecuting and paranoid in-group problem. If it wasn't me who sinned and caused the gods to be angry and desert us, then it must have been somebody else. We'd better find them quick! So let's seek out those individuals in our community who have broken the law and upset the gods and sacrifice them. For instance, in Genesis, Eve is blamed for humans beginning to sin and being expelled from the Garden of Eden, and as a result parts of the Bible can be pretty nasty about women in general. Wanting to persecute the disobedient because you're worried that they'd cause God's desertion or punishment opens the doors to our sadistic, hellish imaginations and concepts of mortal sin. These have terrified many people over many centuries. This behaviour is deeply uncompassionate, but then fear-based archetypes can be like that.

So our deep-rooted fear about life and death and the fragility of it all means that we blame ourselves (or others in our group). The only thing we can do to protect ourselves is to monitor our behaviour (or that of others who could offend the gods and cause problems for us) and try to ensure that we do what we're supposed to do in order to bring the power of the gods on side.

Despite the fact that we understand these processes fairly well now, it's tragic that so many societies and individuals are still caught up in this kind of terror management. Imagine going back in time to one of these societies and explaining to them that there are no gods in the form that they have been imagining them, that the diseases that befall them are rooted in the very flow of life and are part of its design and, in a thousand years' time, humans will understand this and have cures for these diseases, which are not god-given nor god-controlled. You can imagine how they'd treat you; they'd be very frightened of what you're saying because the implications would overwhelm their whole sense of self and meaning. Hmm . . . anyone for a sacrifice with you as the offering? Fear of and obedience to a fantasized dominant male authority in this world or the next remain potentially deeply problematic to us as a species.

Now how do these stories relate to self-criticism, anxiety and depression? Well, in fact, this way of thinking is not so dissimilar to the one I find when I work with depressed people. Their self-criticism has often developed in the context of powerful or threatening others; because of them, they've had to learn to self-blame and monitor themselves very carefully.[12] They keep checking that they're not going to do something that stirs up the anger of those threatening others. If there's nothing you can do to control those other, more powerful people, the only thing you can do is control your own behaviour. This is called an 'involuntary subordinate strategy' because it's the kind of thinking and attentional focus that goes with being a frightened subordinate.

Giving up self-blame and self-criticism can, therefore, feel frightening. And so we see here some rather complex defensive strategies that can operate outside of our conscious awareness and cause us rather a lot of trouble. Depressed people with this problem can only slowly come to understand it because it can overwhelm them. Caught up in this difficulty, they can become very focused on self-blame and a sense of badness and sin. Indeed, in centuries past but sometimes even today, depression is associated with the feeling of having offended God and being pushed away – out of God's love. This is because depression involves a toning down of our positive emotion systems, leaving us with awful feelings of isolation and disconnection. When trying to deal with their anger at life or at the deities that have let them down, or with their rage at their parents who were supposed to be loving and loved, people can be so frightened of their emotions and so want to be loved or protected by parents or partner that they can suffer a kind of inward collapse. So sometimes self-criticism is really a cover for the fact that we feel very angry with others: we're actually in conflict over that and frightened of our anger.

People can also be very frightened of the strength, sadism and vengefulness of their anger. Like Dr Jekyll and Mr Hyde or The Hulk, we are afraid that we can become 'possessed by anger', taken over by it, and run amok. It could become so intense that we'll lose control, and then we'd be back to shame again.

Compassion enables us to stand back and look with kindness at our intense rage while, at the same time, recognizing that we do indeed need to learn how to prevent ourselves from acting out the primitive emotions that swirl around inside us. Indeed, Freud and Jung based much of their thinking on the way in which we construct strategies to hide from our primitive impulses.

The compassionate approach does not simply try to soothe anger away. Compassionate mind training of the type that I'm concerned with here sees anger and hatred as tragedies, not poisons. The concept of a poison is an unhelpful concept with which to approach anger and hatred. This is because anger and hatred are usually linked to hurts and fears and to deep vulnerabilities, sometimes from the past and sometimes even to the whole process of life and death. Anger and hatred are both like a flame – it can cast light, give life-sustaining warmth, inspire and create passion but, unchecked and undirected, can also burn, cause intense pain and consume and turn to ash all that it touches. Anger and hatred should be seen as pointers, telling us to look back to find the source of our hurt and to be honest about our fear. In compassion-focused work, this is often the hardest thing to do, to be honest enough to work with the fear and grief that sits underneath anger.

Kim had severe depression. She believed that her body was diseased and felt that she had a basic badness inside of her. Her parents had brought her up to believe that they were a special loving family, chosen by God. However, when Kim was abused by a neighbour when she was eight years old, at first her family wouldn't believe it and then they implied that Kim must have done something to encourage it. Looking back, she now thinks that they were frightened of the neighbour and also of the potential scandal if they notified the police. She recognized that her parents often buried their heads in the sand or simply prayed if they had difficulties. Within just a few months of the abuse, the special loving relationship that Kim had thought she'd had with her mother had turned to dust. But, of course, she couldn't give it up because her parents had been the centre of her life and Kim so much wanted her mother to love her. Yet how could her mother refuse to believe Kim or to acknowledge her daughter's feelings, and what about her failure to protect Kim from the neighbour's abuse? If only her mother would acknowledge what had happened and apologize, but when Kim tried to broach the subject as an adult, her mother simply denied that it was that important. 'These things happen,' she said and would not discuss it further.

Kim had struggled through and had become a successful lawyer, but when she'd had her own children, the complexities and feelings of becoming a mother reactivated memories of how she herself had been mothered – and, with them, the rage and conflicts she continued to feel. However, when Kim started therapy, she was still completely unaware of her rage against her mother and was, in fact, still trying to impress her. Actually her family clung to each other as best they could but with a fair degree of pretence and delusion through which complex feelings were kept buried. Kim had many suicidal urges, often triggered by feelings of intense anger about some unknown something, feeling overwhelmed and then just wanting to run away. At times, she could be honest enough to admit thinking that maybe her suicide would bring other people to their senses and realize what they'd done to her. After a year or so of working on her anger, understanding it as an important feeling to own up to and link to her hurt and fear but also to move on from, and acknowledging that some of the anger that she directed at herself was actually a cover for anger she felt towards others, her depression lifted.

Now these are complex difficulties that often require professional help. But in less severe depression, it's useful to recognize that we can self-blame because we don't fully acknowledge how cross or angry we are with someone else. This doesn't for a moment mean that we need to act out our feelings or express that anger, but we do need to realize that compassion is not about denial of what we feel or that everything has to be quiet and soothing. Indeed, if you look at compassion, even aggressive images in Buddhism, some of them are extremely active.[13] Compassion is about trying to understand what we feel, working through it as best we can, trying to be honest about what we feel and to recognize that the feelings that flush through us are often coded in our emotional systems. Doing this takes courage, something we're going to explore in the next chapter.

Some compassion–focused exercises

This first set of exercises involves you thinking about the kinds of things that you are typically self-critical about or feel ashamed about. For ease of practice, we'll use the previous example of having guests, rushing out to buy a missing ingredient and burning some of the dishes. This is a fairly mild example, but it's not so much the content that's important as the process.

Exercise: 'Sitting' with your self-criticism

First, look back at Table 3 on page 314. Think of a situation that elicited a sense of shame and self-criticism in you. Using the table as a model, write down some of your worries about what (actual or imagined) was going through the minds of the others present, and then your own thoughts about yourself. Then try to identify your key threats and fears.

The next stage is to engage in a soothing breathing rhythm and bring to mind your compassionate image. This may be the image of your ideal compassionate other (*see* pp. 256–62) or it may be you putting yourself into a compassionate state through the method-acting example described on pages 251–3.

Now look at your self-critical thoughts and just breathe gently, being with your compassionate feelings and seeing what happens to them. If you feel that you're drifting back into feelings of self-criticism, just smile, pull back and refocus on warmth and kindness.

You might want to add to the exercise by imagining compassion flowing into your heart area or actually placing your right hand an inch above your heart and feeling the warmth (*see* pp. 263–4). Experiment to see what helps you.

Practise this a few times and make a note in your journal of what happens to your self-criticism when you just 'sit' with it accompanied by feelings of kindness, warmth and understanding. Remember that self-criticism is often based on fear or disappointment or is caused by echoes from the past.

Exercise: The many parts of me

In this exercise, we're going to use some of the skills of compassionate thinking that we looked at in the last chapter. So once again look at Table 3 on page 314 or perhaps the one that you created for the exercise above. Here are some compassionate and helpful alternatives to try out. For example, using the example of the burned dinner, you might think:

- This was disappointing, what a pain to forget that ingredient! It's understandable to be upset because I wanted to do better, but actually I carried it off pretty well and made a joke of it.

- People were more interested in chatting to each other than they were in marking my performance as a cook.

- My ability to get on with people is linked to how kind and considerate I am, not to whether I forget things.

- It's understandable that I forgot that ingredient because I've been very busy and rushed.

- So the reality is that it was a disappointment and a bit embarrassing, but I have no evidence that I've been rejected or have ended up with no friends. It was my threat system worrying on my behalf but unnecessarily on this occasion.

Okay, these are only suggestions – you may think of others that appeal to you more.

Cognitive therapists suggest that we should never globally rate ourselves because we're made up of lots of little 'I's', different bits and pieces. Take me – there's the guitarist me, the drunk me, the calm father, the angry father, the friend to others, the chooser of red wines, the dedicated therapist, the lazy therapist, the completely knackered therapist, and so on and on. There's no such thing as a single me to rate and judge! So disappointments are normally about specific behaviours or situations or specific elements of ourselves, and it's useful to recognize that specificity. It's also helpful to realize that it's often the level of stress, disappointment or anger that makes us go on the rampage and want to criticize and blame everything. Your compassionate mind will help you get things back into perspective, acknowledging the specific behaviour or thing that you're upset about. You can learn to be accepting of the disappointment or the things or the situations, and not self-criticize or self-condemn.

The trick is to get into the spirit of trying to generate alternatives by standing to one side of your distressing feelings and thoughts. Take a view from the balcony, as it were. You'll find it easy to 'Yes, but' your feelings and thoughts, and the practice is to note these 'Yes, buts' while also generating the alternatives because that's what you might need practice in. Now engage your compassionate imagery and soothing breathing rhythm and, with as much of warmth, kindness and encouragement as you can muster, read through those alternatives again, but this time focus on the warm and supportive feelings in them rather than whether you logically believe them or not.

Exercise: The unreliable self-critic

It's useful to stand back from your self-critical side and think: 'How much is it *genuinely* concerned with my well-being and how much does it have my best interests at heart?' Your self-critic certainly strikes when you feel threatened, disappointed or upset, but is it really interested in your well-being? It may kick you when you're down, and that's not very nice, is it? If you think back to people you've known who had a very critical and harsh attitude towards you, did they seem very loving and caring and genuinely interested in your well-being? If the answers to these questions are 'no', that's another reason to start to pull back from self-criticism. Yours isn't rooted in helping you achieve well-being or indeed the well-being of others. It's unreliable because it's based on threat, anger, fear or disgust.

So in this exercise simply take a piece of paper and write out all the reasons why your own self-criticism is unreliable. Try to really feel how it's threat-, anger-, fear- or disgust-based and doesn't have any kindness or real desire to see you flourish and feel happy. It is, of course, easy to become self-critical through annoyance or fear in the heat of the moment, or if we're very disappointed in our behaviour. But as we calm down we can genuinely decide to refocus on the compassionate and helpful aspects of our thinking rather than dwell on the self-critical. This exercise may help you see that self-criticism, which is always focused on the past and on what goes wrong, is thus very biased, unreliable and unhelpful as a life coach or guide.

Exercise: Your best interests at heart?

Sometimes we can identify key individuals – parents, teachers, bosses, school bullies – who have put us on the road to self-criticism. Try to bring these individuals to mind and then imagine asking them:

- Did you actually have my best interests at heart?

- What right did you have to pass judgement on me?

- What was it in your life that made you such a critic or have such a need to put me down?

Try to create a feeling of genuinely wanting to know, with an assertive expectation of an answer rather than with, say, angry, demanding feelings. You're trying to create inner feelings of 'calm' and 'assured' in this exercise.

These questions, if thought carefully about, will allow you to stand back and realize that the critical people were often themselves struggling in some way. For example, Margaret recognized that some of the envious attacks on her by her mother were probably because her mother had never felt valued as a child. Now this doesn't excuse her mother, of course, but finding this out did help Margaret realize that the attacks were not based on genuine aspects of herself but on her mother's own fragile sense of self. Never accept the judgement of anybody else unless you're convinced that they've got your best interests at heart and they don't just want to put you down to make themselves feel better!

One person I worked with came up with the thought: 'I think I've worked out why my mother used to criticize me so much. Somehow she didn't want me to be happy about the things she couldn't be happy about.' We didn't know positively if that was true, of course, but for this person, it was an important step on her road to reducing self-criticism. So in this exercise, write down who you think your main critics have been in your life or simply those who had a hand in developing your self-criticism. Then work out what might have been going on in their minds and explore whether they really had your best interests at heart. If not, complete this sentence: 'I don't think you had my best interests at heart because . . .'

You might even want to write a letter to your 'recalled critic' from the past, explaining why you don't believe that their criticism was based on genuine concern for you and why you now reject it. In this way, you can clarify in your mind the reasons why you're going to reject their criticism. Letters like this are usually not sent but are rather used to illuminate your own inner position.

Exercise: Writing about our conflicted feelings

If some of your self-criticism is linked to conflicting feelings – for example, you feel very angry with somebody whom you also love – you should recognize this as a *normal* human difficulty. One thing that can help is to write down things about that person that you're angry with. Try putting all this to the individual in a letter. You may choose not to send it or, if you do, only after giving it some thought, because this exercise is for your own exploration rather than for confronting others. Begin your letter with: 'I find this very difficult to write because . . .' or 'I find it very difficult to tell you this because . . .' This will help you articulate your conflict.

Your feelings may be linked to regarding yourself as a kind, lovable or nice person who is not supposed to get angry or have other, similarly upsetting feelings. But do keep in mind that you never designed these feelings; they were designed for you. All you can do is to try to work with them and through them. In time, this may lead you to being more assertive in your behaviour. Or you might find that, as you understand these conflicting feelings better, they change.

When you've expressed your anger in your letter (and go for it – no holding back here), then smile, acknowledging this all-too-human feeling, and take a few soothing breaths. Then write about all the things that you love about that person, the things that you appreciate. Think how you would like that person to flourish, grow and be free from suffering in their life, and write to them about that. Again, these sorts of letters are often not sent, but if you do want to send yours, give yourself time to think about it first.

Of course, there may be no conflict and you are actually angry with somebody you just don't like. Even so, it can be helpful to try to write a few compassionate paragraphs trying to understand him or her. Remember that the point of this letter is to help you concentrate on your criticism over a conflict or strong emotion, to see it as normal but also be able to work with it.

For more details on compassionate letter writing, see page 347.

Exercise: Blaming others and forgiveness

It can sometimes seem that giving up self-criticism is just blame-shifting. We hear people on television and radio going on about the fact that psychotherapists are too much into parent-blaming and foster victim psychology. Sometimes that's true, perhaps, but it is, of course, typical for some powerful adults to look at children and say, 'Don't blame us parents!' and push the blame back on to them. These commentators can continue to perpetuate child-blaming, which is often what children encounter in the first place and which makes them depressed or anxious. In fact, as I've mentioned before, many depressed people actually blame themselves *to avoid blaming their parents*. However, learning to be honest about what has gone on in our lives and our feelings about it is important for change.

None the less, these commentators have a point: coming to understand why we feel as we do, why we tend to be critical of ourselves, and the role that powerful others have played in our lives is to liberate us. It's not about becoming an angry, powerless victim, but about honesty and openness, compassion and forgiveness. So understanding the sources and origins of our self-criticism and acknowledging and working on unprocessed emotions and yearnings are hugely important. However, we have to move on from that anger or yearning.

One way of avoiding simple blame-shifting and victim psychology is to recognize when it arises in you. You can then move from anger to letting go and forgiveness – assuming that you understand what forgiveness is and isn't. Being in a state of non-forgiveness means that you're in a state of anger, with a sense of injustice and wanting recompense. This means that your threat system is active and churning away in you. Forgiveness is a way in which you can change your emotional orientation to those who have hurt you. Forgiving others doesn't mean holding them in your mind in angry, vengeful ways. You may never like the people you forgive nor ever wish to see them again, but forgiveness is a way of releasing yourself from the chains of anger that bind you to those who have hurt you. It's tricky, though, and isn't just a submissive 'What you did to me doesn't matter' approach.

So when you write your letters or become clearer about your feelings towards those who may have been harsh to you, keep in mind that the point of this is to acknowledge and move on. Focus on what's helpful to you. Rather than concentrating on blaming others, which doesn't nurture or calm you, complete relevant statements, such as:

- Given my background, it would be helpful for me to . . .

  ....

- To be compassionate and caring of myself, I have to . . .

  ....

Think about how you might help someone you care about to 'move on'. Another useful exercise is to imagine that you're talking to your ideal compassionate image about these issues.

In this exercise, we're trying to recognize understandable reasons for why we may have become self-critical, look at those afresh, acknowledge our anger or disappointment with others because they were wrong in their judgements or treatment of us, and return our focus to our compassionate development. This helps us avoid the pitfalls of getting stuck in powerless victimhood and instead we seek to take responsibility for our lives and feelings. Be sure to focus on kindness while working through this. Note, too, that as with all these exercises, if you feel that you need the help of others, including a professional therapist, open your heart to that – do the exercise and see if it will help you.

Exercise: Standing up to your self-critic

This exercise is probably best tackled when you've got the hang of the previous six. Here, you're going to try to visualize your self-criticism. If you could take it out of your head and look at it, what would it look like? Would it be human or non human? If human, what would its facial expressions be? What emotions would it direct at you?

Next, imagine you're a wise, compassionate person (*see* pp. 251–3). Now spend a minute or two really getting into that feeling state of mind – it takes time to shift states. When you can feel it, imagine saying to your self-criticism: 'Look, I'm sorry you're angry, upset, frightened and feeling vulnerable and that you want to lash out like this. However, this isn't the way it needs to be. I'm going to be more in charge now.'

What you're doing here is standing up to the critical side of yourself, recognizing that it's linked to threats, disappointments or voices from the past, but also realizing that you've arrived at a point in your life when your compassionate self is going to be more in control. You aren't aggressive or threatening to your critical side – that would be like teaching children not to be violent by being violent to them. If you focus on your compassionate self, you'll find that you just feel more powerful, more mature and wiser than your internal bully and realize that the criticism really stems from fear and sadness. It can be interesting to see how your image of your inner critic changes as you stand up to it. As I've said, the idea here is to create a different emotional texture and not fight with it.

Here is another exercise you can try. Once again engage in your soothing breathing rhythm and imagine yourself as a compassionate person. Then look at the part of you that's critical; see the facial expressions and emotions inside the critical you. Now to stay with those feelings and send compassion to your self-critic. You are not debating or engaging with the critical part of you, simply recognizing its threat- and fear-based feelings and having compassion for them.

A third exercise related to this is to imagine that your ideal compassionate image is with you and is being very compassionate to your critical side. It has a genuine interest in the fears and issues that are of concern to your inner critic (e.g. failure, rejection, etc.). It has compassion for the critic but is also clear that its anger and fear are not helping you pursue your goals. Again, the point of the exercise is to observe how you feel when you do this.

A word of caution: as I've mentioned above, sometimes self-criticism actually hides the desire for vengeance, or it needs to be recognized and acknowledged. In these situations, it can be important to be assertive. For example, Mary recognized that some of her self-criticism stemmed from her mother's criticism of her. Mary recognized that she was disappointed in herself because she couldn't do well enough to stop her mother's criticism or win her praise. To work on this, Mary imagined telling her mother exactly how disappointed she was and that the criticism was very hurtful to her. This is an example where it's important to be clear and assistive to a critic that you've taken into your head.

As I've already noted, sometimes people are very frightened to direct their hostility outwards. It's not uncommon for people who have been abused to blame themselves because they are very frightened of blaming other people. When they think about doing that, they just become very anxious. If that is true for you, you might want to seek professional help.

Exercise: Coping in the moment

In the process of learning to be more attentive to your feelings and thoughts, you might be able to identify just when self-criticism hits you. Then you can learn to cope 'in the moment' (*see* pp. 299–301).

A useful thing to do is to separate clearly from your self-evaluation the anxiety that you might feel when somebody criticizes your work, or the disappointment that you might feel if something doesn't work out as you would like. Try to accept the anxiety as understandable, treat it compassionately, then step to one side of your self-criticism and be mindful of it.

You can also use imagery to practise holding a compassionate feeling in yourself in the face of self-criticism. So try this exercise: Imagine someone criticizing you and then you adopting your compassionate posture and facial expression and acknowledging the criticism but without self-blaming. The idea is that you can begin to bring this 'into the moment', when criticism or conflicts actually occur.

Exercise: Limiting your criticism of others

This may be the hardest exercise of all. Research suggests that some self-critics are also quite critical of other people. Try to monitor how often you have critical thoughts or say critical things about others, either directly to them or behind their backs, or if you simply ruminate on these thoughts. Don't be self-critical about this: observe that it happens and think to yourself: 'What is that about? Why did I need to do that? Where is the fear and vulnerability in me?'

Treat your criticism of others compassionately, and avoid shaming yourself for it because then it will be difficult to work with. At the same time, ask yourself if you want to be different. One of the problems with living in a world in which you're critical of others is that you'll constantly be stimulating your threat/self-protection system. As we saw in Chapter 8, as we can create feelings of compassion and loving kindness for others in ourselves, this action stimulates our brains in a different and positive way. So even if you feel justified in being critical of others, you're still far better off practising generating compassion for others.

Compassionate letter writing

There is now evidence that it can be a great help to learn 'expressive writing'[14] – that is, writing about difficulties, problems and dilemmas. Compassionate letter writing is a way of doing this. The idea is to help you refocus your thoughts and feelings on being supportive, helpful and caring of yourself, rather than self-critical. Practising this can help you access an aspect of yourself that will tone down your more threat-focused feelings and thoughts. Through it, you can get your compassionate mind to think things through with you, and it's a way for you to exercise a certain quality of mind.

Before you begin your letter, try to ensure that you'll have some time when you won't be disturbed. Get a sheet of paper and a pen or pencil, engage in a soothing breathing rhythm, then either bring your compassionate image to mind and imagine it writing the letter with you or put yourself into your compassionate state and imagine yourself as a highly compassionate person (*see* Chapter 8) writing a letter. Spend a few moments really thinking about this and trying to feel in contact with that 'kind' part of you.

As you write your letter, try to allow yourself to have *understanding* and *acceptance* for your situation, difficulty, feelings or distress. For example, your letter might start with: 'I'm sad that you feel distressed' or 'Your distress is understandable because . . .' Or if you're writing from the compassion itself, you might start with: 'It's sad that I'm feeling distressed today, but this is understandable because . . .' It's not known whether it's more helpful to write such a letter from the 'I' (first person singular) point of view or, by imagining a compassionate image or friend writing to you, from the 'you' (second person singular) viewpoint. Just work out what's best for you.

In the next stage, note the reasons for your distress, realizing that it makes sense. This is called 'validation of feelings'. Then perhaps you could continue your letter with: 'I'd like you to know that . . .' – that is, your letter might point out that distress comes with a powerful set of thoughts and feelings, so that how you see things right now may be the distressed rather than the balanced view on things. Given this, we can try to step to one side of the distress and focus (through writing) on how best to cope and what is helpful and balance our minds.

Any number of ideas might appeal to you to be included in your letter. Do *not* feel that you have to cover them all. In fact, you might want to tackle different things in different letters to yourself. With all of these ideas, try to avoid telling yourself what you should or should not think, feel or do. There's no right or wrong way; it's the process of trying to think in a *different* way that's important.

Standing back

Once you've acknowledged your distress, it is useful if, while writing your letter, you can stand back from the distress of your situation for a moment. If you could do that, what would be helpful for you to focus on and attend to? For example, you might think about how you'll feel about the situation in a couple of days, weeks or months, or you might recall that distressing feelings can lift and remember how you'll feel then. It can also be helpful to recall in your letter, thus bringing to your attention, the times when you've coped with difficulties before. If you show a tendency to dismiss them, note this but try to keep your focus on your letter. It will concentrate on your efforts and on what you *are* able to do.

Your compassionate mind might gently help you – with kindness and understanding – to see things in a less black and white way. It's never condemning and will assist you in reducing your self-blaming. If someone has shunned you and you're upset by that, your compassionate mind will enable you to recognize your upset and also that such thoughts as 'That person doesn't like me and therefore I'm unlikable' may be very unfair. So you might write:

> I felt very upset when this person shunned me. But humans occasionally do that, and given some of the things that I've had to contend with in my life, it's understandable why being shunned is particularly upsetting to me. I guess I can see that this person does tend to be like this and can be quite moody – and not just to me. I guess they have difficulties of their own. It can't be much fun being moody like that. I have other friends who don't treat me this way and I'm just going to remember them and the feelings I have when I'm with them.

You might find some of the questions in Chapter 9 useful here.

If you've forgotten to do something, or have made a mistake and are very frustrated and cross with yourself, your compassionate mind will understand your frustration and anger and will also help you to see that the mistake was a genuine one and isn't evidence of you being stupid or useless. Finally, it will assist you in deciding what will be the most compassionate and helpful thing to do in these circumstances. It doesn't offer advice, though, or say, 'You should do this or that,' because in your heart you know this already and you don't need telling. What you do need is understanding and support to do what you think will be helpful to you.

Not alone

When we're distressed, we can often feel that we're different from other people in some way. However, rather than feeling alone and ashamed, remember that many others feel just as anxious, fed up or depressed with negative thoughts about themselves, the world and their future. In fact, at least one person in 20 may be depressed at any one time. So while your depression may be very regrettable, it's far from uncommon and isn't a personal weakness, inadequacy, badness or failure.

So in your letter, you could write:

> It's very understandable to feel upset because this is how our minds tend to work. Sadly it's also part of the human condition for us to have these kinds of feelings. They're difficult but I'm not the only person who has them. They're not a mark of anything bad about me, in particular. And I've had these feelings before and have come through them.

Coping with disappointment, loss and fear

If you're feeling down or disappointed or are being harsh on yourself, note in your letter that self-criticism is often triggered by disappointment (e.g. because you've made a mistake or because you don't look like you want to), loss (e.g. of hoped-for love) or fear (e.g. of criticism and/or rejection). Maybe being self-critical is the way you've learned to cope with these things or to take your frustration out on yourself, but this isn't a kind or supportive thing to do. Understandable, perhaps, but it won't help you to deal with the disappointment, loss or fear. So you need to acknowledge and be sensitive to those feelings, and be understanding and compassionate about the disappointment, loss or fear.

Compassion in action

It's useful to think about what might be the compassionate thing *to do* at this moment or at some time ahead – how might your compassionate part help you do that? So in your letter you may want to think about how you can bring compassion into action in your life. If there are things that you have been avoiding or finding difficult to do, write down some small steps you could take to move yourself forward. Write down ideas that will encourage and support you to tackle the things that you might find difficult. If you're unsure of how to proceed, try brainstorming as many options as you can think of and then decide which ones appeal to you.

Could you ask others for help? Opening our hearts to the help of others and trying to rally as much support as we can when we have difficult things to do are both indicative of a compassionate approach to life.

Dilemmas

If you're in a dilemma about something, focus on the gentle compassionate voice inside you and write down the different sides of the problem. Note that dilemmas are often difficult, and that, at times, hard choices have to be made, so this may take a bit of time to work through. Talking it through with others might be helpful. Sometimes we know in our hearts that we have to change – to give up a lifestyle or even a relationship – and so our compassionate letter will help us think this through and recognize that there may be some grief and loss. Acceptance of the benefits and losses of a decision can take time.

Compassion for feelings

Your compassionate mind will have compassion for your feelings. If you have powerful feelings of frustration, anger or anxiety, then compassionately recognize these. These emotions are part of being human and can become more powerful when we are distressed, depressed or frightened, but they don't make you a bad person – just a human being trying to cope with difficult feelings. We can learn to work with these feelings as part of our 'humanness' without blaming or condemning ourselves for having them – remember: you never built these emotion systems. We can, on the one hand, become mindful and not fight or try to avoid them and, on the other, not ruminate or dwell on them. We become more observant of them, like watching eddies in a river. Your compassionate mind will remind you that we often don't choose to feel negatively and that these feelings can come quite quickly. In this sense, it is 'not our fault', although we can learn how to work with these difficult feelings and take responsibility for them.

Loss of positive feelings

If you're feeling bad because you've lost positive feelings, be compassionate about this loss – it's very sad. Sometimes we lose loving feelings because a relationship has run its course, or we are just exhausted, or depression can block our positive emotion systems. As we recover from the depression, these positive systems can return. Your compassionate letter can help you see this without self-blaming.

What is helpful

Your letter will be a way of practising how to really focus on the things that *you* feel will help you. Other people can come up with all kinds of good solutions and suggestions, but these won't necessarily fit you, even if you think they 'ought to'. If thoughts come to mind that make you feel worse, then notice them, let them go and refocus on what might be helpful – remember, there are no 'I shoulds'. Some people put aside their letters until the next day, when they find that they can think things through in a different way.

When my colleagues and I work with patients, we sometimes find that they're not sure about what would be helpful to them. Learning how to discover what is useful is half the battle, but that takes experimentation, trying this and that. Be prepared for the fact that it may take some time.

Warmth

Now, as you write your letter, try to focus on feelings of warmth and a genuine desire to help. Spend time breathing gently and really try, as best you can, to let feelings of warmth be there for you. If you were writing to somebody else, would you feel that your letter was kind and helpful? Could you change anything to make it more so?

Some cautions

There are various things to look out for when writing compassionate letters – in particular, the validation of your feelings. For example, go back to page 349 where a person was dealing with being shunned at work. Now an invalidating and unhelpful letter might read something like this:

> Dear Me/self/your name,
>
> I'm so sorry to hear that you were feeling distressed and upset because your friend shunned your work. This is upsetting especially given some of the things that have happened in the past. However, you know that it's the past operating through the present and you do have a tendency to make mountains out of molehills. So you should try to get hold of your thinking and achieve a better, more balanced perspective. You clearly won't feel okay if you continue to dwell on your anger. So you must stop this because you know it's bad for you. Be positive and focus on positive things. You need to refocus your attention and do some of those exercises that are in this book . . .

The first bit is okay but the rest of it is awful. To be told that you tend to 'make mountains out of molehills' and 'you should try to get hold' and 'you must stop dwelling on the past' and 'you need to think positively and refocus' – well, you can see that these statements are all very uncompassionate. This letter was written as if by a stern, harsh, cold parent who, full of advice, delivers it in such an unhelpful way that you just feel that you've been 'naughty' for getting upset.

Contrast that letter with this one, focused on compassion and kindness:

> Dear Me/self/your name,
>
> I felt very upset when my friend shunned me. But humans feel upset by such things, and given some of the things I've had to contend with in my life, it's understandable why feeling shunned is particularly upsetting to me. If I stand back a bit, I guess I can see

that this person does tend to be like this and can be quite moody – and not just to me. I guess they've difficulties of their own; it can't be much fun being moody like that. I have other friends who don't treat me this way and I'm just going to remember them and the feelings I have when I'm with them.

I guess I also got upset because life has been a bit of a struggle recently. There have been conflicts with my son and I guess I'm worried about him really. Sometimes we're just at loggerheads . . .

In your letter, you can let your mind and writing flow with your worries and concerns. Remember to make the *emotional tone* as compassionate and as gentle and understanding as you can. You might also find it helpful to go through the checklist in Chapter 9 (*see* pp. 295–7), derived from the compassion circle in Chapter 6. As you write your letter, remember the compassion circle on page 194 and ask yourself:

- Is my motivation genuinely one of caring, nurturing and helping me?

- Am I being sensitive to and observant of my feelings?

- Am I allowing myself to be moved by my distress rather than trying to block it out?

- Am I being mindful and tolerant, recognizing the human condition?

- Am I being empathic, standing back and trying to understand my feelings and the way in which I think?

- Am I being non-judgemental?

- Am I keeping my emotional tone as focused on warmth and kindness as I possibly can?

These are the qualities that you're trying to bring to your letter writing. The compassion skills comprise the ways you use your attention and imagination, your thinking and reasoning, your behaviour and feelings.

When you've written your letter, read it slowly and gently back to yourself. You can do this silently or aloud, using a slow, soft tone of voice. See how you feel about it – does it seem to you to have warmth? It might even make you tearful if you've included things that are painful for you. If your letter leaves you cold in any way or feeling that you 'should' be trying to do something different, then you might have to refocus on compassion a bit. Ideally the letter will help you feel validated, supported, understood and encouraged – if, at times, sadder.

Remember that, although this might occasionally seem difficult to do, you're exercising a part of your mind that can be developed to be helpful to you. The key is your desire and effort to become inwardly gentle, compassionate and self-supportive. The benefits may not be immediately apparent, but like exercising to get physically fit, they'll usually emerge over time with continued practice.

Sometimes people find that, even though they're depressed, they'd very much like to develop a sense of self that can be wise and compassionate to both themselves and others. You can practise thinking about how, each day, you can become more and more as you wish to be. As in all things, there will be good times and times that are not so good. Spend time practising your postures and facial expressions that go with being compassionate, and practise creating compassionate thoughts and feelings inside yourself. This means being open with your difficulties and distress, rather than just trying to get rid of them. Look at your letter and make sure that it's written in the same way as it would be to a friend who is distressed and in exactly your situation and you were trying to help her or him.

Some general points

Moving towards compassion

Self-criticism usually builds up over a long period, by which time it performs various functions for you. In compassion-focused work, my colleagues and I suggest to our patients that they don't have to give up their self-criticism all in one go or even at all if they don't want to.

An alternative way of thinking is to consider that you're *moving towards* a compassionate position, a place that you might come to prefer. You may then find that, as you naturally become more compassionate in your thinking, feeling and behaviour, somehow your self-criticism just doesn't seem as appropriate any more. You haven't had to challenge it, convince yourself to change or fight against being self-critical. It just becomes less appropriate for you. Indeed sometimes when we've learned to be compassionate to our self-critical side, we recognize that it's a very frightened part of us, one that panics over disappointments or struggles to come to terms with the fact that, for example, our body shapes don't fit the social desired norm.

Grief

As we move away from self-criticism and shame, we're also moving away from a sense of isolation and being cut off. This can open up inner feelings of grief because our self-criticism may have started because we wanted to feel wanted, included and loved and we are now beginning to realize what a struggle it's been. It's as if we're starting to recognize just how alone and isolated we've been and maybe there's a possibility of coming home. This isn't an uncommon experience when people begin to feel compassion for themselves. Those who practise mindfulness can also become aware of a sadness that's been sitting somewhere in the corner of their mind. However, if this grief is overwhelming, some people use that as a reason to back off from being compassionate.

If that happens to you, you might like to seek professional help, or find someone who can guide you through it. All the little hurts in our lives can combine and build up into what may seem like an unbearably intense sense of grief, hurt and isolation. And if we're even mildly depressed, that can make grief feel even more powerful. But grief is a very normal and important process, and sometimes just being 'mindfully' with our grief and sadness and acknowledging them allows us to feel again and heal.

Conclusion

We humans are often highly self-judging and self-evaluating beings. This is because we've evolved a sense of self and self-awareness, we're concerned with how we exist in the minds of others and we worry about how we'll fit in with them. It is also because we can treat ourselves as objects. So just as we can get annoyed with others who don't do as we want or aren't as we want them to be, so we can have these feelings and thoughts for ourselves. Our awareness of causing others upset and that it's unkind to be critical may stop us from openly expressing hurtful things to others, but when it comes to ourselves, we may not feel so inhibited. And because it happens inside us, we have immediate access to our critical thoughts – other people only have access if we tell them! So self-criticism is one of the most disruptive inner processes and barriers to happiness and well-being. It is usually linked to disappointment and fear, and stimulates the threat/self-protection system.

The self-compassion approach is to discover the sources of our self-criticism (including, at times, anger that we're too frightened to acknowledge or work with) and to develop understanding of and kindness towards it. In addition, we need to practise switching from shame-based self-criticism to compassion-based self-correction. We start from the position that, as evolved beings, our complex minds can often be extremely confusing, powerful and difficult. This is absolutely not our fault, but only we can take responsibility for trying to do something about having such minds. If we approach the problem with gentleness and kindness, rather than with blame and anger, we'll get much further.

We've explored various ways in which we can identify our self-critical thoughts and what we fear other people might be feeling about us. If we can write these down or articulate them, we can bring our compassionate minds to bear on them. Finally, we looked at developing compassionate letter writing. This gives us a way of expressing our feelings and the things that upset and worry us. We then engage in validating and recognizing the source of them, so that we can be gentle and kind with them in order to heal.

Worksheet 2: From self-criticism to self-compassion

1. If something has distressed or upset you, note the feelings that this produces in your body.

2. Recognize that your body is responding in a way that it's been programmed to respond. You need to help it by focusing. So take a moment to think about your breathing and slowing down. If it helps, put your hand one inch above your heart (*see* p. 263) or hold your soothing stone (*see* p. 264–7) or take out and look at your soothing postcard (*see* p. 286).

3. Now, as best you can, become mindful of any thoughts or feelings that you have about yourself that seem to be associated with your upset. Notice them without, if you can, engaging too much with them. Recognize them as old patterns, perhaps hiding various fears, or maybe it's a voice of someone from the past. If it helps, bring your attention gently back to your breathing.

4. Now allow yourself to focus your attention on your compassionate image, allowing yourself to have a gentle, compassionate smile. Understand the pain of your distress and really attend to the message of support and compassion that you can generate inside yourself. You may not be able to see or sense this clearly, but the act of focusing can help you.

5. Try to bring to mind times when you've felt kind to yourself or others and allow yourself to focus on that feeling. Listen intently to what your compassionate mind is saying to you. Try to feel compassion flowing through you.

6. Notice your thinking and allow that to be compassionate, too. Remember that you are in the flow of life; you did not choose these feelings or your distress. Keep in mind that many humans suffer with self-criticism and distress as you do; it's not your fault. Distinguish clearly between your distress or disappointment and your sense of yourself,

which is a point of self-aware consciousness. Hear the voice in your mind as gentle and warm, kind and wise. There may be things that upset or disappoint you, but these are not judgements of your whole self or being.

Write down your reflections on this process:

In a day or two, revisit this worksheet. Think about how you could improve on what you've done, to make it more effective for you. You're trying to develop compassionate attention, compassionate thinking and reasoning and compassionate behaviour, and to infuse these with warmth, kindness and support.

In the following, complete the sentences and answer the questions:

Helpful and useful compassionate attention for me would be:

Helpful and useful compassionate thinking and reasoning for me would be:

Helpful and useful compassionate behaviour for me would be:

Helpful and useful compassionate practice for me would be:

What would be a helpful way for me to bring this into my life so that I can practise it, even if just a few minutes a day?

What is my greatest challenge in switching from self-criticism to self-compassion and what would be most helpful for me in making this transition in my life?

11 Compassion and Emotions: Working with anxiety, anger and forgiveness

This chapter explores compassionate ways to think about, and work with, our emotions. Originating in brain systems that were built long ago, they can be very fast to arise in us and at times be extremely powerful, pushing us to think and do certain things. Now we can't examine all our emotions, of course, so we are going to focus primarily on our threat/self-protection emotions – anxiety and anger – because these are the ones that can cause us a lot of pain and difficulty. We'll see how our 'new brains/minds', which comprise thinking, fantasizing and reflective self-awareness, can be very helpful or very unhelpful in dealing with emotions, either calming us or driving our emotions to greater intensities.

When exploring any emotion, the key messages are: learn to be honest about it, accept it, discover how to tolerate it and work with it in a kind way. So the first thing is to decide how to approach our emotions. However, there can be confusion because some schools and traditions talk about 'destructive' emotions and the fact that, because we suffer various 'poisons' of fear, attachment, greed, envy, anger and hatred, we must learn to battle with or rid ourselves of these emotions. They can also be seen as 'sinful' feelings. With this way of thinking, it's easy to try to 'de-sin' yourself or try to get rid of your 'bad' and 'poisoning' emotions, desires or fantasies. People may start to have ideas such as 'I shouldn't feel this but I should feel that', 'This is a good feeling but that is a bad one' or 'This feeling makes "me" bad' or 'This feeling makes "me" good.' People try to separate the good from the bad, to purify themselves, something that, in psychological speak, is called 'splitting'. Heaven and hell are the result of splitting – all that's good and pure goes upwards and the nasty bits go downwards. The search for purification and splitting can take us to the road to sadism, as we'll see in our next chapter.

Mindfulness and meditation (which actually means familiarization) can't be used 'to rid' ourselves of things. Rather, it helps us understand, tolerate, cope with and avoid intensifying unnecessarily, and enables us to soothe our feelings. It also helps us understand the power of emotions and how (without training our minds) they can so easily dictate behaviour.

So, don't be confused by suggestions that you should approach your emotions with the intention of purifying yourself. Purification is good for bodies that have to deal with and get rid of viruses and bacteria, but this approach is *no good at all* for dealing with our psychology and emotions. Here we need engagement, integration, transformation, transcendence and healing. People may spend years trying to purify their minds and control their emotions, or stop feeling, wanting or thinking certain things, but developing self-compassion moves us in exactly the opposite direction. Not only is it impossible to get rid of undesirable emotions (any more than you can stop yourself needing food), it is also unhelpful. Research shows that the more we try to suppress or get rid of certain feelings, thoughts or memories, the more they come back as unwanted intrusions into our minds or dreams. Rather it is more useful to go into these painful areas of our minds with openness, acceptance, curiosity and kindness. It's compassionate to recognize that our capacity to feel these things was built for us by our genes and social environments and, in that sense, they are not our personal creations.

Emotions are not poisons to be avoided or got rid of but may, in fact, have important things to reveal to us. For example, a person who becomes addicted to the buzz of internet pornography or shopping may be trying to avoid feelings of desperate aloneness, fear of rejection, social anxiety or perhaps anger. A kind but firm exploration of the *function* of a behaviour, lust or emotion can be useful. So the question to ask ourselves is: 'What would I feel if I stopped acting on my feelings? What do I want to do?' What do you think would happen if you stopped having that glass of wine every night when you come home from work? It's then up to you if you want to work on what you discover from the answer to such a question. The question also invites you to become mindful of your emotions and learn, with an open and curious mind, to observe them and pay attention to how they work in your body and on your thoughts. This isn't always an easy road and sometimes professional help is useful, particularly for anger and anxiety.

Compassionate behaviour

One vital aspect of compassionate behaviour is the way we act when our emotions are aroused. Anger and anxiety are the two most powerful emotions in our brains, and more processing systems are given to each of them than to any other emotion. This is because they have been essential to our (and all mammalian) protection and survival. Anger can alert us to blocks and frustrations, to cheating or injustice and inspire us to change things,[1] while anxiety can warn us of dangers and encourage us to take action to protect ourselves.

However, these basic, primitive emotions are also a source of great unhappiness and possibly even the seeds of our own destruction (*see* Chapter 4). Not only is anxiety very unpleasant, it can make us run away from things and stop us from developing the lives we would like, or prevent us from standing up for ourselves and our values. Anxiety can stop us understanding our minds because we try not to think about things that upset or frighten us. It can also make us go along with things that, in our hearts, we know are wrong, just because we're frightened of shame or rejection, which we'll investigate in our next chapter. As for anger, well, that has obviously been linked to violence against children, spouses, strangers, outsiders and even ourselves. Fear and the inability to turn anger into assertiveness can lurk at the heart of many depressions. Raised levels of anger and irritability are also linked to a range of health problems, especially cardiovascular diseases.

There are also, of course, our 'new brain/mind' abilities of imagination, anticipation, fantasy and rumination. These can drive anxiety and rage into extremes and maintain them over long periods. Our thoughts and imaginations, which can drive our feelings to excess, can be a long way from reality and we can lose contact with what is compassionate, helpful or calming. No doubt at all, then, that anger and anxiety can spell trouble.

Courage

Given that anger and anxiety can wreak such havoc in our lives and the lives of others, one would hope that our education system would offer ways to help us understand and learn to cope with them. Sadly not, because schools are set up to educate us sufficiently to produce goods and services rather than enabling us to develop insight into our minds and learn how to foster our well-being with these tricky brains of ours.

Now perhaps one of the most important lessons we have learned in the last 30 years, especially from the behaviourists, is that powerful threat-based feelings can arise in us very quickly and for many reasons, so we need to be alert and learn how *not* to act on our feelings. The essence of our ability to deal with these painful feelings is *courage*. Now courage isn't easy to define. In fact, in his fascinating book on the subject,[2] William Miller refers to the 'mystery of courage'. People can find themselves behaving courageously automatically and, in those moments, have little fear. Courage can operate with high fear or from a well-considered point of principle. Of the religions, Christianity places courage at its centre and makes it clear that it's not permissible to act out one's fear or desires for vengeance – even to the point of allowing oneself to be tortured and killed. Sadly, though, by the time of the Crusades, this focus for courage had been completely reversed and was now all about conquering and slaughtering.

With all our behaviours, though, the key is to understand their function and intention. This is also the case for compassionate behaviour. This isn't always easy because some of our intentions are unconscious to us. Evolutionists might say that the mother who runs into the burning house to save her baby simply wants to save her genes and is acting out a basic protection strategy. This raises the issue that courage needs to be considered not just as automatic reactions but also as linked to the *choices* that we make. Again function is important here. Teenage males herded into armies and charging at each other using spears, arrows, bullets or bombs could be seen as courageous, but what about suicide bombers who also sacrifice themselves for what they believe to be a valid cause? In both cases, there are issues of social pressure, fear or shame (in refusing), the seeking of social approval, rage, depression or even dissociated states in which one becomes oblivious to the danger and reality of the situation. We will touch on these in the next chapter.

Now we'll be looking at everyday courage and recognize that, in so many areas of our lives, we have to confront feelings of anxiety or anger and doing so requires us to value and develop compassionate courage. To help us, we have to keep a close eye on that fantasy world of ours, on our thoughts, anticipations and interpretations. To put it another way, it's going to be a little easier for you to act against your anxiety or not allow your anger to turn into attacking aggressiveness or criticism if you've developed compassion for your feelings and have a warm, kind voice in your head that understands the power of these emotions and doesn't condemn you for them but enables you to tolerate them without acting them out, and helps you keep a reality check on and balance your thoughts, fantasies and ruminations.

So when we think about compassionate behaviour, we can see that it's far from being just about gentleness, kindness and warmth; we also need courage. The same is true when it comes to self-compassion. Our self-criticism or even desire to hurt ourselves is the result of the aggressive parts of our emotions having more control than is helpful. Be compassionate to them but try to find ways not to act them out. Compassionate action can involve developing our courage to tackle important issues in our personal lives and struggles, to face up to and work on psychological difficulties that we recognize are holding us back. This is usually to do with how our threat/self-protection system is working; feelings of anxiety and anger put blocks in our path to self-fulfilment, well-being and happiness. If anxiety and anger control us rather than us controlling them, we hand our lives over to them to script.

Sometimes working with these difficult feelings means learning how to tolerate them, accept them as part of our lives, but not to act on them blindly. At other times, we have to engage with them and change them, to act against the impulses and behavioural urges of the emotion. Accepting your feelings of anxiety or anger and acting *against* or *in spite of* them can therefore be key to overcoming them. This isn't easy or fair because there may well be genetic influences on our tendencies to feel anxiety and anger, but there's still much we can try.

Action and behaviour

In Buddhist psychology and in a school of Western psychotherapy called *behaviour therapy*, the process of change occurs through action and behaviour. Buddhist psychology has long suggested that, for us to conquer fears, we need to face them. Those who are frightened of death, for example, can be given meditations on the process of death and decay of the body – okay, not my cup of tea either. The more recently devised behaviour therapy is based on research that has shown that our brains are directly changed through our behaviour.

As mentioned on page 279 another therapeutic school, developed by Marsha Linehan,[3] which combines Buddhist and behavioural approaches, is *dialectical behaviour therapy* (DBT). If you type that into a search engine, you'll find out a lot about DBT. The 'dialectic' aspect involves focusing on the opposing processes of, for example, change versus acceptance, or self versus others, and how we balance those conflicts. DBT emphasizes becoming more aware and mindful of the pulls and pushes of emotions, developing acceptance and tolerance of them, and learning how not to act them out. You feel anxious and don't want to go for the interview. But you want the job so you go: you act against your anxiety. You might temporarily feel better by avoiding, but you'll suffer in the long term.

Chapters 2 and 3 explored how our archetypes, social mentalities and emotions are products of millions of years of evolution and how some of them can give us a very hard time indeed. It's important that we learn to listen to our emotions carefully because they have important information for us. Sometimes we don't acknowledge anxiety, anger, frustration or upset because we're just keeping our heads down in order to survive or because we're frightened of these feelings. Learning to attend to and understand the meanings of our emotions and social mentalities can be extraordinarily helpful, which is why, at times, writing compassionate letters to ourselves can enable us to understand what we feel (*see* pp. 347–55).

For example, Kay felt slightly hurt by her fiancé's habit of going out drinking with his friends at weekends rather than spend time with her. However, because she thought she was in love with him, rather than thinking about these feelings she dismissed them and deliberately tried not to pay attention to her upset. However, as her wedding day approached, her negative feelings about this built up and she decided to tackle him about it. He emphatically told her that she wasn't going to 'rule his life' and he would do what he wanted. As a result, she broke off the engagement. She was soon shocked to discover that, far from being upset about this, her boyfriend had actually found another girlfriend within two months. On reflection, she realized that she should have paid attention to her feelings and intuition – that his feelings towards her were rather shallow – much sooner. Sometimes we dismiss what we feel and tell ourselves not to be silly. Compassionate attention can, however, help us think about our feelings in some depth. Sometimes we avoid them because of conflicts or because in our hearts we know something that we don't want to acknowledge. If you have concerns about such a situation, you might want to write yourself a compassionate letter about it. Look at the ins and outs, ups and downs, the hopes and the fears, the advantages and disadvantages.

Working with anxiety

Let's look more closely at how to engage with compassionate behaviour in the face of anxiety. This emotion has been designed to protect you and make you avoid dangerous situations. Although we don't like to be anxious, anxiety isn't your enemy and it's useful if you can see it that way. It sometimes just needs the volume adjusting. So this *helpful* emotion can become confused and get involved with things that are not helpful. There are many anxiety 'disorders' related to fears of specific things such as spiders or animals, fears of social situations, of germs and of abandonment or just a general sense of anxiety. It's our anxiety – for example, of coping alone – that can stop us from moving away from relationships that are actually toxic to us. It's our anxiety that can stop us from reaching out to other people, making friends and sharing our hearts with them. It's anxiety that can hold us back from what we really want in life. It's anxiety about failing that stops us from reaching for success. And, of course, it's anxiety that can prevent us from behaving compassionately or morally.

In what we call 'anxiety disorders', the threat/self-protection system seems to be 'inflamed' and easily activated. In fact, there's evidence that, when we suffer from anxiety and depressed conditions, there is increased sensitivity in the part of our brain called the *amygdala*, which regulates these feelings. Genes, hardships early in life and current stresses can all play roles in lowering the threshold for the amygdala to give us a hard time. But once we know this, and we don't blame ourselves, we're then free to think about how we're going to help that part of our brain settle down, and how we can bring more soothing compassion to our brain.

A ten-step plan to tackle anxiety

The compassionate approach towards anxiety utilizes wisdom that has been gained over many years from careful study and by those who have suffered anxiety discovering for themselves what is helpful. So you'll already have intuitive knowledge of many of the things that I'll outline here – I'll be telling you things that you already know in your heart.

Most therapists agree that it helps to develop a plan to tackle anxiety. Here's an example of a ten-step programme. You may want to add extra steps or alter some of the existing ones to reflect your own needs.

Step 1: Recognize that you have an anxiety problem that might be holding you back or interfering with your life in some way.

Some people are afraid of something but as it doesn't really interfere with their lives, they don't especially want to tackle it. I don't like travelling in long-distance buses (don't ask – it's a long story), but I'm quite happy avoiding such a mode of transport because there are many other ways of travelling. It's when anxiety gets in the way of your life that it's helpful for you to engage with it. Most people are, of course, quite familiar with their anxiety but may not realize how much it might be interfering with their desired lifestyles. Imagining how your life might be different without the anxiety can make it clear in your mind how problematic it is and isn't and also give you a focus and the courage to engage it.

Step 2: Think about whether your anxiety is linked to stresses in your life or perhaps has arisen with depression.

For example, if you are going through a divorce, it's understandable for you to be suffering from increased anxiety, which will settle down once the rest of your life settles down, too. If you think that you're depressed and your anxiety has come with the depression, it's important to work on the depression.

But let's assume that you experience straightforward anxiety about specific situations. The compassionate way of thinking is to recognize that this isn't your fault, you didn't design your brain to be anxious and there may be all kinds of reasons why you have become anxious about certain things. So there's nothing to be ashamed about in feeling anxious. Have compassion and acceptance for your anxiety as a human difficulty. But do check out if you're feeling slightly critical about it.

Step 3: Accept the fact that you may feel more anxiety before you feel less – but this will be more under your own direction and control.

Remember that anxiety tends to flush through us quite quickly and is not easily suppressed by thinking. Rather we need to learn how to understand, face, cope and deal with our anxiety, and this means learning to tolerate some degree of anxiety rather than trying to suppress, stop or inhibit it completely. That, in turn, means that, before we start, we need to accept that this is going to be a little anxious journey. We're going to need courage here, but the motto is: 'Be challenging but not overwhelming.' The idea is to make a commitment to find ways to experience your anxiety, taking these as opportunities to practise tolerating and working with it, but not so it overwhelms or disheartens you.

Psychological approaches are very different to medical approaches, which will involve giving you drugs that will reduce your anxiety by directly affecting your brain. Some people find this extremely effective. The psychological approaches, however, require courage and the desire to change your brain yourself in a kind and skilful way.

Step 4: Examine clearly *why* you want to face your anxiety.

Why do you want to learn how to deal with, tolerate and work through your anxiety? Make a list of all the things that you feel would be improved if you could deal with your anxiety. These will become the things that you'll commit yourself to and will help you focus when working with your anxiety gets tough. It's one of those situations where 'a little pain offers a lot of gain'. Also, when things get tough, you can focus your mind on imagining in as much detail as you can what you're aiming for. If that's not clear in your mind, it'll be easier to give up.

Jeff was a little anxious about flying, but he loved sunshine and desperately wanted to go on holiday with his girlfriend. So he learned some basic anxiety-reduction techniques, such as breathing and relaxing, reminding himself that his anxiety wasn't dangerous and would pass. To focus on his commitment to his goal, he created in his mind pictures of himself having fun and saw himself laughing with his girlfriend in the sunshine. He also thought how pleased she would be that he'd been able to come with her and how important it was to be there for her. These types of things are small ways to give courage a helping hand.

Step 5: Ask yourself whether you might need some help with your anxiety.

Don't put pressure on yourself or tell yourself that you've *got* to sort it out by yourself. The compassionate approach is always to open our hearts to the help of others. If you feel that your anxiety is probably a bit too difficult for you to work on by yourself, go and see your family doctor to find out what help is available. There are now many good psychological approaches for dealing with anxiety problems, and psychology professionals will assess the nature and causes of your anxiety and help you work out a programme to deal with it. Remember there's nothing to be ashamed of in having this difficulty – it's extremely common because of how our brains are designed. So seeking professional help can be the result of compassionate behaviour and courage. Think of it as finding a physiotherapist for your mind. It's understandable, though, that sometimes we worry that our anxiety means that there's something seriously wrong, that we'll be shown to be cowards and weak, that the therapist is going to dig up something from the past that we would rather leave buried or that we'll just be given drugs. If that is the case for you, express these concerns to whoever you go to see; explore if you can trust and collaborate with that person.

Step 6: Make a list of situations in which your anxiety may play a role and the tasks that could help you overcome it.

List them from the least challenging to the most. For example, if you're socially anxious, one of the least challenging situations you might find yourself in could be trying to say a bit more at work each day or to phone your friends more often. The most challenging might be meeting new people, joining a new group such as a slimmers club or giving a speech – say, at a wedding. Let's call this list your 'continuum of difficulty'.

Now think about various tasks of varying levels of difficulty for you personally, which can be placed along your 'continuum of difficulty'. You can use these tasks to practise stimulating and working with your anxiety. For example, if you have social anxiety, you could practise going into shops and asking for information and demonstrations on washing machines or televisions, and then thanking the sales assistants for their help (always show gratitude) – don't buy anything, of course, unless you really need it! If possible, choose a day when the shop isn't busy. Or phone a travel agent and ask for information about a holiday. The idea is not to pester people, of course, but to practise conversing, taking the initiative, asking questions.

Another task would be to find out one new thing each day about the people you work with. Practise asking questions about how they are and the things and people in their lives. Show that you take an interest in them: attend to your posture, practise using your compassionate face when you talk and look them in the eye. Socially anxious people can sometimes appear rather aloof and uninterested and, of course, people pull back from that, which in turn can confirm to socially anxious individuals that people don't like them.

So the approach here is to be creative in developing your 'hierarchy' and range of tasks/exercises. Hierarchies can be developed for all kinds of fears, such as spiders. You might begin by drawing a picture of a spider, then looking at a photograph of one, then holding a toy spider and so forth. If you suffer from agoraphobia (a fear of open spaces), you can have a hierarchy, too – e.g. going out the front door, then a few steps down the road, then further every day. Be as creative as you can. This is no different from learning to drive a car: it's best to just sit in it at first, then drive in the back streets, then drive on the main roads before you go out on the motorways. The key to the process is a commitment to work with your anxiety in compassionate ways rather than avoid it.

Step 7: Prepare for your anxiety situation.

If you know that you are about to face something that triggers your anxiety, there are a number of things you can do to prepare for it. Using your soothing breathing rhythm, bring to mind your compassionate image, place a hand just over your heart and focus on your heart (*see* p. 263) and on the fact that your anxiety is not your fault (nor your enemy) and that you're showing a lot of courage in engaging with it. Allow yourself a compassionate smile. Remember that you've probably had these experiences of anxiety hundreds of times before, and it is your amygdala playing up. However, you'll be pleased to help it settle down. Bring to mind a picture of having gone through it and how happy you were.

Step 8: Write down coping thoughts.

Keep in mind that it's very easy for certain thoughts, fantasies and ruminations to run away with you, increasing your anxiety. Without care, you'll find that it's being driven more by thoughts, interpretations and / or old memories than it is by the approaching event itself. How often, after we've done something that we had been anxious about, have we thought to ourselves, 'Well, that wasn't as bad as I thought it would be' (and, yes, occasionally, 'That was worse!')? Although we know that we can get in a dither and fret about things, we often don't take steps to help ourselves. We say, 'Well, I'm just that kind of person.' Maybe, but by learning to be mindful and 'in the moment' to your thoughts as they arise in you, you can practise the art of compassionate balancing of your thoughts (*see* Chapter 9) and not let them run away with you.

As you set off to engage with your anxiety situations, take a postcard, maybe one that has a soothing picture on it, and write down a number of your coping thoughts. Examples of these might include:

> It's understandable to feel anxious [i.e. start by being sensitive and kind to your distress].

> I have experienced these feelings before and they're unpleasant, but they're *anxiety* and not anything more serious. I know they're anxiety because I can bring them on by putting myself in certain situations or thinking certain things – if these feelings were any more serious, I wouldn't be able to turn them on and off like I can.

> Many people have these anxieties so it's not *my* fault.

> By facing my fear, I'm helping my brain to become more balanced.

> By facing my fear, I enable myself to open up to life more.

> My anxiety always settles down, so this will pass, too.

Try to maintain a focus on the facts if you can. Consider what you'd like somebody who was kind and supportive of you to be saying in your ear, which would support and encourage you while you're having to cope with your unpleasant (okay, possibly scary) anxiety. At all times, remember that these thoughts should be infused with feelings of kindness, support and encouragement as well as facts. Try to keep your facial expressions and body posture in a compassionate mode, along with a compassion smile. See if bringing your compassionate image to mind and imagining having a conversation with it helps you. Experiment and try things out.

Step 9: Engage.

As you engage with your anxiety, remember your soothing breathing rhythm. Keep in mind that, if your anxiety mounts, that's only natural and, in some ways, quite useful because you're gaining experience of how to cope with it. Try to be mindful in the sense of recognizing how anxiety flushes through your body and pulls on your thoughts and behaviours.

An effective task is to build up your confidence so that you can learn that you're able to tolerate anxiety even if it's quite intense. Chances are, if you have an anxiety condition, you've experienced it on a number of occasions. So the main focus here is to remind yourself of your previous courage and that you've coped and tolerated very severe anxiety in the past. It's not pleasant, but you've done it and can do it again. Here you'll learn emotion tolerance – allowing the feeling without acting on what that feeling is trying to pull you into. While doing this, keep the voice in your head as warm, compassionate, encouraging and understanding as you can.

You can now begin to focus on how to try to soothe it, to help your amygdala settle down. Keep your thoughts focused on your breathing and on your postcard with its soothing picture and coping thoughts. If you have used a soothing stone with imagery (see p. 265), you can gently hold that in your hand. Focus on your compassionate reasoning about your anxiety. Continue to imagine that your compassionate self is with you and feel compassion coming into your heart – breathe it in. Keep your facial expressions as compassionate as possible. Remember that this anxiety isn't your fault and that you're showing a lot of courage in working with it. Keep in mind what your goal is, what you'll be able to do if you overcome or learn to cope with this anxiety.

Eve's stress levels had built up and she had become slightly depressed and developed anxiety about new things, such as going into shops or meeting new people. She thought that her friends weren't like this, so something must be wrong with her – this was a sign of weakness or a flaw in her. There were various things in her background that made her sensitive to such feelings. However, with a compassionate approach she was able to think, 'Well, maybe my threat system is over-aroused at the moment because of some things that happened early in my life and because of all the stress I'm under at the moment. So while these anxieties are unpleasant and a pain to have to face each day, they are natural and normal for my situation - it's the way my brain reacts from time to time.'

Eve also became aware of how some of her thoughts – such as 'Why am I like this? What's wrong with me? How bad will it get? I'm letting people down. I should be over this by now' – simply stimulated her amygdala and her threat system and increased her anxiety. She learned how to validate and accept her anxiety, and to recognize that there were good reasons for it occurring. She also found out how to be kind to her anxiety rather than 'wind it up', by carefully noting her thinking and interpretations. She then deliberately worked to switch her attention and thinking to the soothing system.

This is quite a lot to remember, I must admit. But they're all things to have a go at and see if they work for you. Anxiety can wax and wane according to how stressed we are and, for women, throughout their menstrual cycle. All you can do is your best and learn to focus on that. And remember that, at times, professional help can be the best course, so don't struggle on if these basic ideas don't seem to be doing the trick.

Step 10: Reflect on your anxiety after it's over.

First, focus on anything that you felt you did okay or well. Supposing you suffer from agoraphobia and you managed to get to the end of your road, but then had to return home. Now you *could* focus on the fact that you had to return home and feel self-critical, or you could concentrate on the fact you got to the end of the road and that's further than you've managed for a while. And who knows? Maybe you'll get further next time. Sometimes people undermine themselves because they don't do as well as they'd hoped and then they feel like failures. As cognitive therapists point out, you can see the glass as half full or as half empty. It's compassionate to train ourselves to focus on that half-full glass rather than on disappointment. So you should reflect on things that went well for you even if they didn't go as well as you would have liked them to.

Second, think about your tasks and other things you're trying to do. If everything went okay, a bit bumpy here and there but okay, then you've probably got your tasks and expectations about right, but if you were seriously struggling, you may have set the bar too high. Remember that you can start with something very small. The idea is to train your brain in stages, not to scare the hell out of it! If your task proved to be very easy, you may be setting your level a bit too low, although there's nothing wrong with taking it easy from time to time. It's like getting fit, really – you wouldn't run a marathon on the first day at the gym, but you'd like to work up a bit of a sweat.

Third, think about what worked well in helping you cope and face your anxiety. How was the breathing and the imagery? What about the thoughts on your postcard? Do you need to change the latter? Then, once you've identified what worked for you, go on to develop it.

In your reflections, come back to the idea that you're committing yourself to coping with or overcoming your anxiety – and focus on all the reasons for that, which you may have already written down. This is something that many people do. I used to get anxious about exams, but it helped me to focus on the fact that I wanted to have a career in this profession. The famous British actor Laurence Olivier spoke of having panic attacks on stage for the first time at the age of 60. He forgot his lines and felt terrible. However, he so wanted to continue acting that he knew he just had to face this problem, so he'd have somebody stand discreetly at the front of the stage with his lines on a board to help him through. In fact, some actors are so anxious that they actually throw up on their first nights, but they so want to act that they work through their anxiety. So finding things to commit yourself to can be extremely helpful in carrying you along.[4]

Anxiety is so common in our society, and caused by so many things, that there's now a large body of self-help literature and various websites.[5] If you put 'self-help for anxiety' into a search engine, you'll find lots of things. Look also for anxiety support groups. There are various national ones that can give you details of groups in your area. Sharing your problems with others can be extremely helpful.

All the steps above have focused on helping you take opposite action and switch from your threat/self-protection system to your soothing one. Rather than doing what your anxiety dictates, which is usually to avoid and hide or stay quiet, you are compassionately taking control.

Working with anger

Like anxiety, anger can often be a powerful, fast-arising emotion. It can spread through people like a tidal wave and then we see 'anger on the streets' that can spill over into violence. Some people are over-controlled and don't learn assertiveness – in conflict situations, they just go quiet or back away. By contrast, others are under-controlled and don't learn assertiveness either – they just act out their anger or even aggression. Also people can vary from situation to situation. In some, they might be over-controlled and submissive and not give voice to their annoyances (e.g. with the boss), but in other situations (e.g. at home with the children), they will be under-controlled, irritable and angry.

Coping with anger is one of our biggest challenges in our relationships and in the world today. Like many of us, I've been known to have the odd tantrum or two and be irritable and unkind to people. If I've felt a bit ashamed about that sort of behaviour in myself, I've been tempted to blame others: 'You made me cross.' But there's another way to go on this. We can, first, acknowledge openly that we have a brain that has systems for anger and, second, notice when those systems have been triggered. Since these feelings can sweep through us so quickly, it can be difficult to get hold of them; they can take control of us very easily. Now they were designed by evolution to do that, so this is not our fault. Given that, it's untrue and unhelpful to tell ourselves that we're bad for feeling anger, when evolution has made it so easy to feel! It's also unhelpful to tell ourselves that we should not be angry when we are. Self-condemning will only make us depressed and/or more irritable.

So let's drop all the blaming, self-condemning and ruminating on how bad we are and decide instead to try to take genuine control of our powerful, evolved anger emotions. So we learn to spot the anger signals and vulnerable times (which, for me, definitely includes time pressure). We learn to notice our bodies and recognize the touchy topics that can spark anger. We learn to observe the focus of our thoughts and attention as we become angry. Maybe there are understandable reasons for being angry: maybe underneath we're frightened or tired out and at a low ebb, or maybe this is how we, as children, learned to deal with conflict. We now start to think carefully about our trigger points. We become curious rather than shaming. We train our minds with regular mindfulness, relaxation or compassion practice and ease our arousal levels down so that anger becomes less of an uninvited guest. The Dalai Lama has often noted that just because he's a Buddhist doesn't mean that he doesn't have sexual or aggressive feelings; it's how they're expressed through him that is key.

To move in this direction is to have a genuine desire to try to help ourselves cope better with anger. Once we have this, rather than think about what we should or shouldn't do, we start to think about what would be the kindest and most helpful way to deal with our conflicts, disappointments, setbacks, frustrations and anger. These are different for different people – here are a few examples:

- Sally, who was rather submissive, constantly ruminated on how people treated her like a doormat. Eventually she'd explode over something relatively minor, then feel very bad about herself and go back to being submissive. Although it was a frightening prospect at first, with kindness and understanding she decided that she wanted to learn and practise assertiveness skills. That is a compassionate behaviour.

- Tom found expressing his feelings and communicating clearly very difficult. He knew that bottling things up didn't help his relationships, so the compassionate thing to do would be not to remain quiet and trying not to upset people, but to learn the skill of openly discussing emotions, including anger. This meant learning about his own emotions first, focusing on body posture, voice tone, language style and the emerging thoughts that come with emotions, learning how to cope with increasing arousal and so forth.

- Coming from an aggressive family, Kerry felt that her anger protected her and gave her courage – despite the fact that it also stopped her making long-term relationships. She was very reluctant to give it up and was keen to justify it. However, when she became compassionate towards her anger, she recognized that it covered up a lot of fear of not being heard, of being walked over and hurt.

Until we compassionately acknowledge the *purpose* and *function* of our emotions, it can be hard to work with them. Some individuals have been brought up to believe that expressing anger is essential. They think that you must never let other people get one over on you because, as one of my patients said, 'If you let them sit, they shit.' Well, that's not very nice, so no wonder he felt angry. Some people come from very aggressive backgrounds where displays of anger were part of growing up. This is the main way they learned to understand conflict – to shout and threaten. And, of course, anger and aggression, as ways to get what we want and exert our power, have been knocking about as strategies for many millions of years.

One thing that seems clear, though, is that, in spite of us being much better off than we were 50 years ago, we've become more irritable, angry and aggressive. Kim told me how, as a result of various cuts and 'drives for efficiency', there really weren't enough people in her department to do a proper job. They could just about keep going, but with a lot of 'under the table' short cuts. However, the lack of appreciation, expectations of doing more and more with less and less, and her manager's stressed and somewhat bullying approach meant that, when she got home, she'd be irritable and angry. She found it difficult to relate to her husband and children even though she desperately wanted to, because of the state of mind she was in, and she'd get angry with herself. This is extremely common, and we have to face facts: we've allowed the business model to drive us all slightly crazy. This is why we're so irritable; the drive for the 'competitive edge' is doing nothing for our own mental health.

On the other hand, we can say that, because we live in a world of plenty, we've come to expect and want more and more. We are the species we are because of this – always to seek more, to be better and to improve. But we have to be careful because our expectations, desires and wants can become excessive and our fantasies can become detached from reality, and then we'll live in a world of disappointment and frustration in a land of plenty. So anger can be a damaging emotion if left uncontrolled. It doesn't stimulate our brains for well-being because it's linked to both the threat/self-protection system and a rather hyped-up incentive/resource-seeking system. You see this in some individuals who need to be continually on the go and always get their own way. Sometimes they become successful business executives, but they'll have caused a lot of emotional bruises on the way up.

Anger has one other big disadvantage. I've come across individuals who really don't want to give up their anger, and yet in their quieter moments, they realize that they feel very isolated, that all their anger really does is push people away – others are unlikely to love you if you threaten them. However, perversely, this loneliness actually makes angry individuals feel more threatened and thus more prone to anger.

A ten-step plan to tackle anger

As with anxiety, the compassionate approach to anger utilizes wisdom that has been gained over many years, by many people, by careful study. Most therapists agree that it helps to develop a plan to tackle anger. Here's an example of a ten-step programme. You may want to put in extra steps or develop some of the existing ones for your own needs.

Step 1: Recognize whether you have a problem with anger.

You may feel that you become angry too often or your anger may be quite extreme and you're frightened of it. Sometimes you're not the best person to decide if you have an anger problem, so try being open and asking others. Sometimes there are key themes that are your Achilles heel for anger.

Step 2: Determine the nature of your anger.

First, think about whether your anger is linked to stresses in your life, or whether it accompanies depression – are you particularly angry and irritable when you're depressed? If the answer is yes, this means that we need to treat the depression.

But let's assume that your problem is primarily about anger perhaps fed by a low tolerance of frustration – and there are many different types of anger[6] – but it's not so serious that you feel that it's out of control. A compassionate way of thinking is to recognize that *this is not your fault*, you did not design your brain to have anger and there may be all kinds of reasons why you get angry. So there's nothing to be ashamed about in feeling angry. Check to see if you're slightly critical of your anger, or maybe you're trying to justify it. Be honest with yourself: justifying yourself in this way is like trying to tell yourself that it's okay to express whatever anger you want, when in your heart you know it's not okay – you wouldn't want other people doing that to you, would you? So again, it's not your fault that you feel anger, but you do need to take responsibility for what you do with it. Assertiveness, confidence, clarity of message, defending a position, passion for a cause – these are useful forms of this emotion, but 'raw' anger includes certain (scary) facial expressions, voice tones, ways of thinking and behaving that are usually designed to stop or harm others or force them in some way to do what you want. In extreme forms, of course, anger is about destroying the other. If it flushes through you and you leave it 'raw', this is not assertiveness.

Step 3: Learn to tolerate feelings of anger without acting on them.

Now, you can do this. If you're very angry with somebody who's much bigger than you, you'd be cautious and would hesitate before taking any action. If we're honest, we tend to express our anger when we feel safe – e.g. to partners, subordinates at work, people in positions of less power than us or even children, *not* to anyone who has control over us. There's now a lot of research that shows this.[7] We need to recognize this tendency in all of us, without being ashamed of it, but of course, we must take responsibility for it in ourselves. If we let this archetypal process work through us, we're all going to be bullies.

People often say that they can't control their emotions, and especially not anger. However, imagine that someone offered you £5 to control your anger by not expressing any to those around you for a week, instead being nice and patient. Not enough? Okay, £100. Still not enough? Okay, £10,000. Hmmm, you're thinking about it now. Final offer: £1,000,000. Yes, you'll receive £1,000,000 if you control your anger for a week. Do you think you could do it? Evidence suggests that we can control our emotional expressions if we're committed enough to doing so, and of course, potential money in the pocket is a good commitment.

Of course, nobody is going to give you £1,000,000 (sorry – and, yes, that would allow you to retire and then you'd have no more frustration), but it's the principle I want to make clear: you can tolerate a strong emotion without acting it out once you've committed yourself to that task. If you really commit yourself to this goal, you can do it, though it will take effort, courage and practice. In the next chapter, we'll see that anger at injustice and the desire to avenge our group over another one are equally important to understand and not act out.

A number of things can lead us to stray from this commitment. One important one is justifying our anger with such thoughts as: 'Other people deserve my anger' or 'If they can't cope with me, they should go somewhere else.' The point is that we have to commit ourselves to a different philosophy. We need to acknowledge that our anger can stimulate another person's stress system to cause a flush of unhelpful hormones to stream through their body that is harmful to them and their health. So we need to be very thoughtful about whether we really want to release our anger.

Step 4: Think clearly about why you want to learn how to deal with and tolerate your anger.

Make a list of all the things that you feel would be improved if you could cope with your anger in different ways – for instance:

● I might feel better about myself.

● Being prone to anger is associated with a number of health risks.

● People might find me easier to get on with.

● People might be more approachable and nicer to me.

● I might make friends rather than just having people be frightened of me.

● I might make better decisions.

Anger can also be accompanied by an obsessive rumination that can distract us from our well-being – it's certainly not a way to create peace or happiness. Against this, you may worry that people won't take you seriously if you abandon your shows of anger, but that's a call to learn assertiveness.

Step 5: Listen when other people say that you have a problem with anger or that you're a bit of a bully.

Think about whether you need some help. Don't tell yourself that you just have to sort it out by yourself. The compassionate approach is always about opening our hearts to our need for help, and if you feel that your anger is a bit too difficult for you to deal with on your own, go to your family doctor and see what help is available. Remember that there's nothing to be ashamed of in having difficulty with anger; it's extremely common. This is because anger is one of the big players in our brains.

One of my problems has always been a lack of *patience*. In Buddhist approaches to compassion, patience is one of the key qualities to develop, and we do this by recognizing that it's our grasping and trying to force life to give us what we want that makes us impatient. We have a lot of feelings and beliefs of 'must have' and 'need to have now' or, in my case, 'need to do now'. Queuing is my big impatience trigger; I have thoughts like 'Why don't they get enough staff here?', quickly followed by the feeling that 'They don't care enough to bother' and so forth. When we're time pressured, as we increasingly are, poor old patience is the first to suffer. Regular meditation or mindfulness and compassion exercises can help slow us down and give us patience. If this is something that you need to work on, take active steps to do so, using the techniques in this book.

A particular problem you might have, especially if your anger turns to aggression, is with *alcohol*. A lot of domestic and other violence is associated with this. There are, sadly, a number of people, mostly men, who are perfectly civil, reasonable and nice until they've had a few beers; then their threat system, with its sensitivity to criticism, rejection, insult and aggression, comes on line. If you're one of these, you may need help with your drinking, but you may be in denial about it. But the fact is that, either because of your *background* or your *genes* (neither of which are your fault), you're not able to control yourself when you're drunk. A compassionate approach is to face this honestly and truthfully and seek help without shame. There are many places now where you can get support for this kind of problem. It doesn't mean that you're addicted, just that alcohol has a particular affect on your brain state. There's nothing to be proud of or particularly *macho* in losing control of our minds and emotions when we're drunk. I suffer bad migraines with alcohol so I have to be careful. That's not my fault; it's just the way my genes are. The same goes for you maybe, but once you know this, then, of course, it's about taking responsibility to do the best you can to get help.

Step 6: Make a list of the situations that make you angry.

List them from the least to the most challenging. Can you see any patterns? For example, do you get most angry when you think that:

- there's not enough time?

- you could be at fault?

- people criticize you?

- people are trying to cheat you?

- people aren't that bothered about you and not giving you good service?

- people are being unfair?

When you've identified your triggers, write down why these things make you angry. In particular, focus on your greatest fear. Interesting that, isn't it, that we need to turn anger around to look at our fear? This fear might be that others will put you down, reject you, get away with things that they shouldn't, block you in some way, and you'll feel powerless. Or it could be that you think that, if you don't get things done, you'll be letting people down and they'll be disappointed in you.

If you do this exploration, you'll clarify the fact that your anger is often linked to things that actually threaten you in some way. Parents blow up at their children because they, the adults, are time pressured and stressed; they may believe that, unless their children obey them, they'll become wayward; or they may think that the children's behaviour is evidence that they don't love or respect them as parents. One father who used to get angry with his young children had in the back of his mind the thought that their constant demands and nagging made his wife tired, and when she got tired, she'd go to bed early and withdraw from him. So he felt in direct competition with his children. This isn't so uncommon, actually. The couple needed to discuss it openly, without blaming, and work on a solution.

Step 7: Make a commitment to find a way to empower yourself that doesn't involve expressing anger.

You can do this in your imagination. First, engage your soothing breathing rhythm and bring to mind your compassionate image or put yourself into a compassionate state. Now bring to mind one of your anger triggers – for example, it might be somebody criticizing you. Now think of an assertive response that focuses on how you are feeling, making the message clear that you want to get across, and imagine yourself with a posture and facial expressions that say that you are friendly, confident, upright, non-defensive and open rather than aggressive. Now imagine that you're delivering your clear message in a non-aggressive way, but presenting yourself as firm and confident. Reflect on how this feels for you. Notice how you make yourself deliberately slow down and centre and calm yourself.

In some ways, this isn't very different from a martial arts approach, in which practitioners act assertively from a point of calmness within themselves. Learning to act on the world from that position of inner calm gives us the most control. If we allow our anger to direct us, then because it's quite primitive, it's not going to be very thoughtful and we'll only get away with it if we have some power. If we're in a subordinate position, we might simply dwell on our anger, which is also very unhelpful. Clare, for instance, was very angry with her boss but would smile and be submissive. However, in the evening or on weekends, she would ruminate on how she felt and be quite miserable and lose interest in sex. This had a negative impact on her relationship with her children and husband. The message here is not to cling to things that clearly reduce your well-being and stress your brain.

Now using imagery to devise an assertive response can be helpful because it gives you a structure for working and thinking things through. The problem is that it doesn't produce the emotions that you'll have to deal with when anger arises. So the next element of this step is to try to identify minor situations around you that slightly trigger your anger, so that you become familiar with your triggers and how they affect your body. This will help you get in early to deal with your anger.

A major element in handling anger is *learning to deal with conflict* – this may be conflicts with young children, adolescents, parents, partners, people at work, your boss or employer. There are a whole range of skills that can be very useful to learn to enable you to become confident in a creative, helpful and firm way. We can't go into all of these here, but if you type 'assertiveness training' into a search engine, you will find many areas to explore. Clearly, you'll have to decide which skills will be helpful for you. Many people find assertiveness classes useful, but do check out the qualifications of the trainer and only go if you feel it will be good for you. You could try practising with your partner and get feedback. Remember, recognizing that we are struggling with certain types of conflicts in our relationships is absolutely nothing to be ashamed of. Conflicts are common and can be difficult.

Different situations may require different behaviours so I can't be too specific here. The key is commitment and practice. Start actively looking for situations that represent your triggers and practise coping with them. For example, if you have a busy day tomorrow and you know that you've got to get your children off to school and then drive to work through traffic and that you're likely to be a bit irritable, then rather than just hoping that the day will go off okay, see it as a day when you'll be able to practise your new skills. Think to yourself: 'Tomorrow is going to be a stressful day. I'm going to look out for feelings of irritability and observe my thoughts, which will give me a chance to have a go at being compassionate with my feelings and in control of them.' In this way, you can put yourself *into* the situation rather than becoming angry when you find it occurring. As with anxiety, try to be mindful – that is, noticing feelings and thoughts rising in your mind as they happen but standing back from them and just observing them. In a way, your consciousness will be observing your evolved mind at work.

Step 8: Write down some coping thoughts.

Do this on a postcard with a picture that you think might be helpful or soothing. Your thoughts may include something like these:

> It's understandable to get angry [*i.e. start by being sensitive and kind to your distress, acknowledging that anger can be about fear and distress*

386 Building the Compassionate Self: Skills and exercises

in some way]. I've chosen to find a different way of dealing with these feelings rather than being angry, and am practising a 'friendly assertive approach'. When I notice that anger is arising in me, I become more mindful and focus on my breathing. I know that it's important to slow myself down and not be rushed along by my feelings. In this way, I'm helping my brain become more balanced so that I'm in control of my anger rather than allowing my anger to do what it wants to my thoughts and behaviour. By facing up to how anger flows through me, I'm opening up more to life.

Step 9: Learn how to let go and forgive.

There are two basic *behaviours* that can be helpful with resolving anger. The first is: letting go. We often hold on to our anger because we feel that letting go of it or not expressing it will weaken us. For instance, someone I was working with felt that he'd been unfairly dismissed and 'shouldn't let them get away with it'. Ruminating on his anger and also his powerlessness – because there was nothing he could do – simply made him depressed. Realizing that he didn't have to prove himself in this battle, that life *is* unfair and we just have to do the best we can, made him decide to talk to his union and let them get the best possible deal for him. He handed the fight over to them and looked for another job. Within a month, his depression had lifted. He recognized that it was his own inability to let go, because he was telling himself that he was weak if he did, that kept him in a very unhelpful position. So it's important to explore 'letting go' and moving on.

Sometimes letting go involves the second basic behaviour: *forgiving* people who have hurt us. We engage in forgiveness because *it's good for us*, because giving up our anger is good for our brains, our well-being and health. Sometimes, if you've been very angry with somebody, you might have to clarify your thoughts and feelings before you can forgive. To do this, you can write a letter to those whom you're forgiving, putting down all your grievances and feelings (*see* Chapter 10). Usually these letters are never sent, but if you do want to send yours, it's best to put it to one side for a while rather than impulsively send off what you've just written. The main point of the letter is to help *you* with *your* feelings.

Then think about the advantages to *you* of letting go of your anger. Notice how thoughts like 'they mustn't get away with it' are actually like chains holding you to an unpleasant place. Certainly, if you can do something positive, go for it, but usually in these situations, when we're ruminating on our anger, we know we can't. Sometimes we can't let go of our anger because, underneath, there's a desire of some kind. For example, a person may be very angry with a parent but letting go of that anger would also be like saying 'farewell' and breaking a deep connection. What they really want is for that parent to be very loving and attentive. In this situation, letting go can also mean *grieving* for the parent that you wanted to have but who wasn't there. The problem with parents is that we always experience two, in a way, the one who is the actual parent but then there is the parent that we ideally would love to have. If these two match up we're in business but if they get too far apart we can struggle.

Forgiveness doesn't mean that you'll ever like the person you're forgiving, nor does it mean that the person is entitled to your forgiveness. It is purely about letting go of your anger *because it's good for you*. It means that the threat/self-protection system in your brain, which pumps out stress hormones, is not being constantly stimulated by you ruminating on your anger. You know in your heart that dwelling on anger doesn't lead to feelings of well-being, happiness, joy and enthusiasm. If you type 'forgiveness' into a search engine, you'll find many websites that address this issue, but if your anger is great, you may need professional help.[8] Again, don't be ashamed of this: acknowledge it and open your heart to be helped.

Step 10: Reflect on how you're doing.

Try and find some time during the day to think about how you're doing. First, attend to and practise anything that you feel that you did well, no matter how small. If you're struggling in certain areas, try not to be self-critical but recognize these may require more practice. Keep your expectations realistic and recognize that all of us become irritable from time to time. As for anxiety, so with anger: the key is opposite action. Your anger will want you to think and behave in a certain way and so the practice is to do the opposite, to stay friendly rather than aggressive. It's a funny thing, but actually not to act out anger can, in fact, be an act of courage!

Conclusion

Each of us has a brain that has evolved two powerful and protective emotions that urge action: anxiety and anger. There are others, of course, such as disgust, sadness and depression, but anxiety and anger can cause us great difficulty and pain, especially when they feed into and direct our fantasies, anticipations, imaginations and ruminations, qualities of our minds that can intensify and prolong these unpleasant feelings. Anxiety and anger are among the biggest blocks to compassion and kindness, but we can't banish them because they're so fundamental to our emotional brains. So we must work with them by learning to tolerate them, not act them out, and discover how not to get carried away through the thoughts and fantasies that can come with them. Many psychotherapists suggest that unresolved issues and traumatic memories in our past can, along with a genetic disposition, increase our sensitivity to anxiety and anger, which may require professional help to deal with. But there's much that we can do to help ourselves if we recognize the need to change and commit ourselves to becoming more mindful and practise changing.

The compassionate approach always invites us to recognize that difficulties in our minds are often a result of having powerful emotions. We want to shift into a different emotion system, one of soothing and kindness and from this position think of the best way forward. Fear, anger and violence have dominated our minds and our planet for so long and have caused such pain to humanity that the time has come to learn different ways to train and organize our minds. Sometimes, of course, these situations are complex and will take a fair amount of time to work out. Life can be very tough and tragic. Sometimes we have to face things that make us very sad. Learning to do this compassionately can be key to getting through.

So we can see that compassionate behaviour can be more difficult than it at first appears. It can be tough on us because there are all sorts of dilemmas that we have to face; it can be tough on us because it calls on our courage; it can be tough on us because we have to face our own powerful internal emotions; it can be tough on us because it's not always clear what the compassionate way actually is. So the only thing we can do is to be compassionate to the fact that behaving compassionately and facing up to our powerful emotions is tough on us and we can only do our best.

12 Compassionate Behaviour: The cultivation of courage

It's often said that actions speak louder than words, so it's not surprising that we bring compassion into our lives and into the world through our actions. You can be highly motivated to care and be sensitive, tolerant and patient, but without translating those intentions into action, not much will happen. There are, of course, a whole range of kindnesses that don't cost us much, but we must also acknowledge that compassionate behaviour may create dilemmas within us and may require courage. This courage shows itself in many ways, as we will see.

The art of resistance

The last chapter explored how and why compassionate behaviour isn't just about enacting kind feelings but also involves tough actions and courage. We saw that compassion can require engaging with the excesses of our threat/self-protection emotions: anger and anxiety/fear. In this chapter, we're going to look at how compassionate behaviour requires a different kind of courage – the ability to resist our own *desires*, including those associated with wanting to be part of the group and admired by our leaders and the defenders of our tribe. But we'll start with something not too difficult before shifting gears into more morally tricky areas. So the underlying theme in this chapter is resisting the persuasion of our archetypal minds and desires.

A recent television advertisement had smiling people suggesting that we can be kind to ourselves by indulging our wants (tastes) for cream cakes. Making ourselves fat and increasing our cholesterol and our risk of dying from strokes and heart disease is supposed to be kind? Such advertising feeds into our confusion between kindness and the satisfaction of desire – they are absolutely not the same thing! This confusion also exists in our parenting. In our hearts, we know that we feed our children and give them things that are really not in their best interests.

As we noted in Chapter 3, each of us has a brain that has given us a whole range of desires and passions that worked well when we didn't have 'new brain/mind' abilities, when we lived in small, mutually dependent groups and in worlds of scarcity in which we didn't have the mass production we have now. Today, however, with our mental abilities, isolated living and consumerism, compassion is about the art of resistance – about *not* acting on our desires and emotions. If I want to be fit, healthy and live long, I must be cautious of what and how much I eat and drink in this Western world of plenty, and be self-disciplined enough to take exercise (if only!). Treating myself compassionately means saying 'No' to many strongly wanted things and facing that grief (*see* p. 86). My fantasies can create all kinds of desires and set me up for all kinds of disappointment.

It can sometimes help if we make a list of the things that we know we want to resist. For example, if you're trying to work on your eating behaviour, plan each day carefully and do the best you can to stick to that plan. Maybe you can start by cutting out one thing – e.g. biscuits or cakes. Go for small targets, not the big ones. Use your compassionate mind to guide you. Be forgiving if you don't quite make it and joyful when you do. Remember: no shaming or criticism! Compassionate behaviour is also about protecting ourselves from our own drive system and self-criticism – not being passive in the face of our self-focused frustration and anger at not getting what we want, making mistakes or not being as we want to be.

A Muslim commentator has pointed out that Ramadan, a month during which people fast from sunrise to sunset, can be seen in all kinds of ways. It can be viewed as simply obedience to God. However, another way of experiencing it is to think about it as giving people experiences that will show that they *can* resist their temptations and desires if they wish. Moreover, it also gives them some sense of what it's like to feel hungry and so become more open to compassion towards those in the world who go without.

Being compassionate to others can also mean saying 'No' to many strongly wanted things. Men enjoy images and fantasies of sex – not our fault: our brains are designed for it – but to actively pursue those fantasies can feed sex trafficking. We want cheap clothes, but some of the unrealistically inexpensive items on sale will have involved child labour. We like eating meat, but in addition to those who feel that this is intensely cruel to the animals who supply it, some scientists believe that the clearing of the Amazonian rainforest for cattle raising has contributed to global warming. We want to keep as much money as we can and not pay taxes? Fine, but as Britain saw in the 1980s and '90s, with little to pay for their maintenance, the infrastructures of schools, transport systems and hospitals were allowed to crumble and rot away, leaving us with huge problems now. Complex societies need massive investment to maintain quality.

So in every aspect of our lives we're now being called on to think about the consequences of acting on our desires. There's a huge difference between compassionate behaviour and simple indulgence. The reason all Western governments talk about tax cuts, rather than tax investments, is because they want to appeal to our greed, knowing that we've grown up in a world where we've been trained to focus on our indulgences, wants and desires, and to believe that we're entitled to anything just as long as we work hard enough for it.

Resisting others

Compassionate behaviour turns out to be very hard, confusing and, at times, scary work. Not only do we need to understand the link between self-protection and self-resistance and how not to act out our desires, angers and fears, but we also may have to stand up to others, too. We can begin to explore this process by looking at how we can teach children that they can't always have what they want when they want it. This begins with a certain courage on our part, the courage not to be persuaded by misplaced feelings of guilt. So we can start with small acts of courage and build to some more difficult ones.

So let's assume that you're a parent with young children. If you give into their demands to eat only junk food, very soon you'll have very unhealthy and disruptive children on your hands. So you have to be able to tolerate their frustration with you and their complaints, such as 'Other parents allow their children to eat these things,' so you must be a 'not so nice' parent. You have to have the courage of your convictions that *setting boundaries* and saying 'no' to your children is the right thing to do even if they regard you as not the most popular person. If you're feeling slightly guilty at the lack of time you've been spending with them, then out of your own feelings of guilt (and not in their best interests) you might give in. *It takes courage not to act out of guilt but from a genuine belief of what is best for others.* This is true of many things in life, isn't it? And, of course, we can't always be sure what *is* actually in the best interest of others.

Imagine that you're selecting doctors for training. One of the candidates is extremely hard-working and has references showing that they are wonderfully helpful, thoughtful and kind and have many of the personal qualities that you would ideally want in a doctor. You interview this person with high hopes, but they're clearly struggling academically and you look at the references and find that their teachers also suggest that they're unlikely to get good grades. On the one hand, you'd love to accept this candidate and fulfil their dreams, knowing that they'd give 110 per cent and be kind to their patients – yet you also know that they simply wouldn't be up to the job and could make mistakes, compromising the lives of others. You need courage to face being the one who has to tell them. You'll also need courage to be honest about your feelings of sadness for them rather than just becoming detached and hardened to such things.

It's becoming clear, isn't it, that compassionate behaviour cannot possibly be submissive, that *giving in* to what others want simply because they want it isn't kind? And sometimes we have to be honest enough with ourselves and compassionate about the fact that we can't pursue what we want. When we're young, we rely on our parents to give us boundaries and they do so from (we hope) a caring position. If those boundaries have been too tightly drawn, then perhaps we move into adult life with a desire to rebel and do what we want, no matter how bad it is for us. And, of course, the corporate world desperately doesn't want you to put boundaries around yourself or indeed your children; they want you to buy more and more and will try to stimulate your acceptance of doing so.

However, giving in to ourselves is not compassionate, especially when it can actually be harmful. The way we recognize our need to limit ourselves – the food we eat, our consumption of alcohol and other appetites and desires – can be an important step in developing compassionate behaviour. It is about compassionate protection – looking after – not moral self-denial. It takes courage to acknowledge this and work on it.

The concept of 'deserve'

Narcissists find it difficult to experience others as feeling beings like themselves; they have a sense of personal entitlement to use others to satisfy their own desires and ambitions. Such people are highly represented in business and politics. But there are many elements of narcissism that Western society deliberately fosters, especially with concepts like 'you need and deserve' or 'you are entitled to'. Well – more entitled than whom? More deserving or entitled than the child labourer in India or the starving man or woman in Africa? These are unhelpful concepts, employed to entice you to strive and buy. Consider instead the lovely motto: 'Take what you need to give what you can.'

So the first step is recognizing that the concept of 'deserve' can be used in unhelpful ways. We don't live in a world that's based on 'deserve', and in any case, these are arbitrary judgements. Of course, we understand that the concept of 'deserve' is to link effort and 'good' behaviour to reward. Animals and humans do things because of the rewards they will get for doing them - it's basic to life. However, saying that hard work *deserves* rewards is a good capitalist view of life. Certainly we don't like the idea of people being rewarded for their laziness, cheating or privilege, but using justifications and rationalizations such as 'deserve' to indulge ourselves is unhelpful. A couple of years ago, a banker who had been given a £3 million 'golden handshake' genuinely believed she deserved it!

No one *deserves* the diseases they get or their fate to have grown up in a war-torn country or to be flooded out by a monsoon. No one *deserves* the privileges that come because their genes, education or social position have given them an advantage. 'Deserve' often becomes a way of justifying the unfair. It's not a question of whether you deserve a holiday but whether you need one and if it would be helpful to you and your family. It's not a question of whether you deserve compassion but whether it will help you grow and prosper. It's not a question of whether other people deserve compassion but whether that will help them and whether we're prepared to give it. This view is, of course, different from the view of our competitive society and, indeed, the ancient Greek view, which put much store in 'deserve'.

Standing up to bullies (and recognizing them in oneself)

If you're in a position of authority, there will be times when you'll have to point out your subordinates' errors, things that you're unhappy with and things they need to change. One way, of course, is to tell them straight, bully them, ensure that they're slightly frightened of you so that they'll respect you and bow down to you. Not much courage there, really. For bullies, these situations provide opportunities to dominate others and make them feel even stronger. When you realize that you've been putting off addressing problems, you'll require courage to advise people on their faults, especially when this isn't what you're used to. We sometimes think that we're being kind or trying to find a kind way to say things by delaying doing what really needs to be done, but in reality it's because we're in avoidance mode. Compassionate behaviour is all about being sensitive to other people's feelings, of course, and delivering messages in non-aggressive ways, but it's also about delivering *clear* messages and guidance and offering *clear* feedback. It's your intention to help and inform the person, rather than just 'put them in their place' or 'teach them a lesson', that's important. So you have to take a soothing breath and bite the bullet.

If someone is bullying you and this is distressing you, then compassionate behaviour invites you to take action. Try not to stay in environments that are toxic to you; that's not compassionate. You may choose to leave a situation – get a transfer or find another job. If that solution works for you, then all well and good. Don't see this as cowardly running away but as sensible. If you can't get away, you may need to find ways of standing up to this person. First, check on your alliances. Are there other people who have experienced this person in the same way that you have? Would they support you? Could you talk this over with them and maybe together address the issue, see the bully together, demonstrate that you are all sticking together?

If you have to face the bully by yourself, try to find a time when they aren't rushed and hurried – sometimes bullying comes from the bully's own experiences of stress. Then it could be useful to start off with a positive comment: 'I understand that you're stressed and trying to do the best you can for the company, and I'd like you to get the best out of me, too. However, I find some of your critical comments upsetting and they stop me from performing my role well. It would be very helpful to me if you could focus on what you think I do well and build from there . . . I guess we all like appreciation.' Try to keep your tone as friendly as possible while still being assertive. Be aware of the nonverbal signals you're sending: if you give ones that are aggressive or show that you're upset, the other person (or, rather, the amygdala in their brain) will respond to your nonverbal behaviour and not your verbal message. Some bullies are genuinely unaware of their impact on other people, whereas others will back off if you confront them. In a way, taking a friendly but firm position is the kind of dominance that conveys the message that you expect them to change *their* behaviour. But keep in mind that these are only suggestions and you may find better ways through talking with friends, your union or your company's human resources (HR) department.

It takes courage to recognize the bully in ourselves. If you're in a position of authority, stand back and listen to yourself at times. Would you like to be treated in the way that you're treating others? Really spend time imagining yourself as someone who works for you. In group meetings, how often do you use the words 'I' and 'me' rather than 'we' and 'our'? How often do you become irritated when other people are slow, interrupt them, sometimes mid-sentence, and then justify it, of course? Do you see the people who work with you as fellow human beings struggling as best they can? Or do you see them as people who need a 'kick up the bum'?

How do you handle your own stress? If you're stressed, do you make sure everyone knows it? Or are you emotionally polite and don't spew it out on everybody else? If you're in a position of power and authority, you may feel that you have a right to do whatever you like. Indeed, a lot of research shows now that, when people occupy powerful positions, they don't always treat subordinates very well.[1] It takes courage and honesty to recognize that sometimes we're the bullies.

Conflicts: Assertiveness and compassion

Conflicts of interest are built into the very fabric of our lives, operating from the genetic level upwards. In some species of sand shark, for instance, the young compete in the womb until only one survives to be born. Well, that's taking sibling rivalry to extremes! Evolutionists tell us of the conflicts between the strategies of parents and those of their offspring in terms of the amount of time and investment given and wanted. Few relationships are without conflict. There are also many 'new brain/mind' talents that can drive our conflicts with each other. One is to have a strong sense of 'deserve' that brings you up against people who, you believe, are constantly thwarting you. Another aspect of our minds that can fuel and drive our conflicts is our imaginations and fantasies. The world and other people can never be as we fantasize them. Our lovers don't behave as we fantasize they do, and our children rebel and act out and refuse to study.

The *zeitgeist* of the 1960s was to rebel against the old power establishment and structures and become self-determining, self-expressing, 'free' people. This was enthusiastically adopted by business, which believed that people would express themselves by buying more clothes, make-up, guitars, records and so forth. There was also a lot of focus on self-assertiveness – that is, feeling entitled to express yourself, having your say, standing up for yourself, 'becoming your own person', not subject to the dictates and wants of others. This was clearly endorsed by the early feminist thinkers who felt that men had used their power to subordinate women in all kinds of ways. Some good ideas came from this, such as learning to articulate, be clear about and express *your* feelings rather than attack other people.

Here's an amusing story that illustrates something else about assertiveness. An assertiveness trainer was staying in a hotel. When a young man got into the lift with him, the trainer asked him to push the button for Floor 10. The young man smiled, shook his head and said: 'I don't feel I want to.' Surprised, the trainer asked why. The young man smiled again and said: 'I'm doing an assertiveness training course and I only have to do what I want to do.' Now this story is used by assertiveness trainers to describe what assertiveness is *not* – it is *not* about selfishness or bloody-mindedness.

None the less assertiveness does (obviously) have a tendency to focus on the self and the expressions of the self. These skills are extremely important for rather submissive people because it is difficult to be compassionate from a submissive or subordinated position. And, of course, assertiveness requires courage. However, once you're confident in doing it, assertiveness simply in the service of your own self-interest in fulfilment of desire may not help you sort out compassionate decision-making or what is the right thing to do in conflict situations. It also won't necessarily give you the skills for friendship building and caring for others. It can, therefore, be useful to ask oneself: 'What is the compassionate thing to do?' as opposed to the assertive thing to do, in this or that situation or context. Sometimes in a conflict situation, it can help to simply say, 'Look, we both see this issue in different ways and want different things, so let's see how we can work on this together.' This statement starts the process with a recognition of your differences as opposed to each of you feeling that you've got to assert and defend your positions or be (resentfully) persuaded to come over to the other side. As we discussed in Chapter 2, respecting and coping with individual differences between people are very important. And as noted on pages 67–71, differences can be based on claims of justice or on caring compassionate ones.

Conflicts of interest can also pose very real dilemmas for us. Recall some of the dilemmas we saw in our discussion of morality in Chapter 2. Working on and adopting compassion can be difficult because justice and caring concerns can conflict.[2] With regard to public conflicts between people and the tendency for the powerful to exploit the weak, compassion must turn to the rule of law. Compassionate societies have to have appropriate rules and laws, effective ways of policing them, and punishments and deterrents for breaking them. Again, this is linked to the protective functions of compassionate behaviour. As to the latter (and as noted in Chapter 6), we have to choose between *retributive* justice, focusing on condemning, blaming and punishing, and *restorative* justice, focusing on healing, preventing, grief, guilt and remorse. Also we must recognize the social constructions of law breaking: people become unkind, criminal and violent to each other in certain social contexts, such as poverty, a lack of good role models, the need to join a gang for protection, and desires to escape 'the gutter' via profits from drugs. So compassionate approaches need to struggle with the complex issues of freedom, policing, rights and protection and the social conditions that manufacture crime and conflicts. We come back to the point with which we started this chapter – that compassion is not about some 'softy' form of kindness – though it is about kindness. It is also not about submissive behaviour, weakness or only turning the other cheek. I's about coming to important social and personal dilemmas and difficulties with a particular focus and mind-set.

Heroic compassion

There can be times when courage is at the very core of our ability to act compassionately. A well-known example of this can be seen in Steven Spielberg's film *Schindler's List*. Here was a man – Oskar Schindler – who before the Second World War was an ordinary 'wheeler-dealer' and yet his extraordinary courage saved hundreds. Why? Samuel and Pearl Oliner[3] have written a fascinating and important book on rescuer behaviour. Investigating why many people helped Jews during the war, they found that the motives were complex and varied. Some of these acts were based on the rescuer's sense of right and wrong, some on non-prejudiced views, some on religious ideals, some on a sense of justice and moral principle and some on simply having the opportunity to help, while many acts of rescue sprang from caring, sympathy and compassion. Some rescuers were even fairly autocratic to those they helped, insisting the rescued do as they were told. Yet for all these varied motives, one thing shone through clearly: the courage that it had taken to undertake the rescues. Not only did these people put themselves at risk but also their families and associates. What good would compassion have been here without courage?

Sometimes this kind of compassionate behaviour is fuelled by anger, a deep sense of injustice, a feeling that 'this shouldn't be happening'. Indeed, in Buddhist imagery and psychology, compassion (and the images of the compassionate Buddha) can be very fierce.[4] Compassionate behaviour, however, is rarely if ever acted out in anger. This is because anger can make us stray into different territories, can be impulsive and destructive and can cause us to act in unforeseen ways. So anger can be the emotion that *alerts* us to a call to compassion but is not the point from which we enact compassion. Like the martial arts instructor who teaches his karate student to act from a position of calmness, inner stillness and clarity of mind rather than from rage, so too with compassion.

If I were confronted by the same challenge of saving Jewish people in 1943, I would like to think I'd help others too, but there is a voice in my heart that expresses serious doubts. I'm easy to frighten. The problem is that you can never know what you'll do until you're faced with a particular situation. Many research studies have found that we don't know how we'll act in emergencies until one arrives. Consider the woman who was being treated for an anxiety condition, yet one day, when a truck crashed into the front wall of her house, she was, by all accounts, the calmest of all, taking control, notifying the police and finding out if anybody was hurt. Some people, of course, choose careers where they know they'll be at risk. The firefighters in New York on September 11, 2001 had chosen a career of risk. None the less all agree that their courage and altruism in that terrible tragedy, when many died trying to save others, were outstanding. And it wasn't just the firefighters. Many people within the World Trade Center buildings acted in similar ways. Indeed, we find this all over the world – that some people will take extraordinary risks to help others. Importantly those individuals who will risk themselves to save others are not necessarily the gentlest or kindest of people, and indeed sometimes the kind and gentle individuals are not necessarily the bravest.

Combating our tribal and submissive behaviours

It's one thing to talk about resisting desires to eat cream cakes or other self-focused wants, but there are other desires, especially in our social relationships, that are far more destructive if we're not aware of how they're playing out in us. We humans have an enormous need to belong, fit in and feel accepted. The pressure to conform to group values is huge. Be it smoking, drinking, our dress sense or even going to war, people like to be seen as being 'like others' and proving themselves to be worthwhile members of the group. I was desperate to join the smoking group at boarding school. Even though I hated smoking to begin with and managed to set fire to my school jacket, which nearly got me expelled, I persevered because these were the 'cool group', the dominant males – and I wanted to be one of them. Being perceived as different or not up to the challenges of the group, you run the risk of rejection. The emotion that alerts us to possibly 'not fitting in' and being in danger of criticism or rejection is *shame* (*see* Chapter 10). Shame is one of the most important of the social emotions because it's our effort to avoid shame and being shamed that can play such a big part in conformity. The drive towards conformity and the avoidance of shame can block compassion. Sometimes compassion requires us to be able to tolerate being shamed by others – not running from it.

It was both a desire to conform (and avoid the shame of not conforming) and a cultural view of beauty that fuelled such practices as Chinese foot binding, where a young girl would have her feet broken and bound, sentencing her to a life of pain, increased vulnerability to infection and death. Each time the feet were rebound, the pain was intense. In the 1600s, the Qing dynasty tried to outlaw foot binding but it was too deeply entrenched in cultural beliefs and traditions. Billions of women over the centuries were victim to this cultural practice maintained through conformity, shame and shame avoidance, until, following the revolution of 1911, Sun Yat-Sen officially prohibited it. There was nothing evil or bad in the Chinese families who insisted on binding their young daughters' feet, and to believe otherwise is to completely misunderstand the power of shame and social conformity. Female circumcision and other (to Western eyes) barbarous practices are maintained through similar processes, which we must, of course, do what we can to bring to an end.

Our desires for social conformity, acceptance and belonging – desires that might have propelled the evolution of our social intelligence and have been life savers in the last ice age – can also be the source of terrible things now. Psychologists have studied these processes in various ways. Back in the 1950s, the social psychologist Solomon Asch did some very simple but powerful experiments. He handed out cards to his students, on each of which were three vertical lines of different lengths (but not excessively so). Then they were each handed another card with only one vertical line on it. Each student had to announce which of the three lines on the first card matched the single line in length. However, of the students, only one was the true 'subject'; the rest had been primed by Asch to give the same *wrong* answer. This experiment was carried out many times with many different 'subjects'. When the 'subjects' were asked for their answers, they would be very uncomfortable, knowing that the group had all given the same *wrong* answer and not wanting to disagree. In fact, 32 per cent eventually said that they had changed their minds and agreed with the (obviously) *wrong* answer.

The sociologist Thomas Scheff suggests that shame is the emotion of deference and social conformity. Referring to the Asch experiments, he notes:

> A reaction that occurred both in independent and yielding subjects was the fear that they were suffering from a defect and that the study would disclose this defect: 'I felt like a silly *fool* . . . A question of being a *misfit* . . . they'd think I was queer. It made me seem weak-eyed or weak-headed, like a black sheep' [p. 403, italics added].[5]

Group pressure operates everywhere – at school, in fashion, in nationalism and patriotism, in street gangs, in racism and sexism, in humour and in religion. Undoubtedly some people gravitate to groups who already express values they feel in tune with, but these values are likely to have been commonplace while they were growing up. Indeed, in any group, the pressure to conform can be so pervasive and intense that, in fact, one's personal values, beliefs and behaviours are actually socially constructed for you – you just adopt them from others (remember Chinese foot binding?). Some studies on conformity have looked at how our brain works in these conditions and suggest that group pressure may actually affect our perception, not just our judgements or submissive / compliant behaviour.

Two other series of experiments are important to mention here.[6] One is the famous Stanford prison experiment by Philip Zimbardo. In 1971, while a professor of psychology at Stanford University in California, Zimbardo took a group of students, placed them in a mock prison and artificially divided them into 'prisoners' and 'guards'. He found that, with encouragement, the guards quickly began exerting cruel pressure and punishments on the prisoners – so much so that the experiment had to be stopped and has been a source of controversy ever since.

Conformity to authority had earlier been researched by Stanley Milgram who, in 1961, had devised one of the now classic experiments to explore conformity. In the original experiments, conducted in the impressive laboratories at Yale University, volunteers – the 'teachers' – were told by a stern, impassive, 31-year-old researcher, dressed in a grey technician's coat, that they were to take part in an experiment on learning. They would ask questions of another person – the 'learner' – sitting in an adjacent room and were to deliver an electric shock for each incorrect answer. The 'learner' (who was part of the set-up and in on the research) was a pleasant, mild-mannered, 47-year-old accountant who had trained for the role. The shocks were of graded intensity, going from mild to quite severe (450 volts). As more and more questions were answered incorrectly, the shock level rose. In reality, of course, the experiment was a fake, nobody got shocked, but crucially the 'teachers' asking the questions and delivering the shocks didn't know this. The accountant was a good actor and faked distress, even a possible heart attack. In the first round of experiments, 65 per cent of the 'teachers' were obedient and did what they were told by the researcher, administering the horrendous 450 volts even when they could hear (feigned) cries from the 'learner' in the next room.

In subsequent experiments, changes were made to make it easier to challenge the legitimacy of the research, such as moving it out of the Yale University setting and making the researcher act more informally. Another change was not to have the 'learner' in another room but actually interact with the 'teachers'. When touch and physically proximity were included, 30 per cent of the 'teachers' still complied even though they knew that they were (supposedly) causing pain to the 'learner'. Milgram noted that many of the 'teachers' were obviously distressed at what they were asked to do but complied anyway. They weren't able to turn their distress into action, but instead simply handed responsibility to the 'authority' of the researcher.

Recognizing in our hearts how easy it is to abdicate responsibility even when we know that something is wrong is, of course, key for us in trying to develop compassionate behaviour. It can be a useful exercise to think about the things in our own lives that we simply go along with that we actually feel are wrong. Again look at this with kindness rather than criticism and think about making small changes perhaps. But keep in mind, too, that, as we'll see later, some of our feelings of 'right' and 'wrong' aren't as reliable as we'd like to think they are.

Confronting our capacity for cruelty

This is the biggy – the real challenge for the compassionate minded. Like many others, I've suggested[7] that we can't understand and promote compassion unless we also understand the sources of cruelty. When it comes to cruelty, we're dealing with some very old and powerful archetypal processes. The concept of evil doesn't help us here, but understanding the link between 'old brain/mind' and 'new brain/mind' does. In their powerful book *Crimes of Obedience*, Herbert C. Kelman and V. Lee Hamilton[8] outline how many immoral behaviours spring from the action of subordinates and henchmen who sometimes willingly (but sometimes not) conform because of a need to belong and identify with a tribe and to seek the approval of their leaders. We follow leaders for many reasons – because we hope they might protect us, look favourably on us or lead us to better times, or we identify with them in some way. Some rewards for (submissive) following have been called *expansions*, in that the person who follows and obeys leaders avoids the latter's anger or attacks and can be rewarded with love, approval, status, security, a sense of belonging, acceptance, power, privilege and so on, thus becoming more than they were before and gaining from it. For instance, suicide bombers may believe that they will be heroes in their own tribes and gain wonderful rewards in heaven. Becoming a follower can also give us a new sense of self-identity, meaning and purpose in life, which counteracts low self-esteem, depression, existential crisis and fear. However, the desire to win approval and show that we're more willing and able than others to obey orders and work for the benefit of the leader and group can cause seriously immoral behaviour.

Here is one well-publicized event that demonstrates this, but it is one among many, many thousands. As you'll see, there's far more to this example than just the following of orders or defending and avenging one's group. The ease with which moral concerns and compassion can be *turned off* under conditions of threat, plus submissiveness and compliance with orders, are all important elements.

Kelman and Hamilton relate how, on 16 March 1968, a group of US Marines from 'Charlie' Company were dropped by helicopter just outside a Vietnamese village called Son My, at a subhamlet known to the Americans as My Lai. What was to unfold in the next ten hours was to make history in American military law courts. The villagers were massacred by the soldiers almost down to the very last man, woman, child and dog. Even women clutching babies and begging for their lives were shot. The full body count is unknown but is likely to have been 500 or so. Bodies were stacked on each other, many still moaning in their death throes. Later, other Marines who could not stand the noise of the dying walked along the lines shooting, 'to put them out their misery'.

A friend has recently added a perspective to this story that I hadn't noticed before: 'While the slaughter is obviously important, what has always struck me about My Lai was the fact that so many rapes occurred. This seemed to completely negate the statements by the soldiers that they had shot at the villagers because they were frightened. If they were so frightened, how could they have possibly spent the time (or had the physical ability) to rape?'

No one knows the degree to which the events at My Lai were an aberration of the Vietnam war, although judging by the history of other conflicts, they were probably not as rare as we might like to think. Indeed, such atrocities are extremely common in wartime and you can find them occurring thousands of years ago. It has been typical for armies to sack cities and kill all they found there and crucify or enslave those they captured. Such occurrences tell us of how powerful archetypes and social mentalities can be under certain social conditions, *patterning our minds* (e.g. turning off compassion attributes) so that we become simply actors of these old scripts. Even the God of the Old Testament was in favour of the odd genocide or two. What was unusual in the case of My Lai, however, was the role of the media in ensuring that these acts didn't go unnoticed, with no opportunity for social awareness and sanction. Pictures of the massacre's aftermath were flashed around the world and almost certainly played a major part in the subsequent court martial.

'Charlie' Company had been frustrated due to problems with bad orders, failed missions, booby traps and land mines. In fact, on 15 March, just the day before, they'd attended the funeral of one of their sergeants who had been blown up by a booby trap. In his book *Our Own Worst Enemy*, Norman F. Dixon[9] gives a harrowing and moving account of one soldier's involvement with the massacre. When asked at a subsequent hearing why he did it, the soldier answered:

> Because I felt like I was ordered to do it, and it seemed like that, at the time I felt I was doing the right thing, because like I said I lost buddies. I lost a damn good buddy, Bobby Wilson, and it was on my conscience. So, after I did it, I felt good, but later on it was getting to me.

The interviewer seems perplexed by how Americans could do such things and asks the solider to consider his own family. The interviewer asks: 'How do you shoot babies?' and the soldier replies, 'I don't know. It's just one of those things.' The interviewer then asks if the people were doing anything, if they were begging to save themselves. At first, the soldier denies it, then says: 'Right. They were begging and saying "No, no." And the mothers were hugging their children and . . . but they kept right on firing. Well, we kept right on firing. They were waving their arms and begging . . .' (Dixon, pp. 127–8).

Part of this tragic event was fuelled by a desire for recognition and to please authority. Kelman and Hamilton give a good description of the kinds of relationships that operated in 'Charlie' Company, which made the Marines so vulnerable to acting in this way.

> The company's commander, Capt. Ernest Medina, was an upwardly mobile Mexican-American who wanted to make the army his career although he feared he might never advance beyond captain because of his lack of formal education. His eagerness had earned him a nickname among his men: 'Mad Dog Medina'. One of his admirers was the platoon leader Second Lt. William L. Calley, Jr., an undistinguished, five-foot-three-inch junior-college dropout who had failed four of the seven courses in which he had enrolled his first year. Many viewed him as one of those 'instant officers' made possible only by the army's then-desperate need for manpower. Whatever the cause, he was an insecure leader whose frequent claim was, 'I'm the boss.' [p. 2]

Calley, like some men within strong hierarchical male groups, turns out to have been insecure, ready and eager to please and desperate for recognition and approval by his superiors regardless of what was asked of him, provided that he could justify it as 'doing his duty'. Men of this type often have had poor relationships with their fathers. On the day in question, 'Charlie' Company had orders to carry out a 'search and destroy' mission to root out a Viet Cong battalion believed to have their base in or near Son My. Such lack of clarity may have made it possible for a few individual males like Calley to interpret the horrendous actions that followed as desired by, and worthy of approval from, those higher in authority. Although he was tried and convicted, according to a report in the *Guardian* newspaper[10] Lt Calley 'became a right-wing hero and served only three days of his sentence before being transferred to house arrest'.

Indeed, throughout history this type of approval-seeking behaviour and competing for investment from others has often led to atrocity. Hitler was known for giving vague orders, letting his generals compete for his attention and approval like squabbling siblings, with the result that each tried to be more loyal, efficient and ruthless than the others. Sometimes your life can depend on proving yourself loyal and ensuring the approval of the leader. Saddam Hussein would read out lists of those he thought had been disloyal and have them taken outside and killed, allowing their screams to filter back into the room. In many religions, too, gods threaten hell for the disloyal. But Hitler who sent 11 million people to the death camps and Stalin who killed more than 20 million of his own people were not appeased only out of fear; they were also deeply loved and admired by many sections of the population. And these atrocities were all made possible because so many countless thousands of others were prepared to keep doing routine jobs and do as they were told.

As Milgram[11] said of his own research:

> I am forever astonished that, when lecturing on the obedience experiments in colleges across the country, I faced young men who were aghast at the behaviour of the experimental subjects and proclaimed they would never behave in such a way, but who, in a matter of months, were brought into the military and performed without compunction actions that made shocking the victim seem pallid. In this respect they are no better and no worse than human beings of any era who lend themselves to the purposes of authority and become instruments in its destructive process. [p. 180]

Although it is not nearly so extreme, we often hear of how some politicians strive to prove themselves loyal to their leaders and their parties in an effort to progress themselves. Indeed democracy can make party loyalty a virtue rather than fostering free thinking. This is a very worrying way to run a democracy in my view, because tribal psychology opens us up to all kinds of problems, as we saw in the lead-up to the Iraq war.[12]

Cruelty and sadism as virtues

It's clear that the human mind is never far from a fascination with sadism and cruelty. We've seen this in our entertainments over thousands of years – from the Roman games right through to the re-emergence of sadism in computer games, novels and Hollywood fantasies. Many writers on such matters wonder if this is linked to our intense fears and rages about being in a world surrounded by death, decay and disease; with brains that aren't exactly easy to control, we can quickly turn on each other. There are major debates as to how these games and Hollywood movies, scripted only to extract money from us, may be dulling our compassionate senses.

But cruelty operates in many ways, and the reasons for it are complex and multifaceted.[13] It can be a way in which the dominant and powerful instil fear in subordinates and stop rebellion. Some of the punishments handed down to 'criminals' (violators of the social order) have been extraordinarily cruel and often associated with torture. By contrast, subordinate acts of cruelty can be seen as virtues, winning favour in the eyes of the dominant leaders or of God. After all, it's the hand of man that swings the sword, plunges the dagger or puts the flame to the stake. The inquisitors didn't believe that they were being cruel but thought that they were virtuous, doing the will of God. Their fantasized God and his desires seem deluded and cruel to us now, but a fascination with the pain and suffering of others exists in all cultures.

When executions were public, they brought large crowds who had little desire for mercy but would goad the executioner on. The historical record shows that, be it burnings, beheadings, quarterings (which included being disembowelled) or hangings, public interest was often so great that fights could break out as spectators tried to get as close as possible. At times, some of those in the crowd would shout contemptuously at the poor, dying victim and roar with pleasure as the deed was done. In Britain, until the last century, hanging killed by strangulation, which could take as long as 20 minutes. According to Geoffrey Abbott[14] in his book *Rack, Rope and Red-Hot Pincers*, when a more humane way was found to hang victims, by breaking the neck in the fall, the crowd were incensed and threatened to riot for having been robbed of their spectacle. Although women do not act violently to anything like the same extent as men, they can also be attracted to sadism. Indeed, during the 'reign of terror' during the French Revolution, women made up large sections of the crowd and fought to get near the front to watch the nobility being guillotined.

Consider also the invention of the concept of hell. It's usually associated with punishment – because most of us have a strong sense of justice/ retribution and we hate the idea that some folks get away with bad crimes without being punished. However, many cultural versions of hell suggest that these punishments are not just painful but are actually very sadistic, with agony that never ends. This seems to be a case where humans fantasize about horrible things and then can't decide what is *their* fantasy and what might be a reality. People can be drawn to these ideas for different reasons.

There's an interesting sideline here, which is the way that myths about hell often use fire. A plastic surgeon told me that he thought the inventors of hell included burning in a big way because it's the most severe of all pains known to humans. However, it's also the case that, for many centuries, fire was the only way to cleanse the environment of disease – so it's not surprising that cleansing, purification and punishment are all interlocked.

The roles of power plays, enforced obedience, anger, vengeance, deterrents and subordinates 'wanting to please' are fairly easy to spot in our cruelties and how they can drive our fantasies to extremes. However, the emotion of disgust, although not so commonly associated with cruelty, is linked to it in a number of ways, especially the desire for purification. We've evolved disgust so that we'll spit out and get rid of things that taste or smell bad in order to avoid or eradicate the substances that can contaminate and cause infection and disease. We want to purify our water to prevent ourselves getting ill. Now because words like 'poison' describe bodily processes, they shouldn't be used to refer to an emotion, inner state of mind or other people. However, a common way to generate tribal violence is to use the idea of disgust and to see 'the others' as an infection, an illness, a way of contaminating our way of life, destroying us from within, 'racially unpure' and so on. Not only does this arouse the interest of the threat/self-protection system, but that system will guide the brain to try to seek out and eradicate the danger. In a crisis, people can get into excitable and dissociated states in which compassionate brain patterns are firmly turned off.

Some religious people can also want to purify heaven and keep out all the 'bad people'. Those with bad genes, poor upbringing, lusts and 'sinful' behaviour don't pass the 'ones like us' test – they aren't 'pure of heart'. So, again, we're back to splitting people into good and bad. Sadly some people still project their own fears and sadism, using as threats such concepts as mortal sin. Well, of course, these punishments and rules are usually man-made, but with compassion, we can see that we don't have to be frightened by other people's projected fears and sadism or desire to control us. Until about the fifteenth century, it was thought that one of the pleasures of heaven was to be able to watch those in torment below. But around that time there was a shift, as echoed in the sentiment: 'My soul can never rest in heaven while one soul is in torment in hell.' (I agree. Of course, ideally today we would take this same sentiment and apply it to the hell that many people still live in on Earth.) Thankfully many of us are now free of the indoctrination and fear that was only encouraged to prop up a powerful religious hierarchy. However, the idea of trying to purify our minds lives on – but that is not the compassionate path.

In the last chapter, we saw the problems of trying to enact the desire to rid ourselves of emotions and feelings. If it's rage that people are trying to get rid of, this can drive them to be sadistic towards themselves. Cutting and burning yourself are forms of sadism even though their function can be to regulate emotion. The point is that sadistic actions are often designed to regulate someone or something. Consider then that we're confronting increasing rates of depression and self-harming behaviour in our younger population. There are various explanations for this but, to me, it seems that, however we look at them, our increasingly sadistic entertainments, the 'drive for competitive edge', the complete lack of interest in providing adolescents (and adults, too) with a sense of belonging in the adult world, the sacrifice of our human needs to the economics of 'want more' – all these are signs that something quite serious is happening to our mental health.

It's difficult, but the compassionate path requires us to pay attention to possible sources of our 'care-less-ness', cruelty and sadism, not to deny them or condemn them but to transcend them and not act them out. It can be very tough to open our eyes to the potential cruelty in our minds and the world. But always remember that you didn't design your brain like this. Our task is to understand it and find ways of bringing compassionate light to it.

Confronting our shadows

Carl Jung, a contemporary of Freud and developer of the archetype theory (*see* pp. 94–100) was in no doubt that one of our greatest challenges is to confront our shadows – the sources of our fears, anger and violence. There have long been myths, stretching right back to the Greeks and beyond, about the fear of the 'beast within' – a concept that was brilliantly caught in the 1956 film *Forbidden Planet*. On the planet of Altair IV, a race of aliens called the Krell had developed a machine that could make their thoughts become real. However, they hadn't apparently taken into account the destructive impulses that sit alongside the brain's compassionate ones, and so they were done in by the release of their 'monsters from the Id'. The film is really the story of how we also are now capable of making real some of our worst nightmares when we allow our 'new minds' to carry out the wishes of our 'old brains'; warfare is but one obvious example. The problem with many of these myths is, of course, that we think the beast within is released through aggression or our evilness, but it's more complex than that; it's released through our fear, our search for security, belonging and conformity, our tribalism and our submissiveness to leaders.

So the greatest challenge for compassion is to be open and not shaming or blaming about our desire for belonging and recognition from leaders (the pats on the head) and how this can drive our capacity for cruelty. We can allow cruelty to stalk the Earth through our fears, wish for vengeance, tribalism, indifference, desire to prove to ourselves, complicity, denial and self-focused wanting – quite a lot of ways, really, when you think about it. This is because our brains can adopt different patterns where some aspects are turned on and others are turned off. Thus we will risk our lives to save our loved ones or truly grieve for the pain of others on one day, and yet on the next, we can vote in favour of bombing other people and their children. We like to believe that we're independent, self-sufficient, clear-thinking folk, but we're actually one of the most dependent, submissive, easily led species around. Sheep have little on us – we simply hand over our new thinking brains to be guided by those primitive 'old brain/mind' archetypes or emotions and whatever or whoever stirs them.

The eruption and savagery of the Bosnian war reminds us of this. Under the influence of certain leaders, fuelled by tribal psychology, people who had been neighbours and friends for years became enemies and were brutalizing each other within weeks. Only by open and careful psychological study of these processes can we hope to illuminate how to prevent them. Moral shock and puzzlement are unhelpful and suggest a mind in complete denial of human history, brain design and the power of social context. The moment we feel threatened, or special, privileged and entitled, the moment we distance ourselves from 'the other', is the moment we take our first steps on the road to cruelty.

If we believe that we're doing good for our group or our leaders or in self-defence, our capacity for compassion seems to be easily turned off in our brains. When we feel threatened, the brain doesn't want to be bogged down in moral concerns that could undermine its capacity to defend itself. Moreover, defeating one's enemies and making them suffer can be experienced positively – like a reward. It's one of the most problematic designed features of our brain. Mild versions of it occur when whichever sports team we support wins – we very rarely feel depressed for the defeated side. If there's one thing we need from compassion, it's to open our minds to the ease by which we're led to perform immoral acts and then truly believe them to be justified. Humans have been doing this for many thousands of years.

Conscience or compassion?

In the last century, an estimated 200 million people or more were killed by other humans in wars and tribal conflicts. Goodness knows how many more were severely injured, tortured, dispossessed or raped. Billions are spent on weapons to maim and kill other humans and weapons research. Tribal psychology takes us into a kind of madness (and I mean that quite literally) where we lose our sensitivities for our fellow human beings. Throughout the world, minds possessed by the primitive emotions of fear and anger, politically or religiously motivated, seek to spice, stir and focus our tribal psychology – one can almost see the fires burning in the eyes of such people. It's an act of courage to stand back from this and think first not of your tribe or local group but of your humanity.

So compassionate behaviour can require us to be courageous in the face of potential shame, personal uncertainty and fear, to stand against the crowd and to listen to the voice of compassion. It also requires us to recognize that, when we say that we're making decisions with our *conscience*, those decisions may not be compassionate. If we use our religion to guide our conscience and the way we view things, aren't we simply accessing feelings that link to our socially conditioned traditions and values? It's not rocket science to suggest that, if we'd been born in a different time and culture, our values would be quite different, too – and therefore so would our conscience. I'm not sure that the Romans had much of a conscience about slaves being cut to pieces in the arena. The Greek philosophers had no problem with the issue of slavery or that some men were born to rule others. But both the Romans and the Greeks (and all other such groups and civilizations that had cruelty embedded in their social systems) were just like you and me – but in a different culture. What we see as a moral issue can be related to culture – what we collectively come to understand.

Now this is very tough on us, really. There are no easy answers except to say that compassion and your conscience are not the same thing. Compassion requires the skills and attributes we saw in Chapter 6 and also often a degree of courage to break free of your tribe. It's hard and, at times, scary work. 'Conscience' is more likely to refer to an emotional and automatic *feeling* about something, but the origins of such feelings can be difficult to discover. One group of people believe contraception is fundamental to helping the world's problems; another group thinks using it is wicked. One group of scientists believes that stem cell research, including human/animal hybrids of a few hundred cells, is the gateway to discoveries that will help eliminate incredible suffering in the world; a religious group has described this as 'monstrous'. Compassion must play a role in thinking through these dilemmas because conscience, social conditioning and emotional reactions are problematic.

As a self-confessed submissive, I can look back on my life and see times where I could have stood up and didn't. I deeply regret some of that now. So we have to recognize these powerful archetypal forces in ourselves, and the way in which leaders, be they political or religious, manipulate them and try to turn us all into sheep. We need to stand back and think through the compassionate options in any situation, giving ourselves space enough for thought and discussion as we try to avoid being overly persuaded by our *emotional* reactions, no matter how intense they are. It will help us if we remember that we all just find ourselves here, playing out the scripts and dramas of the archetypes in our 'old brains/minds'. But we also need to learn to *take responsibility for our own decisions* and not hand them over to a leader, guru or some mysterious god and obey blindly. Science is gradually bringing us to an end of an era where blind obedience and faith were regarded as virtues (against the resistance of some who fear the loss of their religious versions of life and meaning). It's in the interests of our leaders to try to maintain our fear and obedience. Spiritual searching for meaning, yearning for interconnectedness and wondering about the very nature of consciousness will stay with us because they lie at our heart. We must not let these searches be hijacked by the more primitive and destructive parts of ourselves – and that's going to take courage.

Conclusion

Kindness, generosity and forgiveness are obviously all important compassionate behaviours, but this chapter has taken us into the more complex and difficult areas of compassion, where moral certainties become difficult. In many recent books and in research, compassion has been closely linked to happiness, but I believe that compassion is far, far more than that. A compassionate mind actually takes you on a journey deep into your evolved being – down into the building blocks of your brain and the genes that built it. It takes you on a journey that is both frightening and illuminating. It takes you on a journey into the archetypes and social mentalities that might be writing the scripts of your life and, indeed, that of all of us in our collective dealings.

So we become compassionate to the very fact that we are beings who have emerged in the flow of life, with a peculiar brain, evolved over many millions of years, riddled with passions, desires and archetypal forces that play through us. This is a brain of multiplicities, with the potential for compassion, kindness and love, but also self-focused wants and desires, able to generate unrealistic fantasies and be consumed by vengeance, tribalism and sadistic pleasure. Now there is nothing to be ashamed of in any of this, and once we give up self-blame and shame, we can start to look at these things in ourselves, *expecting* to find them. And then it is up to us which parts of ourselves we choose to train.

Looking to the decades ahead, one thing is clear, I think, and this is that our education system, and indeed the whole fabric of our society, will have to take far more interest in our psychology and the training of our minds if we really want to create compassionate societies and live in harmony with each other and the environment that sustains us. Those individuals who see psychology and gaining deeper insight into the nature of our own minds as having little to offer them, or believe that it's only for wimps or a liberal plot or that it might offend God, need to be challenged because, otherwise, they'll take us to a world of exhaustion, pollution and depletion – with smart weapons and ones of mass destruction. Well, let's be honest, they already have. So compassion is rooted in the *scientific* pursuit of how our minds work and are controlled. In a hundred years from now, we'll know and understand our brains and minds better – and who knows? – we may actually be further forward in building just and compassionate societies because it's these aspects of ourselves we've chosen to feed and understand better how to nourish.

13 Expressing the Compassionate Mind

We've seen that much of what goes on in our minds is related to how we have been genetically built and socially shaped. Rats, rabbits and monkeys have no choice but to live out their lives according to the scripts of their emotions and archetypes and within environmental constraints. They live and die never understanding why they're alive nor even that they *are* 'alive'. We, on the other hand, have become conscious of being alive and existing within the process of life itself. This awakening isn't easy, for we then discover that we live in a world where living things have to eat each other to survive, where viruses maim and kill on a massive scale in their own pursuit of reproduction, where our lives are short and our bodies destined to decay and end, and where we ourselves find it terribly difficult to break free of our genetically scripted archetypes and social conditioning. It's all too easy for us to carry out tribal vengeances, to distinguish between the chosen and unchosen, to be submissive to absentee or callous leaders, to be indifferent to the suffering of others or to get lost in anxiety, depression and paranoia. For thousands of years, these experiences and life themes have been played out over and over again in human minds and in the field of human activity. As Shakespeare said, 'All the world's a stage, and all the men and women merely players . . .'

It's easy for us to pathologize these feelings and themes and believe that, if we're not happy or aren't maximizing our potential, there must be something wrong with us. Do we need Prozac? But 'old brain/mind' feelings and passions evolved for good reasons – to defend, protect and advance us, or at least our genes. So sometimes our less pleasant emotions and feelings about ourselves and others are natural responses to difficult life situations, stress, unresolved issues from the past and so on. We can help ourselves if we learn to tolerate, understand and work with them, to find ways to resolve and cope with them. Evolution has no interest in happiness as an experience in itself. Only self-aware beings can take on the responsibility of seeking to understand the causes of suffering, how to alleviate it and promote happiness and well-being. When we do this, we find that it's our ability to face up to and tolerate our threat emotions, sadness and tragedy and to develop courage that's so important to compassion and, indeed, happiness.

None the less, evolution hasn't left us empty-handed because, in addition to having minds that can think, accumulate knowledge, self-reflect and train themselves, we have also evolved potentials for reaching out to others and for caring for and being cared for by them. Indeed, we now know that love, kindness and compassion actually influence how our brains wire and organize themselves, and many of our most basic physiological processes. The more we try to generate and value compassion, the more we will stimulate those neuronal systems that support positive feelings – and 'neurons that fire together wire together'. Also, if we focus on developing compassionate feelings, values and behaviours, this will influence the interactions we have with each other, which will influence, on one level, our brains and neurons, and, on another, the kinds of society we create (e.g. more sharing and more nurturing of the environment). So we can put compassion at the centre of our motives for self-awareness and goals in life. And once we understand how our brains work, we can start making choices.

Of course, these are difficult to carry through because our threat/self-protection system is so very easily activated. So we have to train our minds for self-compassion and develop relationships and communities that support compassion and societies that value it. Just as if we're in a science fiction movie, perhaps, we may need to learn to *break our conditioning*, to question our values and emotional reactions, to become 'mindful' of our own minds, to learn about them, to search for the compassionate solution, and to practise creating compassion as a preferred brain pattern. This does require courage, to let go of past certainties, open our hearts, challenge our own emotional reactions, study, explore, discover, change and take responsibility and practise. We have to keep in mind that the direction of travel is towards transforming our minds.

Enhancing our lives with compassion

There are three directions of compassion: the compassion that flows into you from others and your openness to it; the compassion that flows out of you to others; and the flow of self-compassion that you create inside of you. Full compassion works to maximize each of these. Self-compassion helps us recognize how easy it is for us to become ashamed, disappointed and self-judgemental when we feel unable to achieve, get or be what we want. We feel that we're missing that 'something' that will help us find acceptance in the eyes of others. Being compassionate about this means understanding it and learning how to stay 'in the moment' with it and with kindness.

Compassionate mind training is about learning to bring balance to our three different types of emotion regulation systems (*see* pp. 21–8) – namely, the system that focuses on threats and self-protection, the incentive/resource-seeking system that focuses on wants and achievements, and the soothing/contentment system that focuses on safeness and connectedness. By bringing balance to these, patterns of brain activity will emerge that create states of well-being, pro-social values and behaviour. In Chapters 6 and 8, we explored the nature of compassion, attributes and compassion skills that are key to bringing balance and, in the subsequent chapters, how to develop them.

Once we understand what these attributes and skills are and we're clear about *why* we want to put compassion at the centre of our being and focus in life (to transform our minds), we're free to begin training our minds. We engage in this with understanding of and insight into how we've emerged in the flow of life and how our brains have been designed, rather than just because we've got a vague wish to be happier. We also engage in training with a sense of playfulness, gentleness and openness to exploration and the discovery of new things. Even though we might frequently be grumpy, anxious, frustrated, argumentative, hung-over or suffering from the windy after-effects of too much curry, we can *always* return to a compassion focus. Each moment is a new moment, and each of those moments can be a moment for compassion, regardless of what previous moments have been about.

It's easy to see, in some spiritual traditions, a rather negative take on human desire. I hope that I've clarified what the 'middle way' is. It's not about living life in some rarefied, self-denying, self-limiting struggle. It's about paying attention in a particular kind of way, learning to savour joys in the simple and small, while also finding ways to be open to losses and tragedies, reaching out to others and exploring the world through the compassionate mind. We live in a society where we're told that maximum pleasure is gained from having the *biggest* portions, the *fastest* cars, the *most beautiful* bodies and partners. But older wisdoms teach us that the greatest happiness comes from experiencing things *right now, in-this-moment, with exactly what you have*. This is not the end of ambition but approaching ambition with a compassionate smile. I still love buying new guitars! The Dalai Lama is known to love gadgets! We learn, however, that such things only give a certain type of pleasure, not the longer sustaining happiness of self-contentment and well-being that we seek.

Insight into these realities is important to help us train but is only the first step. For example, we can have genuine experiences of enlightenment – 'penny dropping' moments of insight. An American friend with whom I had spent an hour explaining cricket suddenly got the point and the game finally made sense to him. But this 'enlightenment' would not make him a good player. The Buddha meditated every day of his life because training and practice are key. Enlightenment is gaining insight but clearly is *not* the end product of, say, 40 years of practice! And in practice we're learning all the time. Training and practice are important because, like playing a musical instrument, you can lose a certain sharpness in your efforts without them. This is why I've given you ideas for training that you can use most days or even every day of your life. We can change our brains.[1] Even if you spend just a few minutes, say, in the bath or before getting out of bed or during breakfast or your lunch break – to compassionately smile, focus on your breathing and try to be 'mindful' and generate compassionate feelings in yourself – that's cool! Little and often can work. Later you may want to dedicate more time to compassionate practice and even start meditating, and as in all things, the more you practise, the better you'll get. You may also want to seek out more advanced teachers than I to take you further.

Worksheet 3 will help you think about practising regularly and reflecting on it. You can copy these pages and write on them about what you find helpful and what you find difficult. In the 'Find out more' section at the end of the book (see p. 490), you'll find references to various CDs that may help you with your practice.

Worksheet 4 offers a quick reference and review for coping with current life difficulties and unpleasant emotions that can arise at certain times. These are ideas to practise and experiment with, to see which ones are helpful and which ones you want to develop. Again, you can copy this form to keep notes of your practice and efforts.

All things considered, we're back to where we started, recognizing that we're a species designed to flourish best in conditions of kindness, support and compassion that flows in, out and within us. The sooner we start training our minds to do this – for ourselves and our children – and try to create societies where this flow of compassion occurs naturally, the happier and more flourishing we'll be.

As we begin to develop a compassionate focus and a compassionate mind, it can be useful to explore how this will help us change and become more as we would like to be. So in the last exercise of this book – Worksheet 5 – see how a compassionate focus will affect many things to do with yourself and others.

Compassion for ourselves and others also requires us to shift away from the worship of the self that's so much part of our Western culture. For example, sometimes we find ourselves in very fortunate places. We may have been born into a life of comparative privilege or have certain positive attributes – say, intelligence, sporting skills, musical talent or a body that stays relatively thin or is good looking. We live in a world where we're encouraged to think of these qualities as 'the self', as if we made them and should be proud of them, flaunt them even. We might even have a sense of entitlement. In fact, they're equally due to luck as to anything else. Feeling that you're better than others because of your abilities or appearance can cause problems. It's preferable for us to think of our talents with delight at and gratitude for our good fortune.

Worksheet 3: Compassionate approaches to life practice

Record your regular practice, choosing an activity.	Personal comments and reflections on your practice
Soothing breathing rhythm and mindfulness: being 'in-the-moment'. Practise looking at things in new ways, noting the things you enjoy and can savour, no matter how small – e.g. the first cup of tea of the day, the warmth of a bath. Consider things you are grateful for in joyous, fun ways, no matter how small.	
When in a place of quiet, focus on your **ideal compassion/caring image**. It has the qualities of wisdom, strength, warmth and non-judging/condemning and gives these unconditionally to you, with the deep desire for you to flourish and be free from suffering. Practise feeling that flowing into you from your image. Remember that images can be fleeting and more felt than seen. Your image is well aware of how difficult our evolved brains/minds and lives can be for us.	
When in a place of quiet, focus on **feeling yourself to be a compassionate person** with the qualities of wisdom, strength, warmth and non-judging / condemning – which you direct unconditionally towards yourself. Also practise directing compassionate feelings towards others. In both cases (directing towards yourself and towards others), focus on the deep desire for you and others to flourish, be happy and free from suffering.	

Record your regular practice, choosing an activity.	Personal comments and reflections on your practice
Compassionate behaviour: choose and enact compassionate behaviour that has the intention and deep desire for you and others to flourish and be free from suffering. This may include letter writing or acts of appreciation or gratitude or courageously doing something you are fearful of but would like to overcome.	
Make a commitment to look after and take care of yourself, as you would a dear friend. Seek out ways to learn assertiveness if you feel this would help you.	
Express your appreciation to others. Make a point of trying to be kind to others and see how you feel when doing that. Pay attention to how different things you do affect your feelings. If you're in conflict with someone or something, work on the most compassionate and helpful (non-submissive) way forward.	
Note any novel ways you have found to develop your compassion-focused lifestyle.	

Learning to be grateful and appreciative of our talents and compassionate to those who lack them is a different way of 'being' with our abilities – we become less interested in self-focused achievement. If you follow more deeply into meditative traditions, you may find that even the notion of an individual self (created by our brains/minds) is somewhat illusory anyway.

Worksheet 4: Compassionate approaches to coping with life's difficulties and upsetting emotions and situations.

This worksheet offers various prompts and ideas designed to help you to practise refocusing your mind if you're distressed, and to access your soothing/contentment system. When threatened or upset, it's easy to become focused on unpleasant feelings, worries or memories. Try to recognize them but also try to rebalance your system.

What issue(s) are causing upset?	Reflections on what helped, what was difficult and what requires practice
Compassionate attention is about our focus and how we create images and memories in our minds: • Engage and attend to your soothing breathing rhythm. • Adopt a compassionate body posture and facial expression. • Become mindful – hold your attention 'in this moment' rather than becoming distracted by 'what ifs?' and ruminations. • Recall times when you've coped. • Recall times when you were happy. • Focus on your compassion image. • Keep in mind that things and feelings change. • Create an image of yourself coping or of you at your best. • Imagine yourself having got through this difficulty – and really focus on that. • Observe thoughts and feelings as *patterns* created in you – and realize that you can experience many different patterns.	

What issue(s) are causing upset?	Reflections on what helped, what was difficult and what requires practice
Compassionate thinking/reasoning is about how we think things through – the kinds of self-talk and conversations that go through our minds: • Notice if you're ruminating and decide to move out of it. • Notice if your feelings or thoughts are self-critical and decide to switch to a kinder and compassionate focus. • Imagine yourself as a compassionate person speaking to a friend. Actually speak out loud with a warm voice tone. • Put yourself in 'compassion self' mode and feel compassion for your upset self. Stay in that compassion mode. • Compassionately speak to your upset self. If it helps, place a hand just over your heart area. Bring as much wisdom, strength, warmth and non-condemning to this as you can. • Bring to mind your common humanity and become aware that many humans can struggle with difficult feeling. Feel at one with them rather than alone or different. • Recognize how often some of what you feel isn't your fault. Focus on the reasons why it isn't (e.g. we did not design our brains or backgrounds). • Assume that others will be helpful until you get evidence that they won't. • Keep in mind the motto: 'The secret of success is the ability to fail.' • Focus on your efforts rather than on results.	

What issue(s) are causing upset?	Reflections on what helped, what was difficult and what requires practice
Compassionate behaviour is behaviour that will help you cope with your difficulty: • Make a commitment to behave in ways that help you move forward in life, even if this means short-term difficulty. • Practise trying out different behaviours and see which ones work for you. • Reach out to others and see if help is available for you. • Keep in mind that confidence develops from engaging with the difficulty, and that this trying time you are going through now may, in the long term, build your confidence. • Recognize your limits, and when you need to rest, slow down or take time out. • If problems seem large, try to break them down into smaller elements.	
Compassionate feeling Whatever you attempt to do, always try your best to do it with kindness so that you feel your efforts to be ones of support and encouragement, in the service of helping yourself cope and flourish. Remember that coping can be hard and can take practice. There are no 'oughts' or 'shoulds' here, no perfect ways to cope, no freeing or ridding oneself of difficult feelings – just basic kindness for life's difficulties that many of us find ourselves in. This won't remove those difficulties but it might ease your path through them – good luck!	

Worksheet 5: The consequences of becoming compassionate to yourself and others

As you begin to develop a compassionate focus and compassionate mind, explore how this will help you become more as you would like to be.

List how a compassionate focus will affect ...

... how you feel about and relate to yourself.
What will be different? How will you notice this happening and build on it?

... how you interact with other people.
What will be different? How will you notice this happening and build on it?

... how you deal with problems in your life.
What will be different? How will you notice this happening and build on it?

... how you choose and work towards goals.

What will be different? How will you notice this happening and build on it? (Your goals can be short term – taking only a few days or weeks – or they can take months, years or a lifetime to achieve.)

... how you deal with setbacks and crises.

What will be different? How will you notice this happening and build on it?

... any other life issues that are important to you.

What will be different? How will you notice this happening and build on it?

Being kind

As we develop self-compassion, we also open ourselves to the pains of others and to our own desire to help – because we all just found ourselves here. Many traditional meditative practices focus on filling the mind with compassion *for others* – and practise activating and working those brain systems. But we can also focus on kind and compassionate behaviour.

Stephan Einhorn[2] has written a lovely book called *The Art of Being Kind,* partly to counteract the growing belief in our society that only if we're ruthless and self-focused can we get ahead. He looks at a number of situations in which we could put kindness into action, and points out that kindness to others is not just a form of altruistic self-sacrifice. There are many personal benefits to being kind. If you're kind to others, they're more likely to be kind to you, you'll receive appreciation in return and avoid conflict, and people are more likely to like and trust you, and you'll feel good about yourself – all of which is good for your brain. Caring relationships impact more beneficially on your body – and especially on your stress hormone levels and immune system – than conflictual ones. When we recognize these self-help effects, it stops us from worrying about our true motives: are we really being kind or are we doing kind things just to satisfy ourselves or to be liked? Most acts of kindness result from a mixture of the selfless and the selfish, so 'pure' kindness is probably rare. But that's not the point: it's the effort we expend in being kind that matters. Sometimes I feel in a kindly mood; other days I'm grumpy and have to work at not spilling my grumpiness over everybody else. Also note that kindness is not the equivalent of submissive giving in, because sometimes we need to be courageous and assertive to be kind.

Kindness, however, is not always easy to define but would certainly involve generosity and effort. Consider the doctor who dedicates him/ herself to curing disease and works all hours but his/her personality is not very warm. Contrast this to a very warm person with good 'person skills' but who is not very dedicated to anything. Indeed, there has long been discussion of different types of kindness. For example, there are those who put themselves out for other people and try to solve their problems; others who have few practical skills but are sensitive to feelings; others who are not good at either but are very generous; and yet others who are very brave when called on. People are not necessarily good at all aspects of kindness, so we should try to appreciate each individual's own ways of kindness.

Working on a close relationship

Let's focus on close relationships and how compassion can help them. In couples and marital therapy, research has shown that, if two people concentrate on creating good, compassionate feelings between themselves, they'll be planting the seeds of a good partnership. I suspect that, in fact, this general principle also holds good for all kinds of partnerships and relationships. John M. Gottman and his colleagues[3] have worked for many years to illuminate the elements that are dangerous to partnerships, which they have called 'the Four Horsemen of the Apocalypse': criticism, defensiveness, contempt and stonewalling. The first three are, I think, self-explanatory. Stonewalling is where people go quiet and won't articulate or work through conflict; they may have brooding resentment that they cover in submissive withdrawal. However, Gottman's work also suggests that, if we just help each other to resolve conflicts and deal with the 'four horsemen', that's often not enough to build a good partnership. Rather we have to ensure that *friendship* and *sharing* both develop. Indeed, if a couple can develop a positive friendship within their relationship, they're likely to get along increasingly well outside any conflict, to be less negative during an upset and to try to resolve problems amicably.

A key element in creating positive flow in a relationship is learning to keep in mind the wants, wishes and needs of your partner – as in meditation, you can take time to think about how to *bring happiness to them*. A second important aspect is learning to *appreciate* the people you live or work with and be able to show that appreciation. As in all things, you can see a glass as half full or half empty, and it's easy to get stuck on the dissatisfactions in our relationships, particularly if they resonate with something in our past. So you gradually focus much less on the positive qualities of your partner, and of course, they pick up on that and this affects how they relate to you.

Compassion for others, then, means behaving in 'valuing' ways, including using verbal expressions that are designed to help them understand that you appreciate them. Learning to employ affectionate and playful phrases, ('darling', 'sweetheart', 'dearest', 'precious one', 'reason for my existence' – okay, let's not go overboard), warm voice tones and facial expressions, to pay attention to the needs and wishes of those around you, to express your gratitude for the things they help you with, to focus on what you like about them rather than what you don't, to acknowledge their strengths to them – these are all ways of building friendship and other positive qualities into a relationship and they need to be practised and used regularly. In many ways, we've come back to Dale Carnegie's 1937 book *How to Win Friends and Influence People*, which we explored in Chapter 2.[4]

Consider also the role of appropriate touching and hugging in relationships. There's now considerable evidence, from both animal and human research, that appropriate touching, stroking, cuddling and hugging have important influences on our brains, can deepen relationships and offer feelings of safeness and can help reconciliation. Even laboratory rats grow up calmer if they are regularly stroked and handled and, of course, the family cat or dog usually becomes calm with being stroked. This type of interpersonal behaviour results in the recipient releasing endorphins (natural painkilling and mood-enhancing chemicals) and the stimulation of the soothing/contentment system. Physical affection can say more than words!

Time and again, my colleagues and I hear stories from our patients of parents who were distant and not physically affectionate, and of the sadness in a marriage because one partner can't be physically affectionate and stays somewhat aloof. Indeed, in schools now there's a re-evaluation of the prohibition on touch, particularly when children are distressed. Depriving them of touch and physical comfort may actually be quite damaging, given that we're *biologically designed* to seek physical comfort when upset. In our terror of paedophilia, we may be depriving our children of important ways to develop brain systems that help regulate their sense of threat, prompt feelings of safeness and trust, and give them body confidence. This is a major research question. The increasing ways in which we are sealing ourselves off from different types of relating – physical and affectionate caring and sharing – in our increasingly fear-focused and hurry-hurry world may be badly affecting our minds, brains and bodies.

As mentioned throughout this book, try to be aware of – and avoid – your anger and frustration being expressed as criticisms of yourself or others. Criticism is undermining most of the time and is very easily spotted as subtle (and sometimes not so subtle) forms of bullying. We all do it, of course, but try to reflect on it and be compassionate about it if it slips out, but also dedicate yourself to seeing if you can deal with conflicts and disappointments in relationships in more compassionate ways. See if you're 'demanding' that the other person be as you want them to be and if you've got caught in trying to force things to be different. Remember that, if you criticize people, they may criticize you back or resent you – even if they're nice to you to your face – and, in extreme cases, withdraw or become depressed.

Fear-based and need-based caring

Some forms of and motives for caring can, however, cause difficulties in relationships. Some people who lack confidence or are socially anxious and need to be loved and valued can behave in very caring ways but are actually seeking the *gratitude* of others. This crops up in couples therapy. One partner has taken on the role of 'rescuing hero' and tries to be kind, understanding and supportive of their partner or others. However, their partner may need to feel independent and not obligated to anybody. You can imagine the clash that's going to occur. The more the rescuer tries to be kind, loving and understanding, the more their partner begins to pull back – at some level, the two of them have detected that this is a 'game'. This becomes deeply distressing to the rescuer because, try as they might, they're unable to get the appreciation they seek or the same degree of caring back. It's particularly sad because both parties have quite unintentionally been playing the 'game'.

There are many varieties of this type of interaction. For example, emotionally sensitive women who've had bad relations with their mothers or fathers can link up with emotionally insensitive men, or people who are rather anxious in their relationships and need reassurance can connect with individuals who appear powerful and confident but who have an affectionate style that allows them to avoid closeness. A lot of our relationships are like this to some degree because we all have slightly different needs and styles.

The point here is that these kinds of difficulties are common. Compassionate behaviour requires us to recognize and try to appreciate our different relating styles and needs and come to various compromises. Keep in mind that we all just find ourselves here, with our needs, fears and styles of relating to each other, doing the best we can. It's important that we don't play a guilt or shame game to try to induce others to give us what we want – although even with the best of intentions we can find ourselves doing this, of course. Compassionate behaviour requires us to recognize our rescuer side or avoidant side and try to see things from the other person's point of view and how our behaviour, needs and styles might affect them.

Pro-social behaviour

We can approach these relating issues in another way by looking at what is called *pro-social behaviour* – that is, behaviour in which one individual gives, helps or shares with another without any hidden goals.

Nancy Eisenberg[5] is one of the leading figures in research on pro-social behaviour in children. In a number of writings, she points out that caring for others is very much related to education: we can educate and create the conditions for children's minds and brains to be oriented towards care-giving and pro-social behaviour. Compassionate behaviour can be promoted by:

- personal competency and general well-being

- role models who attend to, value and reward caring behaviour

- experiencing the benefits of sharing and caring

- opportunities to practise caring behaviour

- acquiring knowledge and skills for developing pro-social forms of conflict resolution

- open discussion with children about the implications of their behaviour on others.

In contrast, if children experience punishment and neglect, this can have detrimental effects on their development of caring and pro-social behaviour. Shame, humiliation, envy and indifference don't promote it, and caring for others just to avoid shame or because you feel you 'ought' or 'have to' can lead to resentment. It's also extremely doubtful that the threat of punishment leads to caring and compassionate behaviour. Think about what's happening in the brain. Punishment will activate the threat/ self-protection system, and while the child will be motivated to avoid the punishment, he or she will not necessarily engage in the behaviour you want or develop the appropriate feelings. The fear of punishment will tend to block soothing and empathy, whereas you want to activate his or her capacity for empathic understanding. So if we do hurt someone else, our ability to experience and tolerate guilt (and not turn it into shame or fear of being punished by others) becomes very important. We're then able to feel sorrow and try to put things right rather than run away, collapse into self-condemning depression or defend ourselves angrily.

Here's a hazy memory from my boarding school days to make this point in a different way. Outside one of our dormitories was a high ledge. As 12- and 13-year-olds, we would dare each other to slip out on to the fire escape after lights out and walk this ledge. Occasionally we got caught, which was a caning offence, but that only made the activity seem more daring and those who did it more brave. One night, a new teacher came into our dormitory, sat on a bed and said that he understood how exciting walking the ledge was, but it was dangerous and we needed to think about how we'd feel if one of us slipped – imagine ourselves or a friend lying there in pain with a broken leg or even dying, imagine how terrible that would be for his family, imagine how we'd feel if we felt we'd encouraged that boy to walk the ledge. By the end of his little talk, we were nearly in tears – and no one walked that ledge again. A compassionate discussion, understanding the excitement but also directing us to think about consequences, had done what caning could not. It helped, of course, that this teacher was kind and so was liked by the boys. That night I gained a new role model.

In recent years, there's been a growing awareness of the need to educate ourselves to become a civilized, caring and moral society, and many researchers have written on these themes. A leading one on empathy, Martin Hoffman,[6] argues that caring behaviour can be promoted when we bring children's attention to it. He suggests:

> One thing moral education can do is to teach people a simple rule of thumb: Look beyond the immediate situation and ask questions such as 'What kind of experiences does the other person have in various situations beyond the immediate one?', 'How will my actions affect him or her, not only now but in the future?' and 'Are there people, present and past, who might be affected by my action?' If children learn to ask questions like these, this should enhance their awareness of potential victims of their actions who are not present and to empathize with them to some extent. To increase the motivational power of empathic identification, children should also be encouraged to imagine how they would feel in the absent victim's place, or to imagine how someone close to them would feel in that person's place.

Thus we can train ourselves to become more pro-social psychologically by learning to ask certain types of questions of ourselves and to be interested in the answers. In addition, we can learn various conflict resolution skills. These skills can and should be taught to children to make them more aware of how our minds work, so they can understand and cope with their emotions and be pro-social with others.

Judging by how my children were educated, this psychological and moral education is not happening at all. Religious education is about telling stories or singing hymns, not learning how to take the perspective of others or empathy training, both of which require guided *practice*.

Educating children for compassion links to the compassion circle on page 194. Being clear in our minds about the qualities, attributes and skills in which we're trying to train ourselves and our children is an important first step in all of us becoming more compassionate. Some schools are now also looking at game playing that requires empathy. We have compassion in us and can develop it if we can create the conditions to train it, value it and make it essential to our social currency.

So putting all the above together, we can see that there are many ways that we can promote compassionate relationships. If you look back at the compassion attributes and skills in Chapter 6, you'll see how the above captures these. There is the *motivation* to be caring: compassionately thinking about other people, thinking about how you might feel if they treated you the way that you treat them – and taking time to really work out your impact on them. To behave compassionately is to learn to be generous, dedicated, helpful but not submissive. We can engage in compassionate attention and behaviour by learning to be appreciative and valuing, and forgiving and understanding. Now, in fact, there's nothing in these attributes and skills that is particularly new and hasn't been written about for centuries. It's just that we need to make an effort to bring them into our lives day in and day out – to place them at the centre of our mind training.

Social policy

Individuals can do a lot to bring compassion into their own lives, into their network of relationships and into the world. However, for many of our more serious problems, we require governments, social organizations and social policies that are compassion focused and which recognize that immoral behaviour commonly grows from immoral and/or unregulated systems and social structures.[7] As we've already seen many times, personal values are shaped by social relationships. Many commentators have no doubt that the psychology and politics of welfare, which permeated Britain in the post-war era of the 1950s and 1960s and resulted in the development of a free education system and NHS, have gradually been dismantled from the 1980s on. In his book *Dancing with Dogma: Britain under Thatcherism,* the former UK government minister Ian Gilmour[8] notes:

> Margaret Thatcher wanted, through her economic polices, to change the heart and soul of the nation. She did achieve a transformation, but not presumably the one she intended. Britain did not change to an enterprise society. The change was in sensibility. British society became coarser and more selfish. Attitudes were encouraged which would even have undermined the well-being of a much more prosperous society.

Gilmour points out that the British government of the 1980s, run by the Conservatives, was in retreat from the post-war consensus that politics should be welfare oriented, concerned with poverty and with reducing the disparities that are inherent under capitalism and amplified by it, not only in this country but in others. Its focus was on deregulation and letting the markets rip – believing them to be self-correcting and that the wealth created by them would 'trickle down'. The Conservatives were wrong, as the recent banking collapses sadly show. The North Sea oil windfall that should have been invested in our infrastructure paid for tax cuts for the rich.

New Labour later made no apology for the fact that it was a government for business and was moving away from old socialist ideals – it was *New* Labour, after all. They seem to have inherited from Thatcher (who believed that 'There's no such thing as society') the same basic philosophy of undervaluing the power and importance of human relationships. While striving for greater efficiencies in public services, they went on a target-focused crusade with a punishing and shaming approach but were to discover that people will strive to avoid the punishments but not necessarily behave in the desired way. And, not surprisingly, people will become stressed, may become bullying and don't like working in such systems. The psychology of engagement in compassionate commitment is quite different to that of punitive enforcing.

It's understandable and proper, of course, that governments seek to have good and efficient services, but again we must be cautious. In my world, patients and staff alike worry about how, in this technical world of fast response and constantly trying to assess technical competence (defensive bureaucratic overkill and paperwork, according to some), we will find time for human feelings and compassion. Moreover, training is not equipping our caring professions for the fact that, for many conditions, there's nothing you can do – you may not always be able to stop the pain, the degeneration and the suffering, or the dying. As we lose faith in the old gods and are left with insight into the biological bases of life, we struggle with our anger at 'just finding ourselves here' like this – suffering and dying as we do. We increasingly insist that medicine sort out our suffering, find the answers, and if we suffer, someone is to blame. 'This shouldn't be happening,' we say. 'Why can't you do something?' Yet it's exactly at these moments that compassion matters most. If carers are struggling with such realities, and with the pain and anger of those for whom nothing can be done, what are we doing to facilitate compassion with and for the caring professions?

Where is the time or space in which to cry or be open with others or reflect on our own feelings? Learning to 'harden yourself' to show that you're tough and up to the job may not actually be what we want from our professionals. If, after a death, the only thing that matters is whether the paperwork is correct or if anyone has made a mistake, how can we wonder that our caring professionals are not as compassionate as we would like them to be? And this goes for many other professions that perform services for us, including the police and teachers. You'll get the best out of them if they feel cared about, emotionally supported and valued. The current government is trying to bring compassion into the health service and hopefully will appreciate how complex and staff-focused this must be.

Other examples of a lack of appreciation for the power of compassionate relationships are Britain's 'children in care' (now often called 'looked-after children'), who are basically thrust out of the orbit of that care once they turn 16. Many children in care have emotional difficulties and require a secure and safe base with individuals who they feel will care for and about them *well into adulthood*. If you ask people who work with children in care, they'll tell you that money is the reason why we don't have facilities for older adolescents and young adults to return to a safe base with others who are familiar to them, to help them when in difficulty. The tragedy is that spending money on *really* looking after young people, offering genuine care and training for them for as long as they need it, would probably save an awful lot of money through helping them stay out of prison, reducing their need for mental health services, making them less likely to become unemployed and so forth. As it is, Britain has more locked-up young people than any other country in Europe. Although some adolescents and young adults obviously do have serious mental health problems, what many who drift into using public services actually need are not mental health services but loving, protective homes. And consider: my children had crises and wanted to come home to recover or needed some TLC or money until they were well into their 20s (probably just like yours if you have older ones)! What must it be like for someone as young as 16 to go through a crisis and know that there's nowhere and no one who knows and cares for them to turn to?

Another example of underestimating the role of human relationships can be seen in the British government's and NHS managers' desire to create large 'poly-clinics' of family doctors. The concept looks good because quick access to technically competent medicine is great, of course – and I personally have certainly benefited from it. But there's more to family medicine than access to drugs and surgery (wonderful though these are). The General Medical Council, the medical profession's regulator, is deeply concerned, pointing out that the personal relationship between patient and doctor, built up over years, is also vital to health and caring. It's this relationship that allows patients to develop trust, to discuss things they may be ashamed of, to feel that they're being looked after by somebody who knows and genuinely cares about them. The doctors, for their part, learn about their patients' lives in all their subtlety, about a family's ups and downs – for instance, the nature of a grandmother's dementia and how this is stressing her daughter and affecting the children, which may be a factor in some of the daughter's symptoms. They also understand that a lot of ill health and symptoms emerge within historical and social contexts, which, commonly, involve psychological issues that contribute to, exacerbate or even cause the difficulties. Trust built up over time is priceless to both patient and doctor.

My research unit has been doing some work with Slimming World, a British slimming organization. One of the crucial things that has stood out for us is how people have talked about the things that have helped them. Undoubtedly the lifestyle advice on eating and exercise is immensely valuable, but most participants also mention the sense of support, community and family they received from sharing in their groups. They identify these as being key in helping them get through the difficult times, including some quite obvious depressive episodes. Time and time again, we come back to this experience of being able to get through difficulties in life if we feel understood, supported and cared about by others.

These processes also need to be at the heart of how we work in our communities with a large number of the depressed and anxious people. Drugs and individual psychological therapies can be helpful, but we need to do far more to build supportive, valuing communities that people can return to for understanding, acceptance and support.

Building compassionate societies

Compassion begins in our own hearts as we refocus our attention, thoughts, feelings and behaviours on it. Interestingly, research shows that if people justify the disparities in wealth and hardship between themselves and those less fortunate – that is, literally rationalize them away – they may feel better for doing that. We used to blame such disparities on God – he decided who should be king or pauper – and some still do. So shifting to a compassion focus isn't easy because it means that we can no longer justify disparities and disadvantages. When we open our minds to the suffering of others, we may feel moved, sad or angry, as well as a desire to want to do something. But in being moved, we can also get political.

So it's important for us to think about compassion for others and ourselves within a *social context*. The drive for 'competitive edge' is pursuing its own course, and individuals with a tough and ruthless ability to make difficult decisions and 'get things done' are increasingly sought to take up leadership roles in business. Such folk can become big earners and then support their chosen political parties, which in turn enable them to flourish. The recent financial crash shows what some of them have been up to – compassion for others was not part of their game plan. Millions will suffer from lost jobs and home repossessions because of their activities. The point is, though, not so much to blame individuals, because many of us would follow our own selfish urges if able to, but to recognize how serious the lack of regulation was. It was the failure to create compassionate, fair and ethical financial systems that has got us all in this fix. And these sorts of failures are occurring in many areas of the world. As we saw in Chapter 12, people will simply adapt to the rules and values around them and come to think of them as 'normal' even when, with hindsight, they turn out be seriously misguided, illusory, selfish or even cruel.

Our seeking to build human-serving compassionate societies raises the prospect of a new type of politics. It's one that's not easily located in modern schemes and parties of left and right, for the latter grew out of class conflicts and concerns with wealth creation and distribution. The proposal of using compassion to build societies brings with it the need to stimulate and reward specific social mentalities and psychologies (*see* pp. 100–2). We require our politicians to realize that, unregulated, people are exploitative, so, in a world of new challenges, our leaders really do need to be the guardians of society and the environment, to ensure social fairness and protection of the weak. They can no longer be the handmaidens of business. And if they want 'services' to work well, they need to inspire, not threaten, those working in them. We in turn need to find ways to value our politicians and their skills rather than only having contempt for them and not voting, or voting with our pockets. Although you probably need a certain personality to flourish in politics, many who go into that arena really do want to make a difference to people's lives and have a passionate sense of service. The emergence of leaders like Barack Obama is cause for great hope.

So compassion invites us to open our hearts to the nature, structure and values of society. It is about recognizing how we need to create new social milieu that will affect our minds and brains because they are highly responsive to the social relationships in which we find ourselves embedded. We must endeavour to create social milieux that impact on our personal and working relationships, our values and our goals. Compassion needs to percolate through our economic, health and educational systems. If we continue to pursue only efficiencies, we may have a wonderfully efficient society that's just horrible to live in.

Charity and generosity

But we can't end here. In these days of financial collapse, wars and competitive-edge politics, it's helpful to remind ourselves that many millions of humans are combining all over the world to promote the ethical and compassionate dimensions of life. People have a basic desire to help others – it's as much a part of our make-up as wanting to make money and (once we have enough of that) may be more personally meaningful. So let's not ignore the thousands of charities, international and national, that work with children and against poverty, hardship, disease and violence. These groups involve millions of dedicated people doing fantastic work and raising many billions of pounds. I'm a great believer in the United Nations* as the only sensible approach to world problems. Deeply flawed though it is, it has stimulated much charity work including, of course, its well-known efforts on behalf of children via Unicef and its attempts to work out solutions for debt relief.

In addition to the better-known charities and associations, community foundations and projects all over the world work with disadvantaged people. You can find out more about these from the Trans-Atlantic Association of Community Foundations and, in the UK, from the Community Foundation Network. A good example of one such group, which I'm personally aware of because of the involvement of a friend, is the community action programme in Ottawa called No Community Left Behind.

In this world of dubious investments, the UN has developed key ethical guidelines: *Principles for Responsible Investment*. Some banks have portfolios of ethical investments, and we can all demand the highest ethical standards

---

* You can find out more details of the organizations mentioned in this section in 'Find out more' (p. 490).

of our banks and try to find out whether they have ethical and compassionate policies on what they invest in, how they deal with mortgage defaulters and so on.

We can also think about how to increase compassion in education. Again there are some wonderful projects already in existence, including the Vancouver School Board's *Nurturing Compassion* programme. Compassion for children should not only include comforting them more frequently with physical contact but also teaching them far more about how their minds and emotions work, helping them to understand and work with their emotions and to be kind to each other. We need to better equip teachers who spot children who are clearly emotionally distressed or problematic. Even if teachers worry about some children, they often are unsure about what to do or find it difficult to get help from over-stretched services. Recent research has shown that the British government's Surestart programme, which targets disadvantaged children and families, may be working and that more research and money should be invested in such projects.

With regard to crime and punishment, we all know that some people can do truly terrible things to others and we must stop them, so we need policing that is both effective and efficient. But we also know that a compassionate system must seek to prevent crime through social justice and creating community engagement. For instance, some off-duty police are trying to engage gang members in poor, drug-infested areas with sports and other activities to help them stay out of trouble. And some lawyers are trying to introduce more compassionate and effective systems of justice, such as those advocating restorative justice (*see* pp. 213–17).

Finally, we shouldn't forget the 60 billion animals that are raised each year for food. We need far greater ethical and compassionate engagement with this issue, something that Compassion in World Farming is concerned with.

The organizations mentioned above are just the tip of a huge iceberg of wonderful things that people are doing *compassionately* all over the world.

Each and every one of us can get involved in our work places and as consumers to demand kindness and ethical practice. And here's something we can do all by ourselves: just spend a moment really thinking about this fact:

> *All over the world, many millions of people are working for the betterment*
> *of others.*

Spend a few minutes focusing hard on that and see what happens to your mood. Try it every day. And don't forget your compassionate smile. You will feel quite different to focusing on what the newspapers feed you with – our inhumanity to each other. It is of course about balance.

Spirituality

Spirituality is central to the lives of many. Some biologists, sceptical about the existence of spiritual dimensions in our lives, are reductionists – that is, to them, we and our consciousness are nothing more than the product of neurochemical trickery caused by our genes. Perhaps that is so. However, physicists are more at home with the complexity of the universe and the lack of clarity that exists about the nature of consciousness and what we're all caught up in.[9] They recognize that science progresses in unexpected ways – for instance, Newtonian physics gave way to Einsteinian relativity. The great mystery is why 'something' (a material universe with certain laws) exists rather than 'nothing'. They also understand that, without technologies, we can't investigate; our telescopes, microscopes and atom smashers are essential. So while we can study the brain and its relationship to consciousness, this may be like studying a TV set in relation to radio waves. It could be that our experience of consciousness is only one form of many, but it could be many generations before we have the technologies for studying this and related subjects thoroughly, and so these remain hotly debated issues in science.

Science is the way to a compassionate world. From simple discoveries such as the wheel and the water pump to the complexities of anaesthetics and ridding the world of smallpox, our lives have been transformed. If spirituality involves efforts to reduce suffering, it must include science. If spirituality involves searching for our place in the universe, it must include science. Science is self-correcting and expands our knowledge. However, we need to be aware that using science simply to demolish other people's belief systems, leaving them with nothing other than the lives they have been born into, may be okay for the well educated and privileged but is seriously problematic for the majority of individuals on this planet. We need a spirituality that is both scientific *and* compassionate. If science does not help here, then people will invent whatever spirituality fits their emotional needs – as they always have. Science can direct us away from this.[10]

But even if we're attracted to old religious figures, we must at least be honest and not self-deceptive. It's clear that Jesus didn't support violence, vengeance, retribution and the accumulation of wealth, while he was all for forgiveness, sharing and compassion. However, it's also clear that many who claim to be followers of Jesus have the opposite values or are least are very hazy about these values. A compassionate spirituality requires us to be truthful at least with ourselves. In fact, if we listen to the hearts of all religions, we could find a compassionate song. We just have to decide if we want to sing it, but that's not easy.

Personally, I'm not a believer in God as a creator, but I remain open to the nature of consciousness and the possibility of other forms of consciousness. Our consciousness may be a chemical trick or something more profound, but in the end, I believe that science will help us with this. In the meantime, we can develop a compassionate spirituality based on our sense of community, recognizing that we all just find ourselves here seeking to be loved and valued and searching for a sense of meaning and understanding of our place in the universe and having to confront our own tragedies of life decay and death. So whether we're materialistic, atheists, humanists or believers in gods, have a more *Star Trek*-like spirituality or are just open to the idea that there are more mysteries yet to discover and solve, we can agree that developing a better scientific and personal understanding of the compassionate mind, and how it can be implemented, can be a useful focus for all of us.

Conclusion

Okay, time to go. In this book, I've tried to explain why I think we have a deeply compassionate mind that yearns for expression. We may look at the world as a cruel and horrible place, but we can also see fantastic minds working for the betterment of humanity and other living things. Our compassionate minds emerge from patterns of brain activity that can be easily suppressed by other patterns such as those for anger and anxiety, tribalism and prejudice, desire and lust. Our minds can go into different states that think and feel quite different things, so we need to try to choose what we will focus on, what states of mind we want to train ourselves for. We can't rid ourselves of these 'other' minds but we can balance them. We can focus and attend to the good in the world and the good in ourselves and realize that sometimes the wind will blow us off course but we can just pick ourselves up and return to our direction of travel – to transform our minds in the service of compassion. We can seek to join with others who have the same goals and to share with them a sense of community and belonging. We're back to where the Buddha started all those years ago.

Our world is changing. Unregulated 'competitive edge', possessive and wealth-seeking psychologies have set us (and those who will follow us) really tough challenges and, quite probably, tragedies in waiting. This is no one's fault; it's what happens when we simply act out blindly the selfish passions of our 'old brains/minds'. However, we can no longer allow our minds to be so undisciplined. We require mature compassion-focused politics to help us build a foundation on which we can train our compassionate minds and create compassionate societies, and we need a nourishing spirituality that's science based. In our hearts, we know that most of our problems – of the environment, tribal violence and terrorism, social injustice and human exploitation – are only going to be resolved through our relationships with each other.

Evolution has designed for us a really difficult brain, one that can create heaven or hell, and it's up to each of us to choose which to opt for. Opening our hearts to each other and developing self-kindness based on understanding that 'none of us chooses to be here with this strange mind' is probably not a bad first step.

So may your compassionate mind serve you well.

May you be well.
May you be happy.
May you be free from suffering.
And may you bring these things into the world for others.

Now where's that Merlot . . . ?

Postscript

Within hours of going to press I was able to hear President Barack Obama's passionate inaugural address. He was inspiring. Here at last there seems to be a very intelligent politician who really understands the need to build a fairer and more compassionate society, and the enormous challenges involved in doing just that. Who, along with his young speechwriter Jon Favreau, seems to be operating from a deep sense of compassion.

To quote just a few lines:

> ... we cannot help but believe that the old hatreds shall someday pass; that the lines of tribe shall soon dissolve; that as the world grows smaller, our common humanity shall reveal itself; and that America must play its role in ushering in a new era of peace.

> ... It is the kindness to take in a stranger when the levees break, the selflessness of workers who would rather cut their hours than see a friend lose their job which sees us through out darkest hours. It is the firefighter's courage to storm a stairway filled with smoke, but also a parent's willingness to nurture a child, that finally decides our fate.[11]

So maybe, just maybe, begins a new era.

Notes

These publications are for those who would like to follow up the more technical aspects of the subject and explore where some of the ideas came from.

Introduction

1 Wheen, F. (1999). Blood, sweat and carbuncles. *Weekend Guardian*, 2 October, 9.10–18.

2 Price, J. and Stevens, A. (2000). *Evolutionary Psychiatry: A new beginning*. London: Routledge.

3 Guidano, V.F. and Liotti, G. (1983). *Cognitive Process and Emotional Disorders: Structural approach to psychotherapy*. New York: Guilford Publications.

4 Gilbert, P. (1989). *Human Nature and Suffering*. Hove: Psychology Press.

Chapter 1: Compassion: The start of our journey

1 Cozolino, L. (2007). *The Neuroscience of Human Relationships: Attachment and the developing brain*. New York: Norton. Gerhardt, S. (2004). *Why Love Matters. How affection shapes a baby's brain*. London: Bruner-Routledge.

2 Accessible modern texts include:

- Dalai Lama (1995). *The Power of Compassion*. India: HarperCollins.

- Dalai Lama (2001). *An Open Heart: Practising compassion in everyday life* (edited by N. Vreeland). London: Hodder & Stoughton.

- Sangharakshita, B. (2004). *Living with Kindness: The Buddha's teaching on metta*. London: Windhorse Publications.

- Hopkins, J. (2001). *Cultivating Compassion*. New York: Broadway Books.

I have to say that not all books I've read on compassion are written in a compassionate tone. Some seem almost to recommend practising dissociation from suffering. So stick with what *feels* right to you.

3 Begley, S. (2009). *The Plastic Mind*. London: Constable.

4 Bunting, M. (2004). *Willing Slaves: How the overwork culture is ruling our lives*. London: HarperCollins.

5 Bakan, J. (2005). *The Corporation: The pathological pursuit of profit and power*. London: Constable. Klein, N. (2007). *The Shock Doctrine: The rise of disaster capitalism*. London: Allen Lane.

6 Oliver James has written a number of books on the same theme: linking unhappiness with the creation of competitive dynamics and striving within groups. In *Britain on the Couch: A treatment for the low serotonin society* (London: Century, 1998), he focuses on the way that social dynamics affect brain physiology and values. His more recent work examines the pursuit of affluence and its dark side: *Affluenza* (London: Vermilion, 2007) and *The Selfish Capitalist: Origins of affluenza* (London: Vermilion, 2008). Another work that looks at the same kinds of themes is Graaf, J.E., Wann, D. and Naylor, T.H. (2001). *Affluenza: The all-consuming epidemic*. San Francisco: Berrett-Koehler. It is also worth exploring Kasser, T. (2002). *The High Price of Materialism*. Cambridge, MA: MIT Press.

There is increasing evidence that countries that focus on competitive edge and maximizing profits at the expense of welfare-orientated politics have increasing rates of mental and physical ill health and higher crime rates. Britain, for instance, has the highest prison population per head of population compared with many Western societies. See Arrindell, W.A., Steptoe, A. and Wardle, J. (2003). 'Higher levels of depression in masculine than in feminine nations'. *Behaviour Research and Therapy*, 41, 809–17. Another key area of research has shown that we are creating societies that are making us unhealthy, unhappy and mentally ill: Wilkinson, R. (1996). *Unhealthy Society: The afflictions of inequality*. London: Routledge. Wilkinson, R. (2005). *The Impact of Inequality: How to make sick societies healthier*. London: The New Press.

Our children are among the unhappiest in Europe: *see* the Children's Society website <www.childrenssociety.org.uk>.

7 Naish, J. (2008). *Enough: Breaking free from the world of more*. London: Hodder & Stoughton.

Evolutionary psychology is greatly debated, particularly the way in which social context and cultures create values and dispositions for certain kinds of behaviour (e.g. attitudes towards women, intergroup violence). However, it is being increasingly recognized that we are not blank slates but come into the world with primary needs and dispositions to pay attention to certain things, which are also reflected in our brain physiology.

There are a number of good basic books if you wish to read more: Barrett, L., Dunbar, R. and Lycett, J. (2002). *Human Evolutionary Psychology*. London: Palgrave. Buss, D.M. (2003). *Evolutionary Psychology: The new science of mind* (2nd edn). Boston, MA: Allyn & Bacon. Ridley, M. (2000). *Genome: The autobiography of a species*. London: Fourth Estate. Gilbert, P. (1989). *Human Nature and Suffering*. London: Lawrence Erlbaum Associates.

Two thoughtful and cautious accounts are: Laland, K.N. and Brown, G.R. (2002). *Sense and Nonsense: Evolutionary perspectives on human psychology*. Oxford: Oxford University Press; and Malik, K. (2000). *Man, Beast and Zombie: What science can and cannot tell us about human nature*. London: Weidenfeld & Nicolson.

If you're interested in the Jungian archetype approach that's based on evolution theory, see: Knox, J. (2003). *Archetype, Attachment and Analysis*. London: Routledge.

8 *See* note 7.

9 If you are interested in the way that evolution has created various vulnerabilities to illness, you may enjoy Nesse, R.M. and Williams, G.C. (1995). *Evolution and Healing*. London: Weidenfeld & Nicolson; and Smith, E.O. (2002). *When Culture and Biology Collide: Why we are stressed, depressed and self-obsessed*. Piscataway, NJ: Rutgers University Press.

Cordelia Fine's 2007 book *A Mind of Its Own: How your brain distorts and deceives* (Cambridge: Icon Books) offers a highly readable overview of how our evolved brain can lead us astray in all kinds of ways.

10 Sapolsky, R.M. (1996). 'Why stress is bad for your brain'. *Science*, 273, 749–50. Sapolsky, R.M. (2000). 'Glucocorticoids and hippocampus atrophy in neuropsychiatric disorders'. *Archives of General Psychiatry*, 57, 925–35.

11 Schore, A.N. (2003). *Affect Dysregulation and Disorder of the Self.* New York: Norton. Teicher, M.H. (2002). 'Scars that won't heal: The neurobiology of the abused child'. *Scientific American*, 286, 3, 54–61.

12 *See* note 9.

13 Smith, E.O. (2002). *When Culture and Biology Collide: Why we are stressed, depressed and self-obsessed.* Piscataway, NJ: Rutgers University Press.

14 Gilbert, P. (2007). *Psychotherapy and Counselling for Depression*, 3rd edn. London: Sage.

15 *See* note 11.

16 Restak, R. (2003). *The New Brain: How the modern age is re-wiring your mind.* New York: Rodale. Pani, L. (2000). 'Is there an evolutionary mismatch between the normal physiology of the human dopaminergic system and current environmental conditions in industrialized countries?' *Molecular Psychiatry*, 5, 467–75.

17 Cohen, D. (2001). 'Cultural variation: Considerations and implications'. *Psychological Bulletin*, 127, 451–71.

This important paper shows how the distribution of resources and the nature of the social environments in which people live have very major impacts on their attitudes and values, especially on whether they develop trusting or cheating relationships with each other. People are not consciously choosing their strategies to be trusting or not but are operating with non-conscious rules and strategies.

18 Gilmore, D.D. (1990). *Manhood in the Making: Cultural concepts of masculinity.* New Haven, CT: Yale University Press.

19 Barrett, L., Dunbar, R. and Lycett, J. (2002). *Human Evolutionary Psychology*. London: Palgrave. Smith, E.O. (2002). *When Culture and Biology Collide: Why we are stressed, depressed and self-obsessed*. Piscataway, NJ: Rutgers University Press.

20 Matthieu, R. (2006). *Happiness: A guide to developing life's most important skill*. New York: Atlantic Books. Lyubomirsky, S. (2007). *The How of Happiness*. New York: Sphere.

21 The *Journal of Happiness Studies* (vol. 9, no. 1) has dedicated a whole edition to different approaches to well-being. The authors distinguish between a happiness-focused psychology, typical of Buddhist approaches, and what they call *eudaimonic psychological well-being*. In the latter, well-being is linked to a range of competencies such as: the ability to pursue goals for the intrinsic pleasure of doing so rather than for the indirect results of goals, such as fame, money and power; being able to develop feelings of relatedness with others but also feelings of autonomy; and feeling in control of one's life rather than trapped and controlled by others. In my view, compassion helps in the pursuit of eudaimonic forms of well-being because it is linked to particular brain patterns that coordinate social mentalities, behaviours, feelings, thinking and ways of creating a self-identity, which are all conducive to well-being.

Chapter 2: The Challenges of Life

1 Depue, R.A. and Morrone-Strupinsky, J.V. (2005). 'A neurobehavioral model of affiliative bonding'. *Behavioral and Brain Sciences*, 28, 313–95. The basic science for the three emotion regulation systems is given in this paper. You might also like to look at: Panksepp, J. (1998). *Affective Neuroscience*. New York: Oxford University Press; LeDoux, J. (1998). *The Emotional Brain*. London: Weidenfeld & Nicolson. My outline in this book is a very simplified and crude summary of Depue's work. The way emotions work in our brain and how they co-regulate each other are, of course, more complicated than just the three systems.

A very accessible book is Stein, K. (2007). *The Genius Engine: Where memory, reason, passion, violence and creativity intersect in the human brain*. New York: Wiley. Stein is very good at delineating the role of the frontal cortex. If you want to read more on the soothing and social affiliative system, see Carter, C.S. (1998). 'Neuroendocrine perspectives on social attachment and love'. *Psychoneuroendocrinlogy*, 23, 779–818.

2 *See* note 1.

3 As noted for Chapter 1, there are a number of interesting books here. Naish, J. (2008). *Enough: Breaking free from the world of more*. London: Hodder & Stoughton. Restak, R. (2003). *The New Brain: How the modern age is re-wiring your mind*. New York: Rodale. Pani, L. (2000). 'Is there an evolutionary mismatch between the normal physiology of the human dopaminergic system and current environmental conditions in industrialized countries?' *Molecular Psychiatry*, 5, 467–75.

4 Damasio, A.R. (1994). *Descartes' Error: Emotion, reason and the human brain*. New York: Putman. *See also* Panksepp, J. (1998). *Affective Neuroscience*. New York: Oxford University Press.

The idea that much of what goes on in our minds is unconscious and our conscious mind simply responds to decisions made non-consciously is, of course, an old one that stretches back to Freud and before. What we are getting at here is the idea of us having an old brain and new brain, a theme that has been explored by John Birtchnell in his 2003 book *The Two of Me: The rational outer me and the emotional inner me* (London: Routledge). There is also an excellent paper on how we often use our thoughts to back up positions we have made emotionally and outside consciousness: Haidt, J. (2001). 'The emotional dog and its rational tail: A social intuitionist approach to moral judgment'. *Psychological Review*, 108, 814–34. Mark Baldwin's 2005 book *Social Cognition* (New York: Guilford) also explores these aspects in relation to non-conscious processing in social relationships. If you want to get deep into the heart of the research into non-conscious processing and old brain vs new brains ideas, have a look at Hassin, R.R., Uleman, J.S. and Bargh, J.A. (2005). *The New Unconscious*. New York: Oxford University Press.

5 Goodall, J. (1990). *Through a Window. Thirty years with the chimpanzees of Gombe*. London: Penguin.

6 Geary, D.C. and Huffman, K.J. (2002). 'Brain and cognitive evolution: Forms of modularity and functions of the mind'. *Psychological Bulletin*, 128, 667–98. Suddendorf, T. and Whitten, A. (2001). 'Mental evolution and development: Evidence for secondary representation in children, great apes and other animals'. *Psychological Bulletin*, 127, 629–50.

7 *See* note 6.

8 Gilbert, P. (2007). *Psychotherapy and Counselling for Depression*, 3rd ed. London: Sage. Gilbert, P. (2000). *Overcoming Depression*. London: Robinson. The third edition of the latter, which will contain much more on compassion, is due out in July 2009.

9 Leary, M.R. (2003). *The Curse of the Self: Self-awareness, egotism and the quality of human life*. New York: Oxford University Press.

10 McGregor, I. and Marigold, D.C. (2003). 'Defensive zeal and the uncertain self: What makes you so sure?' *Journal of Personality and Social Psychology*, 85, 838–52. I have also explored this in my chapter on compassion and cruelty in P. Gilbert (2005). *Compassion: Conceptualisations, research and use in psychotherapy*. London: Routledge.

11 *See* note 10.

12 Some studies have looked at changes in the brain, especially a shift to the left frontal cortex that can result from focusing/practising on 'filling one's mind with compassionate thoughts and feelings'. Davidson, R.J., Kabat-Zinn, J., Schumacher, J., Rosenkranz, M., Muller, D. *et al.* (2003). 'Alterations in brain and immune function produced by mindfulness meditation'. *Psychosomatic Medicine*, 65, 564–70. Lutz, A., Brefczynski-Lewis, J., Johnstone, T. and Davidson, R.J. (2008). 'Regulation of the neural circuitry of emotion by compassion meditation: Effects of meditative expertise'. *Public Library of Science*, 3, 1–5. Rein, G., Atkinson, M. and McCraty, R. (1995). 'The physiological and psychological effects of compassion and anger'. *Journal for the Advancement of Medicine*, 8, 87–105. These researchers found that anger images and fantasies had a detrimental effect on the functioning of the immune system, whereas compassion-focused fantasies and images had a very positive effect. You'll also find a review of lots of studies of how mind training affects the body in Begley, S. (2009). *The Plastic Mind*. London: Constable.

13 Cozolino, L. (2007). *The Neuroscience of Human Relationships: Attachment and the developing brain*. New York: Norton.

14 *See* note 13.

15 Mikulincer, M. and Shaver, P.R. (2007). *Attachment in Adulthood: Structure, dynamics, and change*. New York: Guilford.

16 Schore A.N. (2003). *Affect Dysregulation and Disorder of the Self*. New York: Norton. Teicher, M.H. (2002). 'Scars that won't heal: The neurobiology of the abused child'. *Scientific American*, 286, 3, 54–61.

17 Baumeister, R.F. and Leary, M.R. (1995). 'The need to belong: Desire for interpersonal attachments as a fundamental human motivation'. *Psychological Bulletin*, 117, 497–529.

18 Restak, R. (2003). *The New Brain: How the modern age is re-wiring your mind*. New York: Rodale. Pani, L. (2000). 'Is there an evolutionary mismatch between the normal physiology of the human dopaminergic system and current environmental conditions in industrialized countries?' *Molecular Psychiatry*, 5, 467–75.

19 Seddon, John (2008). *Systems Thinking in the Public Sector: The failure of the reform regime . . . and a manifesto for a better way*. Axminster, Devon: Triarchy Press.

20 Carnegie, D. (1937/1993). *How to Win Friends and Influence People*. London: Vermilion. This is a fantastically insightful book and really puts the importance of focusing on the other person centre-stage in the building, maintaining and flourishing of relationships.

21 Straub, E. (1999). 'The roots of evil: Social conditions, culture, personality, and basic human needs'. *Personality and Social Psychology Review*, 3, 179–92. Shermar, M. (2004). *The Science of Good and Evil*. New York: Times Books. Baumeister, R.F. (1997). *Evil: Inside human violence and cruelty*. New York: Freeman.

22 Gilbert, P. (2007). *Psychotherapy and Counselling for Depression*. London: Sage. Gilbert, P. (2000). *Overcoming Depression*. London: Robinson. The third edition of the latter, which will contain much more on compassion, is due out in July 2009.

23 Gay, P. (1993). *The Cultivation of Hatred*. London: Penguin.

24 Wakabayashi, A., Baron-Cohen, S., Wheelwright, S. *et al.* (2006). 'Development of short forms of the Empathy Quotient (EQ-Short) and the Systemizing Quotient (SQ-Short)'. *Personality and Individual Differences*, 41, 929–40.

25 Buss, D.M. and Malmuth, N.M. (1996). *Sex, Power and Conflict: Evolutionary and feminist perspective*. New York: Oxford University Press. Diamond, J. (1997). *Why Sex is Fun: The evolution of human sexuality*. New York: Phoenix.

26 Gilbert, P. and Irons, C. (2005). 'Focused therapies and compassionate mind training for shame and self-attacking'. In P. Gilbert (ed.) *Compassion: Conceptualisations, research and use in psychotherapy*. London: Routledge, pp. 263–325.

27 Gilbert, P. (August, 2009). *An Introduction to the Theory and Practice of Compassion-focused Therapy*. London: Routledge.

28 Haidt, J. (2001). 'The emotional dog and its rational tail: A social intuitionist approach to moral judgment'. *Psychological Review*, 108, 814–34. This offers an excellent airing of key issues.

29 I reviewed some ideas on this in Gilbert, P. (1989). *Human Nature and Suffering*. Hove: Lawrence Erlbaum. Paul Bloom's 2003 *Descartes' Baby: How child development explains what makes us human* (London: Arrow) gives a very readable account of moral development in children.

30 Batson, C.D., Klein, T. R., Highberger, L. and Shaw, L.L. (1995). 'Immorality from empathy-induced altruism: When compassion and justice conflict'. *Journal of Personality and Social Psychology*, 68, 1042–54.

31 Gilligan, C. (1982). *In a Different Voice: Psychological theory and women's development*. Cambridge, MA: Harvard University Press. This was

based on interviews with women exploring their dilemmas when having an abortion.

32 Taylor, S.E., Klein, L.B., Lewis B.P., Gruenwald, T.L., Gurung R.A.R. and Updegaff, J.A. (2000). 'Biobehavioural responses to stress in females: Tend and befriend, not fight and flight'. *Psychological Review*, 107, 411–29. This paper argues that men and women are adapted for different challenges in life and to cope with them in different ways.

33 Jaffee, S. and Hyde, J.S. (2000). 'Gender differences in moral orientation: A meta-analysis'. *Psychological Bulletin*, 126, 703–26. Fascinating airing of gender differences in moral thinking and behaviour.

34 *See* note 28.

35 Hinde, R.A. (1999). *Why Gods Persist: A scientific approach to religion.* London: Routledge. There are, of course, many works on the functions of religion, how they have grown from the evolution of our capacities to imagine and think about other minds, and the fact of the dangers and tragedies of life – and how we try to make sense of them. It is useful to keep in mind that, in many religions of a few thousand years ago, gods were seen as pretty fickle and malevolent: *see* Armstrong, K. (2006). *The Great Transformation: The world in the time of Buddha, Socrates, Confucius, and Jeremiah.* London: Atlantic Books. Other authors stress the role of the need to feel a sense of belonging, attached and being cared for, and especially a sense of union, as a way of coping with death as an end. Kirkpatrick, L.A. (2005) *Attachment, Evolution, and the Psychology of Religion.* New York: Guilford.

36 Gillath, O., Shaver, P.R. and Mikulincer, M. (2005). 'An attachment-theoretical approach to compassion and altruism'. In P. Gilbert (ed.). *Compassion: Conceptualisations, research and use in psychotherapy.* London: Routledge, pp. 121–47. This chapter offers a good review of current evidence. Mikulincer, M. and Shaver, P.R. (2007). *Attachment in Adulthood: Structure, dynamics, and change.* New York: Guilford: this is one of the most comprehensive and up-to-date texts on the forms and values of caring behaviour.

37 Davidson, R. and Harrington, A. (eds) (2002). *Visions of Compassion:* *Western scientists and Tibetan Buddhists examine human nature.* New York: Oxford University Press. A key element of this book points out that, while Buddhist psychology focuses on loving kindness and compassion, Western psychology has focused on studying pro-social behaviour and moral behaviour – which overlap considerably with Buddhist notions of compassion. The same view is taken in *Compassion* (2005), which I edited.

Nancy Eisenberg is one of the world's leading authorities on the development of pro-social behaviour in children. A good review of her work is given in Eisenberg, N. (2002). 'Empathy-related emotional responses, altruism, and their socialization'. In R. Davidson and A. Harrington (eds). *Visions of Compassion: Western scientists and Tibetan Buddhists examine human nature* (pp. 131–64). New York: Oxford University Press. *See also* Emler, N. and Hogan, R. (1991). 'Moral psychology and public policy'. In W.M. Kurtines and J.L. Gewirtz (eds). *Handbook of Moral Behavior and Development* (vol. 3).

38 There is now a lot of evidence for the value of compassion and compassion meditations on well-being. A useful review can be found in Begley, S. (2009). *The Plastic Mind.* London: Constable. One of the leading authorities on the study of *self*-compassion is Kristen Neff, whose work can be found on her website <www.self-compassion. org>. For some fascinating studies, see Leary, M.R., Tate, E.B., Adams, C.E., Allen, A.B. and Hancock, J. (2007). 'Self-compassion and reactions to unpleasant self-relevant events: The implications of treating oneself kindly'. *Journal of Personality and Social Psychology, 92,* 887–904. My own approach has been to build a compassion focus into psychotherapy (addressing the difficulties and pitfalls). Our study on group therapy shows promising results: Gilbert, P. and Procter, S. (2006). 'Compassionate mind training for people with high shame and self-criticism: A pilot study of a group therapy approach'. *Clinical Psychology and Psychotherapy, 13,* 353–79.

39 Nassbaum, M.C. (2003). *Upheavals of Thought: The intelligence of emotions.* Cambridge: Cambridge University Press. This contains a most fascinating discussion of compassion, exploring historical and philosophical positions including those of Aristotle. It makes clear the importance of emotion and emotion identifications in the experience of compassion.

Chapter 3: Placing Ourselves in the Flow of Life

1 Gerhardt, S. (2004). *Why Love Matters: How affection shapes a baby's brain*. London: Bruner-Routledge. There is now quite a lot of research looking at the way in which early experiences shape the brain and the patterns of neuronal networks. Experiences work in such a way that 'neurons that fire together wire together'. *See also* Cozolino, L. (2007). *The Neuroscience of Human Relationships: Attachment and the developing brain*. New York: Norton.

2 Klein, R. (1993). *Cigarettes are Sublime*. London: Picador.

3 Sagan, C. (1977). *The Dragons of Eden: Speculations on the evolution of human intelligence*. New York: Ballantine Books.

4 Bailey, K. (1987). *Human Paleopsychology: Applications to aggression and pathological processes*. Hillsdale, NJ: Lawrence Erlbaum Associates, Inc. *See also* Panksepp, J. (1998). *Affective Neuroscience*. New York: Oxford University Press. Stein, K. (2007). *The Genius Engine: Where memory, reason, passion, violence and creativity intersect in the human brain*. New York: Wiley.

5 Armstrong, K. (2006). *The Great Transformation: The world in the time of Buddha, Socrates, Confucius and Jeremiah*. London: Atlantic Books.

6 There are a number of good books that will help you understand archetype approaches to psychology. A very readable introduction is C.S. Hall and V.J. Nordby's 1973 *A Primer of Jungian Psychology* (New York: Mentor). Anthony Stevens's *Archetype Revisited: An updated natural history of the self* (London: Routledge, 1999) is also an easy-to-understand introduction. For more technical insights and consideration of the debates within archetype theory, see Knox, J. (2003). *Archetype, Attachment and Analysis*. London: Routledge. Modern evolutionists tends to think more in terms of strategies, but actually the overlap

with archetypes is significant: Gray, R. (1996) *Archetypal Explorations: An integrated approach to human behaviour*. London: Routledge. Stevens, A. and Price, J. (2000). *Evolutionary Psychiatry: A new beginning*. London: Routledge (2nd edn). If you want to contextualize Jung with the other psychodynamic theorists of the time, a beautifully written book full of fascinating historical insights is H. Ellenberger's 1970 *Discovery of the Unconscious* (New York: Basic Books).

7 Stevens, A. (1999). *Archetype Revisited*. London: Routledge.

8 Mikulincer, M. and Shaver, P.R. (2007). *Attachment in Adulthood: Structure, dynamics, and change*. New York: Guilford.

9 Campbell, J. (1993). *The Hero with a Thousand Faces*. London: Fontana.

10 Booker, C. (2004). *The Seven Basic Plots: Why we tell stories*. London: Continuum.

11 For more detail on social mentalities, see: Gilbert, P. (1989). *Human Nature and Suffering*. Hove: Lawrence Erlbaum Associates. Gilbert, P. (2005). 'Social Mentalities: A biopsychosocial and evolutionary reflection on social relationships'. In M.W. Baldwin (ed.). *Interpersonal Cognition*. New York: Guilford (pp. 299–335). In this chapter and in Chapter 12, I turn my attention to our capacity for both compassion and cruelty. More detailed academic and referenced work can be found in my chapter Gilbert, P. (2005). 'Compassion and cruelty: A biopsychosocial approach'. In P. Gilbert (ed.). *Compassion: Conceptualisations, research and use in psychotherapy*. London: Routledge (pp. 9–74).

Gilbert, P. (1989). *Human Nature and Suffering*. Hove: Psychology Press: This also outlined a lot of different approaches to evolutionary ways of thinking about human behaviours, including those of the interpersonal theorists. Since the work of Timothy Leary in the 1950s, the latter distinguish between two key dimensions: love–hate (say, running horizontally) which is intersected by a dimension of dominance–subordination. This gives rise to all combinations of these two motives. More recently, Price, J. and Steven, S. (2000). *Darwinian Psychiatry: A new beginning*. London: Routledge (2nd edn) focuses on just two archetypes linked to attachment and rank. The evolutionary psychiatrists

M. McGuire and A. Troisi, in their 1998 *Darwinian Psychiatry* (New York: Oxford University Press), do not use the concepts of archetypes or social mentalities but focus purely on innate strategies, especially those linked to rank and forms of altruism.

12 *See* note 11.

13 Mendes, W.B., Gray, H.M., Mendoza-Denton, R., Major, B. and Epel, E.S. (2008). 'Why egalitarianism might be good for your health.' *Psychological Science*, 18, 991–8.

14 A review of a range of studies that looked at the effects of harnessing cooperative behaviour, versus competitive or individualistic behaviour, in over 17,000 subjects showed that cooperativeness is by far preferable for many reasons including its positive effects on health, achievement and social relationships. See Roseth, C.J., Johnson, D.W. and Johnson, R.T. (2008). 'Promoting early adolescents' achievement and peer relationships: The effects of cooperative, competitive, and individualistic goal structures'. *Psychological Bulletin*, 134, 223–46.

15 My colleagues and I have been very interested in how the competitive and social rank mentality underpins psychopathology and, especially, feelings of anxiety and depression. You can read more on this in Gilbert, P. (2000). 'Varieties of submissive behavior: Their evolution and role in depression'. In L. Sloman and P. Gilbert (eds). *Subordination and Defeat: An evolutionary approach to mood disorders*. Hillsdale, NJ: Lawrence Erlbaum Associates. This book has a number of chapters exploring rank psychology. For a short review *see*: Gilbert, P. (2006). 'Evolution and depression: Issues and implications (invited review)'. *Psychological Medicine*, 36, 287–97. With regard to social anxiety, *see* Gilbert, P. and Trower, P. (2001). 'Evolution and process in social anxiety'. In W.R. Crozier and L.E. Alden (eds). *International Handbook of Social Anxiety: Concepts, research and interventions relating to the self and shyness*. Chichester: J. Wiley & Sons (pp. 259–79). How the social rank mentality can be a focus in psychotherapy can be found in Gilbert, P. (2007). *Psychotherapy and Counselling for Depression*. London: Sage (3rd edn). With regard to people feeling under competitive pressure to

strive to avoid inferiority, see Gilbert, P. *et al.* (2007). 'Striving to avoid inferiority: Scale development and its relationship to depression, anxiety and stress'. *British Journal of Social Psychology,* 46, 633–48.

16 Keltner, D., Gruenfeld, D.H. and Anderson, C. (2003). 'Power, approach and inhibition'. *Psychological Review,* 110, 265–84. This fascinating account of research shows just how power can affect us and change the way we feel, think and behave. It's a good example of what Jung would have called 'being taken over by an archetype' or, in more modern language, an evolved strategy and mentality.

17 Vonk, R. (1998). 'The slime effect: Suspicion and dislike of likeable behavior toward superiors'. *Journal of Personality and Social Psychology,* 74, 849–64. David Owen has suggested that unfortunately we've suffered various governments with this type of psychology: *see* Owen, D. (2007). *The Hubris Syndrome: Bush, Blair and the intoxication of power.* London: Politico's. It's not uncommon to see this in people who strive for fame, get it and then are very contemptuous of those around them and become known as 'difficult personalities', completely losing control to the 'archetype of power' and their sense of entitlement.

18 *See* note 17.

19 Buss, D.M. and Malmuth, N. (1996). *Sex, Power, Conflict: Evolutionary and feminist perspectives.* New York: Oxford University Press. Diamond, J. (1997). *Why Sex is Fun: The evolution of human sexuality.* New York: Phoenix.

20 In 1999, Robert Hinde, a professor of ethology at Cambridge University, wrote the wonderful and accessible book *Why Gods Persist: A scientific approach to religion.* London: Routledge. If you're interested in the interaction of the innate and social in religious belief and experience, then this is a book you may enjoy.

With regard to archetypal processes, there have been many efforts to look at religious feeling and beliefs from an evolutionary point of view. Not least, of course, is Jung's own work, encapsulated in his famous book: Jung, C.G. (1952, 2002). *Answer to Job* (trans. R.F.C. Hull). Hove: Psychology Press. A very readable text that looks at evolutionary psychology and archetype theory is by Brant Wenegrat (1990). *The Divine Archetype*. Lexington, MA: Lexington Books. Another excellent book that examines religion from the evolution-of-attachment approach is by Lee A. Kirkpatrick (2004). *Attachment, Evolution and the Psychology of Religion*. New York: Guilford. If you're interested in how religious beliefs change and emerge to fit social conditions, have a look at Armstrong, K. (2006). *The Great Transformation: The world in the time of Buddha, Socrates, Confucius, and Jeremiah*. London: Atlantic Books.

21 *See* note 20.

22 Richard Dawkins, the Oxford University biologist, has popularized and made very accessible the insights and implications of Darwin's discoveries and of genes as sources of inheritance. His classic book *The Selfish Gene* (Oxford University, 2006) is now in its third revised edition.

Chapter 4: Threat and Self-protection: The good, the bad and the really difficult

1 Depue, R.A. and Morrone-Strupinsky, J.V. (2005). 'A neurobehavioral model of affiliative bonding'. *Behavioral and Brain Sciences*, 28, 313–95. The basic science for the three emotion regulation systems is given in this paper. However, the way emotions work in our brain and how they co-regulate each other is, of course, more complicated than just the three systems, and as a result, this is a very simplified and crude summary of Depue's brilliant work. You might also like to look at Panksepp, J. (1998). *Affective Neuroscience*. New York: Oxford University Press. LeDoux, J. (1998). *The Emotional Brain*. London: Weidenfeld & Nicolson. Stein, K. (2007). *The Genius Engine: Where memory, reason, passion, violence and creativity intersect in the human brain*. New York: Wiley.

2 Marks, I.M. (1987). *Fears, Phobias and Rituals: Panic, anxiety and their disorders*. Oxford: Oxford University Press. I have also written on this: *see* Gilbert, P. (2001). 'Evolutionary approaches to psychopathology: The role of natural defences'. *Australian and New Zealand Journal of Psychiatry*, 35, 17–27. J. LeDoux's *The Emotional Brain* (London:

Weidenfeld & Nicolson, 1998) offers insight into how the brain processes threats. Loewenstein, G.F., Weber, E.U., Hsee, C.K. and Welsch, N. (2001). 'Risk as feelings'. *Psychological Bulletin*, 127, 267–86. Tobena, A., Marks, I. and Dar, R. (1999). Advantages of bias and prejudice: An exploration of their neurocognitive templates. *Neuroscience and Behavioral Reviews*, 23, 1047–58. Gilbert, P. (1998). 'The evolved basis and adaptive functions of cognitive distortions'. *British Journal of Medical Psychology*, 71, 447–63.

3 Anger can take many different forms and can be triggered by many different things. It is also an important element of a range of disorders including depression and paranoia. DiGiuseppe, R. and Tafrate, C. (2007). *Understanding Anger Disorder.* New York: Oxford University Press.

4 Ferster, C.B. (1973). 'A functional analysis of depression'. *American Psychologist*, 28, 857–70. Leahy, R.L. (2002). 'A model of emotional schemas'. *Cognitive and Behavioral Practice*, 9, 177–90. Freud, S. (1917). 'Mourning and melancholia'. In *Completed Psychological Works*, vol. 14 (standard edn). Translated and edited by J. Strachey. London: Hogarth Press.

5 Shweder, R.A., Much, N.C., Mahapatra, M. and Park, L. (1997). 'The "big three" of morality (autonomy, community and divinity) and the "big three" explanations of suffering'. In A.M. Brandt and P. Rozin (eds), *Morality and Health.* New York: Routledge (pp. 119–69).

6 Panksepp, J. (1998). *Affective Neuroscience.* New York: Oxford University Press. LeDoux, J. (1998). *The Emotional Brain.* London: Weidenfeld & Nicolson. Brewin, C.R. (2006). 'Understanding cognitive behaviour therapy: A retrieval competition account'. *Behaviour Research and Therapy*, 44, 765–84.

Chris Brewin's work has focused on different types of memories: those that operate through the body and the sensory system, versus those that focus on the event and are verbally accessible. These two types of memories and memory processing systems can become mismatched in trauma. Brewin's work is very important in understanding how we lay down threat memories.

The body is important in the experience of emotion and, in particular, when we lay down memories of frightening events. *See* Ogden, P., Minton, K. and Pain, C. (2006). *Trauma and the Body: A sensorimotor approach to psychotherapy*. New York: Norton. Rothschild, B. (2003). *The Body Remembers Casebook: Unifying methods and models in the treatment of trauma and PTSD*. New York: Norton. Van der Hart, O., Nijenhuis, E.R.S. and Steele, K. (2006). *The Haunted Self: Structural dissociation and the treatment of chronic traumatization*. New York: Norton.

7 *See* note 4.

8 Gray, J.A. (1979). *Pavlov*. London: Fontana. This excellent book takes us back to the classical conditioning research that is often forgotten these days but is still so important. It shows us how powerful conditioning is in the way that we learn about things, as well as creating physical changes in our body. We've also forgotten just how powerful and disorganizing to our brains strong conflicts can be; indeed, they can even knock out our ability to think logically. Buddhism does not have any theories like classical conditioning, and yet in our work on compassion with people who have mental health problems, classical conditioning concepts are indispensable. For instance, suppose when a child wanted warmth and sought out a parent, he/she was rejected or hurt. Then the feelings of wanting warmth become associated with rejection. If you start to reactivate these feelings in therapy, you also reactivate the conditioned emotional memories. This is why, for some people, getting in contact with feelings of wanting connectedness or warmth for others actually makes them frightened. This is an example of emotional conditioning and how it overrides logical thought.

9 Gilbert, P. (2007). *Psychotherapy and Counselling for Depression*. London: Sage (3rd edn). Many of the technical aspects of depression that are linked to our evolved tendency to become depressed – the role of conflicts, entrapment and blocks in depression – can all be found here, along with recommendations for psychotherapy interventions. Gilbert, P. (1992). *Depression: The evolution of powerlessness*. Hove: Lawrence Erlbaum/New York: Guilford. For a review paper, see Gilbert, P. (2006)

'Evolution and depression: Issues and implications [invited review]'. *Psychological Medicine*, 36, 287–97.

10 *See* note 9.

Chapter 5: The Pleasures and Contentments of Life: The two types of good feelings and your compassionate mind

1 Keep in mind that these systems are rough approximations that are useful ways of thinking about how our emotion systems work. There are other ways of thinking about them, and as always with these things, the devil is in the detail. The key paper behind these ideas is: Depue, R.A. and Morrone-Strupinsky, J.V. (2005). 'A neurobehavioral model of affiliative bonding'. *Behavioral and Brain Sciences*, 28, 313–95. The basic science for the three emotion regulation systems are given in this. You might also like to look at: Panksepp, J. (1998). *Affective Neuroscience*. New York: Oxford University Press. LeDoux, J. (1998). *The Emotional Brain*. London: Weidenfeld & Nicolson. Stein, K. (2007) *The Genius Engine: Where memory, reason, passion, violence and creativity intersect in the human brain*. New York: Wiley.

2 Epstein, M. (2006). *Open to Desire: The truth about what the Buddha taught*. New York: Gotham Books. As I have mentioned before, I'm not a scholar of Buddhism, but I am familiar with its ideas and gratefully recognize my academic and personal debt to this psychology. If you want to find out more about Buddhism, an excellent place to start is with Jonathan Landaw and Stephan Bodian's 2003 book *Buddhism for Dummies*, published by Wiley. Don't be put off by the title – this really is very clearly written and full of fascinating insights. You'll learn more about the different types of Buddhism, including the Theravada, Mahayana and Vajrayana schools (the last sometimes referred to as the 'tantric' school).

3 Restak, R. (2003). *The New Brain: How the modern age is re-wiring your mind*. New York: Rodale. Pani, L. (2000). 'Is there an evolutionary

mismatch between the normal physiology of the human dopaminergic system and current environmental conditions in industrialized countries?' *Molecular Psychiatry*, 5, 467–75.

4 Smith E.O. (2002). *When Culture and Biology Collide: Why we are stressed, depressed and self-obsessed*. Piscataway, NJ: Rutgers University Press. Fine, C. (2007). *A Mind of Its Own: How your brain distorts and deceives*. Cambridge: Icon Books. Dixon, N.F. (1987). *Our Own Worst Enemy*. London: Routledge.

5 Schwartz, G. (2005). *The Paradox of Choice: Why more is less*. New York: HarperCollins. *See also* Gilbert, D. (2007). *Stumbling on Happiness*. New York: Harper Perennial.

6 Yalom, I.D. (1980). *Existential Psychotherapy*. New York: Basic Books. Early in my career, this book impressed me and influenced me greatly. Beautifully written and easy to understand, it discusses many of the dilemmas, dramas and confusions of living and our struggles to make sense of them all.

7 Gilbert, P., Broomhead, C., Irons, C., McEwan, K., Bellew, R., Mills, A. and Gale, C. (2007). 'Striving to avoid inferiority: Scale development and its relationship to depression, anxiety and stress'. *British Journal of Social Psychology*, 46, 633–48.

8 Dunkley, D.M., Zuroff, D.C. and Blankstein, K.R. (2006). 'Specific perfectionism components versus self-criticism in predicting maladjustment'. *Personality and Individual Differences*, 40, 665–76.

9 Bakan, J. (2005). *The Corporation: The pathological pursuit of profit and power*. London: Constable. Klein, N. (2007). *The Shock Doctrine: The rise of disaster capitalism*. London: Allen Lane.

10 Depue, R.A. and Morrone-Strupinsky, J.V. (2005). 'A neurobehavioural model of affiliative bonding'. *Behavioral and Brain Sciences*, 28, 313–95. The basic science for the three emotion regulation systems are given in this paper.

A very useful paper that charts the rise of attachment and the soothing system can be found in Bell, D.C. (2001). 'Evolution of care-giving behavior'. *Personality and Social Psychology Review,* 5, 216–29. Much has now been written on the specificity of the soothing system: *see* Carter, C.S. (1998). 'Neuroendocrine perspectives on social attachment and love'. *Psychoneuroendocrinology,* 23, 779–818. Uväns-Morberg, K. (1998). 'Oxytocin may mediate the benefits of positive social interaction and emotions'. *Psychoneuroendocrinology,* 23, 819–35. Kosfeld, M., Heinrichs, M., Zak, P.J., Frisbacher, U. and Fehr, E. (2005). 'Oxytocin increases trust in humans'. *Nature Neuroscience* [letters], 435, June, 673–6. So oxytocin is a *very* important modulating hormone that underpins feelings of affection. Its influence in compassion has yet to be studied.

11 *See* note 10.

12 Geary, D.C. (2000). 'Evolution and proximate expression of human parental investment'. *Psychological Bulletin,* 126, 55–77. Bell, D.C. (2001). 'Evolution of care-giving behavior'. *Personality and Social Psychology Review,* 5, 216–29. These papers provide some of the technical aspects.

A key person who brought attention to the importance of attachment was John Bowlby: *Attachment and Loss:* vol. 1: *Attachment* (1969), vol. 2: *Separation, Anxiety and Anger* (1973), vol. 3: *Loss: Sadness and Depression* (1980). London: Hogarth Press. Bowlby's ideas stimulated a huge amount of research and influenced psychotherapy.

Mikulincer, M. and Shaver, P.R. (2007). *Attachment in Adulthood: Structure, dynamics, and change.* New York: Guilford. This is one of the most comprehensive and up-to-date texts on the forms and values of caring behaviour.

13 Geary, D.C. (2000). 'Evolution and proximate expression of human parental investment'. *Psychological Bulletin,* 126, 55–77. Bell, D.C. (2001). 'Evolution of care giving behavior'. *Personality and Social Psychology Review,* 5, 216–29.

14 Cozolino, L. (2007). *The Neuroscience of Human Relationships: Attachment and the developing brain.* New York: Norton. Gerhardt, S. (2004). *Why Love Matters: How affection shapes a baby's brain.* London: Bruner-Routledge.

15 Gilbert, P. (2005) 'Compassion and cruelty: A biopsychosocial approach'. In P. Gilbert (ed.). *Compassion: Conceptualisations, research and use in psychotherapy*. London: Routledge (pp. 9–74).

16 Sapolsky, R.M. (1994). *Why Zebras Don't Get Ulcers: An updated guide to stress, stress-related disease, and coping*. New York: Freeman (p. 92).

17 Field, T. (2000). *Touch Therapy*. New York: Churchill Livingstone. You can also find important reviews of research findings on the role of early parental experiences and brain development in a number of books: Gerhardt, S. (2004). *Why Love Matters. How affection shapes a baby's brain*. London Bruner-Routledge. *See also* Cozolino, L. (2007). *The Neuroscience of Human Relationships: Attachment and the developing brain*. New York: Norton

18 *See* note 17.

19 *See* note 14.

20 Gilbert, P. (2007). 'The evolution of shame as a marker for relationship security'. In J.L. Tracy, R.W. Robins and J.P. Tangney (eds). *The Self-Conscious Emotions: Theory and research*. New York: Guilford (pp. 283–309).

21 *See* note 10.

22 Begley, S. (2009). *The Plastic Mind*. London: Constable & Robinson.

23 Haidt, J. (2001). 'The emotional dog and its rational tail: A social intuitionist approach to moral judgment'. *Psychological Review*, 108, 814–34. This is an excellent paper on how we often use our thoughts to back up positions we have made emotionally and outside consciousness. Mark Baldwin's 2005 book *Social Cognition* (New York: Guilford) also explores these aspects in relation to non-conscious processing.

If you want to get deep into the heart of the research into non-conscious processing and old brain/new brain ideas, have a look at Hassin, R.R., Uleman, J.S. and Bargh, J.A. (2005). *The New Unconscious*. New York: Oxford University Press.

The idea that we actually have two selves wrapped up as one, where one self operates the emotional strategies and the other thinks and reflects and tries to regulate the emotional self, has been explored by John Birtchnell in his 2003 book *The Two of Me: The rational outer me and the emotional inner me* (London: Routledge). In his view, the rational thinking self knows an awful lot about the emotional self, but the emotional self knows nothing about the thinking self. Going back to the early Greeks and beyond, this problem of the interaction of old brain and emotions and new brain and thinking haunts us and remains our greatest challenge. It was on this issue that N.F. Dixon wrote his 1987 book *Our Own Worst Enemy* (London: Routledge) – the title says it all.

24 *See* note 22.

Chapter 6: Compassion in the Context of Old and New Brains and Minds

1 The ability to create something by first seeing it in one's mind – i.e. imagining it – is key to creativity and is an evolved human ability: Lock, A. (1999). 'On the recent origin of symbolically mediated language and its implications for psychological science'. In M.C. Coballis and M.E.G. Lea (eds). *The Descent of Mind: Psychological perspectives on humanoid evolution*. New York: Oxford University Press (pp. 324–55). Visual and auditory imagery 'in imagination' has been used extensively in psychotherapy, and to encourage and help sports people: *see* Singer, J.L. (2006). *Imagery in Psychotherapy*. Washington DC: American Psychological Press. Imagery is, of course, very important in a whole variety of religious rituals. Imagination can, however, lead us astray and always needs to be checked out with 'the facts' – what we imagine to be the case often is not. *See* Gilbert, D. (2006). *Stumbling on Happiness*. New York: Harper Perennial.

2 Gilbert, P. and Irons, C. (2005). 'Focused therapies and compassionate mind training for shame and self-attacking'. In P. Gilbert (ed.). *Compassion: Conceptualisations, research and use in psychotherapy*. London: Routledge (pp. 263–325). These simple ideas were the basis for my development of

compassion-focused work in therapy. I introduced them into cognitive approaches in the early 1990s. See Gilbert, P. (1997/2000). *Overcoming Depression*. London: Robinson. Gilbert, P. (2000). 'Social mentalities: Internal 'social' conflicts and the role of inner warmth and compassion in cognitive therapy'. In P. Gilbert and K.G. Bailey (eds) (2000). *Genes on the Couch: Explorations in evolutionary psychotherapy*. Hove: Psychology Press (pp. 118–50). There is also a CD of *Overcoming Depression: Talks with your therapist*, available on Amazon, if you want to listen to my voice droning on a bit.

3 Hamlin, K., Wynn, K. and Bloom, P. (2007). 'Social evaluation by pre-verbal infants'. *Nature*, November, pp. 557–60 [letters].

4 Dalai Lama (1995). *The Power of Compassion*. India: HarperCollins. Dalai Lama (2001). *An Open Heart: Practising compassion in everyday life* (edited by N. Vreeland). London: Hodder & Stoughton.

5 As we go to press, the *Journal of Happiness Studies* has dedicated a whole issue (vol. 9, no. 1) to different types of or approaches to well-being. The authors distinguish between a happiness-focused psychology, typical in Buddhist approaches, and what they call *eudaimonic psychological well-being*. In this, well-being is linked to a range of things such as: the ability to pursue goals for their own intrinsic pleasure rather than seeking to achieve them for the results they can bring, such as fame, money and power; being able to develop feelings of competence, relatedness and autonomy; and feeling in control of one's life rather than trapped and controlled by others. In my view, compassion will also help in the pursuit of eudaimonic forms of well-being because it is linked to particular brain patterns that coordinate social mentalities, behaviours and feelings. Compassion can also be a focus for creating a self-identity that is conducive to well-being.

6 Davidson, R.J., Kabat-Zinn, J., Schumacher, J., Rosenkranz, M., Muller, D. *et al.* (2003). 'Alterations in brain and immune function produced by mindfulness meditation'. *Psychosomatic Medicine*, 65, 564–70. Rein, G., Atkinson, M. and McCraty, R. (1995). 'The physiological and psychological effects of compassion and anger'.

Journal of Advancement in Medicine, 8, 87–105. These researchers found that anger images and fantasies had a detrimental effect on immune system functioning, whereas compassion-focused fantasies and images had a very positive effect. You'll also find a review of lots of studies on how mind training affects the body in: Begley, S. (2009). *The Plastic Mind*. London: Constable.

7 Gilbert, P. (1989). *Human Nature and Suffering*. Hove: Lawrence Erlbaum Associates. Gilbert, P. (2000). 'Social mentalities: Internal "social" conflicts and the role of inner warmth and compassion in cognitive therapy'. In P. Gilbert and Bailey, K.G. (eds). *Genes on the Couch: Explorations in evolutionary psychotherapy*. Hove: Brenner-Routledge (pp. 118–50). Gilbert, P. (2005). 'Compassion and cruelty: A biopsychosocial approach'. In P. Gilbert (ed.). *Compassion: Conceptualisations, research and use in psychotherapy*. London: Routledge (pp. 9–74).

8 Fogel, A., Melson, G.F. and Mistry, J. (1986). 'Conceptualising the determinants of nurturance: A reassessment of sex differences'. In A. Fogel and G.F. Melson (eds). *Origins of Nurturance: Developmental, biological and cultural perspectives on caregiving*. Hillsdale, NJ: Lawrence Erlbaum Associates Inc. (pp. 53–67). This book had a great influence on me in the 1980s. The authors pointed out that caring could be directed towards many things, such as people, animals, one's garden, even a car, and it is associated with motivation and an understanding of what the other requires for them to flourish. It also requires us to modify behaviour and thinking in line with change in the other.

Since that time, further research has been conducted on caring behaviour. There are a number of chapters in a book I edited: Gilbert, P. (2005). *Compassion: Conceptualisations, research and use in psychotherapy*. London: Routledge. Those interested in the specific attachment-linked approach should have a look at: Gillath, O., Shaver, P.R. and Mikulincer, M. (2005). *An attachment-theoretical approach to compassion and altruism* (pp. 121–47). London: Routledge. It has a good review of current evidence.

Mikulincer, M. and Shaver, P.R. (2007). *Attachment in Adulthood: Structure, Dynamics, and Change*. New York: Guilford – one of the most comprehensive and up-to-date texts on the forms and functions of caring behaviour.

9 *See* note 4.

10 Borenstein, E. and Ruppin, E. (2005). 'The evolution of imitation and mirror neurons in adaptive agents'. *Cognitive Systems Research*, 6, 229–42. Decety, J. Chaminade, T. (2003). 'Neural correlates of feeling sympathy'. *Neuropsychologia*, 41, 127-38.

11 Baumeister, R.F. (1997). *Evil: Inside human violence and cruelty*. New York: Freeman. Shermar, M. (2004). *The Science of Good and Evil*. New York: Times Books. Sober, E. (2002). 'Kindness and cruelty in evolution'. In R. Davidson and A. Harrington (eds). *Visions of Compassion: Western scientists and Tibetan Buddhists examine human nature*. New York: Oxford University Press. Straub, E. (1999). 'The roots of evil: Social conditions, culture, personality, and basic human needs'. *Personality and Social Psychology Review*, 3, 179–92. Gilbert, P. (2005). 'Compassion and cruelty: A biopsychosocial approach'. In P. Gilbert (ed.). *Compassion: Conceptualisations, research and use in psychotherapy*. London: Routledge (pp. 9–74).

12 Mikulincer, M. and Shaver, P.R. (2007). *Attachment in Adulthood: Structure, dynamics, and change*. New York: Guilford. These authors give some chilling observations about current Western leaders and their rather detached emotional styles. The way these personalities managed to gain power is also quite worrying. *See also* Lee-Chai and Bargh, J.A. (2001). *The Use and Abuse of Power: Multiple perspectives on the causes of corruption*. London: Routledge.

Westen, D. (2007). *The Political Brain: The role of emotion in deciding the fate of the nation*. New York: Public Affairs. This very sobering account shows how politicians have worked out that we're easily swayed by our emotions and are trying to find various manipulative sound-bites and 'images' that will stimulate them. They are rather keen on stimulating fear and offering themselves as strong saviours.

Achieving positions of power and dominance changes our feelings, behaviour and what we pay attention to, and we become rather dismissive of subordinates and expect our will to be done. Research into this has been well reviewed by Keltner, D., Gruenfeld, D.H and Anderson, C. (2003). 'Power, approach and inhibition'. *Psychological Review*, 110, 265–84. These tendencies can be seriously accentuated by certain personality types and 'crises', as was the case with George W. Bush and Tony Blair, which is examined in depth by neurologist and politician Dr David Owen in his 2007 book *The Hubris Syndrome: Bush, Blair and the intoxication of power* (London: Politico's). As Dr Owen points out, Bush's and Blair's hubris and contempt for those below them filtered down to various sections of society, and was often at the heart of reorganizations of different services.

Leaders can also suffer a range of physical and emotional health problems that can affect their decisions – with major implications for the rest of us. D. Owen's 2008 *In Sickness and in Power: Illness in heads of government during the last 100 years* (London: Methuen) is a chilling outline of this. No one has an answer to these difficulties; ordinary folk like you and me would probably struggle with the pressures of modern political life at the top. The problem is that those who *can* cope may well do so at some cost to themselves and us! See also Freeman, H. (1991). 'The human brain and political behaviour'. *British Journal of Psychiatry*, 159, 19-32. Barack Obama may yet prove the exception: compassionate and emotionally resilient.

13 Margulies, A. (1984). 'Toward empathy: The uses of wonder'. *American Journal of Psychiatry*, 141, 1025–33. This is a lovely paper on the subtleties and importance of empathy in our relationships. It invites us to remain curious, to want to know rather than interpreting or guessing. Unlike sympathy, empathy requires effort – trying to imagine what it must be like to be another person, putting a picture together in your mind from your observations and from what that person is telling you. Empathy has been one of the kingpins of the psychotherapy world, but we now understand that it is complex with different definitions and meanings. *See* Duan, C. and Hill, C.E. (1996). 'The current state of empathy research'. *Journal of Counselling*, 43, 261–74. There are also new neuroscience insights on how empathy works in our brains. An excellent review of this work can be found in: Decety, J. and Jackson,

P.L. (2004). 'The functional architecture of human empathy'. *Behavioral and Cognitive Neuroscience Reviews*, 3, 71–100.

14 Hoffman, M.L. (1991). 'Empathy, social cognition and moral action'. In W.M. Kurtines and J.L. Gewirtz (eds). *Handbook of Moral Behavior and Development: Vol. 1: Theory*. Hillsdale, NJ: Lawrence Erlbaum Associates (pp. 275–301).

15 Many of these social issues are discussed by a number of authors in the 2005 book of which I was the editor: *Compassion: Conceptualisations, research and use in psychotherapy*. London: Routledge.

Chapter 7: Mindful Preparations on the Road to Compassion

1 If you have a look at our website – www.compassionatemind.co.uk – you'll find lots of links to other websites including those about mindfulness. As for books, T.N. Hanh's 1991 *The Miracle of Mindfulness* (London: Rider) is regarded as a classic. You could also look at Jon Kabit-Zinn's *Coming to Our Senses: Healing ourselves and the world through mindfulness* (London: Piatkus, 2005). A helpful introduction to the origins and nature of mindfulness is Bhante Henepola Gunaratana's 2002 *Mindfulness in Plain English* (Boston, MA: Wisdom Books).

For some useful CDs that will guide you, see recommendations on pages 492–2.

2 *See* note 1.

3 Hanh, T.N. (1995). *Peace is Every Step: The path of mindfulness in everyday life*. New York: Rider. Offers a variety of insights and exercises by which we can use and bring mindfulness to everyday life. See also his *The Long Road Turns to Joy: A guide to walking meditation* (New Delhi: Full Circle, new edn 2004).

4 Williams, M., Teasdale, J., Segal., Z. and Kabat-Zinn, J. (2007). *The Mindful Way Through Depression: Freeing yourself from chronic unhappiness*. New York: Guilford.

5 If you want to listen to this exercise as you go through it, you can find it on my CD *Overcoming Depression: Talks with your therapist* (London: Robinson), available from Amazon.co.uk.

6 Gilbert, P. and Procter, S. (2006). 'Compassionate mind training for people with high shame and self-criticism: A pilot study of a group therapy approach'. *Clinical Psychology and Psychotherapy*, 13, 353–79.

7 *See* note 4.

Chapter 8: Compassionate Mind Training through Imagery

1 Leighton, T.D. (2003). *Faces of Compassion: Classic bodhisattva archetypes and their modern expression*. Boston, MA: Wisdom. This fantastic book is a scholarly exploration of compassion imagery, which can be gentle but also fierce. It also looks at the way in which imagery can be seen as a process for developing archetypes and brain states.

Vessantara (1993). *Meeting the Buddhas: A guide to Buddhas, bodhisattvas and tantric deities*. New York: Windhorse. This is another excellent book that shows how Buddhist practice provides students with a range of specific images and how these are used relationally, as sources of soothing, and also to stimulate archetypes and patterns in the mind. The book also implies that these images are actually linked into attachment systems: people come attached to them and they operate like inner soothing figures.

If you want to look at Buddhist works on developing compassion, then Jeffrey Hopkins' book *Cultivating Compassion* (New York: Broadway Books, 2001), which I think is about to come back into print, is a helpful overview with some useful exercises.

Rinpoche, Ringu Tilku and Mullen, K. (2005). 'The Buddhist use of compassionate imagery in Buddhist mediation'. In P. Gilbert (ed.). *Compassion: Conceptualisations, research and use in psychotherapy*. London: Brunner-Routledge (pp. 218–38). Outlines some very interesting imagery cycles based on compassion.

2 Begley, S. (2009). *The Plastic Mind*. London: Constable. *See also* Davidson, R.J., Kabat-Zinn, J., Schumacher, J., Rosenkranz, M., Muller, D. *et al.* (2003). 'Alterations in brain and immune function produced by mindfulness meditation'. *Psychosomatic Medicine*, 65, 564–70. Rein, G., Atkinson, M. and McCraty, R. (1995). 'The physiological and psychological effects of compassion and anger'. *Journal of Advancement in Medicine*, 8, 87–105. These researchers found that anger images and fantasies had a detrimental effect on immune system functioning whereas compassion-focused fantasies and images had a very positive effect.

3 Dagsay Tulku Rinpoche (2002). *The Practice of Tibetan Meditation: Exercises, visualizations, and mantras for health and well being*. Rochester, VT: Inner Traditions. This book offers a very useful set of postures and exercises along with a CD of mantras and instructions.

4 *See* note 1.

5 Frederick, C. and McNeal, S. (1999). *Inner Strengths: Contemporary psychotherapy and hypnosis for ego strengthening*. Mahwah, NJ: Lawrence Erlbaum Associates. This excellent book is mainly for therapists but is easy to read and shows the use of a whole range of different imagery processes, including imagining an inner helper, guide and friend. Edwards, D. (2007). 'Restructuring implicational meaning through memory-based imagery: Some historical notes'. *Journal of Behavior Therapy and Experimental Psychiatry*, 39, 306–16. Leighton, T.D. (2003). *Faces of Compassion: Classic Bodhisattva archetypes and their modern expression*. Boston, MA: Wisdom. This gives a very scholarly overview of the use of compassion in imagery and icons in Buddhism.

6 Begley, S. (2009). *The Plastic Mind*. London: Constable.

7 Rein, G., Atkinson, M. and McCraty, R. (1995). 'The physiological and psychological effects of compassion and anger'. *Journal of Advancement in Medicine*, 8, 87–105. These researchers found that anger images and fantasies had a detrimental effect on immune system functioning whereas compassion-focused fantasies and images had a very positive effect.

8 Leighton, T.D. (2003). *Faces of Compassion: Classic bodhisattva archetypes and their modern expression.* Boston, MA: Wisdom. This gives a very scholarly overview of the forms and uses of compassion imagery and icons in Buddhism. Ringu Tilku Rinpoche and Mullen, K. (2005). 'The Buddhist use of compassionate imagery in Buddhist mediation'. In P. Gilbert (ed.). *Compassion: Conceptualisations, research and use in psychotherapy.* London: Brunner-Routledge (pp. 218–38). This outlines some very interesting imagery cycles based on compassion.

Another excellent book on how Buddhist practice provides students with a range of specific images to practise, and how these images are used relationally, as sources of soothing, and also to stimulate archetypes and patterns in the mind, is Vessantara (1993). *Meeting the Buddhas: A guide to Buddhas, bodhisattvas and tantric deities.* New York: Windhorse.

Deborah Lee, who works with people who have suffered trauma and related difficulties and has been using the compassion-focused approach to therapy, has coined the term 'perfect nurturer' to describe the compassionate image. She's developed a range of worksheets that people can use to think about that image. Lee, D.A. (2005). 'The perfect nurturer: A model to develop a compassionate mind within the context of cognitive therapy'. In P. Gilbert (ed.). *Compassion: Conceptualisations, research and use in psychotherapy.* London: Brunner-Routledge (pp. 326–51).

9 *See* note 8.

10 *See* note 8.

11 Dandeneau, S.D., Baldwin, M.R., Baccus, J.R., Sakellaropoulo, M.P. and Pruessner, J.C. (2007). 'Cutting stress off at the pass: Reducing vigilance and responsiveness to social threat by manipulating attention'. *Journal of Personality and Social Psychology,* 93, 651–66.

12 *See* note 1.

13 Childre, D. and Martin, H. (1999). *The HeartMath Solution.* New York: HarperOne.

My colleagues and I at the Mental Research Unit in Derby and from Bristol and Manchester have recently conducted some research using heart-rate variability. We found that, while some people show increased variability when engaged in compassionate imagery, others go in the opposite direction. This underlines the fact that some people find compassion difficult and, indeed, stressful. We're currently engaged in research to try to work out if training people who find it stressful obtain any benefits from compassion-focused work. Rockliff, H., Gilbert, P., McEwan, K., Lightman, S. and Glover, D. 'An exploration of heart-rate variability and salivary cortisol responses to compassion-focused imagery'. *Journal of Clinical Neuropsychiatry*, 5, 132–9.

14 Porges, S.W. (2007). 'The polyvagal perspective'. *Biological Psychology*, 74, 116–43.

15 *See* note 13.

16 Lee, D.A. (2005). 'The perfect nurturer: A model to develop a compassionate mind within the context of cognitive therapy'. In P. Gilbert (ed.). *Compassion: Conceptualisations, research and use in psychotherapy*. London: Brunner-Routledge (pp. 326–51).

17 *See* note 3.

Chapter 9: Compassionate Thinking

1 Beck, A.T. (1967). *Depression: Clinical, experimental and theoretical aspects*. New York: Harper & Row. Beck, A.T. (1976) *Cognitive Therapy and the Emotional Disorders*. New York: International Universities Press.

2 Ellis, A. and Whiteley, L.M. (eds) (1979). *Theoretical and Empirical Foundations of Rational Emotive Therapy*. Pacific Grove, CA: Brooks/Cole. For a more up-to-date and easy-to-understand introduction to rational emotive behaviour therapy (as it is now called), *see*: Dryden, W. (2008). *Rational Emotive Behaviour Therapy: Distinctive features*. London: Routledge.

3 Horney, K. (1945). *Our Inner Conflicts: A constructive theory of neurosis*. New York: Norton.

4 One of the most prolific writers on this approach is Windy Dryden; you'll find many of his books on Amazon. A useful overview is Windy Dryden and Michael Neenan's 2006 book *Rational Emotive Behaviour Therapy: 100 key points & techniques*. London: Routledge.

5 If you want to explore the NICE guidelines for various disorders, go to www.nice.org.uk.

6 Constable & Robinson have a huge range of books that are based on cognitive behaviour therapy, and if you want to learn how CBT trains attention, the *Overcoming* series would be very helpful. There are also, of course, many Buddhism-based books and those focusing on mindfulness, which will also teach you about training attention.

7 James Pennebaker has been researching the value of expressive writing (i.e. writing about things that happen to us and our feelings about them) for many years. You might want to look at this book: Pennebaker, J.W. (1997). *Opening Up: The healing power of expressing emotions*. New York: Guilford. The following is more technical: Smyth, J.M. and Pennebaker, J.W. (2008). 'Boundary conditions of expressive writing'. *British Journal of Health Psychology*, 13, 1–95.

8 See my CD *Overcoming Depression: Talks with your therapist*, which you can get from Amazon.co.uk.

Chapter 10: From Self-criticism to Self-compassion

1 For reviews on self-criticism, see Gilbert, P. and Irons, C. (2005). 'Focused therapies and compassionate mind training for shame and self attacking'. In P. Gilbert (ed.). *Compassion: Conceptualisations, research and use in psychotherapy*. London: Routledge (pp. 263–325). Zuroff, D.C., Santor, D. and Mongrain, M. (2005). 'Dependency, self-criticism, and maladjustment'. In J.S. Auerbach, K.N. Levy, C.E. Schaffer (eds). *Relatedness, Self-Definition and Mental Representation: Essays in honour of Sidney J. Blatt*. London: Routledge (pp. 75–90). For an exploration of the importance of emotion in self-criticism, *see*: Whelton, W.J. and

Greenberg, L.S. (2005). 'Emotion in self-criticism'. *Personality and Individual Differences*, 38, 1583–95.

For our research on self-criticism, see: Gilbert, P., Baldwin, M., Irons, C., Baccus, J. and Palmer. M. (2006). 'Self-criticism and self-warmth: An imagery study exploring their relation to depression'. *Journal of Cognitive Psychotherapy: An international quarterly*, 20, 183–200. Gilbert, P., Clarke, M., Kempel, S., Miles, J.N.V. and Irons, C. (2004). 'Criticizing and reassuring oneself: An exploration of forms, style and reasons in female students'. *British Journal of Clinical Psychology*, 43, 31–50.

2 I have reviewed these ideas in a number of articles: Gilbert, P. (1998) 'What is shame? Some core issues and controversies'. In P. Gilbert and B. Andrews (eds), *Shame: Interpersonal behavior, psychopathology and culture.* New York: Oxford University Press, pp. 3–38. Gilbert, P. (2003). 'Evolution, social roles, and differences in shame and guilt'. *Social Research: An international quarterly of the social sciences*, 70, 1205–30. Gilbert, P. (2007). 'The evolution of shame as a marker for relationship security'. In J.L.. Tracy, R.W. Robins and J.P. Tangney (eds). *The Self-Conscious Emotions: Theory and research.* New York: Guilford (pp. 283–309). This last book, by Tracy and colleagues, will give you a very good overview of current thinking on self-conscious emotions. For those who are researching shame, they have a very useful appendix that discusses a number of different measures of shame.

3 *See* notes 1 and 2.

4 Whelton, W.J. and Greenberg, L.S. (2005). 'Emotion in self-criticism'. *Personality and Individual Differences*, 38, 1583–95.

5 An excellent review can be found in Baldwin, M.W. and Dandeneau, S.D. (2005). 'Understanding and modifying the relational schemas underlying insecurity'. In M.W. Baldwin (ed.). *Interpersonal Cognition.* New York: Guilford (pp. 33–61). See also Baldwin's website at McGill University in Canada: www.mindhabits.com.

6 MacDonald, G. and Leary, M.R. (2005). 'Why does social exclusion hurt? The relationship between social and physical pain'. *Psychological Bulletin*, 131, 202–23. These authors argue that rejection, exclusion and marginalization actually operate through the brain systems as pain.

7 The fear of giving up self-criticism because it is counter to a parental style and the resulting fear of rebellion are discussed in more detail in: Gilbert, P. and Irons, C. (2005). 'Focused therapies and compassionate mind training for shame and self-attacking'. In P. Gilbert (ed.). *Compassion: Conceptualisations, research and use in psychotherapy.* London: Routledge (pp. 263–325).

8 Dunkley, D.M., Zuroff, D.C. and Blankstein, K.R. (2006). 'Specific perfectionism components versus self-criticism in predicting maladjustment'. *Personality and Individual Differences*, 40, 665–76.

9 Reynolds, M. and Brewin, C.R. (1999). 'Intrusive memories in depression and posttraumatic stress disorder'. *Behaviour Research and Therapy*, 37, 201–15. Chris Brewin has been at the forefront of research on intrusive memory and how memory operates through different types of processing systems, such as an emotional memory that affects our body and an event memory system that tells us when things happened. A technical outline of his ideas can be found in: Brewin, C.R. (2006). 'Understanding cognitive behaviour therapy: A retrieval competition account'. *Behaviour Research and Therapy*, 44, 765–84.

10 Holt, J. (1982). *How Children Fail*. New York: Penguin. The first edition of this book came out in 1964, with a revised edition in 1982. I read it in the 1970s and was very struck by Holt's ability to identify the subtle and sometimes not-so-subtle shaming that goes on in our relationships with each other and at school.

11 Ellenberger, H. (1970) *Discovery of the Unconscious*. New York: Basic Books.

12 For a more detailed discussion of this dynamic, see: Gilbert, P. and Irons, C. (2005). 'Focused therapies and compassionate mind training for shame and self-attacking'. In P. Gilbert (ed.). *Compassion: Conceptualisations, research and use in psychotherapy*. London: Routledge (pp. 263–325). It is also discussed with regard to depression in: Gilbert, P. (2007) *Psychotherapy and Counselling for Depression*. London: Sage (3rd edn).

13 Leighton, T.D. (2003). *Faces of Compassion: Classic bodhisattva archetypes and their modern expression.* Boston, MA: Wisdom. This fantastic book is a scholarly exploration of compassion imagery, which can be gentle but also fierce. It also looks at the way in which imagery can be seen as a process for developing archetypes and brain states.

14 An easy access to this work, which was developed by James Pennebaker, can be found in his book for a general readership: Pennebaker, J.W. (1997). *Opening Up: The healing power of expressing emotions.* New York: Guilford. For more technical and up-to-date research on expressive writing, see: Smyth, J.M. and Pennebaker, J.W. (eds) (2008). 'Boundary conditions of expressive writing'. *Health Psychology* (special section). *British Journal of Health Psychology*, 13, 1–95.

Chapter 11: Compassion and Emotions: Working with anxiety, anger and forgiveness

1 Baumeister, R.F., Bratslavsky, E., Finkenauer, C. and Vohs, K.D. (2001). 'Bad is stronger than good'. *Review of General Psychology*, 5, 323–70. Gives an excellent review of how negative and positive emotions work in different ways and why our threat-based negative emotions are more powerful and can have a much greater impact on us and our lives than our positive ones.

2 Miller, W.I. (2000). *The Mystery of Courage.* Cambridge, MA: Harvard University Press.

3 Linehan, M. (1993). *Dialectical Behavior Therapy.* New York: Guilford.

4 Steve Hayes has developed what he has called 'acceptance commitment therapy'. If you put this into Google, you'll find various websites and articles about it. If you're interested in his self-help manual, look at Hayes, S.C. (2005). *Get Out of Your Mind and into Your Life: The new acceptance and commitment therapy.* New York: New Harbinger. You may also be interested in another guide based on acceptance commitment therapy, Harris, R. (2008). *The Happiness Trap.* London: Constable & Robinson.

5 Mansell, W. (2007). *Coping with Fears and Phobias: A step-by-step guide to understanding and facing your anxieties.* Oxford: Oneworld. This is a lovely book, written in a compassionate style, although it is also very cognitive behaviour focused. For problems of worry and rumination, you may also want to look at Robert Leahy's 2006 book *The Worry Cure* (London: Piatkus).

6 Anger can take many different forms and can be triggered by many different things. It is also an important element of a range of disorders including depression and paranoia. DiGiuseppe, R. and Tafrate, C. (2007). *Understanding Anger Disorder.* New York: Oxford University Press.

7 Fournier, M.A., Moskowitz, D.S. and Zuroff D.C. (2002). 'Social rank strategies in hierarchical relationships'. *Journal of Personality and Social Psychology*, 83, 425–33. The way in which anger tends to flow down from higher-power people to lower-power individuals has also been explored by Keltner, D., Gruenfeld, D.H. and Anderson, C. (2003). 'Power, approach and inhibition'. *Psychological Review*, 110, 265–84.

8 If you want more information on self-help, there are a number of books that you can consult. Just put 'Anger' into, say, the Amazon search engine and you'll come up with quite a few, many of which will be accompanied by readers' recommendations. In particular, *The Dance of Anger: A woman's guide to changing the pattern of intimate relationships* by H.G. Lerner (London: Thorsons, 1999) is very useful to understanding the way in which anger operates within relationships. In his book *Overcoming Anger and Irritability* (London: Robinson, 2000), William Davies gives a cognitive behavioural approach. The key point is that you're making a decision to work on your anger and then following it up by exploring various leads and using those that are most helpful to you. And don't be ashamed to seek professional help.

Chapter 12: Compassionate Behaviour: The cultivation of courage

1 Keltner, D., Gruenfeld, D.H. and Anderson, C. (2003). 'Power, approach and inhibition'. *Psychological Review*, 110, 265–84. *See also* Fournier, M.A., Moskowitz, D.S. and Zuroff D.C. (2002). 'Social rank strategies in hierarchical relationships'. *Journal of Personality and Social Psychology*, 83, 425–33. A fascinating paper by R. Vonk (1998) – 'The slime effect: Suspicion and dislike of likeable behavior toward superiors'. *Journal of Personality and Social Psychology*, 74, 849–64 – shows the way that some bullies are incredibly appeasing to those above them but unpleasant to those below (this is called 'downward kicking and upward licking'). This is a real problem because many of us believe that the way in which such individuals obtain positions of power within organizations is increasingly problematic. To their superior managers, they can appear extremely enthusiastic, keen to meet deadlines and so on, yet those below them have terrible morale.

2 Batson, C.D., Klein, T. R., Highberger, L. and Shaw, L.L. (1995). 'Immorality from empathy-induced altruism: When compassion and justice conflict'. *Journal of Personality and Social Psychology*, 68, 1042–54.

3 Oliner, S.P. and Oliner, P.M. (1988). *The Altruistic Personality: Rescuers of Jews in Nazi Europe*. New York: Free Press. There is now more research on 'rescuer behaviour', and if you type that into an internet search engine, you'll get quite a few interesting pieces to explore.

4 Leighton, T. D. (2003). *Faces of Compassion: Classic Bodhisattva archetypes and their modern expression*. Boston, MA: Wisdom.

5 I have long suggested that shame taps into our rank systems and social mentalities, and the way we think about ourselves in terms of inferior–superior and engage in submissive behaviour (*see* Gilbert, P. and McGuire, M. [1998]. 'Shame, status and social roles: The psychobiological continuum from monkeys to humans'. In P. Gilbert and B. Andrews [eds]. *Shame: Interpersonal Behavior, Psychopathology and Culture*, New York: Oxford University Press, pp. 99–125).

In complete contrast, guilt is about caring and avoiding harm. This is also brought out in various publications: Scheff, T.J. (1988). 'Shame and conformity: The deference–emotion system'. *American Review of Sociology*, 53, 395–406. You can find a good review and update on these studies at http://en.wikipedia.org/wiki/Asch_conformity_ experiments (accessed 9 November 2008). You can find more in Bond, R. and Smith, P. (1996). 'Culture and conformity: A meta-analysis of studies using Asch's line judgment task'. *Psychological Bulletin*, 119, 111–37. The way in which our sense of self is constructed through our group identity can also be explored through the writings of Abrams, D., Cochrane, S., Hogg, M.A. and Turner, J.C. (1990). 'Knowing what to think by knowing who you are: Self-categorization and the nature of norm formation, conformity and group polarization'. *British Journal of Social Psychology*, 29, 97–119; Robinson, W.P. (1996). *Social Groups and Identities*. Oxford: Butterworth-Heinemann.

6 Zimbardo, P. (2007). *The Lucifer Effect*. New York: Rider. For over 40 years, Philip Zimbardo has been trying to understand and study how ordinary people can engage in cruel behaviour. He's been an important contributor to many congressional committees exploring cruelty in various aspects of life but, in particular, the military and more recently some of the abuses in Iraq. His is a chilling book in many ways, plotting his research experiences and observations over the years.

Milgram, S. (1974). *Obedience to Authority*. New York: Harper & Row. This book had an enormous impact when it first came out, showing how so many of us are highly submissive to authority and will commit cruelties if asked to. There were (worrying) complaints by some folk that Milgram's research was immoral. Unfortunately, some of the lessons learned through this research in the 1960s and '70s have been allowed to fade away, and we now seem constantly amazed at how easily people can become engaged in cruel and immoral behaviours, prefer simplistic explanations and fail to understand how *we* create the conditions for cruelty. An excellent book that also addresses these issues is Dixon, N.F. (1987). *Our Own Worst Enemy*. London: Routledge.

A somewhat controversial article on Zimbardo's work and ideas is Haslam, S.A. and Reicher, S.D. (2008). 'The banality of evil'. *The Psychologist*, 21, 16–19.

7 Gilbert, P. (2005). 'Compassion and cruelty: A biopsychosocial approach'. In P. Gilbert (ed.). *Compassion: Conceptualisations, research and use in psychotherapy*. London: Routledge, pp. 9–74.

8 Kelman, H.C. and Hamilton, V.L. (1989). *Crimes of Obedience*. New Haven, CT: Yale University Press. As someone interested in all the pathologies and problems associated with our subordinate and submissive behaviour, I can highly recommend this. Only by facing up to the fact that we are highly submissive can we find freedom from it – a theme taken up more than 50 years ago by Erich Fromm in his book *Fear of Freedom*.

9 Dixon, N.F. (1987). *Our Own Worst Enemy*. London: Routledge. An excellent book that also addresses these issues, including the fact that a major source of our troubles is the way our old brain and new minds work together. We often use our intelligence to do the bidding of primitive emotions.

10 Kettle, M. (1998). 'US honours hero who defied Vietnam atrocity'. *Guardian*, 5 March, p. 2.

11 *See* note 6.

12 Cockburn, P. (2006). *The Occupation: War and resistance in Iraq*. London: Verso. This book makes clear that the war was pursued with a mixture of over-ambition and sheer incompetence in post-invasion planning. There are times when one simply can feel only despair at the appalling quality of the leaders in the Western world, their moral ineptitude and their ability to manipulate business and money.

13 I wrote a chapter on cruelty for a book called *Living Like Crazy*. It was never published, but you can download some of it from the *Compassionate Mind* website (www.compassionatemind.co.uk), including that chapter on cruelty.

14 Abbott, G. (1993). *Rack, Rope and Red-Hot Pincers: A history of torture and its instruments*. London: Headline.

Chapter 13: Expressing the Compassionate Mind

1 Begley, S. (2009). *The Plastic Mind*. London: Constable.

   As noted earlier Richard Davidson and his colleagues have been at the forefront of the examination of how compassion meditation affects our brains and bodies. Davidson, R.J., Kabat-Zinn, J., Schumacher, J., Rosenkranz, M., Muller, D. *et al*. (2003). 'Alterations in brain and immune function produced by mindfulness meditation'. *Psychosomatic Medicine*, 65, 564–70. Lutz, A., Brefczynski-Lewis, J., Johnstone, T. and Davidson, R.J. (2008). 'Regulation of the neural circuitry of emotion by compassion meditation: Effects of meditative expertise'. *Public Library of Science*, 3, 1–5.

   Rein, G., Atkinson, M. and McCraty, R. (1995). 'The physiological and psychological effects of compassion and anger'. *Journal for the Advancement of Medicine*, 8, 87–105. These researchers found that anger images and fantasies had a detrimental effect on the functioning of the immune system whereas compassion-focused fantasies and images had a very positive effect. You'll also find a review of lots of studies on how mind training affects the body in Begley's book.

2 Einhorn, S. (2006). *The Art of Being Kind*. London: Sphere.

3 Gottman, J.M., Driver, J. and Tabares, A. (2002). 'Building the sound marital house: An empirically derived couple therapy'. In A.S. Gurman and N.S. Jacobson (eds). *Clinical Handbook of Couple Therapy*. New York: Guilford Press, pp. 373–99.

4 Carnegie, D. (1937/1993). *How to Win Friends and Influence People*. London: Vermilion. This very insightful book really puts the importance of focusing on the other person centre-stage in building and maintaining relationships so they will flourish. It was written long before the new emergence of positive psychology!

5 Nancy Eisenberg is one of the world's leading authorities on the development of pro-social behaviour in children. A good review of her work is given in Eisenberg, N. 'Empathy-related emotional responses,

altruism, and their socialization'. In R. Davidson and A. Harrington (eds) (2002). *Visions of Compassion: Western scientists and Tibetan Buddhists examine human nature*. New York: Oxford University Press, pp. 131–64. *See also* Eisenberg, N. and Mussen, P.N. (1989). 'The Roots of Prosocial Behavior in Children'. New York: Cambridge University Press.

Questions on moral and pro-social development can also be found in a major edited trilogy with a range of key authors: Kurtines, W.M. and Gewirtz, J.L. (eds) (1991). *Handbook of Moral Behavior and Development. Vol. 1: Theory. Vol. 2: Research. Vol. 3: Applications*. Hillsdale, NJ: Lawrence Erlbaum Associates. A recent review can be found in Bierhoff, H.W. 'The psychology of compassion and prosocial behaviour'. In P. Gilbert (ed.) (2005). *Compassion: Conceptualisations, research and use in psychotherapy*. London: Routledge, pp. 148–67.

6 Hoffman, M.L. 'Empathy, social cognition and moral action'. In Kurtines, W.M. and Gewirtz, J.L. (eds) (1991). *Handbook of Moral Behavior and Development. Vol. 1: Theory*. Hillsdale, NJ: Lawrence Erlbaum Associates, pp. 275–301.

7 Emler, N. and Hogan, R. 'Moral psychology and public policy'. In W.M. Kurtines and J.L. Gewirtz (eds) (1991). *Handbook of Moral Behavior and Development. Vol. 3: Application*. Hillsdale, NJ: Lawrence Erlbaum Associates. Wilkinson, R. (2005). *The Impact of Inequality: How to make sick societies healthier*. London: New Press.

8 Gilmour, I.I. (1993). *Dancing with Dogma: Britain under Thatcherism*. London: Simon & Schuster, p. 340.

9 There are many websites that debate the nature of consciousness – some extremely technical and easy to get lost in. You might be interested in Ricard, M. and Thuan, T.X. (2001). *The Quantum and the Lotus*. New York: Three Rivers Press. And also Goiswanis, A. (1993). *The Self-aware Universe*. London: Simon & Schuster. Keep in mind that these are hotly debated issues.

10 Hinde, R.A. (1999). *Why Gods Persist: A scientific approach to religion*. London: Routledge.

Another fascinating book that explores the evolved psychological mechanism supporting religious belief and experiences is Brant Wenegrat's 1990 *The Divine Archetype. The sociobiology and psychology of religion* (New York: Free Press). There are, of course, many works on the functions of religion, how they have grown from the evolution of our capacity to imagine and think about other minds and how dangerous and tragic life is – and how we try to make sense of it. Other authors stress the role of the need to feel a sense of belonging, of being attached and cared for, and especially a sense of union, as a way of coping with death as an end. *See* Kirkpatrick, L.A. (2005). *Attachment, Evolution, and the Psychology of Religion*. New York: Guilford.

11 A full transcript of President Obama's inaugural address can be found at <http://news.bbc.co.uk/1/hi/world/americas/obama_inauguration/7840646.stm>

Find out more

Books

Meditation

Two useful book/CD combinations:

- Jack Kornfield (2004). *Meditation for Beginners*. New York: Bantam Books.
  A nice introduction.

- Dagsay Tulku Rinpoche (2002). *The Practice of Tibetan Meditation: Exercises, visualisations, and mantras for health and well being*. Rochester, VT: Inner Traditions.
  This book offers a very useful set of postures and exercises, along with a CD of mantras and instructions.

Mindfulness

There are lots of books on mindfulness. Two classics are:

- Thich Nhat Hanh (1991). *The Miracle of Mindfulness*. London: Rider.

- Jon Kabit-Zinn (2005). *Coming to Our Senses: Healing ourselves and the world through mindfulness*. New York: Piatkus.

The Dalai Lama

The Dalai Lama is the spiritual head of Buddhism, which can be seen as both spiritual approach and a basic psychology. It's particularly useful for its psychology and insights built up over thousands of years of meditation and introspective observation.

- Dalai Lama (1995). *The Power of Compassion*. London: Thorsons.

- Dalai Lama (ed. N. Vreeland) (2001). *An Open Heart: Practising compassion in everyday life*. London: Hodder & Stoughton.

Other books

Two books that I've found particularly inspiring and beautifully written are:

- Bikshu Sangharakshita (2008). *Living with Kindness: The Buddha's teaching on metta*. London: Windhorse Publications.

- Jeffrey Hopkins (2001). *Cultivating Compassion: A Buddhist perspective*. New York: Doubleday.

If you want a more technical approach, have a look at:

- Paul Gilbert (2005). *Compassion: Conceptualisations, research and use in psychotherapy*. London: Routledge (pp. 148–67).

- Richard J. Davidson and Anne Harrington (eds) (2002). *Visions of Compassion: Western scientists and Tibetan Buddhists examine human nature*. New York: Oxford University Press.

CDs

Some useful CDs that will guide you:

- Pema Chodron (2007). *How to Meditate: A practical guide to making friends with your mind*. Boulder, CO: Sounds True.
  She offers a comprehensive programme based on mindfulness.

- Jeffrey Brantley (2003). *Calming Your Anxious Mind: How mindfulness and compassion can free you from anxiety, fear and panic*. New York: Harbinger.

- Mark Williams, John Teasdale, Zindel Segal and Jon Kabat-Zinn (2007). *The Mindful Way through Depression: Freeing yourself from chronic unhappiness*. Boulder, CO: Sounds True.

Jon Kabat-Zinn has also issued his own set of CDs called *Guided Mindfulness Mediation* (Boulder, CO: Sounds True, 2005). You can find more of his work by typing his name into a search engine.

Websites

Compassionate Mind Foundation
www.compassionatemind.co.uk

In 2007, a number of colleagues and I set up a charity called the Compassionate Mind Foundation. On this website, you'll find various essays and details of other sites that look at different aspects of compassion. You'll also find a lot of material that you can use for meditation on compassion.

Mind & Life Institute
www.mindandlife.org

The Dalai Lama has formed relationships with Western scientists to develop a more compassionate way of living. More information on this can be found on this website.

Self-Compassion
www.self-compassion.org

Dr Kristin Neff is one of the leading researchers into self-compassion.

The Greater Good
www.greatergood.berkeley.edu/greatergood

This is a website and magazine set up by researchers at the University of California, Berkeley to promote and notify people about compassion research. It is excellent.

Building compassionate societies

Community Development Framework: No community left behind
http://www.nocommunityleftbehind.ca/

Community foundation
http://en.wikipedia.org/wiki/Community_foundations

Community Foundation Network
http://www.communityfoundations.org.uk/

Compassion in World Farming
www.ciwf.org.uk/

Nurturing Compassion: An elementary school-wide theme
http://www.vsb.bc.ca/districtinfo/organization/ls/compassion/
Elementary CompassionTheme.htm

Principles for Responsible Investment
www.unpri.org/principles/

Restorative Justice Consortium
www.restorativejustice.org.uk/

Restorative Justice 4 Schools
http://restorativejustice4schools.co.uk

SureStart
www.surestart.gov.uk

Transatlantic Community Foundation
http://www.tcfn.efc.be/whats_new.php

United Nations Foundation
www.unfoundation.org/about-unf/

Index

NEW YORK TIMES BESTSELLER

THE
PLASTIC
MIND

NEW SCIENCE REVEALS OUR EXTRAORDINARY
POTENTIAL TO TRANSFORM OURSELVES

FOREWORD BY THE DALAI LAMA
PREFACE BY DANIEL GOLEMAN

SHARON BEGLEY

New York Times Bestseller

THE PLASTIC MIND

NEW SCIENCE REVEALS OUR EXTRAORDINARY POTENTIAL TO TRANSFORM OURSELVES

SHARON BEGLEY

Is it possible to change the structure of the brain, and alter how we think and feel?

In late 2004, leading Western scientists joined the Dalai Lama at his home in Dharamsala, India, to address that very question – and set in train a revolution in our understanding of the human mind.

For decades, conventional neuroscience held that the hardware of the brain is immutable. Now, pioneering experiments in neuroplasticity, a new science studying the brain's potential for chance, reveal that it is capable not only of altering its structure but also of generating new neurons, even into old age. There is clear evidence that the brain can adapt, heal and renew itself after trauma and compensate for disability.

In this bestselling book, Sharon Begley illuminates this most important advance in our understanding of how the brain and the mind interact, opening a new window on what it means to be human.

Foreword by the Dalai Lama.

'A fascinating exploration of the ways the mind can change the brain.' *Publishers Weekly*

'A clearly written account of recent discoveries about brain plasticity as presented by leading neuroscientists at meetings with the Dalai Lama.' *New Scientist*

'Not only fascinating, but uplifting and inspiring.' Jon Kabat-Zinn, *Coming to Our Senses*

Constable
£9.99
978-1-84529-674-2

www.constablerobinson.com

More psychology titles from Constable & Robinson

Please visit www.overcoming.co.uk for more information

No.	Title	RRP	Offer Price	Total
	Overcoming Anger and Irritability	£9.99	£7.99	
	Overcoming Anorexia Nervosa	£9.99	£7.99	
	Overcoming Anxiety	£10.99	£8.99	
	Overcoming Body Image Problems	£10.99	£8.99	
	Bulimia Nervosa and Binge Eating	£9.99	£7.99	
	Overcoming Childhood Trauma	£9.99	£7.99	
	Overcoming Chronic Fatigue	£9.99	£7.99	
	Overcoming Chronic Pain	£9.99	£7.99	
	Overcoming Compulsive Gambling	£9.99	£7.99	
	Overcoming Depersonalization and Feelings of Unreality	£9.99	£7.99	
	Overcoming Depression *New edition published July 2009.*	£10.99	£7.99	
	Overcoming Depression: Talks with your Therapist (audio)	£9.99	£7.99	
	Overcoming Grief	£9.99	£7.99	
	Overcoming Insomnia and Sleep Problems	£9.99	£8.99	
	Overcoming Low Self-Esteem	£10.99	£8.99	
	Overcoming Mood Swings	£9.99	£7.99	
	Overcoming Obsessive Compulsive Disorder	£9.99	£7.99	
	Overcoming Panic and Agoraphobia	£10.99	£8.99	
	Overcoming Paranoid and Suspicious Thoughts	£9.99	£7.99	
	Overcoming Problem Drinking	£9.99	£7.99	
	Overcoming Relationship Problems	£9.99	£7.99	
	Overcoming Sexual Problems	£9.99	£7.99	
	Overcoming Social Anxiety and Shyness	£10.99	£8.99	
	Overcoming Traumatic Stress	£9.99	£7.99	

	Overcoming Weight Problems	£10.99	£8.99	
	Overcoming Worry	£9.99	£7.99	
	Overcoming Your Child's Fears and Worries	£9.99	£7.99	
	Overcoming Your Child's Shyness and Social Anxiety	£9.99	£7.99	
	Overcoming Your Smoking Habit	£9.99	£7.99	
	The Happiness Trap	£9.99	£7.99	
	The Glass Half-Full	£8.99	£7.99	
	I Had a Black Dog	£6.99	£5.24	
	Living with a Black Dog	£7.99	£5.99	
	Manage Your Mood: How to Use Behavioral Activation Techniques to Overcome Depression	£12.99	£9.99	
	P&P	**FREE**	**FREE**	
	TOTAL			

Name (block letters): _____

Address: _____

_____ Postcode: _____

Email: _____ Tel No.: _____

How to pay:

1. By telephone: call the TBS order line on 01206 255 800 and quote COMPASSION. Phone lines are open between Monday–Friday, 8.30am–5.30pm.

2. By post: send a cheque for the full amount payable to TBS Ltd, and send form to: Freepost RLUL-SJGC-SGKJ. Cash Sales/Direct Mail Dept, The Book Service, Colchester Road, Frating, Colchester, CO7 7DW.

Is/are the book(s) intended for personal use □ or professional use □? Please note this information will not be passed on to third parties.

Constable & Robinson Ltd (directly or via its agents) may mail or phone you about promotions or products. Tick box if you do not want these from us □ or our subsidiaries □.